OECD/G20 Base Erosion and Profit Shifting Project

Tax Challenges Arising from Digitalisation – Report on Pillar One Blueprint

INCLUSIVE FRAMEWORK ON BEPS

OECD
BETTER POLICIES FOR BETTER LIVES

Please cite this publication as:
OECD (2020), *Tax Challenges Arising from Digitalisation – Report on Pillar One Blueprint: Inclusive Framework on BEPS*, OECD/G20 Base Erosion and Profit Shifting Project, OECD Publishing, Paris, *https://doi.org/10.1787/beba0634-en*.

ISBN 978-92-64-73198-1 (print)
ISBN 978-92-64-28932-1 (pdf)

OECD/G20 Base Erosion and Profit Shifting Project
ISSN 2313-2604 (print)
ISSN 2313-2612 (online)

Photo credits: Cover © ninog – Fotolia.com.

Corrigenda to publications may be found on line at: *www.oecd.org/about/publishing/corrigenda.htm*.

Foreword

The integration of national economies and markets has increased substantially in recent years, putting a strain on the international tax rules, which were designed more than a century ago. Weaknesses in the current rules create opportunities for base erosion and profit shifting (BEPS), requiring bold moves by policy makers to restore confidence in the system and ensure that profits are taxed where economic activities take place and value is created.

Following the release of the report Addressing Base Erosion and Profit Shifting in February 2013, OECD and G20 countries adopted a 15-point Action Plan to address BEPS in September 2013. The Action Plan identified 15 actions along three key pillars: introducing coherence in the domestic rules that affect cross-border activities, reinforcing substance requirements in the existing international standards, and improving transparency as well as certainty.

After two years of work, measures in response to the 15 actions were delivered to G20 Leaders in Antalya in November 2015. All the different outputs, including those delivered in an interim form in 2014, were consolidated into a comprehensive package. The BEPS package of measures represents the first substantial renovation of the international tax rules in almost a century.

Implementation is now well underway. The BEPS package was designed to be implemented via changes in domestic law and practices, and in tax treaties. With the negotiation of a multilateral instrument (MLI) having been finalised in 2016 to facilitate the implementation of the treaty related BEPS measures, over 90 jurisdictions are covered by the MLI. The entry into force of the MLI on 1 July 2018 has paved the way for swift implementation of the treaty related measures. OECD and G20 countries also agreed to continue to work together to ensure a consistent and co-ordinated implementation of the BEPS recommendations and to make the project more inclusive. Globalisation requires that global solutions and a global dialogue be established which go beyond OECD and G20 countries.

As a result, the OECD established the OECD/G20 Inclusive Framework on BEPS (Inclusive Framework) in 2016, bringing together all interested and committed countries and jurisdictions on an equal footing in the Committee on Fiscal Affairs and all its subsidiary bodies. The Inclusive Framework, which already has more than 135 members, is monitoring and peer reviewing the implementation of the BEPS minimum standards as well as completing the work on standard setting to address BEPS issues. In addition to its member jurisdictions, other international organisations and regional tax bodies are involved in the work of the Inclusive Framework, which also consults business and civil society on its different work streams.

Addressing the tax challenges arising from the digitalisation of the economy has been a top priority of the BEPS Project and the Inclusive Framework since 2015 with the release of the BEPS Action 1 Report. At the request of the G20, the Inclusive Framework has continued to work on the issue, delivering an interim report in March 2018. In January 2019, members of the Inclusive Framework agreed to examine proposals in two pillars, which could form the basis for a consensus solution to the tax challenges arising from digitalisation. Pillar One is focused on nexus and profit allocation whereas Pillar Two is focused on a global minimum tax intended to address remaining BEPS issues. A programme of work to be conducted on Pillar One and Pillar Two was adopted in May 2019 and later endorsed by the G20 in June 2019. As part of the programme of work, the OECD Secretariat was mandated to carry out an economic analysis and impact assessment of the Pillar One and Pillar Two proposals. In July 2020, the G20 mandated the Inclusive Framework to produce reports on the Blueprints of Pillar One and Pillar Two by the G20 Finance Ministers meeting in October 2020.

This report was approved by the Inclusive Framework on 8-9 October 2020 and prepared for publication by the OECD Secretariat.

Table of contents

Cover Statement by the OECD/G20 Inclusive Framework on BEPS on the Reports on the Blueprints of Pillar One and Pillar Two

Digital transformation spurs innovation, generates efficiencies, and improves services while boosting more inclusive and sustainable growth and enhancing well-being. At the same time, the breadth and speed of this change introduces challenges in many policy areas, including taxation. Reforming the international tax system to address the tax challenges arising from the digitalisation of the economy, restore stability to the international tax framework and prevent further uncoordinated unilateral tax measures has therefore been a priority of the international community for several years, with commitments to deliver a consensus-based solution by the end of 2020.

The current context of the COVID-19 pandemic makes the need for a solution even more compelling than when it was first considered. Governments have responded through increased spending on healthcare and by providing unprecedented levels of financial support to both businesses and workers to cushion them from the economic blow of this crisis. However, the time will come when governments will need to focus on putting their finances back on a fair and sustainable footing.

A consensus-based solution comprised of two pillars (Pillar One focused on nexus and profit allocation whereas Pillar Two is focused on a global minimum tax intended to address remaining BEPS issues) can not only play an important role to ensure fairness and equity in our tax systems and fortify the international tax framework in the face of new and changing business models; it can also help put government finances back on a sustainable footing. The public pressure on governments to ensure that large, internationally operating, and profitable businesses pay their fair share and do so in the right place under new international tax rules has increased as a result of the current COVID-19 pandemic. At the same time, a consensus-based solution could provide businesses with much needed tax certainty in order to aid economic recovery.

Against this background, despite their differences, and the COVID-19 pandemic, which has had an impact on the work, the members of the OECD/G20 Inclusive Framework on BEPS (Inclusive Framework) have made substantial progress towards building consensus. The Inclusive Framework is releasing today a package consisting of the Reports on the Blueprints of Pillar One and Pillar Two, which reflects convergent views on a number of key policy features, principles and parameters of both Pillars, and identifies remaining political and technical issues where differences of views remain to be bridged, and next steps.

We approve the *Report on the Pillar One Blueprint* for public release. It is designed to deliver a sustainable taxation framework reflective of today's digitalising economy, with the potential to achieve a fairer and more efficient allocation of taxing rights. The Blueprint reflects the extensive technical work that has been done. Though no agreement has been reached, the Blueprint nevertheless provides a solid foundation for a future agreement that would adhere to the concept of net taxation of income, avoid double taxation and be as simple and administrable as possible. The Blueprint offers a solid basis for future agreement and reflects that:

- in an increasingly digital age, in-scope businesses are able to generate profits through participation in a significant/ active and sustained way in the economic life of a jurisdiction, beyond the mere conclusion of sales, with or without the benefit of local physical presence and this would be reflected in the design of nexus rules while being mindful of compliance considerations;
- the solution would follow the policy rationale set out above and allocate a portion of residual profit of in-scope businesses to market/user jurisdictions ("Amount A");
- the solution would be targeted and build in thresholds so that it minimises compliance costs for taxpayers and keeps the administration of the new rules manageable for tax administrations;
- Amount A would be computed using consolidated financial accounts as the starting point, contain a limited number of book-to-tax adjustments and ensure that losses are appropriately taken into account;
- in determining the tax base, segmentation would be required to appropriately target the new taxing right in certain cases, but with broad safe-harbour or exemption rules from segmentation to reduce complexity and minimise burdens for tax administrations and taxpayers alike;
- the solution would contain effective means to eliminate double taxation in a multilateral setting;
- the work on Amount B will be advanced, (a fixed rate of return on base-line marketing and distribution activities intended to approximate results determined under the arm's length principle) recognising its potentially significant benefits including for tax administrations with limited capacity as well as its challenges;
- the Pillar One solution would contain a new multilateral tax certainty process with respect to Amount A, recognising the importance of using simplified and co-ordinated administrative procedures with respect to the administration of Amount A;
- a new multilateral convention would be developed to implement the solution, recognising that it would offer the best and most efficient way of implementing Pillar One.

We will now focus on resolving the remaining political and technical issues, including issues around scope, quantum, the choice between mandatory and safe harbour implementation, and aspects of the new tax certainty procedures with respect to Amount A, and the scope and form of new and enhanced tax certainty procedures for issues beyond Amount A.

We also approve the *Report on the Pillar Two Blueprint* for public release. It provides a solid basis for a systemic solution that would address remaining base erosion and profit shifting (BEPS) challenges and sets out rules that would provide jurisdictions with a right to "tax back" where other jurisdictions have not exercised their primary taxing rights, or the payment is otherwise subject to low levels of effective taxation. These rules would ensure that all large internationally operating businesses pay at least a minimum level of tax. We acknowledge that jurisdictions are free to determine their own tax systems, including whether they have a corporate income tax and the level of their tax rates, but also consider the right of other jurisdictions to apply an internationally agreed Pillar Two regime where income is taxed below an agreed minimum rate. Though no agreement has been reached, the Blueprint provides a solid basis for future agreement on:

- the Income Inclusion Rule (IIR), the Undertaxed Payments Rule (UTPR), the Subject to Tax Rule (STTR), the rule order, the calculation of the effective tax rate and the allocation of the top-up tax for the IIR and the UTPR, including the tax base, the definition of covered taxes, mechanisms to address volatility, and the substance carve-out;
- the IIR and UTPR as a common approach, including an acceptance of the right of all members of the IF to implement them as part of an agreed Pillar Two regime. It would nevertheless be recognised and accepted that there may be members that are not in a position to implement these rules. However, all those implementing them would apply them consistently with the agreed Pillar Two vis-à-vis all other jurisdictions (including groups headquartered therein) that also join this consensus. Furthermore, given the importance that a large number of IF members, particularly developing countries, attach to an STTR, we recognise that an STTR would be an integral part of a consensus solution on Pillar Two;
- the basis on which the United States' Global Intangible Low Taxed Income Regime (GILTI) would be treated as a Pillar Two compliant income inclusion rule as set out in the Report on the Blueprint on Pillar Two;
- the development of model legislation, standard documentation and guidance, designing a multilateral review process if necessary and exploring the use of a multilateral convention, which could include the key aspects of Pillar Two.

We welcome stakeholder input into this process on both pillars, in particular on administration and simplification rules, which would help inform the further development of the consensus-based solution.

Next steps

We agree to swiftly address the remaining issues with a view to bringing the process to a successful conclusion by mid-2021 and to resolve technical issues, develop model draft legislation, guidelines, and international rules and processes as necessary to enable jurisdictions to implement a consensus based solution.

1 Executive summary

1.1. Introduction

1. Digital transformation spurs innovation, generates efficiencies, and improves services while boosting more inclusive and sustainable growth and enhancing well-being. At the same time, the breadth and speed of this change introduces challenges in many policy areas, including taxation. Reforming the international tax system to address the tax challenges arising from the digitalisation of the economy has therefore been a priority of the international community for several years, with commitments to deliver a consensus-based solution by the end of 2020.

2. These tax challenges were first identified as one of the main areas of focus of the OECD/G20 Base Erosion and Profit Shifting (BEPS) Project, leading to the 2015 BEPS Action 1 Report (the Action 1 Report).[1] The Action 1 Report found that the whole economy was digitalising and, as a result, it would be difficult, if not impossible, to ring-fence the digital economy. In March 2018, the Inclusive Framework, working through its Task Force on the Digital Economy (TFDE), issued *Tax Challenges Arising from Digitalisation – Interim Report 2018* (the Interim Report)[2] which recognised the need for a global solution.

3. Since then, the 137 members of the Inclusive Framework have worked on a global solution based on a two pillar approach.[3] Pillar One is focused on new nexus and profit allocation rules to ensure that, in an increasingly digital age, the allocation of taxing rights with respect to business profits is no longer exclusively circumscribed by reference to physical presence. Globalisation and digitalisation have challenged fundamental features of the international income tax system, such as the traditional notions of permanent establishment and the arm's length principle (ALP), and brought to the fore the need for higher levels of enhanced tax certainty through more extensive multilateral tax co-operation. These transformational developments have taken place against a background of increasing public attention on the taxation of highly digitalised global businesses, which has in turn reinforced the political pressure and imperative to address the issue.

4. Members of the Inclusive Framework agreed that any new rules should be based on net basis taxation, should avoid double taxation and should be as simple as possible. They stressed the importance of tax certainty and the need for improved dispute prevention and dispute resolution tools. The members are mindful of the need to ensure a level playing field among all jurisdictions: large or small, developed or developing. Also mindful of limiting compliance and administrative burdens, Inclusive Framework members agreed to make any rules as simple as the tax policy context permits, including through the exploration of simplification measures.

5. Following a proposal made by the Secretariat,[4] the Inclusive Framework agreed upon an outline of the architecture of a "Unified Approach" in January 2020 as the basis for the negotiation of the Pillar One solution (the "Outline").[5] Since January, and in spite of the outbreak of COVID-19, all members have worked on the technical development of all the building blocks that make up Pillar One. This is a Report on the blueprint for Pillar One (the "Blueprint"). It describes, in detail, the main features of the building blocks of Pillar One and identifies the areas where political decision is needed. It shows that there has been significant progress towards a global agreement, and contains proposals to bridge remaining divergences. It recognises that further technical work will be required to finalise some aspects of Pillar

One, for example to reduce complexity, improve administrability, and meet the available capacities of both developed and developing economies.

1.2. Pillar One Blueprint

6. Pillar One seeks to adapt the international income tax system to new business models through changes to the profit allocation and nexus rules applicable to business profits. Within this context, it expands the taxing rights of market jurisdictions (which, for some business models, are the jurisdictions where the users are located)[6] where there is an active and sustained participation of a business in the economy of that jurisdiction through activities in, or remotely directed at, that jurisdiction.[7] It also aims to significantly improve tax certainty by introducing innovative dispute prevention and resolution mechanisms. Pillar One seeks to balance the different objectives of Inclusive Framework members and result in the removal of relevant unilateral measures.

7. Consistent with the Outline, the key elements of Pillar One can be grouped into three components: a new taxing right for market jurisdictions over a share of residual profit calculated at an MNE group (or segment) level (Amount A); a fixed return for certain baseline marketing and distribution activities taking place physically in a market jurisdiction, in line with the ALP (Amount B); and processes to improve tax certainty through effective dispute prevention and resolution mechanisms. Eleven building blocks have been identified as essential to the construction of Pillar One, and constitute the bedrock of this Blueprint.

Figure 1.1. Building Blocks of Pillar One

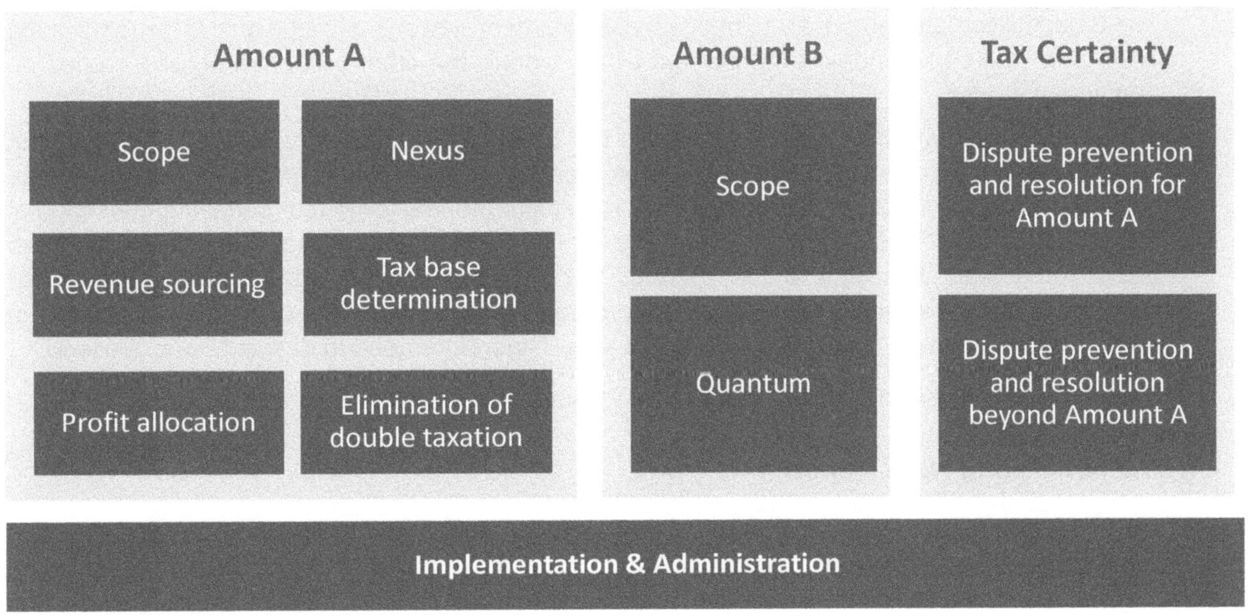

8. While the technical work on the Pillar One building blocks is very advanced, Inclusive Framework members recognise that there are a number of open issues on key features of the solution that can only be resolved through political decisions. To complete the package, political decisions are required on a number of issues including the following:

- **Scope**: With the Outline agreed in January 2020, the Inclusive Framework tried to bridge the gap between those members seeking to focus Pillar One on a narrower group of "digital" business models and those insisting that a solution should cover a wider scope of activities. As a result, two categories of activities to be included in the scope of the new taxing right created by Pillar One were identified: Automated Digital Services (ADS) and Consumer Facing Businesses (CFB). As discussed below, considerable technical work has been done on how these categories could be defined, but to date political agreement has not been reached on the use of these categories, and the scope issue is not yet solved. In order to deliver a solution in 2020 in accordance with the G20 mandate, some members have advocated for a phased implementation with ADS coming first and CFB following later. One member proposed implementing the new taxing right on a "safe harbour" basis, which would enable an MNE group to elect on a global basis to be subject to Pillar One.[8] The scope of Amount A remains to be settled upon.

- **Amount of profit to be reallocated (the "Quantum")**: Agreement on how much residual profit would be reallocated under the new taxing right, which depends on the determination of different threshold amounts and percentages for the purpose of scope, nexus and profit allocation (the formula),[9] is conditioned on agreement on scope. However, much work has been completed on the impact of different threshholds and percentages of profit to be allocated so that a political decision could be taken quickly as part of an overall political agreement. Also, some Inclusive Framework members are of the view that, beyond residual profit, a portion of routine profit should also be allocated to market jurisdictions in the case of remote marketing and distribution activities facilitated by digitalisation. Other members proposed "differentiation mechanisms" in order to increase the quantum of profit reallocated to market jurisdictions for certain business activities (for example, ADS), or a scalable reallocation depending on the profitability of the business (profit escalator). These variations to the Amount A profit allocation rules proposed by some Inclusive Framework members have not been decided upon.
- **Extent of tax certainty**: While all members have agreed on the need for an innovative solution to deliver early certainty and effective dispute prevention and resolution for Amount A, there continue to be differences of view on the scope of mandatory binding dispute resolution beyond Amount A. The Blueprint contains proposals to bridge these divergent views. A decision on this issue will need to be part of a comprehensive agreement also covering the other two open political issues on quantum and scope.
- **Scope and application of Amount B**: While this Blueprint contains an outline of a solution that assumes that in-scope distributors are to be identified based on a narrow scope of baseline activities, there is interest by some members to explore the feasibility of broadening the scope of Amount B. Some Inclusive Framework members have expressed the need to further refine the design of Amount B such that the intended simplification benefits are achieved, and further consider that implementation through a pilot programme at first may allow for some evaluation of the benefits in practice. The Inclusive Framework will therefore need to decide how to proceed.

9. Subject to these pending political issues, the Pillar One Blueprint is described below.

1.2.1. The new taxing right (Amount A)

10. The new taxing right (Amount A) would be an overlay to the existing nexus and profit allocation rules. It would apply broadly and would not be limited to a small number of MNEs in a particular industry. However, given its innovative features, Inclusive Framework members are mindful of the need to keep the number of MNEs affected at an administrable level and have agreed to consider thresholds and other features that help keep the approach targeted while minimising compliance costs and being mindful of capacity considerations for tax administrations. The key design features of the new taxing right would include:

- A **revenue threshold** based on annual consolidated group revenue coupled with a **de minimis foreign in-scope revenue** carve-out. These thresholds are intended to minimise compliance costs and keep the administration of the new rules manageable for tax administrations. To avoid tax administrations being overwhelmed with the initial operation of the new taxing right, one option under consideration is to implement these thresholds on a phased approach. This could start with higher thresholds that could either be gradually reduced over a number of years or be applied for a longer period and then only start the reductions after a post-implementation review has been undertaken. A phased approach may help to make the new rules manageable for both tax administrations and businesses and will allow both to gain practical experience before expanding coverage to a wider set of MNEs. Other approaches that seek to achieve these objectives could also be explored, including the option of a threshold based on in-scope revenues. No decision has yet been taken on the number of the revenue thresholds, the amount of these thresholds or the use of a phased approach.

- **Scoping rules** covering ADS and more broadly CFB. This includes businesses that are able to have significant and sustained interactions with customers and users in a market jurisdiction.
- The use of a **new nexus rule** to identify market jurisdictions eligible to receive Amount A. The nexus rules balances the interests of smaller jurisdictions, in particular developing economies, in benefiting from the new taxing right with the need for low and proportionate compliance costs, where appropriate in light of the overall balance, while avoiding spill-over effects in other tax and non-tax areas.
- The nexus rules are supported by detailed **sourcing rules** that are reflective of the particularities of digital services and consumer-facing businesses and balance the need for accuracy with the ability of in-scope MNEs to comply and the cost of doing so. It has been proposed that this may be achieved through due diligence rules subject to a clearly defined hierarchy, likely to be of particular importance in connection with third party distribution.
- An administrable approach for **reallocating residual profit.** Eligible market jurisdictions will receive a portion of (X%) of residual profit (income exceeding an agreed level of profitability of (Y%)) using a formula. To strike a balance between simplicity and accuracy, the calculation of the relevant measure of profit will rely as much as possible on published consolidated financial accounts. Book-to-tax adjustments (similar to those required for Pillar Two) and segmentation will be limited to a minimum. In practice, most MNEs will compute their Amount A profit (the tax base) on the basis of their consolidated accounts (including groups with out-of-scope activities), but only the portion of that group profit determined by a formula corresponding to in-scope revenue will end up being allocated to market jurisdictions. Accuracy and ensuring a level playing field between different MNEs (e.g. in-scope business line with a significantly different profitability from other business lines) may require the determination of the relevant measure of profit on a segment basis, but only in limited cases where the MNE will likely already prepare segmented accounts for financial reporting purposes. Further simplifications will be available for MNEs that compute a segmented tax base, such as the allocation of indirect costs through a revenue-based allocation key. In total, it is expected that only a small number of groups would be required to segment their tax base under Amount A.
- **A loss carry-forward regime** to ensure that there is no Amount A allocation where the relevant business is not profitable over time. To ensure Amount A applies only to economic profit, consideration will be given to MNEs in scope being allowed to bring existing losses incurred prior to the introduction of Amount A into this loss carry-forward regime. The regime will rely on an earn-out mechanism to enable offsetting past losses against future profit. Amount A losses will be preserved and carried forward in a single account at the level of the group (or segment level where relevant), and not allocated to individual market jurisdictions.
- In addition to the proposed mechanism to eliminate double taxation, different options are being considered to adjust the allocation of Amount A to market jurisdictions where an MNE already leaves residual profits under the existing ALP-based profit allocation rules (so-called "double counting" issues), including **a marketing and distribution profits safe harbour**. This approach would conceptually consider the income taxes payable in the market jurisdiction under existing taxing rights and Amount A together, and adjust the quantum of Amount A taxable in a market

jurisdiction, limiting it where the residual profit of the MNE is already allocated to that jurisdiction as a result of the existing profit allocation rules. Under the safe harbour, groups that already allocate profits to market jurisdiction in excess of the safe harbour return would in some instances not pay Amount A or apply the mechanism to eliminate double taxation and thus could continue to allocate profits under the current rules. Other approaches considered to deal with double counting issues, next to the mechanism to eliminate double taxation, include the domestic business exemption.

- The **mechanism to eliminate double taxation** will have two components: (i) identification of the paying entities; and (ii) the methods to eliminate double taxation. To identify the entity or entities that will bear the Amount A tax liability, the "paying entities", a process with up to four steps is contemplated. First, a qualitative activities test to identify entities that earn residual profit using a positive and negative list of indicia (which will be applied based on existing transfer pricing documentation). A profitability test would then be applied to ensure these entities have the ability to pay Amount A. As a priority rule, the Amount A tax liability for a market jurisdiction would first be allocated to paying entities that are connected to a market jurisdiction. But, where the paying entities connected to a market do not have sufficient profits to bear the full liability, any outstanding liability could be apportioned between other paying entities (not connected to a market) on a pro-rata basis, or on other alternative "back-stop" bases that are being considered. Consideration will also be given as to whether and how this process could be simplified by eliminating the first (activities) and/or third (market connection priority) test and applying a more strictly quantitative and formulaic approach. Having identified the entity or entities that would bear an Amount A tax liability, a residence jurisdiction would then use the exemption or credit method to relieve double taxation.
- Where an MNE is subject to the new taxing right, a **simplified administrative process** will be developed to minimise the complexity, burden and cost of filing and payment, which is aimed at benefitting tax administrations and taxpayers alike.
- The **new Amount A taxing right would be implemented** through changes to domestic law, and by way of public international law instruments, in particular, a multilateral convention would be required. The domestic law and multilateral convention would be supplemented by guidance and other instruments where necessary.

1.2.2. The fixed return for defined baseline marketing and distribution activities (Amount B)

11. The purpose of Amount B is two-fold. First, it is intended to simplify the administration of transfer pricing rules for tax administrations and lower compliance costs for taxpayers. Second, Amount B is intended to enhance tax certainty and reduce controversy between tax administrations and taxpayers. For this reason, it has been acknowledged by a number of Inclusive Framework members and MNEs as a key deliverable of Pillar One on the presumption that the intended benefits may be achieved.

12. Amount B will standardise the remuneration of related party distributors that perform "baseline marketing and distribution activities" in the market jurisdiction. The definition of baseline marketing and distribution activities covers distributors that (i) buy from related parties and resell to unrelated parties; and (ii) have a routine distributor functionality profile.

13. Further, the activities in scope are first defined by a 'positive list' of typical functions performed, assets owned and risks assumed at arm's length by routine distributors (based on a narrow scope, akin to limited risk distributors). A 'negative list' of typical functions that should not be performed, assets not owned and risks not assumed at arm's length by routine distributors are also used to qualitatively measure the additional factors that would deem a distributor as being outside the scope of Amount B. Certain quantitative indicators are then used to further support the identification of in-scope activities.

14. Amount B is intended to approximate results determined in accordance with the ALP, and therefore would be based on comparable company benchmarking analyses under the Transactional Net Margin Method (TNMM) with the quantum potentially varying by industry, as well as region, provided any such variation is supported by the relevant benchmarking analysis.[10] As a result Amount B could have a number of ranges of potentially appropriate fixed returns. Each fixed return provided to remunerate baseline marketing and distribution activities under Amount B is intended to deliver a result that approximates results determined in accordance with the ALP.

15. While some members view that Amount B may provide certain benefits, in terms of tax certainty and as a simplification of the ALP, there remain divergent views on the breadth of baseline activities that should be included in its scope. This Blueprint assumes that in-scope distributors are to be identified based on a narrow scope of baseline activities, which is a view shared by a group of Inclusive Framework members. However, there is another group of members, particularly developing countries, that consider the rule will be only be effective in its policy objective if it is broad in scope and wish to explore broadening the scope of Amount B. There is also some interest in exploring the implementation of Amount B through an initial pilot programme, in order to measure how simplification benefits may be achieved. The precise definitions of regions, industries and the relevant activities and indicators is to be finalised through further technical work.

1.2.3. Improved tax certainty processes

16. Tax certainty is a key component of Pillar One and is core to this Blueprint which provides for innovative dispute prevention and dispute resolution mechanisms.

Dispute prevention

17. The new taxing right will be determined by the application of a formula to a newly defined tax base, corresponding to a portion of the residual profit of large MNEs' in-scope activities. The Blueprint embeds a mechanism to ensure that the application of the new taxing right to a particular MNE group is agreed among all interested jurisdictions. A panel mechanism would be put in place for tax administrations, working with the relevant MNEs, to agree on: (i) the tax base, in particular where there is business line segmentation; (ii) the result of the implementation of the formula, and (iii) any other feature of the new taxing right, including the paying entities and elimination of double taxation. It is also recognised that the resource implications of the multilateral process are significantly less than the resources that would be required by unilateral uncoordinated compliance activities.

18. As described in section 1.2.2, Amount B is intended to enhance tax certainty and reduce controversy between tax administration and taxpayers, particularly in jurisdictions where there are constraints in dealing with transfer pricing disputes. It does so by standardising the remuneration of related party distributors that perform 'baseline marketing and distribution activities'.

Figure 1.2. Overview of the process map for Amount A

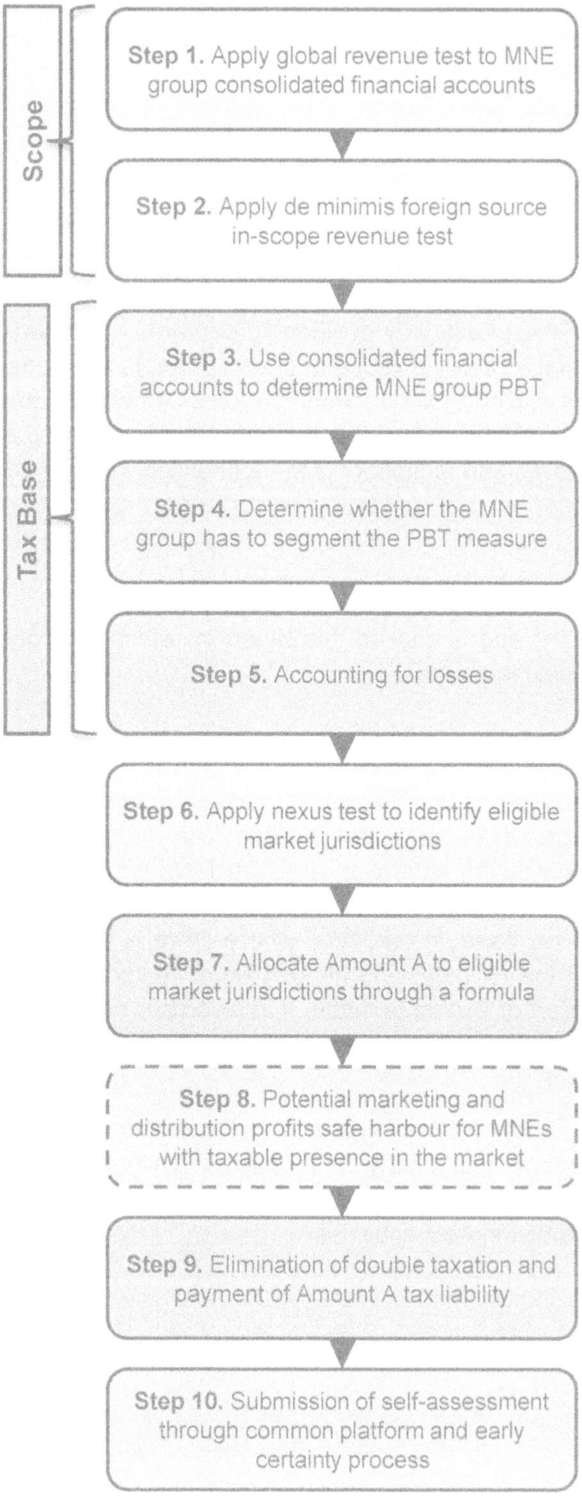

1. Global revenue test
Only MNE groups with revenue exceeding EUR [X] are potentially in scope of Amount A.

2. Apply de minimis foreign source in-scope revenue test
Only MNE groups with aggregated foreign source revenue from in-scope activities exceeding EUR [X] are taken into account for Amount A liability.

3. Use consolidated financial accounts to determine PBT measure
Identify eligible consolidated GAAPs and apply tax adjustments to compute MNE group standardised PBT.

4. Segmentation of PBT
MNE groups will only be required to segment the PBT measure if they do not qualify for the exemption / safe harbour and display the segmentation hallmarks.

5. Accounting for losses
If the group/segment has a loss, this is reported and carried-forward to offset again future profits. If the segment/group has a profit, available carry-forward losses can be offset.

6. Nexus test in each market jurisdiction
Nexus test applied (market revenue threshold, and other factors for CFB) to determine the market jurisdictions eligible for Amount A.

7. Formulaic calculation and allocation of Amount A
The quantum of taxable Amount A results from a three-step formulaic calculation (i.e. profitability threshold, reallocation percentage and allocation key) applied to the group/segment tax base after step 5.

8. Potential marketing and distribution profits safe harbour
For MNEs with taxable presence in eligible market jurisdiction, an option under consideration is to adjust the quantum of Amount A under step 7 to avoid any duplicative allocation of residual profit to that jurisdiction.

9-10. Identification of relieving jurisdictions, payment of Amount A tax liability and early certainty process
If Amount A tax is due, identify the jurisdiction(s) within the MNE group required to relieve double taxation and the entities that have to pay Amount A tax liability through simplified administrative procedure together with a early certainty process.

Dispute resolution

19. In addition to the innovative dispute prevention mechanisms, the Blueprint includes innovative dispute resolution mechanisms. Members of the Inclusive Framework agreed that, in the event a dispute related to Amount A might arise that is not dealt with by the Amount A dispute prevention process, appropriate mandatory binding dispute resolution mechanisms will be developed.[11] Members of the Inclusive Framework also agreed to explore mandatory binding timely dispute resolution mechanisms for disputes not related to the application of the new taxing right. These mechanisms should be respectful of jurisdictions' sovereignty, with consideration paid to the case of certain developing economies with no or low levels of mutual agreement procedure (MAP) cases. As indicated above, agreement on the scope of mandatory binding dispute resolution beyond Amount A is still pending.

1.2.4. Process map

20. To illustrate how the Blueprint would apply in practice, the below contains an overview of the process map to apply its various elements (focusing on Amount A). More details on the different steps described in this process map are available in Annex A.

Notes

[1] OECD (2015), *Addressing the Tax Challenges of the Digital Economy*, Action 1 – 2015 Final Report, OECD/G20 Base Erosion and Profit Shifting Project, OECD Publishing, Paris.

[2] OECD (2018), *Tax Challenges Arising from Digitalisation – Interim Report 2018*, Inclusive Framework on BEPS, OECD/G20 Base Erosion and Profit Shifting Project, OECD Publishing, Paris.

[3] *Addressing the Tax Challenges of the Digitalisation of the Economy – Policy Note*, as approved by the Inclusive Framework on BEPS on 23 January 2019, OECD 2019.

[4] Public Consultation Document, *Secretariat Proposal for a "Unified Approach" under Pillar One*, 9 October 2019 – 12 November 2019.

[5] OECD (2020), *Statement by the OECD/G20 Inclusive Framework on BEPS on the Two-Pillar Approach to Address the Tax Challenges Arising from the Digitalisation of the Economy – January 2020*, OECD/G20 Inclusive Framework on BEPS, OECD, Paris.

[6] For the purpose of this paper, user/market jurisdictions (henceforth "market jurisdictions") are jurisdictions where an MNE group sells its products or services or, in the case of highly digitalised businesses, provides services to users or solicits and collects data or content contributions from them.

[7] Conversely, to ensure elimination of double taxation, this new taxing right will reduce the taxing rights of jurisdictions where MNE entities entitled to residual profits under the existing profit allocation rules are resident.

[8] On 3 December 2019, the US Treasury Secretary, Steven Mnuchin sent OECD Secretary General Ángel Gurría a letter, which, while reiterating the US support for a multilateral solution, proposed that Pillar One be implemented on a 'safe harbour' basis.

[9] It should be noted that other features of Pillar One will have an impact on quantum, such as the question of whether the Amount A loss carry-forward regime is extended to "profit shortfalls", the treatment of pre-regime losses, the issue of double counting (and possible inclusion of a marketing and distribution safe

harbour), the process for identifying the "paying entities" (to eliminate double taxation). All these features will be relevant in the discussion of the quantum of Amount A.

[10] Relevant industry categories could include: fast moving consumer goods (FMCG), motor vehicles, ICT, pharmaceuticals and general distribution.

[11] This will require reaching consensus on such dispute resolution mechanism.

2 Scope

2.1. Overview

21. The new taxing right established through Amount A only applies to those MNE groups that fall within the defined scope of Amount A. The scope of Amount A is based on two elements: an activity test and a threshold test.

2.1.1. In-scope activities

22. The definition of the scope responds to the need to revisit taxing rules in response to a changed economy. The existing international tax rules generally attach a taxing right to profits deriving from a physical presence in a jurisdiction. However, given globalisation and the digitalisation of the economy, businesses can, with or without the benefit of local physical operations, participate in an active and sustained manner in the economic life of a market jurisdiction, through engagement extending beyond the mere conclusion of sales, in order to increase the value of their products, their sales and thus their profits. Such participation is attributable to the nature of what is being supplied, how it is being supplied and the active interaction or engagement with market jurisdictions. This means that the allocation of taxing rights and taxable profits can no longer be exclusively circumscribed by reference to physical presence.

23. As such, the Outline has proposed that the scope for the application of Amount A be based on an activity test. The definition of the in-scope activities reflects the types of activities where this policy challenge is most acute: ADS and CFB. Within each, the definitions are designed with sufficient breadth to accommodate new business models (and thus ensure a level playing field over time). Considerable technical work has been devoted to defining ADS and CFB activities. However, as noted in the executive summary, scope is one of the key pending political issues and the section needs to read within this context.

2.1.2. Automated digital services

24. The approach to defining ADS recognises that certain MNEs can generate revenue from the provision of ADS (including revenue from the monetisation of data) that are provided on an automated and standardised basis to a large and global customer or user base and can do so remotely to customers in markets with little or no local infrastructure. They often exploit powerful customer or user network effects and generate substantial value from interaction with users and customers. They often benefit from data and content contributions made by users and from the intensive monitoring of users' activities and the exploitation of corresponding data. In some models, the customers may interact on an almost continuous basis with the supplier's facilities and services. The ADS scope is not limited with respect to whether the services are provided to consumers, but goes beyond this, given that the possibilities for significant and sustained engagement in the market by ADS businesses is not dependent on the type of customer.

25. The definition of ADS is comprised of a positive list of ADS activities; a negative list of non-ADS activities; and a general definition. Providing a positive list and a negative list provides certainty to MNEs and tax administrations in respect of existing business models; as well as flexibility for the future, as the

lists can be updated from time to time as business models evolve. The general definition ensures that a rule remains in place to address rapidly changing business models not otherwise addressed by the positive or negative list. In practice, businesses and tax administrations will apply the rules by going through the following process. First, they will identify whether an activity is on the positive list (i.e. included); if it is, it is an ADS business. Second, if the activity is not on the positive list, they will need to check whether it is on the negative list (i.e. excluded); if it is on the negative list, it is not an ADS business. Only if an activity is not on either list is it necessary to consider whether it meets the conditions in the general definition. Finally, all questions of scope are covered by the early tax certainty process discussed in Chapter 9(including cases where an MNE ceases to be in scope).

26. The general definition of ADS (which also informs the positive and negative lists) is built on two elements:

- automated, i.e. once the system is set up the provision of the service to a particular user requires minimal human involvement on the part of the service provider; and
- digital, i.e. provided over the Internet or an electronic network.

27. The first part, "automated," reflects the fact that that the user's ability to make use of the service is possible because of the equipment and systems in place, which allow the user to obtain the service automatically, as opposed to requiring a bespoke interaction with the supplier to provide the service. In determining whether a service requires minimal human involvement the test only looks to the supplier of the service, without regard to any human involvement on the side of the user (e.g. where the user may input certain parameters into an automated system to obtain a customised result). The definition focuses on the provision of the service and therefore does not include human interventions in creating or supporting the system, such as setting up the system environment needed for the provision of the service, maintaining and updating the system environment, dealing with system errors, or making other generic, non-specific adjustments unrelated to individual user requests. Typically, such businesses have an ability to scale up and provide the same type of service to new users on an automated basis with minimal human involvement, with nil or minimal marginal cost.

28. The second part, "digital," distinguishes it from other service provision methods, such as the on-site physical performance of a service.

29. The positive list includes online advertising services; sale or other alienation of user data; online search engines; social media platforms; online intermediation platforms; digital content services; online gaming; standardised online teaching services; and cloud computing services.

30. The negative list of non-ADS activities includes customised professional services; customised online teaching services; online sale of goods and services other than ADS; revenue from the sale of a physical good irrespective of network connectivity ("Internet of things"); and services providing access to the Internet or another electronic network.

2.1.3. Consumer-facing businesses

31. The inclusion of a broader group of CFB in the scope of Amount A recognises that the ability to participate in an active and sustained manner in the economic life of a market jurisdiction goes beyond businesses that provide ADS. Although this set of businesses includes traditional businesses that have been disrupted to a lesser degree by digitalisation, CFB are able to engage with consumers in a meaningful way beyond having a local physical presence and can thereby substantially improve the value of their products and increase their sales. This significant and sustained engagement is able to take place and create value for consumer-facing MNEs because of the broader digitalisation of the economy, as technology facilitates more targeted marketing and branding, and the collection and exploitation of individual consumer data – all of which can be achieved with greater efficiency and remotely. Consumer relationships, interactions with users and consumers and wider consumer-facing intangibles drive value

for these businesses. However, the current tax rules allow them to earn residual profits associated with such intangibles remotely and without a commensurate share assigned to the market jurisdiction.

32. The inclusion of CFB in the scope of Amount A not only reflects this principle, but also recognises that in some cases, including both ADS and CFB can ensure consistent treatment of different business models that are sometimes combined. For example, certain online intermediation platforms provide both a marketplace for the sale of third parties' goods to consumers (in scope as ADS) as well as their own inventory of similar goods (in scope as CFB); music, films and certain software may be delivered online (in scope as ADS) and the same material delivered by the MNE on a physical medium (in scope as CFB); entertainment companies may directly make their content available online (in scope as ADS) as well as license the same material to others (in scope as CFB). For activities that may be both ADS and CFB, the ADS definition applies.

33. CFBs are defined as those businesses that generate revenue from the sale of goods and services of a type commonly sold to consumers, including those selling indirectly through intermediaries and by way of franchising and licensing. This definition can be further broken down into the following elements:

- "Consumer" means an individual (whether or not the direct purchaser) who acquires a good or service for personal purposes, rather than for commercial or professional purposes.
- "A good or service is "of a type commonly" sold to consumers if the nature of the good or service is such that it is designed primarily for sale to consumers. This presupposes that the good or service is made available in ways capable of being for personal consumption (such as in portions, in sufficiently finished or usable form, or at purchase points accessible by an individual, as opposed to bulk or raw material accessible to wholesale traders or other businesses only). To be designed primarily for sale to consumers means that the MNE developed the goods or services to be regularly, repeatedly, or ordinarily supplied to consumers (whether directly or indirectly), such as by engaging in consumer market research, marketing and promoting it to consumers, using consumer / user data, or providing consumer feedback or support services (irrespective of the location in which such activities take place). Conversely, an unusual or infrequent transaction with a consumer does not affect the characterisation of the goods or service.
- "Sold to" includes sale, lease, license, rent or delivery, whether directly or indirectly (e.g. through a broker, agent, intermediary or representative). This means that the product or service may still be a consumer good or service even if the contracting party to the sale is not the final consumer (such as a sale via a third party distributor, or where a franchisor has created a product but the sale is contracted by the franchisee). It also covers cases where the nature of the product is such that to be exploited it is licensed, rather than sold (e.g. rights to music), if it is otherwise of a type commonly licensed to consumers.
- CFB are (i) the MNE that is the owner of the consumer product / service and holder of the rights to the connected intangible property (including franchisors and licensors), i.e. the MNE whose "face" is apparent to the consumer; and (ii) the MNE that is the "retailer" or other contractual counterparty of the consumer (if separate from the "owner"), as they have a direct relationship to the consumer (and including franchisees and licensees that sell the consumer product directly). It does not include other third party MNEs, such as manufacturers, wholesalers and distributors, which have no relationship with the customer – whether contractual or otherwise.

34. Guidance has also been developed to clarify the possibilities for applying the definition to the pharmaceutical sector; to show how this concept applies to capture certain in-scope intermediaries, franchising and licensing; to provide guidance on certain products that could be characterised as both for consumers and businesses ("dual category"); and to delineate the situations in which a component product can be in scope. This guidance is set out in this chapter below under the "activity tests."

2.1.4. Exclusions from scope

35. As a consequence of articulating the in-scope activities and the policy rationale underpinning the approach, this chapter also identifies certain businesses that are not intended to be in scope of Amount A. The exclusions from scope and scope clarifications provide certainty for those sectors where the policy challenges of the digitalised economy do not present themselves. Sectors not in scope of Amount A include certain natural resources; certain financial services; construction, sale and leasing of residential property; and international air and shipping business.

Thresholds

36. The second element of defining the scope is the threshold test. An MNE can only be in scope of Amount A if it meets the activity test described above and two thresholds: the MNE's consolidated revenue is above a certain threshold; and its in-scope revenue earned outside its domestic market is also above a certain threshold. This ensures that Amount A focusses on the largest MNEs that generate residual profit available for reallocation under Amount A, and that the compliance and administrative burden is proportionate to the expected tax benefits. This will also keep the number of MNEs affected at an administrable level for tax administrations (including the early tax certainty process).

37. Having regard to the economic impact assessment,[1] setting a threshold below [EUR 750 million] would lead to substantial compliance burdens but without commensurate benefits in terms of the available reallocation for market jurisdictions. At the same time, even at that threshold, there is a significant number of MNEs that would be in scope, and consideration needs to be given to operating the new Amount A system, including the early certainty process, as efficiently as possible particularly in the initial years. As such, an option to operate the thresholds on a transition or phase in basis is being considered, whereby the two thresholds are initially set at a higher level and gradually reduced over time.

2.2. Activity tests

38. The activity tests proposed in the Outline align the scope of Amount A with its policy objective. They are designed to capture those MNEs that are able to participate in a sustained and significant manner in the economic life of a market jurisdiction, without necessarily having a commensurate level of taxable presence in that market (as based on existing nexus rules). This covers MNEs under the broad categories of ADS and CFB. The definitions of each are discussed in turn, followed by a discussion of the sectors that are excluded from the scope of Amount A.

2.2.1. Automated digital services

39. The proposed definition for ADS is comprised of a general definition; a positive list of services that are in any event in scope of ADS business and a negative list of services that are not in scope of ADS business.

40. The general definition, supported by updatable lists, provides certainty combined with flexibility. The benefit of using a general definition supported by updateable lists is that it will be capable of accommodating rapid changes in technology that give rise to new types of ADS not otherwise contemplated by the positive or negative list, and allow the new Amount A rules to stand the test of time. As it would not be possible for legislators to continuously maintain exhaustive positive and negative lists that keep pace with these developments, the general definition ensures that there is a rule in place to bring in scope (or exclude from scope) business models that are not otherwise explicitly contained on the positive list or negative list, until a new or evolved business model can be included on the positive or negative list.

The application of the general definition will be supported by an early certainty process, to ensure that MNEs and tax administrations have certainty and consistency in the application of the scope.

41. The benefit of using the positive and negative lists is that it provides certainty and precision with respect to the business models that are currently known, and avoids the need for those businesses to apply the general test. As these lists are then updated as jurisdictions gain experience with the rules (including being informed by the early certainty process) and new business models evolve, those lists will also continue to provide certainty over time.

42. In practice, businesses and tax administrations could generally apply the rules by going through the following process. First, identify whether an activity is on the positive list (i.e. included); if it is, it is an ADS business. Second, if the activity is not on the positive list, identify whether it is on the negative list (i.e. excluded); if it is, it is not an ADS business. Only if an activity is not on either list is it necessary to consider whether, on first principles, it meets the conditions in the general definition. It is noted that if an MNE does not fall within the definition of ADS following this approach, it may however be in scope as consumer-facing business. The legal implementation of the positive and negative lists and the general definition (such as in a multilateral convention) remains under consideration, as well as more broadly the process and implementation of changes to the lists.

43. Although the general definition would apply only in residual cases of activities that are not identified in either the positive or negative list, and therefore as a backstop to those lists, the principle itself has informed the creation of those lists. For this reason, this chapter first presents the general definition, and then the content of the positive and negative lists, a discussion of dual category / bundled ADS, and finally other definitions that apply for ADS. In each case, the rule appears in the first box, followed by the accompanying commentary in the second box.

Box 2.1. ADS – General definition

An ADS[2] is one where:

- The service is on the positive list; or
- The service is
  - automated (i.e. once the system is set up the provision of the service to a particular user requires minimal human involvement on the part of the service provider); and
  - digital (i.e. provided over the Internet or an electronic network); and
  - it is not on the negative list.

Box 2.2. ADS – Commentary

The definition of ADS is structured around a general definition, combined with both a positive list, and a negative list. An activity on the positive list is an ADS business. An activity on the negative list is not an ADS business.[3]

The first condition, being whether the service is automated, reflects the fact that that the user's ability to make use of the service is possible because of the equipment and systems in place, which allow the user to obtain the service automatically, as opposed to requiring a bespoke interaction with the supplier to provide the service.

In determining whether a service requires minimal human involvement the test only looks to the supplier of the service, without regard to any human involvement on the side of the user (e.g. where the user may input certain parameters into an automated system to obtain a customised result). Furthermore, the definition focuses on the provision of the service and therefore does not include human involvement in creating or supporting the system, such as setting up the system environment needed for the provision of the service, maintaining and updating the system environment, dealing with system errors, or making other generic, non-specific adjustments unrelated to individual user requests. Finally, the threshold of minimal human involvement would not be crossed where the provision of the service to new users involves very limited human response to individual user requests / input at the service delivery point or where in individual cases involving particular, more complex problems, the programmes running the system direct the customer to a staff member.

A general feature of the concept of "automated" is whether there is an ability to scale up and provide the same type of service to new users with minimal human involvement. This feature aims to identify ADS businesses that benefit from significant economies of scale, rather than to suggest that there is no human involvement required in the business. For many ADS businesses, developing the system that delivers the offered service may require a large degree of upfront human involvement and capital inputs (such as creating algorithms to deliver the automated service including such features as tailoring the offering to the user's preferences). It distinguishes ADS businesses by looking to whether the marginal cost in terms of additional human involvement of providing the same services to additional users is nil or almost nil. In other words, once the offered service of an ADS business is developed (such as the music catalogue or social media platform), then the business can provide that service to one user, or to one thousand users, on an automated basis with the same basic business processes and therefore benefit from scale without mass in the market jurisdiction; whereas many non-ADS businesses would have material per unit costs in connection with providing the services to new customers.

With respect to the second condition of the general definition (i.e. that the service is digital), it is inherent in the nature of ADS that it will be provided over the Internet or an electronic network. This distinguishes it from other service provision methods, such as the on-site physical performance of a service. For example, an online intermediary platform website that provides the service of bringing users and hotel offerings together and allowing users to book a hotel online, derives revenue for providing that online intermediation service. It is in scope as ADS. This is different from the case of the hotel itself, which earns revenue for providing physical accommodation, which is not provided over the Internet. Although the hotel may have an online booking service on its website, it is not deriving revenue from providing that function as a service per se but from providing the accommodation (and the online booking is of no use without the main activity of providing that accommodation). It is not in scope of ADS (but would be in the scope of CFB). This condition does not distinguish between different Internet or electronic network transmission methods. It is also not affected by whether or not the service provider owns, leases or otherwise controls the transmission equipment.

The third condition is that the service is not on the negative list, noted above. This ensures that the negative list takes precedence over the general definition.

Positive list

44. As noted above, the approach to defining ADS starts with the proposition that if an activity is on the positive list, it is an ADS (with no need to additionally apply the general definition). The positive list currently contains the following nine categories of services.

- Online advertising services;
- Sale or other alienation of user data;

- Online search engines;
- Social media platforms;
- Online intermediation platforms;
- Digital content services;
- Online gaming;
- Standardised online teaching services; and
- Cloud computing services.

45. The categories are not mutually exclusive and may overlap (for example, a digital content service could be funded in whole or in part by online advertising). Thus, an ADS business may be comprised of multiple ADS – some of which are directly revenue generating and others of which are not. As another example of such a two-sided business model, an online advertising service may obtain a higher price for its advertisements by targeting them based on data about viewer interests obtained by providing the viewers with “free” access to a search engine or social media platform. As discussed in the chapter on revenue sourcing, ADS will be categorised for revenue sourcing purposes according to the nature of the revenue source for the service. The definitions of each category, supported by a commentary to provide further guidance, are set out in turn below.

Box 2.3 Online advertising services – Definition

This means online services aimed at placing advertisement on a digital interface,[4] including services for the purchase, storage and distribution of advertising messages, and for advertising monitoring and performance measurement. It includes related systems for attracting potential viewers of the advertisements and collecting content contributions from them and data regarding them, including via the provision of access to a digital interface, such as search engines, social media platforms or digital content services.

Box 2.4. Online advertising services – Commentary

This category is drafted to be broad and to cover automated online services throughout the online advertising value chain. This includes direct advertising services, such as where social media platforms, online search engines, online intermediation platforms and digital content providers directly sell advertising inventory for display on the digital interfaces they operate. It also extends to the automated systems and processes for the purchase and sale of advertising inventory (such as demand-side platforms, supply-side platforms, ad exchanges, ad verification services, etc.). Given the broad definition of “digital interface” it also includes online advertising displayed on an Internet-connected good (“Internet of things”) provided that there is such an identifiable advertising revenue stream.

Box 2.5. Sale or other alienation of user data – Definition

This means selling,[5] licensing or otherwise alienating to an unrelated third party customer user data generated by users of a digital interface.[6]

Box 2.6. Sale or other alienation of user data – Commentary

This category is drafted to capture business models that monetise user data generated on a digital interface by selling, licensing or otherwise alienating it to unrelated third parties.

It applies to data generated by users on a digital interface. The definition of a digital interface is intended to be broad, and would cover Internet-connected interfaces embedded in a physical good (i.e. the Internet of things) regardless of whether the sale of that good itself is within the scope of Amount A.

"User data" includes information such as a user's habits, spending, location, environment, usage of services, hobbies, or personal interests, including anonymised and aggregated data (including geolocation information and user traffic levels).

Further consideration is being given to the extent to which user data would also include the provision of data such as industrial, scientific, statistical, or other data not linked to natural persons (such as businesses that acquire and disseminate information about investments and financial markets, or scientific research). As the definitions of ADS are not mutually exclusive, such businesses could already be captured under digital content services, where they provide that data in an automated way, such as an online database or online library.

The source of data may be collected as raw data by the MNE itself (e.g. the manufacturer/seller of a home heating system collecting data about energy use, or a social media company collecting data about its users) or it may be acquired from another business. The source of the data would not be relevant for determining scope provided that it is generated by a user through a digital interface.

To the extent that the data is provided as part of a customised service, such as a professional marketing service, the guidance to be provided as set out below under dual category ADS and bundled services would apply.

Box 2.7. Online search engines – Definition

This means making a digital interface available to users for the purpose of allowing them to search across the Internet for webpages or information hosted on digital interfaces.

Box 2.8. Online search engines – Commentary

Many online search engines are monetised through online advertising services and/or services transmitting data about users. To the extent these services are funded via online advertising or the sale of data, such revenue would be treated under those respective categories (including for revenue sourcing purposes).

This category would extend to instances where an online search engine charges users for access, for example under a subscription model, or where online search engine technologies are provided for incorporation into a third-party host website (e.g. a "search box").

This category would not include services such as online databases or 'internal' website search functions that are not monetised, where the search results are limited to data hosted on that same digital interface (or related digital interfaces). However, if an online database or an 'internal' website search function service involves monetisation of services and it falls under the positive list or meets the general definition of ADS, it will be covered under ADS.

Box 2.9. Social media platforms – Definition

This means making a platform available on a digital interface to facilitate the interaction between users or between users and user-generated content.

Box 2.10. Social media platforms – Commentary

This category would include a range of activities that rely on an active and engaged user base to create value, such as social and professional networking websites, micro-blogging platforms, video or image sharing platforms, online dating websites, platforms dedicated to sharing user reviews, as well as online call and messaging platforms, some of which could overlap with online intermediation platforms.

This category would extend to instances where the social media platform charges users for access, for example under a subscription model. To the extent these services are funded via online advertising, the sale of data, or subscription models (which follows the business model for digital content services), such revenue would be treated under those respective categories (including for revenue sourcing purposes).

This category does not extend to instances where user interaction is merely incidental to the core purpose of the digital interface, for example where a company sells its own inventory online and the website allows users to post comments or reviews or where a website allows a user to engage in an online chat with a sales representative.

Box 2.11. Online intermediation platforms – Definition

This means making a platform available on a digital interface to enable users to sell, lease, advertise, display or otherwise offer goods or services to other users. It does not include the online sale of goods and services of the platform's own inventory.

Box 2.12. Online intermediation platforms – Commentary

This category would apply where the service enables the interaction between third party users, irrespective of the nature of the interaction, the characteristics of the users involved, whether an underlying transaction is itself in scope, or the extent of the service provider's activities in facilitating the interaction.

This category would extend to instances where the online intermediation platform charges users for its online intermediation services, for example through commission, listing or subscription fees. To the extent the intermediation service is funded via online advertising or the sale of data, such revenue would be treated under those respective categories (including for revenue sourcing purposes).

The definition would include intermediation services, and would not include the online sale of goods and services which form part of the platform's own inventory (which may however be captured under CFB). This result would also be achieved through the requirement in the definition that there must be more than one user (i.e. the reference to "users" in the plural), read together with the definition of a "user" which specifically excludes the provider of the service or any entity in the same group. The online sale of goods and services other than ADS (e.g. the direct sale to consumers by an MNE of its own inventory on its own website) is also confirmed as out-of-scope in the negative list.

However, there may be exceptional cases where an MNE does sell its own goods or services, while essentially performing an intermediation service and remaining insulated from inventory risk. As such, further consideration is being given to address instances where an online intermediation platform such as an online marketplace operates on a resell model, without incurring the ordinary commercial risks associated with the provision of the underlying product (such as where the business only takes flash-title and is insulated from inventory risk, is fully indemnified against product liability risk and credit risk). For example, after a user secures a reservation for a car rental service through an online platform, the platform service provider may purchase the car rental service itself, after receiving the customer's order, before immediately reselling it to the customer. However, the platform service provider is not incurring any of the ordinary commercial risks associated with the provision of the underlying car rental service (e.g. inventory risk) and its service arguably remains, in essence, one of intermediation.

Box 2.13. Digital content services – Definition

This means the automated provision of content through digital means, whether by way of online streaming, accessing or downloading digital content (e.g. music, books, videos, texts, games, applications, computer programmes, software, online newspapers, online libraries and online databases), whether for access one time, for a limited period or in perpetuity.

Box 2.14. Digital content services – Commentary

This category is drafted to capture the different forms which digital content can take when acquired by a user. This category includes, for example, music, books, videos, texts, games, applications, computer programmes, software, online newspapers, online libraries and online databases (such as subscription-based statistical or academic online databases).

It does not include simply making a digital interface available to users. The purpose from a user's perspective in a digital service transaction is the acquisition of the digital content, whether for access one time, for a limited period or in perpetuity.

It includes streaming, accessing or downloading digital content. By way of background, the streaming and downloading consists of the same process of transmitting data, either as a continuous flow (in effect like a temporary download) or as a file saved to the user's device available for later use. A number of streaming services allow both temporary streaming and downloading, but from the perspective of the ADS provider, the process is essentially the same. Therefore, for the purposes of the scope of Amount A, digital content streaming should include accessing and downloading, under the inclusive heading of "digital content services." Otherwise, distorted and administratively burdensome results would follow if streaming series were only included in scope to the extent that users were temporarily "streaming" rather than downloading the material.

The sale of software was enumerated as a CFB in the Outline. However, the sale of software also meets the general definition of ADS where the provision of that software is automated requiring minimal human involvement to make it available to users and the software is delivered over the Internet. As such, software that is accessed or downloaded over the Internet would therefore qualify as ADS under the "digital content services" category (or it may also qualify as ADS under the "cloud computing" category ("Software-as-a-service").

There are two exceptions to this. First, to the extent that software is acquired as a tangible product (e.g. a packaged product on a CD that does not require any connection to the Internet to access the software), then it would not be an ADS (although it could be included as a CFB alongside other physical, offline items such as music, films, books or computer games purchased on a physical medium.) In order not to create distortions, where the tangible medium has no other purpose than to provide the user with information required to access the digital content via Internet or electronic network (such as a printed access code for downloading the material), then it would remain as ADS.

Second, reflecting the discussion above and the "automated" aspect of the definition, highly customised software that has been designed for a particular businesses' needs (and which may be negotiated with tailored pricing depending on the software package chosen and various elements incorporated) would not be included as ADS, even if the final product is made available online. This is because it would require significant human involvement, more akin to professional services, and would not reflect the same idea of there being limited additional unit costs to make the software available to additional users. This refers to customisation undertaken at the specific request of one customer, in response to its unique requirements. Where software has been designed with particular options or features, which a customer can choose or personalise without any significant human involvement on behalf of the service provider during the online purchase, such software would be in scope of ADS. Thus, the degree of customisation and the level of human involvement should be the primary factors to characterise the provision of software as ADS or otherwise. If the provision of the software was bundled, comprising standardised modules and customised modules, the guidance to be provided as set out below under dual category ADS and bundled services would apply.

Box 2.15. Online gaming – Definition

This means making a digital interface available for the purposes of allowing users to interact with one another in the same game environment.

Box 2.16 Online gaming – Commentary

This category would apply irrespective of whether the access to the game is by way of fee or available for free. It applies to all multiplayer gaming enabled by the Internet, such as massively multiplayer online (MMO) games, or other games that enable multiplayer functionalities, and regardless of the device or platform the game is accessed through.

The provision of in-game purchases, or any other online purchases within the game would also be in scope under this category.

This category would not generally include single-player games (which if streamed, accessed or downloaded over the Internet would be in scope of digital content services) or the purchase of a game sold on tangible media (as above for software, and which would be in scope of CFB).

Box 2.17. Standardised online teaching services – Definition

This means the provision of an online education programme provided to users, which does not require:

(i) the live presence of an instructor; or

(ii) significant customisation on behalf of an instructor to a particular user or limited group of users, whether with respect to the curriculum, teaching materials, or feedback provided.

Box 2.18. Standardised online teaching services – Commentary

This category would include pre-packaged, non-customised education products such as a pre-recorded series of lectures, and the content of which is not customised to each individual user (e.g. massive open online courses). Although these services may allow users to discuss the course content with each other on discussion forums within the platform, there is no or only limited interaction with instructors. Another key feature of standardised teaching services is that coursework completed by the user is generally not marked by the instructors, but either marked automatically, or by other users. Non-ADS online teaching services may be captured under consumer-facing business.

This category would not cover online education products that are customised to a student, or to a limited group of students, which may incorporate certain ancillary elements that are automated (e.g. a pre-recorded lecture offered as part of a customised education package; automatically graded assignments accompanying a live-streamed lecture). Such services would also not meet the general definitions of ADS, and as such are included in the negative list under the category of customised online teaching services.

Box 2.19. Cloud computing services – Definition

This means the provision of network access to on-demand standardised information technology (IT) resources, including infrastructure as a service, platforms as a service, or software as a service (such as computing services, storage services, database services, migration services, networking and content delivery services, webhosting, and end-user applications and software).

Box 2.20. Cloud computing services – Commentary

The network access to on-demand standardised IT resources includes all types of standardised cloud computing services, including computing services, storage services, database services, migration services, networking and content delivery services, webhosting, and end-user applications and software.

- Computing services include virtual servers in the cloud, the ability to run and manage web apps using remote computing, the ability to run code on remote computers in response to events and the ability to run batch code jobs at scale;
- Storage services include storage in the cloud and data transport;
- Database services include data warehousing, database management and caching systems;
- Migration services include database migration and data transport;
- Networking and content delivery services include access to a virtual private cloud (an isolated cloud that the customer can control) and use of a global content delivery network (whereby content such as videos are transferred to viewers at high transfer speeds);
- Web hosting services include website and webpage hosting; and
- End-user applications and software services include systems permitting users to develop access or use software and applications.

Cloud computing services[7] are typically provided in a standardised and highly automated way. Standardised cloud computing services may be 'assembled' or configured together for a particular customer (whether by the service provider or by the customer on a self-serve basis). For example, a business may choose to obtain a certain combination of data storage, data security and web-hosting services from a cloud computing provider. Each such cloud computing service is standardised, irrespective of the particular combination of services chosen by the client. In other words, although a customer's activities may be different (e.g. making available different music on their platform or hosting a different website), from a cloud computing company's perspective the act of providing the data storage or hosting the website in the cloud is essentially the same.

Some cloud computing services, however, involve a high degree of human involvement to customise the service to the needs of a particular client. For example, a hospital may hire a cloud computing service provider to develop a bespoke cloud-based IT system to manage its complex operations (e.g. software to track patient care and medical records, IT security solutions to respect the applicable legal requirements for patient confidentiality, etc.). Such services are closer to engineering and consulting services, i.e. professional services, which are on the negative list.

In order to ensure that the cloud computing services category on the positive list only captures those that reflect the principles of ADS, the proposed definition refers to 'standardised' cloud computing services. This way, a bespoke cloud solution involving a high degree of human involvement on behalf of the provider's staff (e.g. engineers or consultants) to create a new computing solution (as opposed to configuring existing solutions) would not be included. To the extent that the human involvement relates only to the configuration of standardised cloud computing products, the integration of standardised cloud computing products into a customer's existing IT architecture, or ancillary customer support, the human involvement will be considered ancillary to the cloud computing service, which would be covered by this category.

Where a cloud computing service provider is in the business of providing a bundled service comprising both standardised and customised services (including where customised services are built upon standardised modules), the guidance to be developed under "dual category ADS and bundled services" below would apply.

Negative list

46. If an activity is not on the positive list, the next step would be to determine if it is on the negative list. If so, it is not an ADS. The proposed negative list currently contains the following five categories of services:

- Customised professional services;
- Customised online teaching services;
- Online sale of goods and services other than ADS;
- Revenue from the sale of a physical good, irrespective of network connectivity ("Internet of things"); and
- Services providing access to the Internet or another electronic network.

47. This section proposes definitions for the services that would be contained on the negative list, together with a Commentary.

Box 2.21. Customised professional services – Definition

This means customised professional services, whether provided individually or as a firm, such as legal, accounting, architectural, engineering and medical services.

Box 2.22. Customised professional services – Commentary

This category confirms that customised professional services are not within the general definition of ADS. Although such services may be delivered online (e.g. legal advice sent by email, an architect sending drawings in PDF format; or an accountant sending calculations in a spreadsheet), they require customisation to each client, through the tailored exercise of professional judgment and bespoke interactions. These services are not automated and require more than minimal human involvement on behalf of the professional individual or firm. They would also not be scalable without additional human involvement.

Where a professional service relies heavily on ADS, for example if a law firm relies on artificial intelligence software (AI) to conduct due diligence, or an architect's firm to draw plans, revenue from the provision of the professional service itself will remain out-of-scope of ADS. This is because human involvement is required on behalf of the professional to use the AI and exercise professional judgment in order to provide the final service product to the client. Payments made by such a firm to a third-party AI provider, however, will generally be captured under ADS (as cloud computing or digital content services).

By contrast, where a user directly accesses an automated service online that may be equivalent to a professional service (e.g. if a user self-serves legal advice on a dedicated platform) then such service would qualify as ADS to the extent that it meets a category on the positive list or the elements of the general definition.

Box 2.23. Customised online teaching services – Definition

This means live or recorded teaching services delivered online, where the teacher customises the service (such as by providing individualised, non-automated feedback and support) to the needs of the student or limited group of students and the Internet or electronic network is used as a tool simply for communication between the teacher and student.

Box 2.24. Customised online teaching services – Commentary

This category confirms that customised teaching services delivered online would not be within the general definition of ADS where the Internet or electronic network is used as a tool simply for communication between the teacher and student.

This includes online education packages that are significantly customised to a student, or to a limited group of students, even where certain ancillary elements of the product are automated (e.g. a pre-recorded lecture offered as part of a customised education package; automatically graded assignments accompanying a live-streamed, customised lecture).

However, standardised online teaching service with ancillary interaction with an instructor is contained in the positive list.

Box 2.25. Online sale of goods and services other than ADS – Definition

This means the sale of a good or service completed through a digital interface where:

- the digital interface is operated by the provider of the good or service;
- the main substance of the transaction is the provision of the good or service; and
- the good or service does not otherwise qualify as an ADS.

Box 2.26. Online sale of goods and services other than ADS – Commentary

This category would apply to sellers that use a digital platform to sell their own non-digital goods and services to customers. While the sale can be transacted over the Internet, these businesses are sellers of non-digital goods and non-digital services, rather than offering a digital service per se. Applying the general definition of ADS, the provision of the intended good / service (e.g. the use of the hotel) is not of a type that is automated but requires additional human interventions to make that service available to additional users. As such, for the sake of clarity, the sale of an MNE's own goods and services where the order / booking and processing is done electronically are included on the negative list.

See also above on the positive list for online intermediation services.

Box 227 Revenue from the sale of a physical goods, irrespective of network connectivity ('Internet of things") – Definition

This would apply irrespective of the network connectivity of that physical good, provided that there is no separately identifiable ADS revenue stream attached to that physical good (either at the time of purchase or a later date).

Box 2.28 Revenue from the sale of physical goods, irrespective of network connectivity ('Internet of things") – Commentary

Increasingly, physical goods may be connected to the Internet, or bundled with an online service. There are broadly three categories for analysing that service, as follows:

First, beyond the sale of the physical good, such goods can be additionally monetised with a customer beyond the purchase of the physical good through different revenue streams (whether at the outset at the time of purchase or at a later date), and those revenue streams are captured by existing ADS categories on the positive list. Common examples include:

- Sale or other alienation of user data. The monetisation of data collected from the connected object is ADS, where that meets the definition above. For example, if an automobile maker designs an Internet-connected car that collects location data and the company sells the data about the user's habits, location and so forth to third parties for marketing purposes, this would meet the definition above, including because the definition of digital interface above is sufficiently broad to capture the monetisation of information collected from an Internet of things device.
- Online advertising services. Online advertising revenue relating to advertisements displayed on the connected object is ADS, captured under online advertising services (e.g. supermarket adverts displayed on an Internet-connected fridge's interface). This is because the definition of online advertising refers to displaying an advert on a digital interface, which is defined in a sufficiently broad way to include Internet connected devices.

- Other ADS. The user of the connected object may pay for different types of ADS relating to, and/or to be accessed through, the connected object (e.g. subscription payments for a tracking application to be used on a personal bracelet; streaming music through a virtual assistant device; online purchase of upgraded software to activate or enhance a product). These would be captured under the relevant ADS category (e.g. digital content services), which apply regardless of the type of physical good that supports the network connection through which such ADS is delivered.

To the extent that these revenue streams are separately identifiable from the sale price of the physical good, that ADS revenue stream would be captured as ADS. Some typical cases where this is likely to arise are noted in the commentary on the relevant ADS definitions on the positive list above. Further consideration is required to address cases where a separate revenue stream can be inferred even if not explicitly identified as such. For example, if the good is sold in two versions in which the main distinguishing feature is that one includes a subscription to a digital service and the other does not, the price difference may be treated as the revenue associated with the digital service.

Second, there are certain types of machinery and industrial products that may contain a digital component. For example, monitoring the performance of an engine and providing remote technical support. This will typically require significant human involvement to provide the core function, which is using that information to conduct maintenance and repairs on the machinery. This is related to the operation of the machinery, rather than the service provider separately monetising that data in an automated way with a third party. This means that even if the Internet-enabled functionality of the machinery were separately tested under the dual category ADS and bundled services analysis, it would not meet the general definition of ADS or any item on the positive list, meaning the entire item is out-of-scope. For the purpose of certainty, this will be added to the negative list, and revisited at a future point in time if any changes are required.

Third, there are certain consumer products, known as the Internet of things, that provide a network of everyday devices, appliances, and other objects equipped with computer chips and sensors that can collect and transmit data through the Internet, which enables additional features of the product to be used. For example, fitness trackers may give access to an online platform that analyses data, allows interaction with other users, and provides information on workout programmes. It may be that many consumer goods now contain some software and may in the future be Internet-enabled, and bringing all such items into the scope of ADS would be over-broad having regard to the general definition of ADS above, given that the sale of a physical good is not ADS because it is not a service, nor is it provided over the Internet or through an electronic network. One option to address this would be to say that where the physical good embodies an ADS, part of the sale price of that physical good could nevertheless be attributable to that ADS. However, treating a portion of Internet of things goods as within the scope of ADS would be difficult in practice and highly fact intensive for every given product that exists or will exist – and would be likely to generate disputes – as it would require trying to separate the value of the digital component of the service as the ADS, as opposed to the value created by the other parts of the good / service. In any case, the sale of the object, to the extent it is otherwise a consumer-facing product, would already be included in scope under CFB.

Based on the three categories above, the scope of ADS would include the revenue from the Internet of things to the extent separately identifiable as another ADS on the positive list (the first category above), and to exclude the revenue from the physical sale of goods such as industrial or consumer goods. This could be revisited in the future as the Internet of things evolves.

Box 2.29. Services providing access to the Internet or electronic network – Definition

This would apply to the provision of access (i.e. connection, subscription, installation) to the Internet or electronic network, irrespective of the delivery method.

Box 2.30. Services providing access to the Internet or electronic network – Commentary

This category is drafted to clarify that services providing access to the Internet or to an electronic network would be out-of-scope of ADS. This is in line with the policy of Amount A as the provision of such services typically requires a degree of local infrastructure and is subject to local telecommunication regulations. This category covers the provision of access (i.e. connection, subscription, installation) to the Internet or electronic network irrespective of the delivery method, namely over wire, lines, cable, fibre optics, satellite transmission or other means, although this could be revisited if needed as technology advances.

Internet Service Packages (ISPs) in which the Internet access component is an ancillary and subordinate part (i.e. a package that goes beyond mere Internet access comprising various elements (e.g. content pages containing news, weather, travel information; games fora; web-hosting; access to chat-lines etc.)) would not be covered by this category. In such cases, the rules applicable to dual category ADS and bundled packages would apply.

Dual category ADS / bundled packages

48. Where an MNE is engaged in multiple activities, and those are clearly identifiable as separate, stand-alone services by reference to revenue streams, the definitions apply to each activity separately. This includes cases where an MNE provides more than one type of ADS (e.g. an online intermediation platform could be simultaneously operating the intermediation service and running online advertising).

49. However, some MNEs may be engaged in activities that are not clearly severable, and represent a "dual category" or "bundled package." There are two ways that dual category ADS or bundled services can occur: (i) an aspect of the service meets the ADS definition, but it comes with a non-ADS service; (ii) a physical good that comes with a service, where that service may or may not meet the ADS definition. For example, in the first case, a cloud computing MNE may provide a package that is built on standardised modules, but where a customer can also select highly customised elements which would require significant human involvement. An example of the second case is an Internet-connected physical device, which is discussed further above under the negative list.

50. In some cases, and perhaps increasingly in the future, the ADS and non-ADS elements may be highly integrated and thus be considered to be a single service. Where ADS represents a substantial part of the overall service, and the non-ADS elements derive significant benefits from their connection to the ADS elements, then the overall service might be considered as ADS. By contrast, where the ADS elements are merely ancillary or a technical support feature for the rest of the service (e.g. an automated chat function to screen a user's request as an entry point to the service), and the rest of the service requires human involvement to provide the service as described above, the overall service may not be considered to be ADS, given the relative substantive contribution of the ADS within the bundled package.

51. Work is ongoing to address this issue. The starting point being contemplated is whether there are multiple supplies that are identifiable and substantive in their own right (which could be evaluated, for

example, by whether such supplies generate a separate revenue stream or are invoiced or priced separately for the customer, having regard to the need to avoid planning opportunities, such as arbitrary splitting of invoices), in which case each individual supply would be tested against the definitions. If the supplies are not separately identifiable and substantive in their own right, there could be an evaluation of the supply as a whole. Further guidance will be developed to determine the appropriate materiality threshold above which the ADS element may be considered to be a "substantial part" or highly integrated as part of an overall service, or where elements are ancillary. Consideration is also being given to whether there are ways to provide certainty where a substantive part of the supply is on either the positive or negative list. Guidance will take into account the need to have simple, administrable and implementable rules that create certainty and consistency, as well as the documentation requirements to substantiate the application of the guidance in a given case.

Other definitions for ADS

Box 2.31. Other definitions

For the purposes of ADS, the following definitions would apply:

"Digital interface" means any programme or other system allowing access by users to software, content or other information that is accessible by users online, such as websites and mobile applications, regardless of the type of physical support enabling such access. The definition of a digital interface is intended to be broad, and would cover Internet-connected interfaces embedded in a physical good (i.e. the Internet of things) regardless of whether the sale of that good itself is within the scope of the new taxing right of Amount A.

"Online" means over the Internet or an electronic network;

i. "User" means any individual or business accessing a service, but does not include the provider, or a member of the same MNE group as the provider, of that service;

ii. an employee of a person referred to in paragraph (i) acting in the course of that person's business.

2.2.2. Consumer-facing businesses

Defining consumer-facing businesses

52. CFBs would include businesses that generate revenue from the sale of goods and services of a type commonly sold to consumers, i.e. individuals that are purchasing items for personal use and not for commercial or professional purposes.

53. The proposed definition of CFB breaks down the elements of "commonly sold to a consumer" as well as provides clarity on the types of MNE businesses that are "consumer-facing."

Box 2.32. Consumer-facing business – General definition

A consumer-facing business is a business that supplies goods or services, directly or indirectly, that are of a type commonly sold to consumers, and / or licenses or otherwise exploits intangible property that is connected to the supply of such goods or services.

"Consumer" means an individual (whether or not the direct purchaser) who acquires a good or service for personal purposes, rather than for commercial or professional purposes.

A good or service is "of a type commonly" sold to consumers if the nature of the good or service is such that it is designed primarily for sale to consumers. This presupposes that the good or service is made available in ways capable of being for personal consumption (such as in portions, in sufficiently finished or usable form, or at purchase points accessible by an individual, as opposed to bulk or raw material accessible to wholesale traders or other businesses only). To be designed primarily for sale to consumers means that the MNE developed the goods or services to be regularly, repeatedly, or ordinarily supplied to consumers (whether directly or indirectly), such as by engaging in consumer market research, marketing and promoting it to consumers, using consumer / user data, or providing consumer feedback or support services (irrespective of the location in which such activities take place). Conversely, an unusual or infrequent transaction with a consumer does not affect the characterisation of the goods or service.

"Sold to" includes sale, lease, license, rent or delivery, whether directly or indirectly (e.g. through a broker, agent, intermediary or representative). This means that the product or service may still be a consumer good or service even if the contracting party to the sale is not the final consumer (such as a sale via a third party distributor, or where a franchisor has created a product but the sale is contracted by the franchisee). In other words, an MNE is in scope based on the nature of the product / service and this is not altered by the role of a third party in the distribution channel; but this does not mean that such third party itself is a consumer-facing business, as set out below. It also covers cases where the nature of the product is such that to be exploited it is licensed, rather than sold (e.g. rights to music), if it is otherwise of a type commonly licensed to consumers.

A service that is included as an ADS, being the more specific definition, is excluded from the definition of consumer-facing businesses. This avoids duplication and recognises the fact that a single classification is needed as it has implications for other aspects of Amount A, such as the appropriate nexus test.

An MNE would be regarded as being a "consumer-facing business" if the MNE is the owner of the consumer product / service and holder of the rights to the connected intangible property (including franchisors and licensors). This is the MNE whose "face" is apparent to the consumer. The term "owner" in this context does not refer to any party that at some point holds legal title to a consumer good, as there may be several legal owners in the supply chain. To be an "owner" in this context, the MNE must own the product and the related brands.

In addition, the "retailer" or other contractual counterparty of the consumer (if separate from the "owner") would also be in scope, as they have a direct relationship to the consumer. In other words, they are perhaps the most obvious case of a "consumer-facing" business. The profit of the retailer will be different from that captured for the "owner," thus there is no duplication caused by the inclusion of two different MNEs in the value chain. This category may also include franchisees and licensees that sell the consumer product directly, as described further below.

Other third party MNEs, such as manufacturers, wholesalers and distributors, which have no relationship with the customer – whether contractual or otherwise – and are therefore not in scope. While revenue and profitability thresholds may in any event exclude those types of intermediaries, they are already excluded as they do not have an active and sustained engagement in a market jurisdiction (beyond the mere conclusion of sales) without necessarily investing in local infrastructure and operations.

An MNE that meets the definition may, however, be (in whole or part) out-of-scope as provided in the specific exclusions, as set out further below. These exclusions are based on policy factors, such as where for specific reasons associated with a sector the residual profits are already captured in the market.

54. The test must be applied by the MNE. The test is to be applied with respect to the intended market. For example, where the MNE makes sales to a market that has unique tastes, preferences, regulatory or cultural requirements, and the product or service is not available in many other markets, it can still be a consumer-facing product.

55. For borderline cases, the early tax certainty process will be available to provide clarification and ensure consistent treatment across the Inclusive Framework.

56. The following sections discuss the application of the definition to the following particular sectors and business models: pharmaceuticals, franchising, licensing, dual use goods / services, and dual use intermediate products and components.

Pharmaceuticals

57. Broadly speaking, the pharmaceutical industry sells medications and medical devices.[8] To the extent that medical devices are products of a type commonly sold to consumers, these will be in scope. This remainder of this section discusses pharmaceuticals (i.e. drugs).

58. In some jurisdictions, funding from governments and compulsory insurance schemes play a large role in purchasing pharmaceuticals, particularly for those medicines dispensed in hospitals and those available by prescription only. For example, on average, these schemes covered 58% of spending on retail pharmaceuticals in OECD countries,[9] although the situation varies from one country to another.

59. It is noted that with respect to drugs, the government can regulate the prices at which drugs can be sold. It is recognised that pricing of drugs can be impacted by governments and insurance companies and are not exclusively based on consumer demand (e.g. where government directly acquires the drugs, or regulates the pricing). However, this does not change the fact that products are sold to and used by consumers (whether directly or indirectly), and that these products are generating (in some cases, e.g. when the drug is still patented) substantial profits for pharmaceutical MNEs. Therefore, even if the size of that profit may be influenced by the regulator, this regulation does not by itself take pharmaceuticals out-of-scope.

60. The analysis below contains two possible approaches for considering the extent to which pharmaceuticals would be in the scope of Amount A as a CFB:

- All drugs that are sold or administered to a consumer are in scope; or
- The scope is based on whether the drugs are sold over-the-counter (OTC) or by prescription.

61. These two options are discussed in turn.

Option 1 – All drugs in scope

62. The first approach starts from the notion that all pharmaceuticals are ultimately consumed / used by individual consumers. Taking this approach would mean that all drugs used by patients / consumers would be in scope, irrespective of whether they are prescribed and individually acquired by the consumer or are acquired in the course of seeking broader medical treatment. It would also apply irrespective of whether the products are bought by consumers themselves, or bought on their behalf by governments, hospitals or insurance companies, and irrespective of whether and to what extent the consumer paid for the drug (e.g. in some jurisdictions consumers do not pay for drugs at all, regardless whether they are OTC drugs or prescription drugs).

63. This approach would look to the more indirect engagement with the consumer, which, although in most jurisdictions does not happen by direct consumer engagement (such as by marketing), does occur through (in some cases, significant) marketing directed to the medical professionals, insurers and drug purchasing authorities which act on behalf of the consumer in prescribing, purchasing or funding the drug.

Such marketing efforts and activities directed at regulatory compliance in a market (which can be very significant given the consumer safety issues associated with pharmaceuticals) could be seen as evidence of a sustained engagement with the market, representing significant expenditures for the pharmaceutical maker, and an important contributor to profitability.

64. This approach would also be consistent with the approach taken more generally of not limiting the notion of a CFB to cases where there is a direct contractual sale to the consumer, but a broader concept of how the MNE places its products in the market and engages with a consumer, including indirectly (such as the case for franchising and licensing, and through sales via third parties) – in other words, looking to the nature of the product, and not to the specific supply chain.

65. Pharmaceuticals are designed for personal use by individuals. Pharmaceutical drugs are accessible to consumers for personal consumption (e.g. being prepared in a package and with instructions for use, as opposed to being a bulk chemical compound), albeit with the support of the medical professional for safety reasons. Further, the MNE has developed the goods or services to be regularly, repeatedly, or ordinarily supplied to consumers, including by undertaking research as to consumer needs and being available for providing consumer support. Finally, it could be argued that pharmaceuticals are sold to consumers, indirectly as part of a broader delivery of a medical service noting that this could have wider implications for the CFB scope.

66. The approach may be simple to administer, as there would be no need to separate products based on the particular supply channel.

67. It would also have the benefit of being applied in a more consistent way across jurisdictions. For a range of reasons, jurisdictions make different decisions as to the designation of a given drug as prescription only or OTC. Drugs that are sold OTC in one jurisdiction can be prohibited altogether in other jurisdictions. There is no world-wide, general definition of OTC or prescription only drugs (and creating such a uniform list would be virtually impossible, both in the first instance and to update over time). Applying an inclusive approach whereby all drugs were included in scope would mean the same drugs would be in scope in every country, irrespective of a local regulatory designation. This would give each jurisdiction the possibility to receive an allocation of Amount A, irrespective of the regulatory approach taken.

68. In addition, Inclusive Framework members advocating the inclusion of prescription drugs within the definition of CFB take the view that the businesses that manufacture and distribute such products typically benefit from much higher profit margins than for OTC drugs because of the value of the legally protected intangibles often associated with prescription drugs. They believe that such high profit margins and mobile intangibles have facilitated significant base erosion and profit shifting out of market jurisdictions and into low tax jurisdictions. Proponents of including prescription drugs within the definition of CFB also consider that it would be counter-intuitive to exclude such products that have been the subject of aggressive international tax planning while including only OTC drugs, which pose a lesser risk of base erosion and profit shifting.

Option 2 – OTC drugs in scope

69. The second approach under consideration is that prescription drugs would be out-of-scope and non-prescription (OTC) drugs would be in scope, for the reasons that follow.

70. OTC drugs present features in common with other consumer goods, such as:

- They can be obtained at the customer's choosing, as no prescription is needed;
- Advertising is permitted in many jurisdictions, and there are significant efforts to build sustained customer relationships including through targeted marketing and branding undertaken by pharmaceutical companies in respect of this type of product; and
- The acquisition of the drug is not generally a component part of a service of providing medical care.

71. This approach would exclude prescription drugs on the basis that, as compared with OTC drugs, they have specific features that do not fit as easily into the notion of a CFB. In particular:

- They are prescribed by physicians or other medical professionals based on their assessment of patients' needs and delivered as a part of the service of health care ;
- The choice to consume a prescription drug is made by a physician, who may prescribe a different drug from the one known to the patient because it is better for them, or the one the patient knows about is not covered by their insurance;
- In most jurisdictions (other than the United States and New Zealand, for example), advertising prescription drugs to consumers is not permitted (although significant marketing may take place directly to physicians which in turn may influence the choices available to the patient); and
- The patient normally pays only a small proportion of the cost of the drug, with governments or insurance companies paying the rest.

72. These factors could be taken to suggest that the consumer relationship between the MNE producing the prescription drug and the consumer is more indirect than for other CFB, and as such, prescription drugs could be treated as out-of-scope. Applying the definition of CFB above, OTC drugs are "of a type commonly sold to consumers," in that they are designed for individuals' personal use, by being made available in ways capable of being for personal consumption (in individual portions, in finished form, and at purchase points accessible by an individual) and where the pharmaceutical MNE has developed the goods or services to be regularly, repeatedly, or ordinarily supplied directly to consumers (including through marketing and promotion), and the products are sold directly to consumers.

73. In addition, some Inclusive Framework members in favour of Option 2 are of the view that pharmaceutical drugs in general are acquired or used by consumers chiefly for their inherent characteristics.

74. However, the administration of this approach will be further considered, including based on further discussion with stakeholders. Given the different definitions of OTC and prescription drugs that vary from one jurisdiction to another, there could be significant difficulty for an MNE to apply the scope rule, and the Amount A allocation to a market will be smaller for those members that take a stricter regulatory approach to prescription drugs. In addition, some drugs are sold as both OTC drugs and as prescription drugs in the same country, for example where the dose is higher or when a specific drug is prescribed in combination with other drugs. This could lead to administrative difficulties to track and trace whether a particular drug was in scope in a given case and could also involve significant administrative costs for tax authorities and compliance costs for taxpayers in order to comply with the second approach. However, members in favour of this approach take the view that the compliance burden could be addressed, for example, by following the classification of a particular drug as prescription or OTC based on the approach in the majority of Inclusive Framework members or whether a substantial part of the revenue is from prescriptions.

Franchising

75. The proposed scope of Amount A would extend not only to businesses that sell goods and services directly to consumers, but also to those that sell consumer products indirectly through third-party resellers or intermediaries. In this sense, *facing* the consumer is broader than strictly *contracting* with the consumer, and as such, goods and services can be in scope irrespective of the particular distribution channel or selling agent.

76. For this reason, franchise models and licensing arrangements in respect of consumer goods and services are included within the scope. This means that the basic concept of CFB applies, even where the income is earned from franchising or licensing rather than direct sale to the consumer.

77. This is reflected in the definition of CFB above, which includes as a CFB one that licenses or otherwise exploits intangible property that is connected to the supply of goods or services that are otherwise of a type commonly sold to consumers. As franchising involves earning a return from making intangible property available to the franchisee (as described in the franchising models below), this language is intended to capture franchising arrangements. It does not mean that to be in scope, the consumer must be directly acquiring licensing or franchising rights. For example, where an international chain of restaurants operates through a franchise model, the local restaurant franchisee would be in scope as being a directly consumer-facing business. The MNE that is responsible for the franchising and earning franchise fees would also be in scope as a CFB, even though their revenue model is different from the local restaurant (or if the MNE also owns the local restaurant, that revenue would also be in scope as well as other franchising fees earned).

78. By way of background, there are broadly two franchising models: business format franchise and product distribution franchise. Product distribution franchising can be further divided into three sub-categories: manufacturer-retailer; wholesaler-retailer; and manufacturer-wholesaler. These categorisations are not mutually exclusive and some franchise arrangements may be covered by more than one category. However, the categorisations are helpful to understand the range of arrangements that are in scope. The analysis below describes a range of different formats for how franchising may take place. The question of scope does not focus on the legal form of commercial arrangements, but whether the MNE is supplying goods or services commonly sold to consumers, or licensing or otherwise exploiting intangible property that is connected to such goods or services. If the rights forming the franchise arrangement are connected to an underlying product or service of a type commonly sold to consumers as per the definition of CFB above, then the franchisor and franchisee will each be a CFB (provided that they are otherwise subject to Amount A, including with respect to the gross revenue threshold (see below) and profitability thresholds (see Chapter 6).

Business format franchising model

79. In the business format franchising model, the franchisor provides the ready-made business model, while the franchisee is responsible for day-to-day operations in accordance with the franchisor's operational directions. This model is commonly used in the fast food and restaurant sector.

80. One of the key features of a business format franchising model is the level of authority the franchisor can exercise over the franchisee in respect of how the franchisee operates its business. In addition, the franchisee generally has continued access to intangibles owned by the franchisor (know-how, trademarks, etc.) and can obtain advice and assistance from the franchisor. The level of authority the franchisor exercises over the franchisee combined with the franchisee's right to access the franchisor's intangibles, assistance and advice ultimately provides a platform for the franchisor to engage with the consumer. Although there is no direct legal agreement between the consumer and the franchisor, there is significant engagement between them. Business model franchising in respect of CFB is therefore distinguished from other types of business to business arrangements where the supplying business does not have any engagement with the end consumer.

81. In this model, the franchisor's revenue can include technical fees (for training), contributions to advertising, upfront fees, renewal fees and 'franchise fees' (including royalties) which are paid periodically as a percentage of total sales generated by the franchisee.[10]

82. Applying the general definition above, where the franchised rights are connected to a good or service commonly sold to consumers (e.g. burgers), the franchisor is in scope as the owner of the brand being monetised (via the intangible property made available to the franchisee), and the franchisee is in scope as the seller of the consumer product.

Product distribution franchising

83. Product distribution franchising is typically divided into three sub-categories:

- Manufacturer-retailer franchising where a franchisee sells the franchisor's products directly to consumers. For example, manufacturer-retailer franchising is often used to sell new cars. Depending on the legal agreement, the franchisee may be permitted to sell competing products. Under these arrangements, the franchisee sells and operates under its own name although the franchisor's trademarks are generally displayed. The franchisee sells the products using its own business systems and methods but the franchisor may require the franchisee's store or showroom to be fitted-out to a particular specification. No special training on a business system will be required but the franchisee must be familiar with the product range, its capabilities and any follow-up services that are available, and training in this respect will be provided by the franchisor, in some cases on a paid basis. The franchisor may charge an initial fee for becoming a franchisee and may also charge on-going fees (often calculated as a percentage of sales) and contributions to advertising. Separately, the franchisee will purchase stock from the franchisor and may be required to place minimum orders. The franchisor may provide recommended retail prices to the franchisee.
- Wholesaler-retailer franchising, where the retailer as franchisee purchases products for sale to consumers from a franchisor wholesaler. Depending on the legal agreement, the franchisee may be permitted to sell competing and / or complementary products. Wholesaler-retailer franchising is often used as a model to sell car fuel and is also common where a cooperative of franchisee retailers form a wholesaling company through which they are contractually obliged to purchase (for example, hardware and automotive product stores). The franchisor may charge an initial fee for becoming a franchisee (in a cooperative model, this may be a subscription for shares or membership interests) and may also charge on-going fees (often calculated as a percentage of sales) and contributions to advertising. Separately, the franchisee will purchase stock from the franchisor and may be required to place minimum orders. The franchisor may provide recommended retail prices to the franchisee.
- Manufacturer-wholesaler franchising, where the franchisor manufactures an intermediary product that the franchisee assembles into the end product and distributes to customers.[11] For example, many soft drinks businesses use manufacturer-wholesaler franchising, where franchisee bottlers mix, package and distribute the beverage. The franchisee will be required to assemble the end product in compliance with the franchisor's prescriptive procedures and often will acquire equipment from the franchisor to facilitate assembly. Depending on the legal agreement, the franchisee may contract exclusively with the franchisor. The franchisor will manage the overall brand strategy and often will manage key global customer relationships. In some cases, the franchisee might pay the franchisor a franchise fee but in other cases the price paid by the franchisees for the intermediary product can be determined by reference to a number of factors, including, but not limited to, the franchisee's revenue and pricing. Under the latter type of arrangement, different franchisees pay different per unit prices for the manufactured product and the franchisor's return will fluctuate depending on the franchisee's revenue.

84. Similar to business model franchising, under each of the product distribution franchising sub-categories the franchisor exercises a relatively high level of authority over the franchisee in respect of how the franchisee deals with the franchisor's product. In addition, the franchisee generally has on-going access to specified intangibles owned by the franchisor (knowhow, trademarks, etc.) and can obtain advice and assistance from the franchisor (whether on a paid basis or otherwise), for which the franchisor earns a return. Similar to the business model franchise, the product distribution franchising provides a platform for the franchisor to engage with the consumer. As is the case for business format franchising, provided the franchised rights are connected to a good or service commonly sold to consumers (such as cars and beverages), the franchisor is in scope as the owner of the brand being monetised (via the intangible

property made available to the franchisee). The franchisee may also be in scope if it sells directly to consumers, goods or services that are of a type commonly sold to consumers.

85. Further work is underway more generally with respect to how Amount A applies to franchising, such as how to apply the nexus test, what revenues should be regarded as in scope, interaction with withholding taxes, and so forth.[12]

Licensing

86. Although in some cases, licensing shares some of the characteristics of franchising, licensing generally covers a much broader spectrum of commercial agreements. On one hand, certain intangible property can itself be of a type commonly sold to consumers (such as a music) and which by its intangible nature must be licensed to be exploited rather than strictly "sold." This is noted in the general definition above, in connection with the meaning of "sold."

87. There is a second type of category, where an MNE has made available its intangible property to a licensee, to be incorporated in another consumer good or service. For example, providing the rights to a cartoon character or logo to appear on clothing or in a game. The proposal is that this will only apply to an MNE that otherwise supplies (or has in the past supplied) a consumer-facing good or service (such as entertainment or clothing), and makes the rights to intangible property connected with that good or service (such as a consumer brand) available through a licensing arrangement (although further consideration on marginal cases may be required, such as where a non-CFB (e.g. a maker of an industrial product) earns returns from licensing its brand to a CFB such as clothing).[13] In these cases, the intangible is "connected" to the supply of the consumer-facing goods or services otherwise supplied by the licensor, and allowing it to be out-of-scope would distort the scope based on legal form rather than according to the relationship created with the consumer. This does not mean that to be in scope, the licensee must be a CFB. For example, the licensees may be providing ADS (such as digital content or online gaming in which the licensed cartoon character appears). The inquiry is whether the licensor has a consumer-facing product that is being licensed; if so, the licensor is in scope of CFB.

88. There are a number of commercial arrangements by which the MNE licensing the intangible property may derive revenue. At one end of the spectrum are licence agreements that effectively replicate franchise agreements, where the licensor licenses intangibles to the licensee in return for a royalty that is based on the level of sales achieved by the licensee. Trademarks and brand names are often licensed in this way to sell consumer goods. Typically, the licensor will retain strict control over how the licensee uses the licensed mark or name and the quality of products produced by the licensee using the licensed intangibles. For example, a number of luxury brands license their trademarks and logos to perfume and eyewear manufacturers. The licensor will generally impose strict quality controls on the licensees, may obtain rights to audit the licensee's use of the licensed materials and will often impose restrictions on how the intangibles may be used. Royalties for such licenses are typically commensurate with sales or returns earned by the licensee.

89. At the other end of the spectrum are rights that are licensed to licensees for a fixed fee. In those circumstances, the licensor has no entitlement to share in the revenues earned by the licensee and is entitled to a fixed fee regardless of how successful the licensee is in commercialising the licensed material. Film rights and television rights may be licensed in this way for a fixed period in a particular territory or territories. The licensor will typically have limited rights to control how the licensee operates in respect of the licensed material (although there will be strict controls preventing the licensee from altering that material).

90. In other cases, a licensee may agree to pay a royalty to the licensor based on revenues earned by the licensee. Although the licensor may not have significant authority to prescribe how the licensee operates in respect of the licensed material, the licensor is incentivised to ensure success of the licensee in commercialising the material (as this enhances the licensor's return). In those cases, it would not be

unusual for the licensor to market the licensed material in the jurisdictions covered by the licence. Music, films or other content provided to a platform are often licensed in this way, with royalties tied to the number of views / streams / downloads.

91. Although the degree of control over the licensee's operations and the revenue models may vary, the principle is if the licensor has made available intangible property that is connected to a CFB, then it should be in scope even if it is leveraging the licensee to have that distributed rather than doing this within the same MNE group. If the licensed product / service meets the definition of a consumer-facing good or service, then the licensing arrangement is in scope.

92. Therefore, as with franchising, although licensing arrangements involve a different set of legal arrangements in how the goods are made available to the consumer, these methods of exploiting a consumer-facing good or service through the controls over the licensed item being exploited by the licensee would be in scope of CFB. Further consideration will be given to how this approach interacts with other elements of Amount A, such as withholding tax on royalty arrangements.[14]

Dual use finished goods / services

93. Once a good or service meets the test of being of a type commonly sold to consumers, all sales of goods or services of that type of product will be entirely within scope (subject to the analysis below on dual use intermediate products / components). This remains true, even if the product is sold to a business customer. These are "dual use" products that can be sold to both consumers and businesses. For example, passenger cars, personal computers and some medical products (such as blood pressure monitors) fall in this category. Applying the general definition above, an unusual or infrequent transaction would not re-characterise the goods or service, such as where a product otherwise intended to be B2B is unusually acquired by an individual.

94. There are three reasons for taking this approach.

95. First, at a general level, it is difficult given the nature of these dual use goods to say which parts are consumer-facing and which are business-facing. In the case of the passenger car or personal computer, there is nothing conceptually to distinguish one car or computer from another because it is already a finished product designed for consumers. The design features of the car are the same, whether sold to a consumer or to a business.

96. A more practical concern is that tracking revenue according to the nature of the purchaser for every given transaction may be very challenging – and even impossible – for businesses to do. Apart from the administrative burden of recording the consumer purchasers versus business purchasers, that very distinction is not necessarily always apparent. The lines between personal and professional use are becoming less distinct, with a changing economy that allows more business activity to take place with personal items, such as working from home on a personal laptop or participating in the sharing economy. In addition, these goods are marketed to consumers, and ultimately used by an individual. This may influence the individual's future choices and therefore build a relationship with that person, even if they originally are not the purchaser (e.g. where a person uses a laptop provided by their employer, becomes familiar with it, and therefore chooses that same brand when it comes time to purchase a laptop for personal use). It would therefore not always be possible on a practical level to distinguish the line of business according to who makes the purchase on a given occasion.

97. Third, if dual use goods were only in scope to the extent of the amount of consumer purchases in practice, it could give rise to a need for look-through or anti-abuse rules to address cases where sales were intentionally not made directly to consumers, which would add complexity for business and tax administrations.

98. For these reasons, where the good is of a type commonly sold to consumers, the full amount of sales that are of this type of product / service would be in scope, irrespective of whether a given purchaser is a business or an individual.

Dual use intermediate products and components

99. The Outline notes that businesses selling intermediate products and components that are incorporated into a finished product sold to consumers would be out-of-scope. Examples include wood pulp, steel rods, bulk fabric, and electrical parts within a laptop or phone. These do not meet the test of a CFB – neither when considering the nature of the MNE's relationship with the consumer (which will be one of an intermediate manufacturer of component parts), or the type of product itself (which will not be of a type commonly sold to consumers).

100. However, some intermediate products / components are dual use. That is that they are of a type that is also designed for use by consumers. If such intermediate products / components meet the general definition above, they would be in scope. Possible examples include a car tyre, some replacement parts, batteries for consumer products, and some types of medical products such as bandages. However, they would be in scope only to the extent of the sales to consumers (unlike the analysis above for dual use finished products, which are entirely in scope).

101. This approach would give the most accurate result for two reasons.

102. First, the nature of an intermediate product / component has differences whether being sold to businesses or to consumers. For example, the packaging, pricing and distribution channels will be different (e.g. where packaging for consumers contains branding and instructions for consumer use, where packaging is in smaller individual lots rather than in bulk, or where price points are higher for retail sale, or where there is a separate distribution channel directed to consumer sales). These features make it inherently a consumer product and not a component; but the sales to business retain features of a component part.

103. Furthermore, including only the sales actually made to consumers is a much simpler compliance approach. The alternative would be to include in scope even the sale of component parts to businesses on the basis that sometimes they can be directly acquired by a consumer. This would be a significant compliance burden, and would require difficult revenue sourcing rules to be developed. This is because a component part when sold to a business would then need to be traced through what may be a complex supply chain. For example, in the case of a car tyre, this may be shipped to the location of the factory where all tyres are stored, to the factory where the cars are assembled and further manufactured, and through the distribution channel to locate the place where the tyre is ultimately sold to a consumer as part of the car. Instead, the obligation would only be to source those sales made to consumers, which should be feasible because of the different nature of the product when sold to consumers, as noted above.

104. However, the compliance burdens and benefits associated with this approach are being further considered in order to inform the approach, as well as whether simplification measures should be included and whether further guidance can be provided on delineating dual use finished goods from dual use intermediate products / component. It is noted that some Inclusive Framework members would, in the interests of addressing the compliance costs, favour removing all component / intermediate products from scope (even those that are otherwise consumer products); while one member favours including all component / intermediate products that are dual use, irrespective of sale to business or consumers in scope.

2.2.3. Exclusions and carve-outs

105. This section sets out the types of activities that are proposed to be specifically excluded from Amount A. These are: (i) natural resources; (ii) financial services (iii) construction, sale and leasing of residential property; and (iv) international airline and shipping businesses.

106. Many of the goods and services sold in these sectors would already be out-of-scope of Amount A because they are neither consumer products nor ADS. For clarity, specific exclusions are set out for the whole or, as appropriate, parts of these sectors.

107. This section sets out the rationale for exclusions by reference to the ADS and CFB criteria indicated in the above sections of this chapter, and delineates how far the exclusion applies to each sector.

108. The scope exclusions would apply on a segment basis, which means that for an MNE group with multiple business lines, some may fall within a scope exclusion, and some may not.

Natural resources

109. The term "natural resources" encompasses non-renewable extractives (such as petroleum and minerals), renewables (such as agricultural, fishery and forestry products) and renewable energy products and similar energy products (such as biofuels, biogas, green hydrogen).

110. As stated in the Outline, extractive industries[15] and other producers and sellers of raw materials and commodities, including commodity traders, will not be within the consumer-facing business definition, even if those materials and commodities are incorporated further down the supply chain into consumer products. Taxes on profits from the extraction of a nation's natural resources can be considered to be part of the price paid by the exploiting company for those national assets, a price which is properly paid to the resource owner.

111. Natural resources, such as agricultural and forestry products, are generally generic goods which are sold, and whose price is determined, on the basis of their inherent characteristics, rather than on other factors such as marketing. Where premium prices exist (which could lead to residual profits), they tend to be a function of aggregate supply and demand dynamics for the commodity. As natural products of the earth, all are closely linked with the place of production and quality is highly dependent on location-specific factors. Due to local environmental impacts including the sustainability of the resource itself, production is usually regulated in the local jurisdiction.

112. Other policy considerations may also support the conclusion that these generic and undifferentiated natural resource products should be out-of-scope of Amount A. These include the close connection with the place where the resources are found and transformed (reflected in current tax treaty treatment of immovable property); the capital intensity of their production; and the high volume of the products used as raw materials in other industries.

113. The vast majority of natural resources would already be outside of the scope under the general CFB and ADS definitions. These materials are not of a type commonly sold to consumers, nor are they automated services provided digitally.[16]

114. At the other end of the production chain are products that incorporate natural resources, such as jewellery and chocolates, which would be within the general definition of CFB.

115. Between these two points are borderline cases, which are discussed below.

Non-renewable resources (extractives)[17]

116. Some final products derived from hydrocarbons are sold to consumers. Products like natural gas, liquefied petroleum gas and kerosene have many industrial uses but also may be sold to consumers, e.g.

for heating and cooking. Similarly, fuels such as petrol (gasoline), diesel, and aviation gasoline are used by both industry and consumers for transportation purposes.

117. Despite being commonly sold to consumers, however, they have features which distinguish them from other types of consumer products and may bring them within the scope of the exclusion for natural resources and commodities. While these products have undergone a degree of processing, the processing is largely standardised, meaning that the products may be considered generic, undifferentiated and sold on the basis of their inherent characteristics. Indeed, given their standardised characteristics, some of these products such as natural gas and petrol are sold on commodity exchanges. As such, to a consumer, even if sometimes these products are sold under a brand name, there is generally little that distinguishes one MNE's product from another's. This seems to imply that there is limited scope for an MNE to build consumer relationships and interactions and create consumer-facing intangibles to increase value and sales. In determining the importance of firm-specific intangibles, it could be relevant to consider such factors as the degree of retail competition, whether there are material prices differences across supplier, the size of retail profit margins, etc. Fuel retailing also relies on extensive local infrastructure, meaning profits are typically realised locally. However, given questions about the role of branding, advertising and level of processing, in such cases as automobile lubricants, petrol or diesel, further work is required.

118. Likewise, precious gemstones (diamonds, emeralds, non-mineral crystals such as opals) are sometimes sold to consumers. Cut and polished gemstones could be seen as "dual use intermediate products / components" in that they are most often sold to jewellery manufacturers but are sometimes sold directly to consumers. Consideration is being given to whether they ought to be treated as falling outside the natural resources exclusion and instead within the general rules for CFB (for example, having regard to the marketing effort sometimes associated with consumer sales of gemstones, including online sales channels).

Renewable resources and renewable energy products

119. Most bulk agricultural, fishery and forestry products do not meet the CFB definition.[18] Following further processing and packaging, however, some agricultural, fishery and forestry products become consumer products. However, if the product remains generally generic, undifferentiated and sold on the basis of its inherent characteristics, there is a case that it should be excluded from the scope of Amount A. While work continues to delineate more precisely how far the exclusion extends, further work will be required on the role of relevant factors such as the degree of processing, packaging and branding.[19]

120. Renewable energy products also raise questions about the scope of the resources exclusion. Electricity from water, sun and wind power exploits a renewable natural resource. Even when sold to consumers, the product is homogeneous and purchased for its inherent characteristics. As discussed below under infrastructure services, electricity distribution is already closely tied physically to the market due to the physical infrastructure used. Biogas is very similar to natural gas except that it is produced from non-fossil sources. Renewable transportation fuels (biofuels like ethanol) are substitutes for petroleum products like gasoline and diesel. While the origin is distinct, they have similar characteristics, including retail branding, suggesting a case for parallel treatment.

121. Further work will be undertaken, taking into account the above considerations, to provide greater clarity defining the exclusion for generic and undifferentiated natural resource products and commodities.

Financial services (FS)

122. FS business comprises banking, insurance and asset management. As the issues raised by each of these three sectors in relation to the new taxing right (particularly in relation to CFB) are different, the discussion below considers each FS sector separately in relation to CFB. However, in relation to ADS, the

position is more uniform across the three sectors and accordingly is dealt with immediately below. No separate regime is envisaged for finance companies.

123. Digital functionality is widely used in each of the banking, insurance and asset management sectors. Nevertheless, it is generally used to automate what people used to do (and often still do), whether in conducting conventional FS business or in risk-management functions. As such, human intervention and judgement is normally a feature of the use of digital functionality in FS business. For this reason, and subject to certain detailed work that is outlined below, FS business should not generally involve business of the sort that is properly regarded as ADS business for the purposes of the new taxing right.

124. With regard to CFB, very significant parts of FS business are not consumer-facing. However, there are also significant parts of the FS business that involve CFB. Though the analysis of CFB raises different issues across the three sectors, the central rationale for the exclusion of FS business from the new taxing right is common to each of the three sectors. That rationale stems from the highly-regulated nature of FS business. However, it should be emphasised that this central rationale is not premised on the mere fact of regulation but rather is based on the effects of that regulation. More specifically, the regulations governing the relevant business in each of these three sectors, that may involve CFB activity, generally require that appropriately capitalised entities are maintained in each market jurisdiction to carry on business in the market concerned. Due to this factor, the profits from CFB activities that arise in a particular market jurisdiction will generally be taxed in that market location with the result that there is no further need for any Amount A re-allocation. Additional factors relevant to the analysis of banking, insurance and asset management business are considered below.

Banking Business

125. In banking, there is substantial local regulation, which materially affects the local booking and taxation of banks' consumer business. Accordingly, the central rationale for the exclusion for FS business is clearly relevant to the banking sector. Almost without exception, local regulators will implement banking rules based on the Basel II & III framework with amendments to suit its local environment. Because consumer-facing banks need to have local approval and a local licence, they generally provide their services only to local customers. This results in a taxable presence in the locations where they face their customers. Given the dependence of an economy on the financial sector, most developing economies have also implemented regulations such as exchange controls, which add to the existing compliance burden of conducting cross-border financial transactions. Further, banks in many jurisdictions are the primary transmission mechanism for monetary policy through their borrowing and depository transactions with their central banks, and must abide by the requirements of those central banks.

126. Certain additional technical and practical factors further support the case for an exclusion of the banking sector from the new taxing right. One important consideration is that the use of a profit to sales ratio (which would normally be used in non-FS sectors in the calculation of Amount A) would likely prove unworkable in the banking sector. Operating profit margin (operating earnings/revenue), or profits before taxes, is not an appropriate basis for comparing banks with other industries because: (i) interest expense and cost of inventory, which in effect is equivalent to the cost of goods sold for banks, is not included in the definition of operating income; and (ii) banks report trading revenue net of trading costs, and interest revenue net of interest expense. While reporting revenues net of trading and interest costs artificially decreases the revenue generated by a financial institution, grossing up the revenues by trading costs would cause a typical FS group never to have an operating margin above 1%. The volumes, in financial terms, of bank trading operations are typically in the USD trillions and, if sales were grossed up, (i.e. not netted with the cost of inventory) as they are in other industries, the denominator for computing operating profits would be in the trillions of dollars. These differences materially distort bank operating margins by increasing the numerator and decreasing the denominator in the calculation of the operating profit margin. Failure to accurately account for these costs of doing business in both the numerator and denominator of the calculation would result in a disproportionate taxation burden on the FS industry. Corrected for these

amounts, either through modifying the current proposal or developing an alternative metric for the FS sector, banks' profit margins would be dramatically lower.

127. The nature of bank regulation provides a further "positive" and a "negative" reason to support the exclusion. From a positive perspective, where an industry, such as the banking sector, is subject to robust non-tax governmental regulations consistent with recognised industry standards (e.g. Basel requirements), due regard should be given to the constraints those regulations impose upon them. As a result of such regulations, profits from retail banking operations often arise in the jurisdiction in which those operations are conducted. And the consequences of regulation (rather than the mere fact of regulation itself) mean that those jurisdictions will often be the ones that tax the resulting profit. From a negative perspective, there is potential for a clash between the way that Amount A works and such non-tax regulatory regimes because the regulatory objectives may seek to protect the local regulated entities, e.g. from the insolvency of affiliates. This might mean that regulators could refuse to accept the existence of intercompany payments made under Pillar One, or require that an affiliate reimburse the local regulated bank, or require that additional capital be held. This would result in an undermining of the agreed regulatory regime and potentially also in inefficient allocations of capital and liquidity, resulting in increased costs for ordinary financial transactions.

128. Consideration of the application of an exclusion in the context of the banking sector has led to the review of a number of additional matters, specifically the status of Fintech and private banking business and the practical operation of EU passporting.

129. Fintech is broadly finance enabled or provided via new technologies, meaning the application of new technologies to FS. A Fintech business may be developed either by banks or dedicated Fintech firms. Most of the Fintech firms are intermediaries between banks and customers. Some Fintech firms are lightly regulated or may not be subject to any regulatory regime under their national law. However, Fintech firms that wish to provide regulated FS have two options: (i) they can conclude a partnership with a bank, or (ii) they can request a banking licence, in which case they are subject to the same regulations that apply to banks, and thus to the same obligations such as minimum regulatory capital, reporting requirements, cross-border activities limitations or infrastructure obligations that require them to have a physical presence in the local market jurisdiction. Banking regulation is mandatory for four types of Fintech activities: e-money, payment, credit, and full banking licences. Other products and services supporting financial activities provided by Fintechs in some areas (hardware, software, middleware) remain excluded from banking regulation. That is because these Fintechs are only providing technology to the financial sector to perform activities that otherwise would be performed by individuals. Given that regulated Fintech firms have a specific status, similar to that of the regulated banking sector, their exclusion appears consistent with the policy rationale outlined for FS. These firms should therefore receive a similar treatment to regulated banks. However, as the rules in many jurisdictions governing Fintech are at an early stage of development, the issue will be explored further. The logic of the approach would not be applicable to unregulated Fintech activities.

130. Private banking/wealth management (PB) business is an activity conducted within regulated banking groups that falls on the borderline between retail banking and institutional banking, given that clients include wealthy individuals as well as charities, family offices, trusts, etc. PB is often conducted through entities subject to banking regulation both globally and locally. However, PB may in part be conducted through regional hubs, meaning that the policy rationale discussed above may not be fully applicable. Nonetheless, various factors support the application of the exclusion to PB. First, without a locally regulated presence, a bank generally cannot have an active and sustained participation in a local market; publicly offer services (including digital services); or widely advertise or solicit business. Second, many PB clients are business owners, and PB services may also be provided to the business rather than the individual. Third, in the event that PB business were to be included in the scope of Amount A, there would be certain practical difficulties in identifying and isolating private banking profits. These include: (i) the practical difficulties in segmenting the PB business as a substantial portion of customers will be

charities, foundation, etc. Banks would also need to distinguish between services provided to individual clients, and services provided to businesses owned by their clients; (ii) segmenting the in-scope income streams given that the services and products provided to PB customers involve a variety of activities and income that may be booked across the different divisions/entities within a banking group, and isolating and identifying these highly fragmented income streams would be difficult; and (iii) identifying the market jurisdiction as many contractual relationships (especially institutional client relationships) are centralised. On the basis of the above discussion, it is proposed to include PB business within the exclusion for FS.

131. Consideration has also been given to EU passporting (which enables FS firms that are authorised in one EU member state to trade freely in other member states) to assess whether its practical operation might be in conflict with the central policy rationale supporting the exclusion for FS business. However, due to various regulatory and commercial factors, FS businesses generally enter into CFB transactions in local markets through entities that create a physical presence in those markets and thus that are taxed locally on those profits. Banks operating in the EU thus do in practice have a taxable presence in individual EU Member States for the provision of customer-facing activities. It is therefore considered that the existence of EU passporting does not conflict with the policy rationale discussed above.

Insurance Business

132. The analysis of CFB in the context of the insurance sector is similar in many respects to the position in the banking sector. In the insurance sector, there is, as in the banking sector, extensive regulation of consumer-facing business (retail insurance business) leading to the same effect, namely that the profits from CFB activities that arise in a particular market jurisdiction will generally be taxed in that market location, again with the result that there is no further need for any Amount A re-allocation. Regulation of the industry – especially conduct regulation – makes it very unlikely that consumers could purchase insurance without the insurer having a local presence. In many jurisdictions it is illegal to offer it. The regulatory requirements therefore mean that income from retail insurance business is generated and taxed in the market jurisdiction from which it is derived. The prevalence of insurance regulation, dating back decades, is evidenced in studies and surveys of regulation of insurance regulation in different jurisdictions and regions published by the OECD and other organisations[20]. Since the 1990s, in a similar manner to the Basel Committee in banking, insurance supervisors have developed global standards for adoption into national frameworks. Despite global recognition of the importance of regulating the insurance sector, regulation continues to be executed primarily within the local jurisdictions. For example, jurisdictions do not, generally, recognise licensing outside their own borders, and particularly in matters such as access to domestic markets. Insurance companies operating in Latin America, India and China, for example, are subject to both prudential and conduct regulation.

133. The "positive" and "negative" factors that stem from the highly regulated nature of the business (and that are discussed above in the context of banking business) are also relevant in the case of insurance business. There are also concerns that the measurement of profits in the insurance sector is not comparable to the approach outside the financial sector. Insurers measure income and costs differently than other industries so traditional profit measurements might inaccurately result in excess profits that do not in reality exist. Most industries incur costs such as labour, raw materials, etc. at an early stage in the business cycle, with the corresponding revenues generated later in the process. The opposite is true of insurance: insurers collect premiums upfront but incur unpredictable costs later – sometimes much later – when they pay claims. The effect of these types of losses on the insurance industry is unique. The insurance industry's role is to assume risk over many years, with an uncertain realisation and timing of the insured event. This exposes the industry to volatile profits and losses. Premium rates change over the cycle depending on the availability of capital. During a soft market (when capital is plentiful), competition reduces premium rates. But as the market hardens (when capital becomes scarce, typically after a major catastrophe), premiums rise. This creates a multi-year business cycle unique to the insurance industry. Current year profits are often based on insurance reserve estimates that reflect losses that may (or may

not) occur and are based on complex actuarial modelling techniques. The ebb and flow of the insurance cycle makes the determination of normal returns for the industry difficult. As noted above, for the insurance industry, a local market presence is generally required to sell retail insurance products. This is for the regulatory reasons already covered. This means the relevant local entity will already be taxed in the relevant local market. Together with the some of the technical challenges noted in computing insurance industry profits means it makes little practical sense to include the insurance industry in the CFB definition.

134. Consideration has also been given to the impact of EU passporting in the insurance sector with the same result that is discussed above for the banking sector. There is therefore no conflict with the rationale for the exclusion of the insurance sector.

Asset Management Business

135. The asset management sector contains three main types of participants: fund vehicles, financial intermediaries, and investment managers. This section explains why most (but not all) jurisdictions believe that it is appropriate to exclude the sector from the scope of Amount A.

136. Funds are not active businesses. Their purpose is to pool investor capital, which is then invested in accordance with the fund's investment strategy. The tax neutral and passive status of funds is widely recognised under jurisdictions' domestic law, international tax principles and the OECD's own guidance. Funds are therefore considered to be outside the scope of CFB.

137. Under the predominant retail industry operating model, the indirect model, financial intermediaries comprise third-party banks, financial advisors, or similar businesses that advise investors and offer them investment products. Although interactions between financial intermediaries and consumers may on first principles be within the scope of CFB, they are, as for retail banking, subject to local country regulation. Customer interactions would therefore normally occur locally in the market jurisdiction, and the associated profits would be realised locally. Under the less common direct model, an investment manager distributes investment products through an affiliate that is a broker or similarly regulated entity. But under either model, regulatory requirements focus on investor protection, suitability and transparency and result in a required local presence for financial intermediary business (in so far as it concerns retail investors). This means such business is, owing to its broad-based regulatory regime, in the same position as retail banking and retail insurance business. The activities of financial intermediaries are therefore covered by the central policy rationale for the exclusion of financial sector business.

138. In the context of Amount A, investment management services raise more complex questions. Investment managers normally deal with financial intermediaries rather than directly with underlying individual investors in both the indirect and the direct business model. In the direct model, the financial intermediary that has the direct contact with the investor would be the investment manager's affiliated broker, broker-dealer or similarly regulated entity, which serves the role of the financial intermediary. Additionally, the investment manager is normally engaged by the fund or investment vehicle, rather than investors themselves. The engagement of an investment manager by the fund vehicle generally occurs before any individuals invest in the fund. Whether the business is a CFB therefore depends on how interactions between investment managers and intermediaries are construed and in particular whether they are considered to be direct business-to-business transactions or some form of "indirect" service to consumers, through the medium of the financial intermediary.

139. Based on the analysis of the role of the investment manager, on balance the investment manager's services are properly seen as a component of the service the financial intermediary offers its clients. Businesses selling intermediate products and components that are not commonly sold to consumers (but which are incorporated into a finished product sold to consumers) would be out-of-scope of Amount A. Where intermediate products and services are commonly sold to customers they may be within scope (e.g. where they are branded). But this does not seem to apply for investment managers, as the investment management services are incorporated into the service the intermediary offers, which is then provided, as

a component, to consumers. On this basis, they would not be in scope of CFB. The conclusion that the services of investment managers are an intermediate product is supported by the fact that the financial intermediary makes a meaningful difference to the nature and value of the investment management service as a result of (i) the important role of the intermediary and (ii) the fact that investment manager interacts directly (from a legal and practical standpoint) with the fund, similar to other service providers (e.g. custodian, transfer agent, fund administrator, etc.). These matters are discussed further below. On (i), the financial intermediary performs important functions for the consumer, providing substantial economic value. It uses its knowledge of investment opportunities to provide the consumer with bespoke advice about the best products to buy (typically managed by unrelated investment managers) based on the consumer's needs and risk profile. The intermediary is remunerated by either asset-based or transaction fees, separate from the fee earned by the investment manager. These fees can be substantial. On (ii), the investment manager provides its services (legally and factually) to the funds themselves, not to the investors, and its fees are paid by the funds. A bank or other service provider providing custodial, transfer agency or administrative services to a fund works in the same way. The comparison is relevant as there seems to be no basis to think that these custodial, transfer agency or administrative services amount to services to consumers, given how indirect the benefit is to them. The funds to which the investment managers provide services have a fiduciary duty to act in the best interest of unitholders. Those services are guided by the fund's investment strategy and objectives. The services have no regard to investors' objectives, nor to the inflow or outflow of investors, nor to investors' preferences about timing, diversification, liquidity, currency or anything else. These preferences are managed by financial intermediaries, as described above.

140. In addition, there are in any event practical policy reasons to exclude investment managers from Amount A. These reasons are significant in this case as the conclusion that the investment manager's services are a component of the service the financial intermediary offers its clients may be debated. These practical policy reasons concern access to relevant information and the practicability of the exclusion for FS activities. On information access, in the indirect model, intermediaries often cannot disclose information on underlying investors to an investment manager because of data privacy and regulatory restrictions and the nature of proprietary customer lists. The investment manager therefore often cannot access the information needed to identify market jurisdictions. In addition, there are the practical problems caused by the constant change in the identity of investors in a fund, and the fact that the investor base will often be in a state of constant flux as regards the percentage of retail investors (consumers) and other professional and institutional investors. The process of tracing the identity and balance of the investor mix will be further complicated by the fact that funds commonly invest in other funds. Further, if there were no exclusion for investment management activity, banks and insurance companies (assuming they are out-of-scope) could face complex issues. This is because they also conduct investment management business, and would therefore need to isolate their profits from their investment management services. Another concern would be the extensive practical difficulties in establishing and enforcing a definition of in-scope investment management business. The fungible nature of financial products means there can be economic equivalence between investment management advice and the embedded features and performance of a structured product offered by a bank, like an indexed certificate of deposit or a swap, and a similar investment offered in an insurance wrapper, such as an annuity, by an insurance company. For all these reasons, it is concluded that the activities of investment managers do, and should, fall outside the scope of CFB. However, those jurisdictions which do not support exclusion for asset management sector from the scope of Amount A, believe that the asset management sector is very lightly regulated, which (unlike retail banking) may not ensure that the major part of residual profit is captured in market jurisdictions.

Infrastructure and general construction business

141. Infrastructure construction is the provision of physical structures and facilities such as buildings, roads, bridges, tunnels, power plants, and airports. Infrastructure projects can be broadly categorised into

B2G and B2B projects, where the government or a commercial enterprise acquires the infrastructure for use by the public (e.g. a road) or by the business (e.g. a port).

142. General construction can be broken down into commercial and residential. Commercial real estate includes the provision of office buildings, hotels, factories and warehouses. These are developed and sold or leased for use by other businesses.

143. Neither infrastructure construction nor general commercial construction is within the scope of ADS or CFB based on first principles. They would not fall within the definition of ADS, not being a service delivered over the Internet but by physical delivery, and requiring significant human intervention to provide the services. Construction of commercial real estate would also not fall within CFB. It is inherently of a scale beyond an individual's private need or enjoyment. Although an individual may make use of the infrastructure or building (e.g. driving across a bridge or working in an office building), it is not sold to or otherwise acquired by the individual as a product for their personal use. They are therefore not of a type commonly sold to consumers. Therefore, under the general definition, these are not in scope.

144. The third segment, residential real estate, refers to the construction of buildings for the customer's personal use, such as an apartment or house. Applying the general definition of CFB, MNEs that sell residential real estate would be in scope, given that the nature of the product is of a type commonly sold to consumer. Consumers acquire real estate for personal use; the real estate is designed for sale to consumers (being made available in a form for consumption by individuals, where the MNE has set itself up to supply the real estate to consumers); and it is sold (including leased) to consumers. The MNEs that would be the CFB would be the "owner" of the brand and the direct "retailer" of the real estate (which in both cases may be the developer).[21]

145. However, this outcome does not align with the policy rationale for Amount A. That is (i) MNEs can engage with consumers in a market jurisdiction from a remote location in a way that represents a sustained engagement in the market jurisdiction; and (ii) the current taxing rules, being based on physical presence, do not adequately capture this new engagement.

146. For residential real estate, the first element – the consumer relationship – is not one of remote engagement (such as through the use of marketing) to the same extent as in other CFB. This is because even if the construction business has a well-known brand, ultimately the consumer's decision to buy will be determined by the characteristics of the real estate specific to that market jurisdiction, such as its size, its location (e.g. in a desirable neighbourhood), and its other features (e.g. garage, security, etc.). In addition, given the nature of the relationship to the product, it is difficult to practically extract consumer-facing intangible property and separate it from the jurisdiction of the sale.

147. With respect to the second element – lack of physical presence – a company selling or leasing its interest in residential real estate will require a substantial physical presence in a market to earn its revenue. Existing tax rules attach to this physical presence, including through rules governing the creation of a permanent establishment through construction activities (Article 5 of the Model Tax Convention), and rules governing the income and gains from the rental and sale of immovable property (Articles 6 and 13(1) of the Model).

148. As such, market jurisdictions are already well placed under existing corporate tax rules and treaty provisions to impose taxation on the construction MNE given that there will necessarily be a substantial and taxable physical presence in the market. Finally, were the construction sector and sale of immovable property to be included in the scope of Amount A, the requirement to invest in physical infrastructure in the market jurisdiction makes it in any event unlikely that there would be a material re-allocation of profits under the principles of Amount A, given the revenue sourcing rules would in any case allocate Amount A to the jurisdiction where the real estate is "delivered" which in this case would be where the real estate is physically located.

149. For these reasons, the construction, sale or letting of residential dwellings by businesses that have engaged in the development and construction of the residential real estate is proposed to be excluded from the scope of Amount A.

150. For the purposes of this exclusion, residential dwelling means the structure and land intended to be used or occupied, in whole or in part, as the home of one or more persons. The definition of residential dwelling means that the offering of temporary accommodation, such as hotels, remain in the scope of Amount A. While such businesses will use real property in their business, they are not selling or letting an interest in that property to consumers, but rather providing a service to consumers, and which remains in scope of CFB.

151. The exclusion is limited to those businesses that have engaged in the development and construction of the residential real estate (and therefore have the physical presence in the jurisdiction), and derive their revenue from its sale or leasing. As such, this exclusion does not include businesses that derive commission or service fees that are not based on the sale or leasing of an interest in land, and do not depend on a physical presence in the market location of the real estate. For example, online intermediation platforms intermediating offers of real estate would be within the scope of Amount A. The exclusion would likewise not cover professional services related to construction (such as those provided by architects, designers, lawyers, consultants), or professional services or intermediation services facilitating the sale or leasing of property (such as those provided by real estate agents, mortgage brokers, financial institutions), although they may be otherwise excluded from the scope under the general rules.

152. Further technical work will be conducted to address the link between the type of income that a franchising business may earn (which could include rental income), and the analysis above on commercial real estate, to ensure that revenue from franchising is appropriately included in the scope of Amount A.

153. Apart from these, there are certain sectors related to the operation of infrastructure which is provided as a service to consumers. Further work will be done to consider an exclusion for the operation of infrastructure businesses, such as:

- electricity generation and distribution,
- natural gas and water distribution,
- certain telecommunications (except perhaps satellite phones, which do not require physical presence in a jurisdiction);
- railways, highways, ports and airports; and
- public transportation.

154. While there is both public and private provision of infrastructure services, businesses are increasingly involved, sometimes as part of public-private partnerships (P3).

155. There appear to be good reasons for such an exclusion. Infrastructure services businesses are by definition closely tied physically to the market where the activity is carried out. The source and market are generally the same, so arguably there is no need to apply re-allocation rules, since substantial profits are already allocated to the market. With the possible exception of telecommunications, branding generally is not an important component of profitability for these businesses. In fact, many of these businesses are "natural monopolies" because it is often not efficient for different suppliers to build competing networks in the same place. For this reason, infrastructure businesses are often subject to price regulation to protect consumers. This limits the ability to earn residual profits, providing an additional rationale for exclusion. Further, a general exclusion for all electricity generation and distribution would be consistent and neutral with respect to the exclusion for renewable energy production.

International air and shipping businesses

156. This section sets out the justification for the Inclusive Framework's statement that it would be "inappropriate to include airline and shipping businesses in the scope of the new taxing right".[22]

157. It has long been recognised that the characteristics of international air and shipping businesses give rise to special income tax considerations. Unlike other types of enterprises of one jurisdiction doing business in another jurisdiction, the earnings of international air and shipping enterprises are based upon the use of vessels in operations between multiple tax jurisdictions, much of the time conducted outside any tax jurisdiction – that is, on or over the high seas – raising the prospect of either multiple taxation or considerable income allocation challenges.

158. For this reason, there is a longstanding international consensus that the profits of enterprises operating ships or aircraft in international traffic should be taxable only in the jurisdiction in which the enterprise has its residence. This special treatment, which is applied regardless of whether such an enterprise carries on business through foreign permanent establishments, is reflected in Article 8 of both the OECD and United Nations (UN) Model Tax Conventions[23] and in the vast majority of the 3,500+ bilateral tax treaties currently in force. It reciprocally exempts in each jurisdiction the profits of non-resident international air and shipping enterprises, removing the compliance and administrative burdens (and associated prospect of disputes) that would otherwise arise, especially over the attribution of profits.

159. International air and shipping businesses commonly maintain a physical presence, which would constitute a permanent establishment, in multiple jurisdictions. The exemption enjoyed by these enterprises under Article 8 is therefore a deliberate policy choice, reflecting the unique considerations briefly outlined above, and does not result from increasing scale without mass or other factors arising from the digitalisation of the economy.

160. With the possible exception of the provision of online marketplace platforms, the activities of international air and shipping enterprises (i.e. income to which Article 8 applies) should be outside the proposed definition of ADS as those services are not delivered over the Internet. The nature of those services has not changed as a result of digitalisation and accordingly, the Inclusive Framework sees no reason to adjust how the existing rules apply.

161. Air freight and cargo shipping activities, including mail services, parcel delivery[24] and both bulk and liner shipping, will, as almost exclusively B2B services, be outside the definition of CFB. But passenger transportation services, including pleasure cruises, foot and car ferry crossing services, passenger air travel, and associated services (including those delivered online) are within the definition of CFB.

162. The question therefore is whether in-scope activities of international air and shipping businesses should be taken out-of-scope, on policy grounds.

163. In the special circumstances applying to international air and shipping businesses, it was the allocation of taxing rights, under those normal rules, to the multiple jurisdictions in which physical operations are conducted that gave rise to the particular policy problem to which the consensus solution was and has remained exclusive residence state taxation. Those same positions continue today. Given the present policy choice with respect to this sector, members agree that air and shipping businesses be carved out-of-scope for the purpose of application of new taxing rights.

164. Profits that would fall within Article 8 of the OECD Model Tax Convention would therefore be excluded from the scope of Amount A. This would be the case whether or not a bilateral tax treaty exists between the jurisdictions in question.

2.2.4. Alternative to Activities Based Tests: Applying Amount A on a Safe Harbour Basis

165. As described above, the Outline proposes to base the scope for Amount A on an activities test to include automated digital services and consumer facing businesses, with defined carve outs. The intent is to have Amount A apply to a broad range of businesses that generate profits through active and sustained engagement in market jurisdictions. Although considerable technical work has been devoted to the practical, administrative and definitional issues of such an approach and good progress has been made, this approach has to date not achieved political consensus. The need to define ADS and CFB, together with the need for facts and circumstances determinations to apply such definitions, adds complexity, in particular with respect to CFB which covers a wider and more diverse range of business models. In this context, the United States has proposed that Pillar One be implemented on what it refers to as a safe harbour basis.

166. A safe harbour basis would recognise that greatly enhanced tax certainty and robust mechanisms for the resolution of cross border tax disputes have always been critical components of the design of Pillar One. Such enhanced tax certainty in many cases could make Pillar One attractive to electing MNE groups notwithstanding a marginal increase to their global tax liabilities resulting from allocations of Amount A.

167. Under such a safe harbour implementation, MNE's could elect to have all the components of Pillar One apply to them on a global basis, including the Amount A allocation, the Amount B fixed margin mechanism and the mandatory binding dispute prevention and resolution procedures. By allowing any MNE to elect to apply Pillar One, the need to resolve contentious scoping issues, including the definitions of ADS and CFB, would potentially be reduced. Election procedures could be provided to require that an MNE's election be made on a global, multi-year basis. In the view of the United States, implementing Pillar One on a safe harbour basis could also avoid the political challenges of mandating changes to longstanding international tax principles.

168. The United States contemplates that such a safe harbour implementation of Pillar One would be part of an overall agreement that replaces digital services taxes and similar unilateral measures, with the effect that the benefits of increased administrability, greater tax certainty, and mandatory binding dispute resolution procedures would be the primary motivations for MNEs to avail themselves of Pillar One as a safe harbour.

169. Many other jurisdictions have expressed scepticism about an elective approach. In addition to noting the outstanding questions around how an elective regime would operate, they have argued that the objectives of Pillar One would be frustrated in cases where MNEs do not elect into the new rules, and have noted the perverse incentives it could create for jurisdictions to introduce unilateral measures, or increase the breadth and rate of existing unilateral measures, in order to protect against that outcome. They believe that an optional basis would create inconsistency across similar businesses and lead to distortions. They also take the view that an elective regime would undermine the policy justification for reallocating profit to market jurisdictions, threatening its coherence/sustainability and reducing the likelihood of international consensus. Some have further questioned the legal effect of a safe harbour approach, given that such a safe harbour can only be provided in a coordinated manner by jurisdictions if they have the relevant taxing rights in the first place, which will not be the case for all in a safe harbour approach. Further, others emphasise that the tax challenges of the digitalising economy specifically result from their interplay with longstanding international tax principles which therefore need to be addressed with a view to overcoming political challenges.

2.2.5. Next steps

170. The Inclusive Framework will continue its efforts to bridge the remaining differences as regards scope, recognising the importance of coming to a common understanding, and in a spirit of compromise where needed, reflecting its continuing commitment to working together towards a consensus-based long-

term solution. This includes taking into account the divergent views expressed above, and remaining open to simplifications and innovative approaches that help to achieve the tax policy objective while minimising compliance and administrative costs.

2.3. Threshold tests

171. In defining the MNEs that are in scope of Amount A, there is a recognition that below a certain overall size threshold, a cost-benefit analysis does not justify the imposition of the rules required to apply Amount A. The implementation of Amount A is likely to be associated with additional compliance and administrative costs, especially in the short term, as taxpayers and tax administrations implement the new rules. Large businesses are more likely to possess the financial and human resources and systems in their tax function to manage and implement new rules and bear the additional compliance costs inherent in complying with the new taxing right, whereas smaller MNEs may struggle to assemble the necessary resources. Equally, the Amount A that would be available to be potentially allocated to market jurisdictions from smaller MNEs will be limited in absolute terms, resulting in significant compliance costs in exchange for insignificant benefits.

172. Similarly, even for larger MNEs that may be above a defined size threshold, if they have only a small amount of foreign revenue that is in scope the cost of compliance associated with Amount A may still exceed benefits.

173. The above observations are particularly true when considering not just the compliance cost of the MNE but also taking into account the wider administration cost for tax administrations that would be required to process and verify compliance for a large number of taxpayers, whether as part of the early tax certainty process or otherwise.

174. Against this backdrop, this Blueprint contains two thresholds designed to achieve this:

- a global revenue test; and
- a de minimis foreign in-scope revenue test.

2.3.1. Global revenue test

175. Gross revenue[25] would seem to be the easiest metric to use for determining size. A gross revenue test would allow excluding "smaller" MNEs on the basis of the annual consolidated group revenue, as shown in its consolidated financial statements. This then raises the question of where to set the level of consolidated revenue. Considering the costs and benefits, there may be little advantage in using a threshold below the current EUR 750 million threshold that is used for the purposes of Country-by-Country reporting (CbCR).[26]

176. First, the impact assessment shows that there is very little increase in the residual profit that would be allocated to market jurisdictions from using a lower figure. Second, it substantially increases compliance and administrative costs. A lower threshold brings in a large number of additional taxpayers that need to determine whether they have revenue in scope, and if they do, comply with the new system. This results in burdens not only for those businesses, but equally for the tax administrations of all Inclusive Framework members to manage the additional compliance and administrative costs.

177. Furthermore, going lower than EUR 750 million will substantially increase the number of privately held groups in scope that currently are not required to prepare financial statements, or if they do, they are preparing them on the basis of purely local generally accepted accounting principles (GAAP). Requiring such privately held groups to prepare financial accounts on the basis of a different standard (or adjusting to that standard) solely for the purposes of Pillar One (and one that may then not be subject to audit

requirements) would be difficult and costly for taxpayers, and resource intensive for tax administrations to verify.

178. Finally, a tax certainty process with anywhere near the number of taxpayers that a threshold below EUR 750 million would generate may well go beyond the capacity of tax administrations to operate.

179. Generally, and to avoid tax administrations being overwhelmed with the operation of a new system, including as it relates to tax certainty, it will be important that Amount A is limited to a manageable number of MNE groups. Further, it is difficult to foresee the tax certainty process being applied to review the computation of Amount A for thousands of MNE groups from a standing start. Rather, it is reasonable to assume that the new process will require some time to ramp-up, to allow for identifying and addressing operational challenges before any expansion.

180. At the same time, the threshold needs to ensure that it does not exclude a material part of residual profits otherwise in scope. In light of this, and to minimise compliance costs and keep the administration of the new rules manageable for tax administrations, further work will explore different approaches. One approach could be to implement the threshold on a phased approach. This could start with a higher global revenue threshold that could either be gradually reduced over a number of years or be applied for a longer period and then only start the reductions after a post-implementation review has been undertaken. Other approaches will also be explored.

181. The table below contains some economic analysis on the number of MNE groups that could potentially fall in scope of Amount A at different global revenue levels. (see Table 2.1 below).

Table 2.1. Estimated number of MNE groups above potential global revenue thresholds

Global Revenue Threshold (EUR m) [27]	Estimated Number of MNE groups after applying global revenue Threshold	Estimated Number of MNE groups with a primary activity in ADS or CFB sectors after applying the global revenue threshold
750	~8,000	~2,300
1,000	~6,800	~2,000
2,000	~4,100	~1,300
5,000	~2,000	~620
10,000	~1,000	~350

2.3.2. *De minimis foreign in-scope revenue test*

182. The second threshold relates to MNEs that exceed the gross revenue threshold above, but only have a small amount of foreign source in-scope revenue. In such cases, the total profit to be allocated under the new taxing right would not be material relative to the costs to businesses and tax administrations arising from the application of the Amount A rules. First, for MNEs with less in-scope revenue that than the global revenue test the potential profits allocable to market jurisdictions under Amount A will be relatively small. This reflects the fact that an MNE with in-scope revenue of, for example, EUR 250 million and a profit margin of 20% (which is relatively high) will only have profit before tax (PBT) of EUR 50 million that would be in scope of Amount A. Further, the profits allocable to market jurisdictions under Amount A will be further constrained through the application of the profit allocation formula (i.e. the profitability threshold and reallocation percentages).[28] Second, for MNEs that primarily earn in-scope revenue in a single jurisdiction, applying Amount A is likely to have a limited tax impact, because it is likely that the Amount A formula will allocate taxing rights over an MNE's residual profits to the same jurisdiction that already has taxing rights under the current ALP-based profit allocation rules.

183. For this reason, a secondary de minimis foreign in-scope revenue test would be applied to determine the MNEs in scope of Amount A. This threshold for de minimis foreign in-scope revenue would be set at an absolute number, rather than being relative to the size of a given MNE's domestic business.

This has the benefit of achieving the same outcome for MNE groups that engage in foreign market jurisdictions to a similar extent, irrespective of whether that foreign market engagement is significantly smaller than the domestic business or not (and which may otherwise lead to different outcomes depending on the relative size of the domestic market).

184. This test would have two steps. First, an MNE would apply the activities test to determine whether the group earned more than the de minimis foreign in-scope revenue threshold amount from ADS or CFB activities. MNEs that do not earn more than the de minimis foreign in-scope revenue threshold amount from in-scope activities would be excluded from scope on this basis. Second, the MNE would then need to determine whether it earned more than the de minimis foreign in-scope revenue threshold amount from "foreign" in-scope activities. This will first require an MNE to identify its domestic or home market using a standardised definition, for example, where the group is headquartered or where the ultimate parent entity (UPE) is tax resident. Further work is required to define an MNE Group's domestic or home market in order to prevent manipulation. The MNE would then need to determine whether it derived more than the de minimis foreign in-scope revenue threshold amount in in-scope revenue from jurisdictions outside its home or domestic market, based on the Amount A revenue sourcing rules (see Chapter 4). This would be simple for MNEs that derives all its in-scope revenue from its own domestic market, at which this second step is primarily targeted. But it could also be relevant for other MNEs that generate relatively small amounts of revenue outside their home market. Though the application of the Amount A revenue sourcing rules may be perceived to create complexity for MNEs seeking to apply this test, doing so would allow eligible MNEs to avoid the compliance costs associated with the other aspects of applying Amount A. Further work will be undertaken on this threshold including exploring whether any thresholds should be introduced on a phased basis.[29]

2.3.3. Next steps

185. As a next step, a decision will be necessary to agree the definitive thresholds, including whether a phase in/transition period is appropriate and, if so, its design.

Notes

[1] see CTPA/CFA/WP2/NOE2(2020)10).

[2] The provision of services may need to be defined to provide further clarity.

[3] The definition of ADS draws upon, but is different from, concepts contained in the definition of "electronically supplied services" used in the European Union VAT law. The intention is to avoid conflation between both concepts (and avoid any difficult questions as to the relevance of the associated EU case law for the Inclusive Framework).

[4] See general definitions below for definition of digital interface.

[5] It is recognised that there may be a question of whether the sale or alienation of personal data is a type of "service," or indeed whether it can really be "sold."

[6] See general definitions below for definition of "users."

[7] For the avoidance of doubt, the reference to cloud computing services refers to the MNE that provides the cloud services. Even though from a user perspective, accessing another type of ADS (such as digital content) could be (in an indirect sense) accessing a cloud service, for present purposes the question is about whether the revenue is generated from the business activity of providing cloud computing services,

as opposed to generating revenue from a business activity which is in turn supported by a cloud computing service.

[8] Other sectors are in the medical equipment business, such as selling consumer goods (bandages, blood pressure meters); medical equipment not purchased by consumers (e.g. hip replacement materials); or medical equipment for professional use (e.g. MRI machines, surgical tools). These are outside the scope of the pharmaceutical industry, and the ordinary rules applying to determine the scope of CFB, including the approach to dual use goods and components, will be used to address these sectors.

[9] Retail pharmaceutical refers to those provided outside hospital care, such as those dispensed through a pharmacy or bought from a supermarket.

[10] The income can also include rent (where the site of the franchise operation is leased to the franchisee). However, an exclusion from scope from Amount A is being considered for commercial real estate. If agreed, the interaction between that exclusion and franchising fees may require further clarification.

[11] This is separate from the notion of an intermediary product / component sold B2B, as discussed below. In a product distribution franchising arrangement, the company that sells the intermediate product has a significant degree of control over the manner in which the franchisee company assembles the finished product to the consumer (and the franchisee can only use that intermediate product to assemble the final product as instructed by the franchisor); and the franchisor derives revenues from the sales of the end product. Whereas in a sale of a component part B2B, the seller of the component has very limited control in how the buyer uses the component for assembly in its own finished products (and which may be used in a variety of different types of the buyer's products), and the seller of the component earns revenue from the actual sale of the component as opposed to revenue from the finished product.

[12] See also section 6.4 and section 7.3.

[13] It therefore does not include the licensing of trade intangibles or manufacturing know-how.

[14] See also section 6.4, and section 7.3.

[15] Extractive businesses are those engaged in the exploration for, and extraction from the earth's crust of, non-renewable natural resources such as hydrocarbons and minerals, the processing and refining of those resources into usable commodities, and the sale of those commodities.

[16] While natural resources businesses may make use of digital tools, the product or service they offer is not a digital service itself.

[17] Non-renewable resource include hydrocarbons and minerals. Upstream hydrocarbons extracted from the earth such as crude oil (petroleum) and natural gas are out of scope even under the general CFB definition, as they are not sold to consumers. After processing, intermediate products such as ethane, pentanes, asphalt, etc., are commonly sold as inputs to other industries such as chemical production and construction, and likewise do not meet the test of being sold to consumers. Minerals, including base metals (copper, zinc) and precious metals (gold, silver) are extracted from the earth before being refined and smelted into metals and other mineral commodities. Most mineral products (steel, aluminium, gypsum) are not commonly sold to consumers and so are not within the scope of CFB. Likewise, sale of rough or raw gemstones and those for industrial use would be natural resources that are excluded from scope.

[18] For example, crops (a sack of wheat or green coffee beans), a haul of caught fish (whole cod), and a stack of timber.

[19] Application of the factors, however, will require some nuance. For example, there is a spectrum of processing, packaging and branding when considering agricultural products, ranging from raw fruit (which may carry a brand label for retail sale, but where the product is untransformed, unpackaged and generic), through fruit that has undergone simple processing (e.g. cutting and peeling) before being placed in a branded can, to highly processed and branded food products that are combined with other ingredients like fruit-based confectionary that would be the products in scope of conventional CFB. Other examples that demonstrate the need for nuance include bottled water and speciality cheeses. A similar analysis could be applied to fishery and forestry products. For example, raw logs undergo simple processing into dimensional lumber, paper and cardboard (where value is primarily attributable to the raw material and is determined chiefly by their physical characteristics) but which can also be a type of product commonly sold to consumers, compared with further transformation into wooden furniture (which derives its value mainly from manufacturing and sales) which would fall under the CFB rules.

20. For example, the United Nations (UN) for the Trade and Development Conference (1994) noted Genoa, Barcelona, Bruges, Brussels and Antwerp regulated insurance as early as the fifteenth and sixteenth centuries and that today "in most countries, if not all, there are specific regulations concerning the insurance business." See https://unctad.org/en/PublicationsLibrary/unctadsddins6_en.pdf.

[21] A third party construction company contracted by the developer to build the residence would be the "manufacturer," without a relationship to the consumer, and would be out of scope applying the general definition.

[22] Paragraph 32 of the Outline.

[23] For shipping companies, the UN Model contains an "alternative B", which awards limited source state taxing rights over "an appropriate allocation of the overall net profits derived by the enterprise from its [non-casual] shipping operations". It is little-used.

[24] Where a parcel is delivered to a consumer, the parcel company's customer is invariably the company sending the parcel – it is not the consumer that receives it. Parcel companies receive virtually no revenue from individuals sending parcels abroad.

[25] No decision has yet been taken by the Inclusive Framework on the amount or design of the revenue thresholds for the application of Amount A. Further work will be required to determine if the existing definition of revenue provided by accounting standards and shown in financial statements (which are relied upon for CbCR) could be used for the purposes of applying the global revenue test (as well as to determine the Amount A tax base, see section 6.2.3).

[26] CbCR also refers to Country-by-Country Report in this document.

[27] See also Table 6.1, which reflects the number of MNE groups above a residual profit threshold after applying a global revenue threshold of EUR 750 million.

[28] If it were assume that for the Amount A formula it is agreed that 20% of the MNE's profits in excess of a 10% profit margin would be allocated to the market. Under Amount A, the MNE's residual profits would be EUR 25 million, of which EUR 5 million (20%) would be allocated to market jurisdictions under Amount A. At a 25% corporate tax rate, this would equate to EUR 1.25 million in additional CIT or EUR 125,000 if this amount were split equally between 10 market jurisdictions.

[29] An issue has also been raised about whether it is equitable under the approach outlined in section 2.3 that a larger firm with a small volume of in-scope revenue should be in scope of Amount A, when a smaller

firm with a much higher volume of in-scope revenue may be out-of-scope depending on the amount of the global and de minimis foreign in-scope revenue thresholds. Given this issue, consideration will also be given to a threshold based on in-scope revenues.

3 Nexus

3.1. Overview

186. The new international taxation framework set forth in this Blueprint recognises that in an increasingly digital age, taxing rights can no longer be exclusively determined by reference to physical presence. It therefore contains new nexus rules for in-scope revenue referred to in Chapter 2.

187. As explained in Chapter 2, the scope tests seek to capture those large MNEs that are able to participate in an active and sustained manner in the economic life of market jurisdictions through engagement extending beyond the mere conclusion of sales, in order generate profits, without necessarily having a commensurate level of taxable presence in that market (as based on existing nexus rules). In this regard, Chapters 2 and 3 need to be read together as they translate a common underlying rationale.

188. The nexus rules design intends to protect the interests of smaller jurisdictions, and in particular developing economies, and their desire to benefit from the new taxing right. It recognises the need for low and proportionate compliance costs.

189. The new nexus rules determine entitlement of a market jurisdiction to an allocation of Amount A only. They do not alter the nexus for other tax purposes, customs duties or for any other non-tax area. The new nexus rules will be designed as a standalone provision to limit any unintended spill-over effects on other existing tax or non-tax rules.

190. The new nexus rules could apply differently for ADS and CFB. For ADS, exceeding a market revenue threshold could be the only test to establish nexus. The very nature of the ADS allows them to be provided remotely and such businesses generally have a significant and sustained engagement with the market even if there is not a physical presence, which is one of the key challenges in taxing the digitalising economy.

191. For CFB, the ability to participate remotely in a market jurisdiction is less pronounced. This, together with the additional complexity and compliance costs associated with sourcing revenue derived by CFB (e.g. third party distribution) and the broad acknowledgement that profit margins are typically lower for CFB compared with ADS, could justify a higher nexus standard for CFB. Although many Inclusive Framework members, seeking simplicity, would prefer a nexus threshold based solely on revenue, other members consider that a higher nexus standard for CFB is essential. One approach for satisfying this higher nexus standard is through a higher threshold and the presence of additional indicators ("plus" factors) which would evidence an active and sustained engagement in that jurisdiction beyond mere sales.

192. The Blueprint therefore sets out an approach based on the following elements. A nexus is achieved:

- for ADS:
  - with revenues of more than [EUR X million] a year;
- for CFB:
  - with revenues of more than [EUR X million] a year and;

- a "plus factor" to indicate a significant and sustained engagement with the market. One plus factor could be a subsidiary, or a "fixed place of business" (e.g. a permanent establishment based on the commonalities of the UN and OECD Model definitions), with the requirement that the entity or PE is carrying out activities that are connected to in-scope sales. Consideration will be given to the possibility of treating revenues of more than EUR XX million as a plus factor (where the MNE would be deemed to have an active engagement beyond mere sales). Other plus factors may also be considered (which may be unconstrained by physical presence).

193. Depending on where threshold amounts are set, consideration will be given to using a lower nexus standard for smaller developing economies, with GDP below a certain level while also considering compliance simplifications.

3.2. Features and operation of the nexus rules

194. For in-scope MNEs the new nexus rules would be based on indicators of a significant and sustained engagement with market jurisdictions. In other words, absent this engagement with a jurisdiction, none of a group's profits would be reallocated to that jurisdiction under Amount A. The new nexus rules would operate in a standalone manner to limit any unintended spill-over effects on other existing tax or non-tax rules. Thus they would not be used as a basis to create a nexus for any other taxes, customs duties or for any other non-tax purpose. For example, the new rules will not affect the operation of the existing permanent establishment rules, which will continue to operate as at present. The concrete design of this standalone provision, outside *existing* tax treaties, will be undertaken when the substantive elements of scope and nexus have been settled.[1]

3.2.1. General features: market revenue thresholds and temporal requirements

195. **The market revenue thresholds** will apply to the in-scope revenue of a group (or segment of a group where relevant) generated in a market jurisdiction. The market revenue will be identified and measured in accordance with the revenue sourcing rules (see Chapter 4), and could apply separately to ADS and CFB.[2] The nexus rules will follow any wider segmentation approach, i.e. the nexus will be assessed at the level of a segment where a group segments its operations in computing its Amount A tax base (see Chapter 5).

196. Further work will need to be undertaken to decide whether to apply a **temporal requirement**. Such a requirement would avoid covering isolated or one-off transactions that might not demonstrate a sustained engagement with a market. A duration test could be designed by requiring that the market revenue threshold be exceeded over a period spanning more than one year before establishing a nexus. However, assessing nexus year by year is simple and would be more aligned with other testing periods throughout Amount A.

197. The Outline indicated that the market revenue threshold would be commensurate with the size of each market, measured, perhaps by GDP. But this is likely to add substantial complexity, so the nexus rules could use a simple monetary amount of revenue in the market – one for ADS and one for CFB. However, consideration is being given to using higher thresholds for large markets and lower thresholds for small, developing economies.[3]

198. In determining the level at which to set thresholds, several considerations will need to be taken into account. The data analysis prepared as part of the impact assessment, while subject to significant uncertainty, suggests that a market revenue threshold has an important impact on the Amount A allocation to smaller jurisdictions, in particular developing economies (unlike the global scope revenue threshold)[4]. For the smallest jurisdictions (e.g. jurisdictions with GDP less than USD 5 billion), the analysis suggests

that many MNE groups may not have a nexus in these jurisdictions if a single threshold is set at EUR 5 million or above. On that basis, and the considerations further discussed below, a possibility is to have two separate market revenue thresholds: one for ADS, and one for CFB, noting that the amounts of such thresholds are expected to be set below EUR 5 million. As stated in paragraph 197, consideration is being given to using higher thresholds for large markets and lower thresholds for small, developing economies.

199. Different threshold amounts for ADS and CFB could be justified on the following grounds. First, the ability of CFB businesses to participate remotely in market jurisdictions seems less pronounced compared to ADS. Second, additional complexity and compliance costs associated with sourcing revenue derived by CFB (e.g. third party distribution) compared with ADS also points to a higher threshold amount for CFB. Finally, profit margins are typically lower for CFB compared with ADS, and hence that the threshold amount should be greater for CFB to ensure the same balance between tax benefits for market jurisdictions and overall compliance and administrative costs. However, some jurisdictions prefer that the thresholds be aligned.

200. Further work will be undertaken on the administration and co-ordination of the thresholds used for Amount A to ensure they remain appropriate over time.

201. For ADS, the market revenue threshold would be the only test to establish nexus.

3.2.2. Additional indicator of nexus for CFB

202. For CFB, a level of sales just over the market revenue threshold may not denote the active and sustained engagement with the market beyond the mere conclusion of sales that is envisaged as the justification of the new taxing right. To demonstrate this level of engagement, the presence of additional indicators ("plus factors") may be necessary.

203. Many Inclusive Framework members, seeking simplicity, would be prepared to accept a nexus threshold based solely on revenue, especially since the scope tests already seek to capture those MNEs that participate in a sustained and significant manner in the economic life of market jurisdictions. Other members, however, consider plus factors as essential to a nexus rule for CFB. In order to bridge the gap between the two groups this Blueprint suggests that plus factors could be required for a CFB to demonstrate a nexus. One option being considered is that, where sales in a market have passed a certain level, the MNE can be presumed to have an active engagement. In that case, plus factors would be deemed to exist. As explained later, for many groups there will be a level of sales over which they will in any event want to establish a local presence. The application of plus factors for small, developing economies may need to be considered with the level of the thresholds.

204. Several possible plus factors have been examined. They include having an existing physical presence in the form of a permanent establishment (PE) or the residence of a group entity; a physical presence that falls short of a PE; and the undertaking of material, targeted and sustained advertising and promotion (A&P) activities that support in-scope sales into the market jurisdiction.

"Physical presence" test

205. In the interest of simplicity, the likely indicator used would be just this one. A physical presence test in the form of a subsidiary or PE seems the simplest way to establish a nexus (beyond mere selling), particularly as the PE or resident entity will likely already have filing and reporting requirements in that jurisdiction. In other words, the nexus applicable for one entity (its place of residence or having a local PE) will apply to the whole group.

206. To establish an "active and sustained physical presence", there could be a requirement in this test that the activities carried out are connected to in-scope revenues. This requirement could include not only distribution activities but also activities directly supporting sales into the market, e.g. facilitating billing and

payment in the local currency, collecting indirect taxes and duties, transportation, maintenance of local stock, cross border delivery, after-sales support, repair and maintenance, advertising and promoting and adapting product or services to the particular market. Activities without a sufficient connection to sales, and which would therefore not constitute the sustained physical presence envisaged in the test, could include, for example, research and development functions. However, further technical work will be undertaken to define the nature of such a connection.

207. In more detail, the group-PE test will be met if any entity in the group has a PE in the market (as defined under a standalone definition explained below). It will also be met if a group entity is resident in the jurisdiction. In both cases, the local activities must be connected with the tested sales. An entity established with a view to aiding the group's future expansion would not trigger the nexus test if, for example, it had no premises and no employees.

208. The question is then how to assess whether a group-PE exists. This is an issue because several treaties with different PE definitions may be in play (or there may be no treaty at all).

209. One possibility is to take the PE definition in any tax treaty that exists between the state of residence of a group entity and the market jurisdiction that has triggered the existence of a PE in practice, provided the PE is connected to in-scope revenues. But this option could lead to issues of fairness and risk of distortions:

- Where there is no applicable tax treaty, and the fall-back is the domestic law of a market jurisdiction, an MNE could have a taxable presence from merely selling services, and perhaps even goods, into that market.
- Relying on different PE standards found in existing tax treaties may lead to unfairness where one market jurisdiction (with a standard PE threshold in its tax treaties) may not receive any tax under Amount A from a given MNE, while another jurisdiction – with a lower PE threshold – would collect Amount A taxes from that same MNE (and for the same activities). The same fairness issue arises if the definition relies on domestic legislation.
- If Amount A is conditional on an MNE having a PE under existing treaties or domestic legislation, tax administrations may feel additional pressure to find a PE to exist, increasing the chances of PE disputes between jurisdictions with a potential impact beyond the scope of amount A (increasing the risk of spill over effects).

210. To remove the concerns mentioned above, the preferred approach, is to use a single self-standing group-PE definition, instead of relying on a PE definition in a tax treaty or domestic law. Such a standalone provision will not affect the application of PE rules in existing tax treaties or domestic legislation, which will continue to operate as at present for tax purposes, other than the allocation of Amount A. Ready-made possibilities exist (e.g. in the OECD and UN models). But it seems preferable to use one that is designed for the purpose of Amount A. The starting point for doing this is the two models.[5]

211. The intention, therefore, is to develop a group-PE test taking the basic PE principle shared between the UN and the OECD Models: a fixed place of business through which an in-scope CFB of the MNE group is wholly or partly carried on and applying this to the MNE group. Further work will be undertaken on other aspects of the existing PE definition such as Article 5(4) on preparatory and auxiliary activities and Article 5(5) on "dependent agent". This group-PE definition is only for the purpose of establishing a new nexus for Amount A.

A "deemed engagement" provision

212. As noted above, beyond a certain level of sales, it is increasingly unlikely that a group will be selling into a market with no supporting activities. For many groups, there will be a level of sales over which they will want to establish a local presence, either in the form of a subsidiary or a PE. Depending on the industry, that might be when annual sales reach a certain level. But before then, it is likely that the group's

engagement will increase its sales. One approach could be, therefore, to assume that once a group's CFB sales in a market reach a certain threshold it will no longer be necessary to establish the existence of plus factors (i.e. the group could be treated as having a nexus). This deemed engagement provision would avoid the complexities and uncertainties that more factual and expansive plus factors would create, but further policy discussion is needed.

Nexus rules for small developing economies

213. Depending on where revenue thresholds are set, consideration may also need to be given to using a lower nexus standard for small, developing economies. Given the size of their economies within the context of determining a significant and sustained engagement in the market, and the additional complexity in applying and verifying the plus factors for tax administrations with often very limited resources, both principles and practicalities may argue for further reflection. This may also need to involve considerations relating to compliance simplifications and administrative costs, including for other jurisdictions.

Other technical work

214. A few Inclusive Framework Members have favoured the addition of a test based on a sustained presence of personnel in a market jurisdiction (e.g. 183 days in a year), which could be an alternative way of establishing nexus if the physical presence was not met, e.g. for smaller jurisdictions. Many members, however, questioned the relevance and administrability of this test.

215. A test of advertising and promotion (A&P) expenditure is another test that has been explored. If it were adopted, it would be an alternative way of establishing nexus if the physical presence test were not met.[6] The test could be met where, for instance, A&P expenditure for a jurisdiction exceeded a certain percentage of the market revenue threshold, perhaps with some simplifications: e.g. focusing only on market-specific expenditures (no regional or global expenditures) but including expenditure incurred outside the market where it is directed at the market. The A&P expenditure test could also be useful for franchising and licensing business models. However, such a test may not necessarily be an accurate measure of an active and sustained engagement with a market jurisdiction as expenditures could, for example, fluctuate over the lifetime of a brand. Such a test may also apply differently between established businesses and new businesses, given that penetrating a market with a new brand requires a higher level of A&P expenditures. Further work will therefore be carried out on the technical aspects of this test, noting however, the administrative difficulties and challenges.

3.3. Next steps

216. As a next step, decisions will be needed on the amount of the thresholds, the use of plus factors, and if so, which ones, and whether and how, the rules might be adapted to the needs of small, developing economies.

217. In addition, further technical work will be undertaken on:

- Defining a possible temporal requirement (the period over which an MNE will have to satisfy the above tests: whether reaching the nexus threshold for one year will be sufficient or whether it will be necessary to apply the test over a longer period);
- The precise details of a standalone "physical presence" definition based on the commonalities of the UN and the OECD models;
- The issue of the connection between the plus factors and the in-scope sales;
- Work on possible plus factors, with specific considerations for franchise and licensing business models; and

- Consistent technical definitions and rules applicable to all thresholds along Amount A (currency, timing issues, etc.).

Notes

[1] See Chapter 10 on implementation.

[2] This separate approach was developed to prevent the distortions that an aggregated approach would create in the treatment of mixed revenues. Using thresholds based on revenue from a market is less reliant on complex factual determinations compared with other factors, and therefore will limit compliance and administration costs and provide certainty.

[3] See below paragraph 213.

[4] Due to the lack of comprehensive entity level data on MNE sales in each jurisdiction with which to assess a nexus revenue threshold, a probabilistic modelling approach has been developed to approximate the effect of an illustrative range of potential nexus revenue thresholds. To consider the implications for a range of jurisdictions according GDP size, a range of thresholds (EUR 1m, 3m, 5m and 7m) were considered for ADS and CFB combined. As this approach is inevitably assumption-dependent, results should be considered as illustrative of the orders of magnitude rather than precise estimates. The impact assessment of various nexus thresholds is contained in CTPA/CFA/WP2/NOE2(2020)5.

[5] Although there are differences between them, these may not be material for Amount A purposes. The existence of an insurance PE provision in the UN model would not be relevant, for example, if insurance services are removed from the scope of Amount A. Nor does the presence of "delivery" activities in the OECD Model's list of exemptions make any difference after the BEPS Action 7 changes.

[6] A possibility favoured by some jurisdictions would be to require both the physical presence test and the A&P test to apply as evidence of an active and sustained engagement with the market beyond the mere conclusion of sales.

4 Revenue sourcing rules

4.1. Overview

218. The revenue sourcing rules determine the revenue that would be treated as deriving from a particular market jurisdiction. The rules would be relevant in applying the scope rules, (see section 2.3.2), the nexus rules (see Chapter 3) and the Amount A formula (see Chapter 6). They are reflective of the particularities of ADS and CFB and more broadly were designed to balance the need for accuracy with the ability of in-scope MNEs to comply, without incurring disproportionate compliance costs. This is proposed to be achieved through the articulation of sourcing principles, supported by a range of specific indicators, subject to a defined hierarchy (likely to be of particular importance in connection with third party distribution). This approach of providing a range of possible indicators within the hierarchy recognises the different ways MNEs currently collect information in the context of their business model, while still providing certainty to MNEs and tax administrations that the defined set of acceptable specified indicators can be relied upon to provide acceptable outcomes.

219. To source the relevant in-scope revenue to a market jurisdiction, a sourcing principle would be identified for each type of in-scope revenue, accompanied by a list of the acceptable specific indicators an MNE will use to apply the principle and identify the jurisdiction of source. For example, for the direct sale of consumer goods, the principle would be to source the revenue based on the jurisdiction of final delivery of the goods to the consumer, and the acceptable indicator would be the jurisdiction of the retail store front where the consumer good is sold or shipping address.

220. The acceptable indicators would be organised in a hierarchy. The MNE should generally use the indicator that is first in the hierarchy, as this will be the most accurate. However, an MNE may use an alternative indicator that appears second in the hierarchy, if the first indicator was not reasonably available or if the MNE can justify that the first indicator was unreliable, and so on with the remaining indicators.

221. This approach is intended to ensure that there is sufficient flexibility to accommodate the different ways that MNEs collect information. The rules provide guidance on when an indicator can be considered to be unavailable or unreliable, to reduce the potential for disputes for tax administrations and taxpayers alike.

222. Information would be considered unavailable if it is not within the MNE's possession, and reasonable steps have been taken to obtain it but have been unsuccessful. Information would be considered unreliable if the MNE can justify that the indicator is not a true representation of the principle in the source rule.

223. The MNE would need to justify and document its approach and include it in the standardised documentation package to be developed as part of the broader work on tax certainty (see Chapter 9). It is expected that an in-scope MNE will need to retain documentation:

- describing the functioning of its internal control framework related to revenue sourcing;
- containing aggregate and periodic information on results of applying the indicators, for each type of revenue and in each jurisdiction; and

- explaining the indicator used, and, if relevant, why a secondary indicator was applied instead (such as the steps taken to obtain information or why a primary indicator was considered unreliable).

224. This information will remain systemic level data. MNEs would thus not be expected to keep a record of all data points on the indicators for every transaction (which may cause concerns relating to privacy) or use of the service, but rather to establish a robust internal control framework on which the tax authorities can rely to conduct their audit, supported by the underlying results of applying the indicators at an aggregate level, as well as retaining a sufficient sample of the underlying data points to justify that the internal control framework is robust.

225. As it is critical to understand the sourcing rule (and its list of indicators) in the context of each relevant business model, commentary accompanies the revenue sourcing rules to further explain the meaning of the different indicators, and provide guidance for MNE's administration. The status of the Commentary in the context of implementation will be considered in due course. The Commentary is set out in section 4.3, following the complete set of rules.

4.2. Revenue sourcing rules

226. This section contains draft rules on revenue sourcing. They are categorised under the ADS services and CFB in scope of Amount A. For each type of activity identified as in scope, a sourcing principle is identified, followed by a hierarchical list of the acceptable indicators an MNE may use to locate the jurisdiction of source. In addition, it includes specific rules on documentation requirements for MNEs.

4.2.1. General rules

227. An MNE must apply the revenue sourcing rules set out below that are relevant to each type(s) of revenue(s) it generates.

228. An MNE will apply the indicator that appears first in the hierarchy of indicators, unless this information is unavailable or unreliable as noted within each rule.

229. Information is only considered unavailable if it is not within the MNE's possession, and reasonable steps have been taken to obtain the information but these have not been successful.

230. Information is considered unreliable if the MNE can justify that the indicator is not a true representation of the principle in the source rule.

231. If an indicator is unavailable or unreliable, the MNE should seek to apply the next indicator in the hierarchy. In the event that all of the indicators in the hierarchy are unavailable (after having taken reasonable steps to obtain it) or unreliable, the MNE must apply the sourcing rule based on alternative available information and document the approach taken.

232. An MNE must retain documentation as set out in these rules.

233. The following definitions apply to these rules:

- "Developer" means the party that developed the intangible good or service.
- "Independent distributor" means an independent enterprise that is contracted by the MNE to distribute or resell that MNE's goods.
- "Intangible goods / services" means products or services that are not of a physical nature or delivered in physical form, such as downloaded material or advisory services.
- "Jurisdiction" means country or territory that is a jurisdiction for tax purposes.
- "Ordinary residence" means the place a person habitually resides.

- "Other online purchases" mean online purchases of goods or services that are in scope of ADS, or the purchase of additional features within an ADS for which the user pays.
- "Purchaser" means the party making a payment under a contract to acquire a good or service.
- "Seller" means the party providing the good or service under a contract with a purchaser.
- "Tangible goods" means products that are of a physical nature, such as clothing or household items.
- "Tangible services" means services that are delivered in physical form, such as hotel accommodation or transportation.
- "User" means any individual or business accessing a service, but does not include:
    - the provider, or a member of the same MNE group as the provider, of that service;
    - an employee of person referred to in paragraph (a) acting in the course of that person's business.
- "User profile" means information collected and retained by the MNE about a user.
- "Viewer" means the individual who views an advertisement.

234. All other capitalised terms take their meaning from the Scope of Amount A, in Chapter 2.

4.2.2. Automated digital services (ADS)

235. These rules first set out a non-exhaustive, indicative list of the type of revenues that ADS businesses typically earn and the revenue sourcing rules they would apply for each separately identifiable revenue stream. Then, it sets out the sourcing rule and relevant indicator per type of revenue.

236. As noted above, revenue from online advertising, sale or other alienation of user data and digital content services are prevalent revenue streams for many types of businesses in scope of ADS, whether contained on the positive list or not. For the purpose of revenue sourcing, whenever an MNE derives revenues from any form of these activities, the revenue will be sourced according to the rules for revenue from that particular activity. Further consideration can be given to whether guidance is needed for cases where a revenue stream cannot be clearly separated, or where a single customer contributes to multiple revenue streams which may not be easily distinguishable.

Revenue from online advertising services

237. The ADS business of Online Advertising Services generates revenue including:

- Revenue from Online Advertising Services.

Online advertising services based on the real-time location of the viewer

238. The sourcing rule is the jurisdiction of the real-time location of the viewer of the advertisement.

239. The relevant indicators are:

a. The jurisdiction of the geolocation of the device of the viewer at the time of display; or if unavailable or unreliable

b. The jurisdiction of the IP address of the device of the viewer at the time of display; or if unavailable or unreliable

c. Other available information that can be used to determine the jurisdiction of the real-time location of the viewer.

ADS business	Type of revenue sourcing rules applied
Online Advertising Services	• Revenue from online advertising services
Sale or Other Alienation of User Data	• Revenue from sale or other alienation of user data

Online Search Engines	• Revenue from online advertising services • Revenue from sale or other alienation of user data
Social Media Platforms	• Revenue from online advertising services • Revenue from sale or other alienation of user data • Revenue from digital content services
Online Intermediation Platform Services	• Revenue from online advertising services • Revenue from sale or other alienation of user data • Revenue from online intermediation platform services • Revenue from digital content services
Digital Content Services	• Revenue from online advertising services • Revenue from sale or other alienation of user data • Revenue from digital content services
Online Gaming	• Revenue from online advertising services • Revenue from sale or other alienation of user data • Revenue from digital content services
Standardised Online Teaching Services	• Revenue from online advertising services • Revenue from sale or other alienation of user data • Revenue from digital content services
Cloud Computing Services	• Revenue from online advertising services • Revenue from cloud computing services

Other online advertising services

240. The sourcing rule is the jurisdiction of the ordinary residence of the viewer of the advertisement.

241. The relevant indicators are:

a. The jurisdiction of the ordinary residence of the viewer, based on user profile information:
   i. Information on residence obtained from recurring data on geolocation or IP address of the viewer's device; or if unavailable or unreliable
   ii. Billing address of the viewer; or if unavailable or unreliable
   iii. Mobile country code of the phone number of the viewer; or if unavailable or unreliable
   iv. Information on residence inputted by the viewer; or if unavailable or unreliable
   v. Other available information that can be used to determine the jurisdiction of the ordinary residence of the viewer; or if unavailable or unreliable

b. The jurisdiction of the geolocation of the device of the viewer at the time of display; or if unavailable or unreliable

c. The jurisdiction of the IP address of the device of the viewer at the time of display

Revenue from the sale or other alienation of user data

242. The ADS business of Sale or Other Alienation of User Data generates revenue including:

- Revenue from the Sale or Other Alienation of User Data.

Sale or other alienation of user data based on the real-time location of the user

243. The sourcing rule is the jurisdiction of the real-time location of the user that is the subject of the data being transmitted, at the time the data was collected.

244. The relevant indicators are:

a. The jurisdiction of the geolocation of the device of the user at the time of collection; or if unavailable or unreliable
b. The jurisdiction of the IP address of the device of the user at the time of collection; or if unavailable or unreliable
c. Other available information that can be used to determine the jurisdiction of the real-time location of the user.

Other sale or other alienation of user data

245. The sourcing rule is the jurisdiction of the ordinary residence of the user that is the subject of the data being transmitted.

246. The relevant indicators are:

a. The jurisdiction of the ordinary residence of the user, based on user profile information:
    i. Information on residence obtained from recurring data on geolocation or IP address of the user's device; or if unavailable or unreliable
    ii. Billing address of the user; or if unavailable or unreliable
    iii. Mobile country code of the phone number of the user; or if unavailable or unreliable
    iv. Information on residence inputted by the user; or if unavailable or unreliable
    v. Other available information that can be used to determine the jurisdiction of the ordinary residence of the user; or if unavailable or unreliable
b. The jurisdiction of the geolocation of the device of the user at the time of collection; or if unavailable or unreliable
c. The jurisdiction of the IP address of the device of the user at the time of collection.

Revenue from online search engines

247. The ADS business of Online Search Engines generates revenue including:

- Revenue from Online Advertising Services; and
- Revenue from the Sale or Other Alienation of User Data.

Revenue from social media platforms

248. The ADS business of Social Media Platforms generates revenue including:

- Revenue from Online Advertising Services;
- Revenue from the Sale or Other Alienation of User Data; and
- Revenue from Digital Content Services.

Revenue from online intermediation platform services

249. The ADS business of Online Intermediation Platform Services generates revenue including:

- Revenue from Online Advertising Services;

- Revenue from the Sale or Other Alienation of User Data;
- Revenue from Online Intermediation Platform Services; and
- Revenue from Digital Content Services.

250. The rule on Online Intermediation Platform Services is designed according to the nature of the goods / services being intermediated, which may be intermediation of tangible goods, intermediation of tangible services and intermediation of intangible goods /services.

Intermediation of tangible goods

251. The revenue is sourced based on a 50:50 split between the purchaser and the seller.

Purchaser

252. The sourcing rule with respect to the purchaser is the jurisdiction of the ordinary residence of the purchaser.

253. The relevant indicators are:

a. The jurisdiction of the delivery address of the purchaser; or if unavailable or unreliable
b. The jurisdiction of the billing address of the purchaser;[1] or if unavailable or unreliable
c. The jurisdiction of the ordinary residence of the purchaser based on user profile information:
    i. Information on residence obtained from recurring data on geolocation or IP address of the purchaser's device; or if unavailable or unreliable
    ii. Billing address of the user; or if unavailable or unreliable
    iii. Mobile country code of the phone number of the purchaser; or if unavailable or unreliable
    iv. Information on residence inputted by the purchaser; or if unavailable or unreliable
    v. Other available information that can be used to determine the jurisdiction of the ordinary residence of the purchaser; or if unavailable or unreliable
d. The jurisdiction of the geolocation of the device of the purchaser; or if unavailable or unreliable
e. The jurisdiction of the IP address of the device of the purchaser.

Seller

254. The sourcing rule with respect to the seller is the jurisdiction of the ordinary residence of the seller.

255. The relevant indicators are:

a. The jurisdiction of the principal place of business of the seller (or in case the seller is a natural person, the jurisdiction of the residential address of the seller); or if unavailable or unreliable
b. The jurisdiction of the ordinary residence of the seller based on user profile information:
    i. Information on residence obtained from recurring data on geolocation or IP address of the seller's device; or if unavailable or unreliable
    ii. Billing address of the seller; or if unavailable or unreliable
    iii. Mobile country code of the phone number of the seller; or if unavailable or unreliable
    iv. Information on residence inputted by the seller; or if unavailable or unreliable

v. Other available information that can be used to determine the jurisdiction of the ordinary residence of the seller.

Intermediation of tangible services

256. The revenue is sourced based on a 50:50 split between the purchaser and the seller.[2]

Purchaser

257. The sourcing rule with respect to the purchaser is the jurisdiction of the location of the purchaser at the time of purchase.

258. The relevant indicators are:

a. The jurisdiction of the geolocation of the device of the purchaser; or if unavailable or unreliable
b. The jurisdiction of the delivery address of the purchaser; or if unavailable or unreliable
c. The jurisdiction of the IP address of the device of the purchaser; or if unavailable or unreliable
d. The jurisdiction of the ordinary residence of the purchaser based on user profile information:
    i. Information on residence obtained from recurring data on geolocation or IP address of the purchaser's device; or if unavailable or unreliable
    ii. Billing address of the purchaser; or if unavailable or unreliable
    iii. Mobile country code of the phone number of the purchaser; or if unavailable or unreliable
    iv. Information on residence inputted by the purchaser; or if unavailable or unreliable
    v. Other available information that can be used to determine the jurisdiction of the ordinary residence of the purchaser.

Seller

259. The sourcing rule with respect to the seller is the jurisdiction where the service is performed.

260. The relevant indicators are:

a. The jurisdiction of the address / location where the service is performed; or if unavailable or unreliable
b. The jurisdiction of the ordinary residence of the seller based on user profile information:
    i. Information on residence obtained from recurring data on geolocation or IP address of the seller's device; or if unavailable or unreliable
    ii. Billing address of the seller; or if unavailable or unreliable
    iii. Mobile country code of the phone number of the seller; or if unavailable or unreliable
    iv. Information on residence inputted by the seller; or if unavailable or unreliable
    v. Other available information that can be used to determine the jurisdiction of the ordinary residence of the seller.

Intermediation of intangible goods / services

261. The revenue is sourced based on a 50:50 split between the purchaser and the seller.

Purchaser

262. The sourcing rule with respect to the purchaser is the jurisdiction of the ordinary residence of the purchaser.

263. The relevant indicators are:

a. The jurisdiction of the ordinary residence of the purchaser based on user profile information:
   i. Information on residence obtained from recurring data on geolocation or IP address of the purchaser's device; or if unavailable or unreliable
   ii. Billing address of the purchaser; or if unavailable or unreliable
   iii. Mobile country code of the phone number of the purchaser; or if unavailable or unreliable
   iv. Information on residence inputted by the purchaser; or if unavailable or unreliable
   v. Other available information that can be used to determine the jurisdiction of the ordinary residence of the purchaser; or if unavailable or unreliable
b. The jurisdiction of the billing address of the purchaser; or if unavailable or unreliable[3]
c. The jurisdiction of the geolocation of the device of the purchaser; or if unavailable or unreliable
d. The jurisdiction of the IP address of the device of the purchaser; or if unavailable or unreliable

Seller

264. The sourcing rule with respect to the seller is the ordinary jurisdiction of the seller.

265. The relevant indicators are:

a. The jurisdiction of the principal place of business of the seller; (or in case the seller is a natural person, the jurisdiction of the residential address of the seller), or if unavailable or unreliable
b. The jurisdiction of the ordinary residence of the seller based on user profile information:
   i. Information on residence obtained from recurring data on geolocation or IP address of the seller's device; or if unavailable or unreliable
   ii. Billing address of the seller; or if unavailable or unreliable
   iii. Mobile country code of the phone number of the seller; or if unavailable or unreliable
   iv. Information on residence inputted by the seller; or if unavailable or unreliable
   v. Other available information that can be used to determine the jurisdiction of the ordinary residence of the seller

Revenue from digital content services

266. The ADS business of Digital Content Services generates revenue including:

- Revenue from Online Advertising Services;
- Revenue from the Sale or Other Alienation of User Data; and
- Revenue from Digital Content Services.

Digital content services

267. The sourcing rule is the jurisdiction of the ordinary residence of the purchaser.

268. The relevant indicators are:

c. The jurisdiction of the ordinary residence of the purchaser based on user profile information:
   vi. Information on residence obtained from recurring data on geolocation or IP address of the purchaser's device; or if unavailable or unreliable
   vii. Billing address of the purchaser; or if unavailable or unreliable
   viii. Mobile country code of the phone number of the purchaser; or if unavailable or unreliable
   ix. Information on residence inputted by the purchaser; or if unavailable or unreliable
   x. Other available information that can be used to determine the jurisdiction of the ordinary residence of the purchaser; or if unavailable or unreliable
d. The jurisdiction of the billing address of the purchaser; or if unavailable or unreliable
e. The jurisdiction of the geolocation of the device of the purchaser; or if unavailable or unreliable
f. The jurisdiction of the IP address of the device of the purchaser

Revenue from online gaming services

269. The ADS business of Online Gaming Services generates revenue including:

- Revenue from Online Advertising Services;
- Revenue from the Sale or Other Alienation of User Data; and
- Revenue from Digital Content Services.

Revenue from standardised online teaching services

270. The ADS business of Standardised Online Teaching Services generates revenue including:

- Revenue from Online Advertising Services;
- Revenue from the Sale or Other Alienation of User Data; and
- Revenue from Digital Content Services.

Revenue from cloud computing services

271. The ADS business of Cloud Computing Services generates revenue including:

- Revenue from Online Advertising Services; and
- Revenue from Cloud Computing Services.

272. The rule on cloud computing is designed according to the nature of the customer, which may be an individual or a business.

Individual purchaser

273. The sourcing rule for a cloud computing service sold to an individual customer is the jurisdiction of ordinary residence of the purchaser.

274. The relevant indicators are:

a. The jurisdiction of the ordinary residence of the purchaser based on user profile information:

   i. Information on residence obtained from recurring data on geolocation or IP address of the purchaser's device; or if unavailable or unreliable
   ii. Billing address of the purchaser; or if unavailable or unreliable
   iii. Mobile country code of the phone number of the purchaser; or if unavailable or unreliable
   iv. Information on residence inputted by the purchaser; or if unavailable or unreliable
   v. Other available information that can be used to determine the jurisdiction of the ordinary residence of the purchaser; or if unavailable or unreliable

b. The jurisdiction of the billing address of the purchaser; or if unavailable or unreliable
c. The jurisdiction of the geolocation of the device of the purchaser; or if unavailable or unreliable
d. The jurisdiction of the IP address of the device of the purchaser

Business customer

275. The sourcing rule for a service intended for internal use by a business customer is the jurisdiction of the location where the business uses the service.[4]

276. The relevant indicators are:

a. The jurisdiction(s) of the business' employees benefiting from the service as reported to the cloud computing service provider by the customer; or if unavailable or unreliable
b. The jurisdiction(s) in which the business has operations, determined by the offices and address details contained in the business agreement and/or in records collected for tax purposes (such as value added tax purposes); or if unavailable or unreliable
c. Other available information that can be used to determine the jurisdiction of the location of the business' employees that use the service.

4.2.3. Consumer-facing businesses

Revenue from consumer-facing goods sold directly to consumer

277. The sourcing rule is the jurisdiction of the place of final delivery of the good to the consumer.

278. The relevant indicators are:

a. The jurisdiction of the retail storefront directly selling to consumers; or if not applicable
b. The jurisdiction of the final delivery address of the goods to the consumer.

Revenue from consumer-facing goods sold through Independent Distributor

279. The sourcing rule is the jurisdiction of the place of final delivery of the good to the consumer.

280. The relevant indicators are:

a. The jurisdiction of the place of final delivery to the consumer as reported by the independent distributor, based on:

   i. The jurisdiction of the retail storefront directly selling to consumers; or if not applicable
   ii. The jurisdiction of the final delivery address of the goods; or if unavailable

b. The jurisdiction of the place of final delivery of the good to the consumer as indicated by other information already available to the MNE.

Revenue from consumer-facing services

281. The sourcing rule is the jurisdiction of the place of enjoyment or use of the service.

282. The relevant indicator is:

a. The jurisdiction of the address where the service is performed; or
b. For services delivered online, the jurisdiction of the ordinary residence of the user, based on:
    i. The jurisdiction of the ordinary residence of the purchaser based on user profile information:
        1. Information on residence obtained from recurring data on geolocation or IP address of the purchaser's device; or if unavailable or unreliable
        2. Billing address of the purchaser; or if unavailable or unreliable
        3. Mobile country code of the phone number of the purchaser; or if unavailable or unreliable
        4. Information on residence inputted by the purchaser; or if unavailable or unreliable
        5. Other available information that can be used to determine the jurisdiction of the ordinary residence of the purchaser; or if unavailable or unreliable
    ii. The jurisdiction of the billing address of the purchaser; or if unavailable or unreliable
    iii. The jurisdiction of the geolocation of the device of the purchaser; or if unavailable or unreliable
    iv. The jurisdiction of the IP address of the device of the purchase

Revenue from franchising and licensing

Consumer-facing goods

283. The sourcing rule for revenue from franchising goods or licensing an intangible that is attached to goods is the jurisdiction of the place of final delivery of the good to the consumer.

284. The relevant indicators are:

a. The jurisdiction of the place of delivery or enjoyment as reported by the franchisee or licensee, based on:
    i. The jurisdiction of the retail storefront directly selling to consumers; or if not applicable
    ii. The jurisdiction of the final delivery address of the goods; or if unavailable
b. The jurisdiction of the place of final delivery of the good to the consumer as indicated by other information already available to franchisor / licensor

Consumer-facing services

285. The sourcing rule for revenue from franchising services or licensing an intangible that is used to support the provision of a service to consumers is the jurisdiction of the place of enjoyment or use of the service.

286. The relevant indicators are:

a. The jurisdiction of the place of delivery or enjoyment of the service as reported by the franchisee or licensee, based on:

    i. The jurisdiction of the address where the service is performed; or if unavailable

b. The jurisdiction of the place of enjoyment or use of the service as indicated by other information already available to franchisor / licensor

4.2.4. Documentation

287. The MNE must retain documentation explaining:

a. The functioning of its internal control framework related to revenue sourcing;
b. Aggregate and periodic information on results of applying the indicators, for each type of revenue and in each jurisdiction;
c. The specific indicator used for a given category of revenue; and
d. The circumstances when an indicator lower in the hierarchy was used, including why the indicator higher in the hierarchy was not available (and the steps taken to obtain it) or not reliable (and the information available to confirm the presence of a more reliable indicator).

4.3. Commentary on revenue sourcing rules

288. This section contains the Commentary on the sourcing rules. This provides further context on the relevant business models where this is essential to understand the sourcing rule, and explains the meaning of certain indicators contained in the rules. The Commentary provide guidance on the application of the revenue sourcing rules. This guidance will cover four areas:

a. Hierarchy of the indictors;
b. Guidance on ADS (including an explanation of the indicators and guidance on relevant revenues from in-scope activities);
c. Guidance on revenue from CFB; and
d. Documentation requirements.

4.3.1. Hierarchy of indicators

289. The revenue sourcing rules are designed to ensure the collection of the most accurate information possible. This is achieved by providing a hierarchy of rules, which sets a range of acceptable data points for each given scenario. While it may be ideal to have the revenue sourcing rules based on one uniform indicator only (for example, in the case of online advertising, for the sourcing rules to look to the location of the user viewing an online advertisement and the indicator used would be the geolocation), it is recognised that different business models are used even within one set of activities and which make a different set of sourcing rules more accurate, or that different data points may be available for different users / customers even within the same set of activities. At the same time, the hierarchy of indicators approach recognises that MNEs may not always have the same specific data points, given the different commercial operations that drive the collection of information. This means that prescribing a single preferred indicator may be unworkable for certain MNEs, and may overlook other reliable available data that delivers a similar or more reliable outcome.

290. The range of indicators has been proposed as a way to provide a sound basis for revenue sourcing. In most cases, MNEs have a commercial interest in knowing the location of their final sales, for

example to drive efforts at efficient marketing and identify growth opportunities, which provides assurance that they are likely to be in a positon to give a relatively high level of confidence that the results will be reliable. However, the range of permitted indicators also recognises that the operation of Amount A will in some cases necessarily result in balancing the interest in accuracy with the need to take a reasonable approach to limit the compliance burdens on MNEs.

291. In this hierarchical structure, the first indicator is generally the preferred indicator and the MNE should source the revenue according to this indicator if possible. However, an MNE may use an alternative indicator that appears next in the hierarchy, if it can demonstrate that the first indicator was not available or if it can justify that the first indicator was unreliable, and so on with the remaining indicators.

292. Information would be considered unavailable if it is not within the MNE's possession, and reasonable steps have been taken to obtain it have been unsuccessful.[5] Only once such steps are taken, and the information is not able to be obtained by the MNE may it move to a secondary indicator.

293. Information would be considered unreliable if the MNE can justify that the indicator is not a true representation of the principle in the source rule. The result from the indicator could not reasonably be correct, for example where a disproportionate amount of indicators point to one small jurisdiction (for example because of a use of a virtual private network (VPN)) or where a delivery address is that of a freight forwarder.[6]

294. Where an MNE derives revenue from more than one type of service or activity, the MNE should use the different sourcing rules per type of revenue. Where an MNE has different data points for each individual customer / user in respect of the same service or activity / revenue stream (e.g. where for some users the user profile data is provided by the customer logging into the service, while for others only the device location information is available), it will need to apply different indicators in respect of the same service, applying the hierarchy for each customer / user. However, a de minimis safe harbour could be explored in this regard where the differences in available data points only applies in respect of a small number of customers / users.

295. Similarly, if a business is within the scope of Amount A under the general principle of ADS, and the category of that business is not explicitly provided for in the revenue sourcing rule, it should apply the sourcing rules for the type of revenue that is most analogous to the revenue that it derives. Further guidance on such cases will be developed as needed over time.

4.3.2. Guidance on automated digital services

296. This section of the Commentary sets out an explanation of the various indicators used in the rules, followed by an explanation of the relevant business models and how the indicators apply.

Guidance on indicators for ADS

297. The indicators included in the revenue sourcing rules for ADS are explained below.

Geolocation data

298. Geolocation is based on GPS data or information that could be used to extrapolate a viewer's location from a device. When a user enables location sharing on the device they are using, it is possible for the MNE to determine the precise location of the user. Therefore, when the MNE has geolocation data available, it should always use this as the indicator to identify the real-time location of the user.

299. Broadly, geolocation services use various data points to determine the location of the user. These can include a combination of IP address, GPS-derived location data, cell tower IDs to which the user is connected, as well as data associated with Wi-Fi positioning systems. The use of various data points to

triangulate a user's location results in higher levels of accuracy and is therefore considered the most reliable way to determine a user's location for the purpose of these sourcing rules.

300. For example, a geolocation application programming interface (API) is a feature that is embedded in most modern Internet browsers, which allows websites to request the location of the user in the form of a pop-up window. If the user accepts the prompt, the API locates the user, even if the user is connected to the Internet through a VPN. However, as this feature needs to be enabled on the website or platform the user is connecting to, the data is not always available to MNEs.

301. In the revenue sourcing rules, geolocation may appear both as a standalone indicator and as part of a user profile. When geolocation is included as part of user profile information, it refers to recurring data on a user's location, which can be used to determine the user's ordinary residence. This looks to the data the MNE has available about the repeating, recurring pattern of the user's location over time, and which is therefore a reliable indicator of habitual location. Where such data shows a recurring pattern of location, it can be relied upon, notwithstanding occasional results that evidence a different location (such as where a user travels abroad). If the recurring data evidences one jurisdiction for more than half of a year, this can be treated as reliable.

IP address

302. The Internet Protocol (IP) address (based on Wi-Fi or cellular IP address, depending on how the user is connected to the Internet) can be used to locate the device of the user. It is the number that is assigned to each device connected to a computer network, meaning that every device connected to the Internet has an IP address.

303. Although an IP address does not inherently contain the location of the user, IP address databases are widely used by MNEs to determine the location of the user for business reasons. In such databases, certain ranges of IP addresses are assigned to certain jurisdictions, which allows the MNE to identify the jurisdiction from the IP address. The MNE can use different products or methods to track the IP address, all of which could be used for the purpose of apply the revenue sourcing rules.

304. When the IP address appears as part of user profile information, the same considerations apply as set out in the discussion of geolocation data above for recurring data on IP address.

VPN

305. It is possible for users to elect to change the location associated with their IP address through the use of a VPN, which assigns a new IP address to the user in the country of their choosing (where a VPN server is located) and make it appear as an IP address in this other country. This can be done for privacy or security reasons, for business reasons, or to access specific content available in a given country. For example, a user located in Country X may decide to use a VPN to connect to Country Z, in order to access desired content on a streaming platform. In this case, the location associated with the IP address that the user connected to the streaming platform with would be in Country Z, rather than Country X.

306. The use of the VPN can be more widespread in some jurisdictions than others. In some cases, although far from a standard practice or commercial requirement for all ADS providers, "geoblocking" may occur (e.g. as a way for the MNE to protect and enforce the licensing arrangements it has in place), which means that the digital content available in such a market is limited. To have access to wider content available in other markets, users might be willing to use VPN more frequently. Certain ADS providers take specific steps to limit the access to their service via VPN. This involves testing the IP addresses of users accessing their service against information in databases listing known VPN addresses, and is more common for digital content services. However, it is not entirely accurate given that VPN addresses can change. In any case, attempting to break through a VPN is not technically feasible, and if it were so, it

would contradict the purpose of the service provided, for example, where a commercial feature of cloud computing is to provide security of the computing service.

307. In cases where an MNE has the ability to detect VPN usage by their users, it may still be possible for it to make an assumption of the user's location based on historical IP address data. Users may not use a VPN all the time when accessing a platform. This is most likely due to the disadvantages of VPNs, such as slower connection speed. If the MNE logs IP address data for each connection a user makes, it may be possible for the MNE to make a reasonable assumption as to the ordinary residence of the user, provided the user does not connect to the platform using a VPN at all times.

308. To balance the interest in accuracy with the recognition of the limit to which MNEs can address this issue reliably and efficiently, the revenue sourcing rules use a hierarchy of indicators that decrease the dependence of sourcing rules on IP address as an indicator of the location of the user.

309. In many cases, the commercial interest of the MNE is to have a high degree of accurate information about the user, for example, in order to be able to charge their customers a premium for serving the advertisements precisely to the intended audience. These MNEs should, as part of their business, be relying on more sophisticated information than the IP address, such as a range of user profile details or geolocation information and would be expected to take reasonable steps to obtain this information (as set out in the hierarchy relevant to the type of service).[7]

User profile information

310. MNEs that derive their revenue from the relevant ADS activities often collect personal data on their users, whether through a sign-up process or through remote automated monitoring of the users' activity on the MNE's platform or the Internet (e.g. through cookies).

311. There are two types of user profile information. The first one is created by the MNE, based on information it has available on the user. The second one is created by the user itself. A user profile can include information on the user's historical location at different points in time, their usual residence, demographic characteristics (e.g. age, gender, nationality, or estimated income), as well behavioural characteristics (e.g. purchase history, Internet browsing data, or preferences derived from a user's engagement on an MNE's platform).

312. In order to increase the value of the data, the MNE may create user profiles, which can then be used in targeting the MNE's online advertising, or to create data sets that are then monetised with third parties by way of a sale or licensing user profile information. The information contained in a user profile will depend on the information an MNE collects during each user's sign-up process and on the collection of data on the user's interaction with the MNE's platform or service. Some MNEs may for commercial reasons refrain from over-burdening the sign-up process so as to make customer on-boarding as easy as possible (e.g. digital content streaming), while others will obtain a lot of data as part of the nature of the service (e.g. social media).

313. The MNE can also use the user profile information from the profile that was created by the user itself (e.g. for creating a profile on a social media platform). Information that can be included in this profile, in addition to the profile created by the MNE itself, can be home address, telephone number (for which the MNE can use the country code as an indicator of the user's location) and the location of the bank used for the payment, to locate the jurisdiction.

314. In the revenue sourcing rules, several indicators are listed under user profile information. These indicators refer to information that is contained within a user profile that is available to the MNE. When using user profile information for revenue sourcing, the MNE will first look to the indicators explicitly listed to determine a user's ordinary residence, as set out in the hierarchy in the rules above, which prioritise user profile information created by the MNE. In cases where the MNE does not have information on the listed indicators available, or the indicators are unreliable, it may use "other available information"

contained within the user profile, which can be used to determine the ordinary residence of the user. This recognises the fact that MNEs operating under different business models are collecting different data points on their users and gives the MNE the flexibility to use another indicator contained within the specific framework of the user profile information it collects. The MNE will be required to sufficiently documents its choice of indicator and demonstrate that its results are consistent with the relevant sourcing rule.

315. Furthermore, it is possible for certain indicators to appear more than once in the revenue sourcing rules. For example, the billing address can appear both as an indicator contained within user profile information and as a standalone indicator. This recognises that certain ADS business models may not be collecting user profile information at all, but may only keep data points related to specific transactions. Therefore, although an MNE may not have the billing address available as part of a more comprehensive user profile, it still may have billing addresses linked to individual transactions, which can be used for the purpose of revenue sourcing.

Billing address

316. The billing address may identify where the purchaser usually resides. Its purpose is to pinpoint where the customer is established, has a permanent address or usually resides.

317. It is possible that the MNE will not have the billing information of the customer because the payment service is operated by a third party (e.g. PayPal or the App store). The MNE should take reasonable steps to obtain information from the payment service provider on the jurisdiction of billing address of the customer (e.g. on an aggregated level, without disclosing any personal information on the underlying customer). This may be feasible, for example, as payment service providers may provide a report to reconcile the payments it has collected on behalf of the MNE. Further information may therefore already be available or relatively easy to add. In addition, some MNEs are already obtaining this information for VAT purposes.

318. It is acknowledged that users can move jurisdictions and continue to pay for the service with a bank account that is tied to the former residence address. Because a customer cannot generally open a bank account without proof of address, the use of billing address will not be wholly unconnected from the person. However, if the MNE has reasons to believe that the billing address is unreliable, it should use the next indicator in the hierarchy of indicators.

319. See the previous section above for an explanation of when a billing address may appear in the revenue sourcing rules under both user profile and as a standalone indicator.

Other

320. The use of "other available information" as the indicator for revenue sourcing is generally applicable for cases where the sourcing rule looks to the real-time location of users. This indicator can only be used in a last resort situation where the MNE could not obtain any other information included in the hierarchy of indicators, which would lead to a result consistent with the sourcing rule. In such cases, the MNE should adequately document the reasons why other indicators were not available, to justify its use of this indicator.

321. A similar approach is taken with respect to "other available information" contained within user profile information.

Guidance on revenues from relevant in-scope ADS activities

322. This section explains the relevant business models and the rationale for the sourcing rule, together with guidance on applying the associated indicators.

Revenue from online advertising services

323. Revenue from online advertising services generally comes from fees paid by advertisers. However, the advertisements are directed to viewers, and often targeted using information about viewers collected through such means as online search engines, social media platforms and online intermediation platforms, but also through apps, online games, news websites and blogs and Internet of things devices. The advertising can either be offered as part of an MNE's service offering, or facilitated by third parties, such as through the process of real-time bidding. This category includes all online advertising, through all possible online platforms and services facilitating online advertising.

324. The revenue potential of the advertisement is connected to whether it attracts the attention of the viewer, especially if it is tailored to that viewer. The advertisement can either be viewed or clicked on, and as such, the MNE can earn revenue based on the views, the clicks, or a combination of the both. Regardless of how the advertisement is being "used", the sourcing rule is based on the "eyeballs", meaning that it identifies the location of the viewer of the advertisement, rather than the location of the company that is paying the fee for the advertisement. The MNE will need to monitor the extent to which the advertising has been shown, in order to report back to their customer on how the advertising budget has been spent, and as such it would have access to a range of information in order to do this.

325. The hierarchy of indicators for revenue from online advertising services is based on the use of the most reliable information to determine the location of the user that is viewing the advertisement, in the context of that MNE's business model. As MNEs make use of different information, or a combination of these, for providing online advertising services, the indicators selected by the MNE for the purpose of revenue sourcing can vary depending on the way the MNE targets its advertisement.

326. Where the targeting of an advertisement is linked to the real-time location of the viewer (e.g. when a local restaurant is targeting all users within a one kilometre radius, or when an advertisement is not targeted), the MNE will apply the sourcing rule that looks to the real-time location of the viewer at the time they view the advertisement.

327. Geolocation data is considered the most reliable indicator for the real-time location of the user and is not ordinarily changed in the way that an IP address is through the use of a VPN.[8] However, users may choose to disable geolocation services on their device, and this indicator may not always be available to the MNE. If the information required to use this indicator is not available, the MNE will use the IP address to determine the user's location.

328. The rule for location-based advertising is also used for advertising that is generic and is not targeted based on any parameters relating to specific location or user profiles. In this case, the indicators relating to the geolocation or IP address at the time of viewing the advertisement will be the most accurate and available information.[9]

329. Where the content of the advertisement is directed to viewers based on anything other than the real-time location of the viewer, an MNE generally makes use of a broad set of information that may be contained in a user's profile information in order to serve the advertisement to the users that a customer wants to reach. This indicator is the starting point for the purpose of revenue sourcing for MNEs involved in online advertising and will be most relevant for advertisements that target users based on their usual residence, demographic and behavioural characteristics, or a combination thereof. In cases of last resort, if the MNE does not have this information available, or if the indicators derived from user profile information are unreliable, it may use geolocation or IP address to determine the real-time location of the viewer instead. In such cases, the MNE should adequately document the reasons why other indicators were not available, to justify its use of these indicators.

330. When the MNE uses a combination of information derived from a user profile and information on the real-time location of the user, the MNE should apply the sourcing rule that reflects the type of information which is in general more important for the type of advertising in question. On the other hand,

when the MNE has, for example, one category of advertisements based on geolocation data and another based on other factors, different sourcing rules should generally be employed for each.

331. Furthermore, it is recognised that an MNE involved in the provision of online advertising by way of real time bidding may be in scope as both an online advertising service and a service transmitting data about users. In order to ensure certainty in the application of revenue sourcing rules, the sourcing rules for online advertising and services transmitting data about users are aligned, so that an MNE that finds itself in scope under both categories will use the same hierarchy of sourcing indicators under Amount A.

Revenue from sale or other alienation of user data

332. As more personal data has become available online, such as through the use of social media or through Internet connected devices, MNEs can be in the business of acquiring and monetising that personal data. This is commonly used for sale to a company or campaign that can then target its advertising to the most relevant users. As outlined in the guidance on online advertising, these companies are generally creating an "advertising profile" to facilitate targeted advertising. This profile contains a set of data, which contains pieces of information about users personal attributes (such as age, gender, hobbies, place of residence, marital status, income level), or pieces of information about features of a consumer's device (such as operating system, brand, model, installed software, and device's localisation data).

333. The sourcing rule is based on the information on either the ordinary residence or the real-time location of the users that are the subject of the data being transmitted. This recognises that the value of the data is derived from the information that is contained within the dataset, which could vary depending on what data points are being collected.

334. Therefore, if the data that is being transmitted is about the personal attributes of a user, the ordinary residence of the user is the most relevant sourcing rule, as this will reflect the contribution of that whole person's profile and behaviour, which has been built over time primarily in the residence location. Conversely, if the data that is being transmitted is only about the real-time location of the user at the point of data collection (rather than a more comprehensive user profile), the more relevant sourcing rule will be based on the real-time location of the user at the point of data collection.

335. In cases where the data that is being transmitted reflects a dataset that is primarily about the real-time location of the user, the MNE will use information on the geolocation of the user at the point of collection of the data. To do this, the MNE will prioritise the use of GPS, or other geolocation data available, to determine the location of the user at the point of data collection. If this information is unavailable, the MNE will use the IP address of the user's device to determine the jurisdiction, where the user is located at the point of data collection.

336. When the data in question is based on anything other than the real-time location of the user, the sourcing rule is the jurisdiction of the ordinary residence of the user. The primary sourcing indicator is user profile information, as the revenue from transmitting the data is related to the user's personal attributes and characteristics. The indicators are obtained from the data that is being transmitted, or from any other information the MNE may have on the user that is subject to the data transmitted.

Revenue from online search engines

337. Online search engines are websites that allow users to locate information on the Internet. The search service is free of charge to the user, but there are generally two ways that the provider monetises the service.

338. One is by selling advertising space and promoting certain websites on the search engine. For this type of revenue, the sourcing rules for revenue from online advertising services apply.

339. The second type is collection of data about the users of the search engine, which the provider can sell to advertisers. For this type of revenue, the sourcing rule for online search engines is the same as for revenue from the sale or other alienation of user data.

Revenue from social media platforms

340. This refers to platforms that promote interaction between users. The service is often free of charge to the user, and the revenue is derived from the sale of advertising or the sale of data about the users. As for online search engines, the revenue sourcing rule follows that for revenue from online advertising services or revenue from the sale or other alienation of user data, as applicable.

341. If the service is provided to the user by way of subscription fees, the revenue sourcing rule follows that for revenue from digital content services.

Revenue from online intermediation platforms

342. Broadly, there are three revenue streams for Online Intermediation Platforms Services: (i) Online Advertising; (ii) Sale or Other Alienation of User Data; and (iii) commission / fees for intermediation services. The revenue sourcing rules follow the type of revenue generated. In respect of advertising, the online advertising services rule would apply, as above. For the sale or other alienation of user data, the respective revenue sourcing rules as described above apply. Commission / fees for intermediation services can be, e.g.a portion of the sales price paid by the purchaser, or a fee charged to the seller for a portion of their sales on the site.[10]

343. For the revenue derived from commission / fees, the sourcing rule is a 50:50 split between the seller and the purchaser. This recognises that both the market and the provider of the goods have contributed to the possibility of the platform to generate its revenue. It is also more neutral as between different jurisdictions where a transaction is cross-border, as well as between business models that are essentially similar in substance but may as a matter of form charge differently for similar transactions.

344. The sourcing rule with respect to the purchaser depends on the type of good / service being purchased.

345. For "tangible" goods, the sourcing rule is the ordinary residence of the purchaser, as this is the person that has developed the interest and ability to make the purchase. The indicators look first to the billing address, delivery address, and user profile as likely indicators of the ordinary residence, as these features have some degree of permanence of the connection of the purchaser to the jurisdiction. If this information is not available, then geolocation or IP address is used, which will identify the location of the user at the point of sale. This may often, but not always, correlate to the usual residence, depending for example on how much the purchaser uses the service while travelling abroad.

346. For "tangible" services (such as hotel bookings or other short term location rentals, taxi rides, storage services, food delivery etc.), the sourcing rule is the real-time location of the purchaser at the time of purchase, as these services are generally for one-time use (unlike intangible services below), and this sourcing principle reflects the environment of the market jurisdiction where the purchaser has made the decision to purchase the service. The indicators look first to the geolocation of the purchaser, delivery address of the purchaser (if applicable, for services such as food delivery), and the IP address of the purchaser's device, as these features reflect the jurisdiction of the location of the purchaser at the time of making the purchase. If this information is not available, then user profile information is used, which will identify the location where the user typically uses the service, which may often, but not always, correlate to the real-time location of the user at the point of sale. Although the sourcing principle is the same as for location based advertising and sale of user data, additional indicators are included in this rule, given that an online intermediation platform may have additional information given their role in intermediating transactions.

347. For intangible goods / services (such as the sale of an app, software or a movie through an online intermediation platform), the sourcing rule also looks to the ordinary residence of the purchaser. Intangibles are generally used over a period of time rather than be for one-time use at the location when the purchase is made, and the ordinary residence of the purchaser is most relevant. This is also consistent with the sourcing rule for other intangibles such as digital content services and cloud computing services. The indicators used are the same as for digital content services.

348. The sourcing rule with respect to the seller also depends on the type of good/service being delivered.

349. For tangible goods, the sourcing rule is the ordinary residence of the seller that is the contracting party to the sale. The residence of the seller is indicted by the business address (or, in cases where the seller is a natural person acting in a private capacity, the indicator used is the residential address of the seller). If this information is unavailable or unreliable, the indicator is based on user profile information.

350. For tangible services, the sourcing rule is the location where the service is performed. This is because the relevant contributing market jurisdiction is the place where the purchaser has sought to make use of the service, and not where the owner or provider of the service is themselves located. This means that, for example, if an owner of a property is resident in Jurisdiction R, and the property is located in Jurisdiction P, and the property is rented out to a user of the platform, the appropriate sourcing jurisdiction is Jurisdiction P. Further guidance will be provided in cases where the service is performed in more than on jurisdiction, such as airline transportation or a travel package involving tourism in multiple destinations.

351. For intangible goods / services, the sourcing rule is the residence of the seller. This is an equivalent rule to tangible goods. The residence of the seller is indicated by the business address (or in cases where the seller is a natural person, the indicator used is the residential address of the seller). If this information is unavailable or unreliable, the indicator is based on user profile information.

Revenue from digital content services

352. Digital content services, such as the online access to films, music and software through streaming or downloading, generally generate income by either charging a fee to users or by making the service free to users but generating income for displaying advertising during use of the service and / or selling data about users of the service. In the two latter cases, the revenue sourcing rules for revenue from online advertising or revenue from sale or other alienation of user data would apply.

353. Fee-based Digital Content Services are those where a fee is paid by the user to access services such as online gaming, certain social media platforms or any other type of online subscriptions such as databases. It also includes the sale of software such as mobile applications, computer programmes or games that are in scope of ADS.

354. Furthermore, this category includes revenue from other online purchases that the customer makes when using a service, and has options to make additional features available for a fee. For example, a customer may do this to access particular premium content or when it purchases additional options (for example more expensive articles on top of the monthly subscription).

355. The sourcing rule for Digital Content Services is the place where the customer is ordinarily resident. This is because the person has a direct customer relationship with the service provider as it pays the subscription fee or other purchase to access the content, and so it is the connection to the customer's daily life that represents the value in the market. Although the customer can enjoy the content in multiple locations (e.g. watching or listening while abroad) and one account can be used by multiple users and/or on multiple devices, in most instances the place of residence of the customer and the place of enjoyment will be the same in any case. Further sourcing to every location that every user accessed the service would also entail additional compliance burdens.

356. The indicators look first to the user profile and billing address as likely indicators of the usual residence, as these features have some degree of permanence of the connection of the purchaser to the jurisdiction. If this information is not available, or is otherwise unreliable, the geolocation of the device or IP address is used, which will identify the location of the user at the point of sale. This may often, but not always, correlate to the usual residence, depending for example on how much the purchaser uses the service while travelling abroad.

Revenue from online gaming services

357. Online Gaming Services allow users to interact with one another in the game being played. Broadly, there are three revenue streams relevant to online gaming.

358. One is where the access to the game is free, but there will be advertising within the game. The sourcing rules for revenue from Online Advertising Services applies this model.

359. The second is collection of data about the users of the online game, which the provider can sell to advertisers. For this type of revenue, the sourcing rule is the same as for revenue from Sale or Other Alienation of User Data.

360. The third model is similar to Digital Content Services, where a player will register for a subscription and pay a fee to access the game. In addition, once the player is playing the game, there may be options to purchase additional features ("micro-transactions" such as access to new game levels, or game accessories). The sourcing rule for revenue from Digital Content Services applies to this model.

Revenue from standardised online teaching services

361. Online teaching services that fall within the definition of ADS make available standardised educational material to a large number of potential users. Broadly, there are three revenue streams relevant to online teaching services.

362. One is where the access to the teaching material is free, but there will be advertising within the material. The sourcing rule for revenue from Online Advertising Services Applies for this model.

363. The second is collection of data about the users of the service, which the provider can sell to advertisers or other third parties. For this type of revenue, the sourcing rule is the same as for revenue from Sale or Other Alienation of User Data.

364. The third model is similar to Digital Content Services, where a user will pay to access the service. The sourcing rule for revenue from Digital Content Services applies to this model.

Revenue from cloud computing services

365. Cloud computing is unlike other ADS above, because it is of most relevance to other businesses, although these services can be directed to individual consumers (e.g. for storing personal files). Examples of Cloud Computing Services include providing document management and storage services for a large professional services firm, providing computing power to other businesses, hosting the website through which another ADS provider delivers its services to users, and providing the software for data from highly technical operating machinery such as aeroplanes to be fed into a central base for analysis and monitoring. Cloud computing service providers can also derive revenues from advertising; in this case, the sourcing rule for revenue from online advertising services applies.

366. When the service is sold directly to individual users (such as personal data storage), the sourcing rule is the location of the purchaser. The cloud computing service provider has a more direct relationship with the user, and should be able to identify the ordinary residence of the purchaser, using user profile information or the billing address. If this information is unavailable or unreliable, the service provider may

use geolocation or IP address of the device on which the cloud computing service is being used, to identify the real-time location of the user at the time of purchase of the service.

367. In respect of Cloud Computing Services designed for internal use by a business customer and its employees only, there are difficulties in identifying the end-users of the service with precision. For example, the client businesses may procure their cloud computing service through one entity, and the service can then be configured for use by any number of employees throughout the world in conjunction with the business' internal IT system, and the access to the service may be through a central VPN. The sourcing rule is the location where the business customer uses the service. The hierarchy of indicators looks first to information reported by the customer, as this is likely to be the most reliable, and the most efficient, way of obtaining this information.

368. Alternatively, the cloud computing service provider is required to identify the jurisdiction where the business has operations, using information available from its business agreement with the customer and any records collected for tax purposes to determine the jurisdiction(s). Where the customer has operations in more than one jurisdiction, the MNE must make a fair and reasonable apportionment between those jurisdictions, for example, based on information on relative size of the operations. If this is not practical to do, an equal apportionment between each jurisdiction can be used.

369. If this information is not reasonably available, then the service provider can use other location information that can be used to locate the end-users of the cloud service, namely the business' employees that use the service.

4.3.3. Guidance on consumer-facing business

370. This section of the Commentary provides a summary of the sourcing rules for CFB and sets out how the indicators apply.

Revenue from consumer-facing goods sold directly to consumers

371. Consumer-facing goods are usually finished goods, but can also include component parts, if sold directly by the MNE to the end-customer (e.g. replacement parts). In many cases, tangible goods are made available to a customer directly through a retail store or by shipping directly to the customer. Consumer-facing goods can be made available directly at a storefront or can be purchased online and delivered to the customer's delivery address. The sourcing rule is the place of final delivery to the customer.

372. The indicators apply to two different circumstances. The first one is where the MNE sells through its own retail store, in which case the final delivery is the location of the storefront (being the location of the customer's interaction with the MNE). The second one is where it delivers directly to the customer (e.g. through an online shop), in which case the final delivery is the location of the customer's shipping address. Given the direct relationship of the seller with the customer, the sourcing can be identified with relative ease and no hierarchy of indicators is needed. This approach applies notwithstanding that different entities in the MNE may be involved. As it is between the same MNE, the sourcing rules expect that the MNE will have information on the final delivery even if performed by another group member.

373. Where a consumer purchases a good from a physical retail store, and asks the seller to ship it to a delivery address in a different jurisdiction, the revenue sourcing rule to be applied is the jurisdiction of the retail store.

Revenue from consumer-facing goods sold through independent distributor

374. There are circumstances where the MNE sells and delivers tangible goods using an unrelated intermediary, such as through a distribution arrangement. This can arise in respect of ordinary consumer

goods that are in scope but are sold through a distribution arrangement or by another business (e.g. shoes sold by a distributor or shoes sold to a large retail chain that sells to customers).

375. Where a third party distributor is used, it may resell the goods to consumers (directly or indirectly) located within the same jurisdiction. This may be the case for commercial reasons, such as where the MNE has selected a distributor that is close to the final destination to reduce shipping costs (particularly for perishable goods), or where a distributor is given the right to a sell the goods only within a specific country.

376. However, in some cases a regional third party distributor may be established in one central location and be responsible (direct or indirectly) for distribution within a certain geographic region (e.g. for Europe, for the Asia Pacific region). Distribution arrangements are also in place where one MNE enters an agreement for another to sell its products, for example, beverages being sold by another MNE restaurant chain.

377. As for the previous category revenue from consumer-facing goods sold directly to consumers, the sourcing rule is the place of final delivery of the good to the consumer. In principle, accuracy of identifying the market jurisdiction should be sought, to align the results where the MNE is itself fully responsible for the complete value chain of the good, or in the case that the distribution of the goods is contracted with third party (independent) distributors.

378. The hierarchy of the indicators looks first to the information reported by the distributor as the most reliable and accurate indicator. In some cases, the MNE would already have this information available, for example because of regulatory requirements or for safety reasons, or for commercial interest in knowing the performance of its product in each market. In other cases, the MNE is expected to take reasonable steps to seek a change in the contractual arrangement with the distributor, which would require the distributor to report the information on the aggregate number and type of products sold to each jurisdiction (no sensitive commercial information such as pricing information or specific customer addresses would be required). It is noted that such arrangements may take time to negotiate, and may come at a cost as a broader renegotiation of the contract.[11]

379. Only if the MNE can demonstrate that it has taken reasonable steps to change the contract to obtain the information directly from the independent distributor, but has been unsuccessful in doing so, the MNE would use information that is already available, such as market research for the purpose of management reporting.[12] The same approach would apply where a contract has been amended, but there is a period of time before it becomes operational.

Revenue from consumer-facing services

380. The relevant sourcing rule for consumer-facing services is the place of enjoyment or use of the service. This is because these types of services are generally consumed at the same time as and at the same place where they are physically performed, and the place that the consumer has sought the performance to take place represents the most accurate market jurisdiction. For example, in the case of tourism, it is the benefits offered by the jurisdiction being visited, rather than the residence of the tourist, that justifies a return to the market jurisdiction.

381. The indicator for the place that the service is enjoyed or used is the address where the service is performed. In most cases this will be straightforward, such as the location of the hotel, the location of the tourist site, or the performance of the entertainment, as this will be a key term identified in the service agreement. As such, the sourcing can be identified with relative ease and no other indicators are needed.

382. In respect of consumer-facing services delivered online, the place of enjoyment is the ordinary residence of the consumer. The indicators are the same as for digital content services.

Revenue from franchising and licensing

383. Licensing and franchising arrangements cover situations where the provider of a consumer-facing good or intangible makes their product available through an unrelated third party that has the relationship with the customer. For example, a business licenses the global distribution rights for a portfolio of films to a third party distributor, which subsequently sub-licenses these films to its customers around the world. A similar example is a film or television content owner that licenses its content to a digital content service. Another example is franchising the rights to open a fast food restaurant to a regional franchisee, who in turn agrees the specific local restaurant sites. A fourth example is where an MNE enters an arrangement for its logo to be attached to clothing and sold by a large MNE retailer.

384. The underlying supply will typically be used or consumed in the jurisdiction where the customers of the licensee / franchisee are located, which may be separate from where the licensor / franchisor is located. The licence / franchise payments will be made to the licensor / franchisor and represents a return from the market jurisdiction.

385. The sourcing principle for franchising a business selling consumer-facing goods or licensing an intangible that is attached to consumer-facing goods is similar to the ordinary sourcing rule for consumer-facing goods, which is the place of delivery of the good. The sourcing rule for franchising a business selling consumer-facing services or licensing an intangible that is enjoyed as a service is similar to the ordinary sourcing rule of consumer-facing services, which is place of performance of the service. In principle, accuracy of identifying the market jurisdiction should be sought, to align the results where the MNE is in itself fully responsible for the complete value chain of the good or service, or in the case that the distribution of the goods is contracted with third party unrelated licensees / franchisees.

386. The most accurate indicator is therefore the information reported by the franchisee or licensee, for example as part of the franchising / licensing contract. Under existing contracts, many franchisors / licensors will have information about the location of final customers of their franchisees, such as where agreements contain territorial clauses that only permit the franchisee to sell in a designated area. In other cases, the MNE is expected to take reasonable steps to seek to change the contractual arrangement with the licensee / franchisee, and require them to report the information on the aggregate number and type of products sold / services delivered to each jurisdiction (no sensitive commercial information such as pricing information or specific customer addresses would be required). It is expected that most franchisors / licensors have the right to request this information.[13]

387. It is recognised that there could be an unrelated party involved in the value chain, and therefore a hierarchy applies to the indicators to provide sufficient flexibility. Only if the MNE can demonstrate that it has taken reasonable steps to change the contract to obtain the information directly from the franchisee / licensee, but has been unsuccessful in doing so, the franchisor / licensor would need to provide an approximation based on available information. This could include information collected for internal management reporting, market research, or quality control purposes to comply with local legal requirements (such as censorship or food safety standards). This information could also include information on the location where the franchisee / licensee is performing its operations, under the franchising / licensing agreement. It is expected that the franchisor / licensor have this information already available, or have the right to request this information. The same approach would apply where a contract has been amended, but there is a period of time before it becomes operational.

4.3.4. Documentation

Type of information

388. The MNE must retain documentation evidencing:

- The functioning of its internal control framework related to revenue sourcing;

- Aggregate and periodic information on results of applying the indicators, for each type of revenue and in each jurisdiction;
- The specific indicator used for a given category of revenue; and
- The circumstances when an indicator lower in the hierarchy was used, including why the indicator higher in the hierarchy was not available (and the steps taken to obtain it) or not reliable (and the information available to confirm the presence of a more reliable indicator).

389. This information is all systemic level data. For several reasons, including global privacy rules and administration limitations (considering the significant volume of this information), the MNE should not be expected to keep a record of all data points on the above indicators for every transaction or use of the service. In most cases, data will not be able to be stored long enough for the tax administrations to perform a detailed tax audit.

390. Therefore, it is proposed that the MNE need not keep a record of all individual user's geolocation information, IP addresses, and other information, provided that it has a robust internal control framework on which the tax authorities can rely. As such, the MNE should document these internal controls, as well as keep a record of underlying indicators as set out below.

391. The system should be able to extract the aggregate information about the location – at a jurisdictional level – included in the several sources of information.

392. The hierarchy of rules takes into account that information on the preferred indicator may be unavailable or unreliable. There are several reasons for this, as explained in the guidance above. In addition, the indicators can also be different per type of revenue stream, or even in segments of the same revenue stream, for example where different online advertising businesses will have different approaches to tracking users and maintaining their profiles. It also takes into account that business models may change.

393. If the MNE uses a different indicator than the preferred indicator, it should provide the tax administrations with additional information explaining and supporting why it used another indicator. If the reason for using another indicator lower in the hierarchy is that an indicator was unavailable, the documentation should include an explanation of steps taken to obtain the information and why it was unsuccessful. If the reason for using another indicator lower in the hierarchy is that a primary indicator was unreliable, the other indicators that were available and corroborate the application of the secondary indicator as being reliable should be documented.

Review by tax administrations

394. A separate review of an MNE's revenue sourcing by potentially in excess of 100 jurisdictions where it has operations is impractical and could result in disputes if different conclusions are reached by different tax administrations. As such, Chapter 9 describes a multilateral tax certainty process for Amount A, based on a substantive review of an MNE's self-assessment of Amount A by a review panel of representative tax administrations, which could include a review of relevant aspects of the group's tax control framework. While voluntary on the part of MNEs, it is expected that in the first year(s) of applying Amount A, many of the MNEs within scope of Amount A will seek to make use of this process. Where an MNE does not make a request for multilateral certainty and seeks to rely on domestic remedies, the references below to how a panel may gain comfort would apply equally to the separate reviews conducted unilaterally by tax administrations.

395. The review panel would have different options to perform a compliance review procedure. With respect to giving certainty with respect to the application of revenue sourcing rules, and in light of the above documentation requirements and limitations, it is likely that tax administrations on the review panel would generally look to the quality control systems in place to apply the revenue sourcing rules in an accurate way, rather than generally carrying out an audit of every particular transaction.

396. As a starting point, the overall compliance approach taken by the MNE could be part of the process, whereby the review panel would provide the MNE with certainty on the operation of its internal control framework for which it can then rely on the data being extracted by the system. Whenever substantial changes are made to the MNE's control framework, a review by the panel may take place again.

397. Additionally, or as part of this process, the review panel could perform an (IT) audit on the MNE's internal control framework. This may need to be done on behalf of the review panel by the tax administration in the jurisdiction of the UPE, or jurisdiction of other member(s) of the MNE which has the relevant data in its possession and has responsibility for the compliance process and whose systems would be audited, and outcomes of this audit would be subject to review and agreement by the panel.

398. In their review, the review panel could additionally make use of sampling, whereby the auditor would only test a sample of the detailed data that was collected most recently and has therefore been stored for a limited period, in order to evaluate whether the MNE collected this data in an accurate way.

399. The domestic law issues, costs and benefits, efficiency and other relevant aspects of these approaches will be considered further.

Retention of documentation

400. The MNE is not obliged to keep the underlying data stored. It should however keep the extracted reports in its administration for the period consistent with the requirements of domestic law of the respective jurisdictions. It must be available to the tax administrations upon request. There must be a sufficient sample of the underlying data available to tax administrations in order to be able to justify that the internal control framework is operating in a robust manner.

4.4. Next steps

401. The proposals above will be subject to further discussion and refinement, within the broader context of the pending discussions on scope, including further review of the proposed order of the indicators within each hierarchy, taking into account input on the compliance challenges for the affected businesses, and whether more specific indicators are required in respect of business customers. Specific open issues include sourcing the commission / fees from online intermediation platforms in respect of tangible services and the revenue sourcing rules for cloud computing.

402. In addition, further work will be undertaken to finalise guidance on the extent of the "reasonable steps" that are required to obtain information before it can be considered "unavailable." This will need to provide objective guidelines in order to prevent disputes and could involve safe harbours. This could include, for example, asking the holder of the information (such as the customer or distributor), but would not be expected to include a requirement to incur more than insignificant costs (such as a not insignificant increase in price as part of a renegotiation of a contract). In particular, some jurisdictions remain concerned about the accuracy of information when an independent distributor is used, such as where multiple independent distributors are used and the distributor with a contract with the MNE may not have data on the ultimate delivery of the goods. Consideration is being given to the extent of steps that should be expected of an MNE to amend the contract with such intermediary to obtain information on the final destination of goods, and whether this creates undue burdens or any commercial competitive issues for either the MNE whose goods are being sold or the distributor.

403. Likewise, further work will be undertaken to finalise guidance on when an MNE can justify that an indicator is "unreliable." As for the guidance mentioned above, this will likewise need to provide objective guidelines in order to prevent disputes. This could include, for example, more specific guidance in connection with the use of VPNs (such as where this can be detected and is above a certain threshold),

situations where a delivery address should be considered unreliable (such as the address of a freight forwarder and possibly situations where a post office box is used) and whether safe harbours could be used (such as where an MNE has in its possession two or more additional data points that confirm the jurisdiction of the first indicator). The use of safe harbours could be a particularly important way of reducing the potential for disputes, such as relating to whether information was available or unreliable.

404. In addition, more detailed guidance will be developed on the documentation requirements and the definition of "robust internal control framework", including taking into account the need to ensure privacy of users. In addition, consideration will be given to the action that a tax administration should take in the event of an MNE lacking the requisite internal control framework and documentation.

405. Finally, as the work on the in-scope activity progresses, the revenue sourcing rules will be further developed accordingly. For example, how to determine the categorisation of a service is a "dual category / bundled package" of multiple services or as a service and a good and the implications for revenue sourcing, and to provide revenue sourcing rules for any new categories of ADS added to the positive list.

Notes

[1] See Commentary in section 4.3, and the discussion on user profile and billing address, for explanation of the difference between billing address as a standalone indicator and billing address as part of user profile information.

[2] Consideration is being given to address a proposal raised by some delegates of the Inclusive Framework to source the revenue for such intermediation wholly to the jurisdiction of performance of the service.

[3] The applicability of this indicator for cases where the purchaser is a business requires further consideration.

[4] Consideration is also being given to whether a more specific rule could be created where cloud computing service is provided to host the platform of another ADS provider. Where such provider will be required to collect information on revenue sourcing to comply with their own obligations under Amount A, more precise information will already be available for this purpose. Such a rule would source the revenue to the location of the end users of the ADS platform, given that although they are not the internal personnel directly using the cloud computing service, they do enjoy a direct benefit from the cloud service, such as faster and higher quality access to the service provided by the platform.

[5] See section 4.4 on "next steps."

[6] See section 4.4 on "next steps."

[7] See section 4.4 on "next steps" for further consideration of when the prevalence of VPNs would make an indicator unreliable.

[8] It is possible to use GPS spoofing software, which sets up a fake GPS location for the user. Much like with the VPN, users would appear to be in the location of their choosing, when using this software. However, unlike with the VPN, which can be used to access content in other jurisdictions, GPS spoofing is used solely as a privacy tool and its use does not seem to be as widespread as the use of a VPN.

[9] Further consideration will be given to how the revenue sourcing rules apply for cases of generic advertising where the online advertising MNE may not be charging on a view or click basis but on a fixed fee basis, and whether such MNE may not have the relevant data on the viewers.

[10] Further consideration will be given to the types of fees that may be charged for online intermediation services, such as those that are not tied to transactions, and whether these should fall under the 50/50 revenue rule or be sourced, e.g. as per the rule that applies for digital content services.

[11] See section 4.4 on "next steps" for further work.

[12] Given the proposed approach to nexus for CFB, sales that are below an agreed nexus amount could then also be excluded from the need to determine source. This would be the case where an MNE had information on the jurisdictions of final delivery covering all but a small amount of sales revenue, and that remaining amount was below the nexus threshold. For such cases, this would in practice to leave very few situations where sourcing of consumer-facing goods would be based on an approximation.

[13] See section 4.4 on "next steps".

5 Tax base determinations

5.1. Overview

406. Amount A is a new taxing right over a share of the residual profit of MNE groups that fall within its defined scope. The tax base is therefore determined on the basis of the profits of a group (rather than on a separate entity basis), and it is necessary to start with consolidated group financial accounts. This approach raises three broad categories of issues for the determination of the Amount A tax base. First, there is the need to define a standardised measure of profit as a basis for Amount A, including the extent to which harmonisation adjustments are required to address divergences in existing financial accounting standards. Second, there is the need to address the rationale for, and technical feasibility of, computing Amount A using segmented accounts, on either a business line or geographic basis. Third, the design of loss carry-forward rules is required to ensure that losses are taken into account in the computation of Amount A. This chapter sets out a comprehensive set of rules and guidance for the Amount A tax base determination, taking into account the technical work undertaken thus far on these three broad aspects. These rules and guidance have been designed to minimise, where possible, the additional compliance costs for taxpayers and administrative burdens for tax administrations.

A PBT measure based on consolidated financial accounts

407. The Amount A tax base will be quantified using an adjusted PBT measure that will be derived from the consolidated financial accounts of in-scope MNE groups. In practice, consolidated financial accounts prepared under GAAP that produce equivalent or comparable outcomes to consolidated financial accounts prepared under International Financial Reporting Standards (IFRS) – the "eligible GAAP" – will mainly be used.[1] Where necessary, other GAAP will also be allowed provided their use is permitted by the body with legal authority in the tax jurisdiction of its UPE to prescribe, establish, or accept accounting standards and that its use does not result in material competitive distortions in the application of Amount A. This approach (including the assessment of GAAP equivalence) is aligned with Pillar Two, which has adopted a similar approach.

408. Consistent with Pillar Two, no specific book-to-book harmonisation adjustments (to account for variances between different GAAP) are considered necessary at this stage given the significant additional complexity their introduction would entail; however, the Amount A tax base may incorporate an on-going monitoring process to ensure discrepancies across accounting standards do not produce materially inconsistent outcomes among Amount A taxpayers.

409. For ease of administration, only a limited number of book-to-tax adjustments will apply to determine the relevant measure of PBT, and seek alignment of the tax base for Amount A with the corporate tax base of Inclusive Framework members. These adjustments will include: exclusion of income tax expenses, exclusion of dividend income and gains or losses in connection with shares, and expenses not deductible for Corporate Income Tax (CIT) purposes in most Inclusive Framework jurisdictions for public policy reasons. These adjustments are consistent with the approach under Pillar Two, except potentially for income derived from joint ventures and interest expenses from transactions with related parties that do not belong to the consolidated group under the relevant accounting standard (e.g. investment entities).

410. Further work will be undertaken on the implementation of the proposed framework to use consolidated group financial accounts (e.g. introducing a monitoring mechanism), and to finalise some aspects of the standardised PBT measure (e.g. income from joint ventures).

The segmentation framework

411. The *Outline* recognised that for some groups it may be necessary to compute the Amount A tax base on a segmented basis, but also recognised that using segmentation to determine the relevant PBT measure will create additional compliance costs for taxpayers and extra burdens for tax administrations who will need to review these segmented accounts as part of any compliance activity and within the context of the tax certainty process. The segmentation framework for Amount A aims to provide a balance of the benefits of the additional accuracy and the additional complexity and costs that segmentation would bring.

412. The framework starts from an acknowledgement that though it is feasible for taxpayers to break down their revenue between ADS, CFB and out-of-scope, it may not be possible for them to compute separately the net profits attributable to these activities (i.e. segmentation of the tax base). Nevertheless, as Pillar One applies the principle of net, rather than gross, basis taxation it will still be necessary to only reallocate profits attributable to in-scope activities. The easiest way to achieve this would be to calculate the Amount A tax base on a consolidated basis and use the consolidated profit margin of the group as a proxy for the in-scope profit margin, applying it to in-scope revenues to produce a proxy for in-scope profits. From this proxy, Amount A would be calculated and then allocated among market jurisdictions using the allocation formula.[2] Therefore, the segmentation framework will adopt this simplification as the default rule, while providing that in some circumstances, primarily to maintain a level playing field between taxpayers, the Amount A tax base will be computed on a segmented basis.

413. The framework will be based on the following three-step process:

- First, all MNE groups in scope of Amount A would need to break down their revenue between ADS, CFB and out-of-scope activities, as may be required for the scope and nexus rules.
- Second, to limit the number of MNE groups that are required to segment their Amount A tax base, MNE groups with global revenue less than EUR [X] billion would benefit from a "segmentation exemption" which would require them to compute the Amount A tax base on a group basis.[3] For ease of administration and transition, this threshold would initially be set at EUR [X] billion and reduced over a five-year transition period.[4] Alternatively, this exemption could be designed as a safe harbour, whereby MNE groups below the threshold would have the option to compute the Amount A tax base either on a group or on a segmented basis, subject to the constraints outlined in the third step below.
- Third, those groups not eligible for the exemption or, if designed as a safe harbour did not elect for it, would then test whether they are required to segment their Amount A tax base and on what basis. Consideration is being given to an approach based on the following three sub-steps:
  - MNE groups will apply the "segmentation hallmarks" to determine whether they are required to segment their tax base. If they are not required to segment, they will compute their Amount A tax base on a group basis.
  - For MNE groups that do display these segmentation hallmarks, the disclosed segments in the MNE group financial statements will be tested to ascertain whether they meet the agreed hallmarks. If so, Amount A tax base will be computed on the basis of these segments. There will be an exemption for groups whose disclosed segments have similar profit margins, which will also compute the Amount A tax base on a group basis.
  - Finally, MNE groups that are not eligible to use their disclosed segments will be required to compute the Amount A tax base on the basis of alternative segments. This is expected to be relevant for only a small number of MNE groups. This alternative approach would be

determined based on the definition of a segment for the purposes of Amount A. It would be expected that this alternative approach would in most instances merely require a group to further breakdown the profit or loss account of an existing segment or segments and that the group may have an existing internal reporting framework on which to base this alternative segmentation.

414. Further work will be undertaken to finalise specific aspects of the different steps of this segmentation framework, including the appropriateness of the level of the global revenue thresholds (step 2), the definition of a segment based on the hallmarks (step 3) and the administration of the framework through the early certainty and dispute resolution process, and to explore potential simplifications to ease the administration of the approach.

Loss carry-forward rules

415. Loss-carry forward rules will apply through an earn-out mechanism at the level of the group or segment (as determined by the segmentation framework). This means that losses generated over a given tax period under Amount A, unlike profits, will not be allocated to market jurisdictions. Instead, they will be pooled in a single account for the relevant segment and carried forward to subsequent years, with the result that no profit under Amount A would arise for that segment (and be reallocated to markets) until historic losses reported in that account have been fully absorbed. This carry-forward regime will be kept separate from any existing domestic loss carry-forward rules, and include specific rules to deal with business reorganisations (including changes of the segmentation basis).

416. Some specific design aspects of the loss-carry forward rules will need to be refined. This will include considering a transitional regime for losses incurred prior to the introduction of Amount A (pre-regime losses), and determining whether the loss-carry forward regime should include time limitations and anti-avoidance rules. There is also a separate issue on whether this regime should apply exclusively to economic losses or be extended to cover profit shortfalls (where the profit of a group or segment falls below the profitability threshold), which will be resolved as part of the discussion of the quantum of Amount A (see section 6.2).

5.2. A PBT measure based on consolidated financial accounts

5.2.1. Eligible consolidated financial accounts

417. Given that Amount A is a new taxing right that is determined based on the profits of a group (rather than on a separate entity basis), it is necessary to use consolidated group financial accounts as the starting point for computing the Amount A tax base. This approach also has the advantage that the Amount A tax base is less affected by controlled transactions[5] and, for large MNE groups, that it is based on financial statements that have been subject to external audit,[6] thus providing a reliable source of information that is normally readily available to tax administrations.

418. In general, Amount A would not mandate MNE groups to produce consolidated accounts under a specific accounting standard. The relevant financial accounting standard for computing Amount A tax base would be the financial accounting standard used by the UPE in the preparation of its consolidated financial statements.

419. At the same time, because MNE groups prepare consolidated financial accounts under different accounting standards, this approach requires the resolution of several issues to ensure that the Amount A tax base determination produces comparable results when differing standards are used. These issues include identifying acceptable accounting standards across Inclusive Framework jurisdictions that produce

sufficiently comparable and reliable results for computing Amount A, and clarifying whether specific harmonisation adjustments are required to deal with particular items of income or expenses.

Eligible GAAP

420. Although there are variations between different consolidated accounting standards, the GAAP of many Inclusive Framework members have far more commonalities than differences. To limit compliance costs, MNE groups will therefore be permitted to rely on the consolidated financial accounts produced by their UPE under any GAAP provided this standard produces equivalent or comparable outcomes to consolidated financial accounts prepared under IFRS.[7] Equivalency with IFRS is to be assessed based on the work of the International Accounting Standards Board (IASB) as well as the work of securities regulators that allow other accounting standards in financial reports of publicly accountable companies, consistent with the assessment of GAAP equivalence under the Pillar Two. An initial assessment has shown the GAAP of Australia, Canada, Hong Kong (China), Japan, New Zealand, the People's Republic of China, the Republic of India, the Republic of Korea, Singapore and the United States are eligible GAAP. As illustrated in Figure 5.1 below, these eligible GAAP already cover roughly 90% of MNE groups with consolidated revenue above EUR 750 million and profitability above 10% in 2016.

Figure 5.1. Accounting standards used by MNE groups with consolidated turnover above EUR 750 million and profitability above 10%

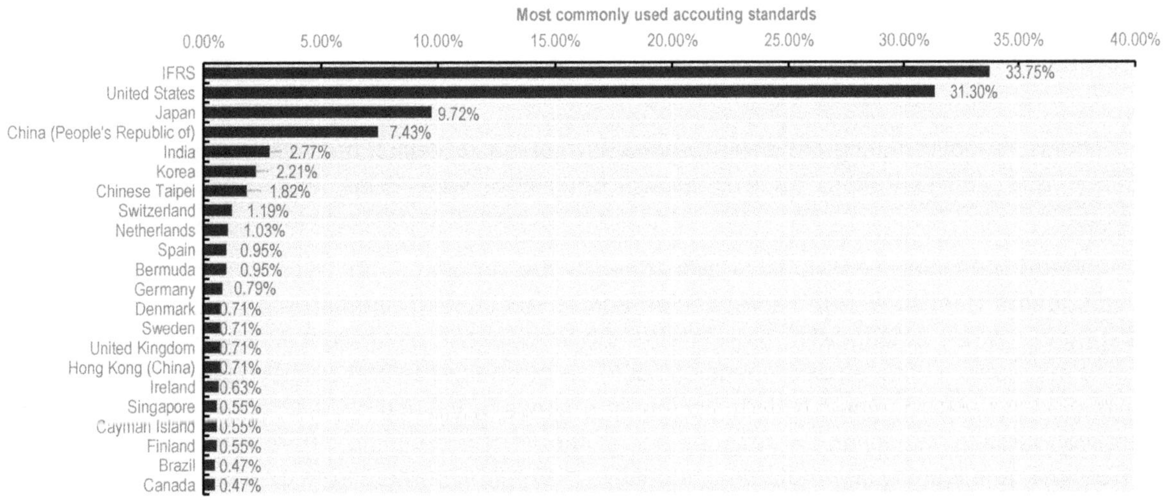

Source: Orbis - Bureau van Dijk and OECD Secretariat.

421. There will be some MNE groups in scope of Amount A whose consolidated financial reports are not prepared under eligible GAAP. Such MNE groups will however be allowed to use other GAAP as a basis for determining the Amount A tax base for ease of administration. These are GAAP permitted by the relevant body with legal authority in the tax jurisdiction of its UPE to prescribe, establish, or accept accounting standards when their use does not result in material competitive distortions in the application of Amount A. This approach needs to be consistent with the determination of acceptable accounting standards under Pillar Two.[8] Further technical work is required to define and measure material competitive distortions.

422. Where an MNE group in scope of Amount A does not produce consolidated financial statements, it would need to prepare consolidated financial accounts and to compute the Amount A tax base under the accounting standards permitted by the body with legal authority in the tax jurisdiction of its UPE to

prescribe, establish, or accept accounting standards for financial reporting purposes, provided that those standards qualify as eligible or, otherwise, do not result in material competitive distortions in the application of Amount A.

Book-to-book harmonisation adjustments

423. The Amount A tax base will not involve any specific harmonisation adjustments to account for differences between different GAAP that could affect the computation of the Amount A tax base.

424. It is recognised that designing and administering harmonisation adjustments would be extremely complex, as the significance of discrepancies across standards varies widely across industries, and even from one MNE group to the next.[9] Examples of such, adjustments could be:

- **Reversal of impairments**: IFRS requires impairment adjustments to be reversed when the reasons for the impairment no longer pertain, except for impairments of goodwill. On the contrary, other GAAP may not allow for the reversal of certain impairments (e.g. inventory, long-lived assets). This could give rise to timing differences, which could be nearly permanent ones depending on the expected time that the underlying items remain in the balance sheet. This issue might be more relevant for industries with particularly long business cycles.
- **Financial assets classification**: Accounting standards may resort to different criteria for classifying financial assets that can lead to permanent differences in profit measurement because classification affects recognition of income. For instance, under certain GAAP, the legal form of a debt instrument primarily determines classification. On the contrary, under IFRS the legal form does not determine classification of debt instruments. Rather, the nature of the cash flows of the instrument and the MNE group's business model for managing the debt instruments are the key considerations for classification.

425. Therefore, not requiring any book-to-book harmonisation adjustment will thus significantly facilitate compliance and administration, as well as be consistent with Pillar Two, and the existing CbCR requirement.

426. Instead of making book-to-book adjustments, the Amount A tax base may however incorporate some safeguards to ensure that discrepancies across accounting standards do not produce materially inconsistent outcomes among MNE groups after the introduction of Amount A. For example, an ongoing monitoring mechanism of these discrepancies could be introduced as part of the implementation of Amount A. This ongoing monitoring could include performing comparisons across MNE groups in scope subject to different standards to identify and assess the actual impact of accounting differences on the Amount A tax base over time, and identify any material competitive distortions derived from existing or future differences across accounting standards that would require specific adjustments. Further technical work will be undertaken to design and explore appropriate mechanisms.

5.2.2. The standardised PBT definition

427. Consistent with the decision to use a standardised PBT figure, the computation of the Amount A tax base will start from the total profit or loss figure from the "profit or loss" (P&L) statement of the MNE group's consolidated accounts. A number of adjustments will then be applied, including the elimination of income tax expenses, to address potential issues that might otherwise arise given the different objectives of Amount A and accounting rules (i.e. book-to-tax adjustments). These adjustments will be consistent with the approach adopted under Pillar Two, except potentially for income derived from joint ventures and interest expenses from transactions with related parties that do not belong to the consolidated group under the relevant accounting standard (e.g. investment entities).

PBT as the selected measure of profit

428. A PBT measure will be used as the basis for determining Amount A as it approximates the measure of profit on which CIT is normally levied. Profit before tax is a comprehensive figure that generally comprises all income and expenses of an MNE group except the income tax expenses. It takes into account all the real costs of doing business, both operating and non-operating expenses (such as finance costs), and is unaffected by the classification of specific items in different sections of the "profit or loss" statement. This makes it the most appropriate metric for use in the calculation of Amount A. Further, its resemblance to the existing CIT base has the advantage of minimising the risk of determining profit for Amount A purposes that is substantially different from the aggregated taxable profit reported by the members of the group under existing rules.

429. PBT is not defined in most GAAP, which typically provide guidance on how various income and expense items should be recognised for accounting purposes. This means that MNE groups have some discretion over which items to include in PBT, and the development for Amount A purposes of a standardised definition (with adjustments) will be necessary to ensure a consistent computation of the tax base across all in-scope groups, which is discussed in the next section.

The determination of a standardised PBT measure

430. As a starting point, all items within the consolidated P&L statement[10] will be taken into consideration.[11] This means the computation of the Amount A tax base will start from the bottom line figure of the P&L statement (i.e. the total for profit or loss). From this point, certain book-to-tax adjustments will be made (such as the deduction of certain items of income and the adding back of certain expenses) to arrive at a standardised PBT figure. For ease of administration and compliance, these adjustments will be kept to a minimum in order to limit complexity, and align with adjustments under Pillar Two.

431. The purpose of these adjustments is to align to the extent possible the Amount A tax base with the corporate tax base of Inclusive Framework jurisdictions. This will be achieved by excluding certain material items that are commonly excluded from the corporate tax base of Inclusive Framework jurisdictions. The exclusion of these items typically reflects the different objectives pursued by tax and accounting rules. .

Income tax expenses

432. Income taxes are the most obvious expense that needs to be added back to determine the standardised PBT under Amount A. Income tax expenses are usually not deductible for CIT purposes in Inclusive Framework jurisdictions.

433. Financial accounting distinguishes between income taxes and other taxes. Income taxes, as defined for financial accounting purposes,[12] are typically reported separately in the P&L statement. Taxes that are not considered income taxes are treated like operating expenses and may not be separately identified in the income statement. Only taxes covered by the definition of income taxes for accounting purposes would be extracted from the "profit or loss" statement, and added back in to compute the Amount A tax base.[13]

Dividend income and gains or losses arising in connection with shares, including income under the equity method

434. In many Inclusive Framework jurisdictions, dividend income and gains or losses from the disposal of shares are excluded, in whole or in part, from the CIT base or benefit from tax relief (such as indirect credit for taxes paid). In some jurisdictions, the exclusion is conditioned on certain ownership and holding period requirements. In other jurisdictions, the exclusion applies without restrictions. These exclusions are

often referred to as participation exemptions, and generally seek to eliminate the double taxation that otherwise would occur if the profit of the investee (i.e. the distributing entity or the entity whose shares are transferred) were to be taxed again at the level of the investor upon the distribution or disposal.

435. Recognising the broad nature of the participation exemptions of many Inclusive Framework jurisdictions, dividend income and gains or losses in connection with shares will be excluded from the Amount A tax base, consistent with the approach adopted under Pillar Two.[14] This exclusion will also apply where, in the absence of any disposal, the P&L statement accounts for gains (or losses) attributable to changes in the value of shares using the fair value method. Some aspects of this adjustment are still under discussion, however, such as the option of introducing some conditions or restrictions to this exclusion (e.g. specific percentage of ownership, holding period). As part of this, the treatment of expenses incurred in connection with dividend income or the generation of gains or losses from shares is also under discussion. This issue will require balancing the challenges associated with tracing these expenses in the financial accounts and the risk of erosion of Amount A tax base (e.g. financial expenses related to funding acquisitions of shareholdings).

436. As a corollary, any profit or loss derived from using the equity method of accounting will also be excluded, consistent with the approach adopted under Pillar Two.[15] Generally, the equity method applies to investments in entities or arrangements in which the investor owns a substantial interest (generally between 20% and 50%) that are not consolidated under financial accounting standards. These ownership interests are effectively treated as transparent, recognising the investor's proportionate share of the entity or arrangement's after-tax income or loss.[16] The Inclusive Framework is, however, discussing whether this adjustment should not apply to income derived from joint ventures, in particular where that income does not represent retained earnings that have already been (or will be) subject to Amount A at the level of the entity or arrangement (e.g. because the revenue of the joint venture falls below the scope revenue thresholds).

437. This issue can be illustrated through the following example. Assume MNE Group A and MNE Group B constitute a joint venture where each group owns an interest of 50%. The joint venture generates revenue below the Amount A revenue threshold and is therefore not in scope of Amount A. Assume further that the joint venture makes a profit of 100 during the first period and Group A and Group B account for 50 profit each under the equity method. There is an argument to support the view that Group A and Group B income under the equity method from the joint venture should not be excluded from the Amount A tax base given that it represents a profit that is not subject to Amount A at the level of the joint venture. However, further work is required on this point to support the rationale of this adjustment and to address potential manipulation.

Expenses that are typically non-deductible or limited for public policy reasons

438. A number of items treated as expenses under financial accounting rules are not deductible for CIT purposes in most Inclusive Framework jurisdictions for public policy reasons. Those expenses are typically associated with behaviours that governments regard as undesirable and will therefore be added back in computing the Amount A tax base. These adjustments would apply to bribes and other illegal payments, and fines and penalties that are due to a public authority for the breach of any legislation. Further work is required to explore whether the deduction of these expenses should be limited only where they exceed a certain amount to reduce the compliance burden.

5.2.3. Next steps

439. As a next step, further work will be undertaken on the implementation of the proposed framework to use consolidated group financial accounts, including:

- Definition of an MNE group for consolidation purposes: the Amount A tax base will follow consolidation rules to delineate the composition of an MNE group in scope of Amount A. As a consequence, entities that benefit from consolidation exemptions, such as investment entities, will not be required to produce consolidated accounts for Amount A purposes. Including interaction with the accounting consolidation test under CbC rules and potential changes in the consolidation group derived from a decision by local accounting regulatory bodies.
- Dual-headed MNE groups: this involves addressing any particular issues for the computation of the Amount A tax base raised by dual-headed structures which can be listed on different exchanges and required to satisfy the accounting and regulatory frameworks of different jurisdictions.
- Changes in accounting estimates and prior period errors: this relates to clarifying the impact on the Amount A tax base of retrospective corrections of material "prior period errors" in the consolidated financial accounts and designing a simple mechanism to adjust Amount A computations.
- Development of a monitoring mechanism to assess differences between GAAP that could lead to material competitive distortions.

440. Further work will also be undertaken to finalise the determination of the standardised PBT measure. Specific areas for consideration include:

- Whether profit or loss derived from joint ventures using the equity method of accounting should be retained in Amount A tax base.
- Whether interest expenses from transactions with related parties that do not belong to the consolidated group under the accounting standard (for example an investment entity that controls an MNE group and advances funds to the group) present a risk of base erosion material enough to consider introducing a specific measure under Amount A.
- Whether gains and losses from exceptional and non-recurring items should be excluded from the Amount A tax base, noting that these items are generally not excluded from the CIT base in Inclusive Framework jurisdictions, nor under Pillar Two or the CbCR requirement.
- Whether items classified in the "other comprehensive statement"[17] should be included in the Amount A tax base, noting that these items are generally not added back to the CIT base in Inclusive Framework jurisdictions, nor under Pillar Two or the CbCR requirement.
- Whether minority interests should be accounted for in computing the Amount A tax base.

441. Important considerations in this work will include simplicity of administration, the ease of compliance, and having a standardised and consistent approach across the two Pillars.

5.3. The segmentation framework

442. The primary reason why it may be necessary to compute the Amount A tax base on a segmented basis is because Amount A will apply only to the profits that groups derive from carrying on in-scope activities. For example, the scope requirements for ADS distinguish between standardised cloud computing services, which would be in scope, and bespoke cloud services, which would not. A group that provides both types of services therefore needs an approach to segmentation that enables it to apply Amount A only to the profits derived from in-scope activities.

443. For the scope and nexus rules, taxpayers will need to separate their revenue between that attributable to CFB, ADS and out-of-scope activities. It is reasonable to expect that a taxpayer could prepare, and tax administrations could review, a breakdown of revenue on this basis. However, it would be more complex for a taxpayer to segment these different types of activities to calculate a measure of PBT. This is because it would require groups to apportion costs between these different types of activities in a way that is unlikely to reflect their existing external or internal reporting, and the reliance on allocation

keys for such an apportionment brings into question whether the segmented PBT for each of these separate activities would accurately reflect the underlying economic reality of each business.[18]

444. Nevertheless, as Pillar One applies the principle of net, rather than gross, basis taxation it will still be necessary to compute the profits attributable to in-scope activities. The easiest way to achieve this would be to calculate the Amount A tax base on a consolidated basis, and use the consolidated profit margin of the group as a proxy for the in-scope profit margin, applying it to in-scope revenues to produce a proxy for in-scope profits. From this proxy, Amount A would be calculated and then allocated among market jurisdictions using the allocation formula. Therefore, as the default a group should be able to compute the Amount A tax base on a group basis.

445. However, there are some circumstances where this would not seem appropriate, or where doing so might fail to maintain a level playing field between taxpayers. For example, where a large group operates two substantially independent businesses, with different profit margins, computing the Amount A tax base on a segmented basis would ensure that a taxpayer cannot reduce or eliminate a potential Amount A tax liability by combining profits from high and low margin activities. In these circumstances, the segmentation framework could require a taxpayer to compute the relevant measure of PBT using segmented accounts.

446. The segmentation framework seeks to balance these competing pressures. In recognition of the need for an approach to Amount A that is as simple as possible, while retaining the integrity of the overall policy, a set of rules to determine whether segmentation is required, and where applicable how to arrive at a segmented PBT, is outlined below. Further work will be undertaken to develop this segmentation framework,[19] and once agreement has been reached detailed guidelines will be published for taxpayers and tax administrations.

5.3.1. Overview of the different steps of the segmentation framework

447. The segmentation framework seeks to provide a balance between the additional accuracy and the additional complexity brought by the segmentation of the tax base. It establishes the following three-step process to evaluate the basis for segmentation, including providing for exemptions to the requirement to segment for ease of administration and compliance:

- First, all MNE groups would break down their revenue between ADS, CFB and out-of-scope activities, as may required for the scope and nexus rules;
- Second, to limit the number of MNE groups that are required to segment, MNE groups will compute the Amount A tax base on a group basis when their revenue falls below an agreed threshold; and
- Third, any remaining groups will then test whether they should be required to segment and on what basis. Consideration is being given to an approach based on the following three sub-steps:
    - MNE groups will apply the "segmentation hallmarks" to determine whether they are required to segment – the Amount A tax base will be computed on a group basis if they are not required to segment.
    - For groups that do display these segmentation hallmarks, the disclosed segments in the consolidated financial accounts will be tested to ascertain whether they meet the agreed hallmarks. If so, the Amount A tax base will be computed on the basis of these segments, subject to an exemption where the disclosed segments have similar profit margins.
    - MNE groups that are not able to use their disclosed segments but are required to segment will be required to compute the Amount A tax base on the basis of alternative segments. This is expected to be relevant for only a small number of in-scope MNE groups, as a consequence of the application of the earlier steps.

448. The steps are outlined in detail below.

5.3.2. Step one: Separating revenue from CFB, ADS and out-of-scope activities

449. As a simplification, the exclusion of profits arising from out-of-scope activities will in most instances be delivered through the revenue-based allocation key of the Amount A formula (see section 6.2.3), rather than by requiring an MNE group to segment its accounts between in and out-of-scope activities to arrive at the relevant PBT measure. The Amount A formula is designed to ensure that only the portion of the Amount A tax base corresponding to in-scope revenue sourced in a given market jurisdiction is allocated to that market jurisdiction. This means that even in instances where the calculation of the Amount A tax base does not distinguish between in and out-of-scope activities, market jurisdictions will be allocated a proxy Amount A profits related to in-scope revenue sourced in their jurisdiction calculated by assuming that the profitability of in-scope activity is equal to the profitability of the group as a whole. Further work will be undertaken to address potentially material distortions where, for instance, an MNE group has highly profitable or highly loss-making out-of-scope activities which could affect the reliability of the approach. This will include consideration of whether, in some circumstances, taxpayers should be required to calculate net profit for in- and out-of-scope activities (or ADS, CFB and out-of-scope activities) separately.

450. To apply the Amount A formula, an MNE group would simply need to separate its revenue between that attributable to CFB, ADS and out-of-scope activities, noting that such break down would also be necessary to apply the Amount A rules on scope (see Chapter 2) and nexus (see Chapter 3).

5.3.3. Step two: Exemption or safe harbour from segmentation based on global revenue

451. The segmentation framework for Amount A includes an exemption or safe harbour to limit the number of groups that will be required to calculate Amount A on a segmented basis. This will reduce compliance costs and ease the burden for tax administrations who will need to review a business' segmentation as part of the tax certainty process.

452. The exemption would exempt smaller groups, with global revenue below an agreed amount, from applying Amount A on a segmented basis. This means that segmentation will be required only for large groups that are more likely to operate a number of largely independent businesses, with different profits margins and different geographic profiles. It is for these businesses, which earn the highest profits, that calculating Amount A on a segmented basis will have the greatest tax impact. Consequently, MNE groups with global revenue less than EUR [X] billion would compute the Amount A tax base on a group basis (i.e. a "segmentation exemption" would apply). For ease of administration and transition, this threshold could initially be set a higher at EUR [X] billion and reduced over a transition period e.g. five years.

453. Alternatively, this exemption could operate as a safe harbour. This means that MNE groups below the threshold would have the option to compute the Amount A tax base either on a group or on a segmented basis (subject to the constraints outlined in the third step below). Such optionality could however substantially increase the number of MNE groups that could compute the Amount A tax base on a segmented basis, including potentially situations where the costs of this segmentation process would largely outweigh the tax revenue at stake.

454. The Inclusive Framework will consider the development of exceptions or safeguards to limit access to the segmentation exemption or safe harbour in certain circumstances. For example, this could include excluding groups that have out-of-scope revenue in excess of [x%] of total revenue and a group profit margin below the agreed profitability threshold or where a group below the threshold has two disclosed operating segments, one that falls within scope of Amount A and one that falls out-of-scope.

5.3.4. Step three: Determining the relevant PBT measure on a segmented basis

455. Businesses that are not eligible for the segmentation exemption or safe harbour (under Step Two) may be required to compute the Amount A tax base on a segmented basis, though it is recognised that

this will not be appropriate in all instances. Step Three will determine whether a taxpayer is required to compute the Amount A tax base on a segmented basis, and, where it is, define the relevant segments for which the relevant measure of profit or loss will be computed separately.

Step 3(a): Testing whether segmentation is required

456. It is expected that in most instances, it will be appropriate for a group that is required to segment its Amount A tax base to do so based on the operating segments it discloses for financial reporting purposes (see below). However, it is also recognised that the objectives of segmentation for financial reporting purposes differ from the objectives of applying Amount A on a segmented basis. In a financial reporting context, segmentation should enable the users of financial statements to better understand a group's business. In contrast, segmentation for Amount A purposes should ensure the new taxing right delivers acceptable outcomes and ensures a level playing field for businesses in comparable circumstances. In addition, concerns have been raised that applying Amount A to disclosed operating segments could allow groups to influence or alter the application of Amount A by changing the way information is communicated to the chief operating decision maker, which under IFRS and US GAAP determines how segments should be disclosed.

457. Consequently, specific tests are being developed to determine if a group is required to compute its Amount A tax base on a segmented basis, or whether it would be more appropriate to compute its tax base on group basis. These tests will establish an objective and standardised definition of a segment for the purposes of Amount A based on "segmentation hallmarks". Under one possible approach, this definition of a segment could be based on International Accounting Standard (IAS) 14, which preceded IFRS 8.[20] This previous accounting standard provides a useful starting point for defining a segment for the purposes of Amount A, as it is based on the nature of a group's business, rather than the basis on which the chief operating decision maker reviews a business.

458. IAS 14 defines a business segment as "*a distinguishable component of an entity that is engaged in providing an individual product or service or a group of related products or services and that is subject to risks and returns that are different from those of other business segments. Factors that shall be considered in determining whether products and services are related include:*

a) the nature of the products or services;

b) the nature of the production processes;

c) the type or class of customer for the products or services;

d) the methods used to distribute the products or provide the services; and

e) if applicable, the nature of the regulatory environment, for example, banking, insurance, or public utilities."[21]

459. For some businesses, notably those that are primarily managed on a regional basis, it may be appropriate to calculate the Amount A tax base on a regional basis. In order to permit this the "segmentation hallmarks" could also include an alternative or supplementary definition of a "geographical segment".[22] However, it could also be argued that it is inconsistent with the nature of Amount A as an allocation of group-wide profits, with an agreed allocation key based on relative in-scope revenues in in each jurisdiction, to sub-divide in-scope businesses on a regional basis.

460. For some MNE groups, particularly those that have a relatively homogenous business, the "segmentation hallmarks" may show that it would be most appropriate to compute the Amount A tax base on a group basis. For other groups, the "segmentation hallmarks" will show that they should calculate the Amount A tax base on a segmented basis, and further will define the most appropriate approach to segmentation.

461. As part of the implementation of this framework, and to help taxpayers applying this definition in practice, this definition will be supported by a commentary, including examples, in order to clarify areas that may create uncertainty or give rise to dispute.

Step 3(b): Computing Amount A based on disclosed segments

Using disclosed segments as a rebuttable presumption

462. It is expected that the vast majority of groups that are required to compute the Amount A tax base on a segmented basis will rely on the disclosed operating segments included in their financial statements. This reflects the fact that most groups will disclose operating segments in their financial statements that meet the "segmentation hallmarks" outlined above. Hence, there will be a rebuttable presumption that Amount A will be applied on this basis. This presumption could be rebutted by either the group itself or a tax administration (e.g. through the tax certainty process) and therefore when an MNE groups disclosed segments do not meet the "segmentation hallmarks" it would not be able to calculate its Amount A tax base on this basis.

463. This approach means that where a group does not disclose any operating segments in its financial statements, there would be a presumption that Amount A should be applied on a group basis. Though these groups would still need to show this approach is consistent with the "segmentation hallmarks". Similarly, where a group discloses business line segments, there would be a presumption that Amount A should be applied on that basis. There remains an important outstanding question whether there will be a presumption that a group disclosing regional segments should apply Amount A in all instances, particularly for groups that also have large pools of unallocated central research and development (R&D) or other costs. The final design of the definition of a segment for the purpose of Amount A will be particularly relevant for these businesses, which could allow businesses that operate on a regional basis to calculate their Amount A tax base on a regional basis.

Exemption for segments with comparable profit margins

464. There may be some situations, notably where profit margins vary little across the segments of a group, where the tax impact of applying Amount A either on a group or segment basis will be minimal. In these instances, in order to minimise the compliance costs and administrative burdens associated with segmentation, taxpayers could be required to apply Amount A on a group basis. This exemption would apply where the profit margin of the disclosed segments (at the profit level shown in the financial accounts, which may be at a gross or operating level) varies by less than an agreed number of percentage points. As with the exemption for segmentation based on global revenue, this exemption could be turned into a safe harbour and become optional.

Determining profit before tax on a segment basis

465. Where a taxpayer computes the Amount A tax base on the basis of its disclosed segments it will still need to allocate a pool of central or unallocated costs between segments in order to arrive at the relevant PBT measure for each segment. In many instances, it may prove difficult, if not impossible, to allocate these costs directly between segments. Therefore, again as a rebuttable presumption, these costs will be apportioned between segments using revenue as an allocation key. To prevent this rebuttable presumption giving rise to distortions, a safeguard rule could be introduced with the effect that the option of using a revenue-based allocation of costs would be available only where the proportion of central costs to be allocated between segments falls below a given percentage of total group or segment costs. Above this threshold, there would be a requirement to allocate costs using a more accurate, less approximate method. Where taxpayers compute their Amount A tax base on a segmented basis there will also be a

requirement to reconcile the aggregated PBT (as calculated for the purposes of Amount A) at a segment level, with the PBT reported at a consolidated level.

466. When applying Amount A on a segmented basis, the treatment of intersegmental transactions remains to be determined. There may be instances where groups recognise intersegmental transactions in their segmented financial statements, or where a specific approach to segmentation requires the recognition of intersegmental transactions. Intersegmental transactions will be eliminated as part of the preparation of consolidated financial accounts. However, these transactions may have a direct impact on the reported profitability of different segments. This could, where Amount A is applied on a segmented basis, create incentives for groups to use intersegmental transactions to shift profits to segments that are primarily out-of-scope of Amount A (or conversely losses to segments that are primarily in scope of Amount A).

467. The simplest way to guard against this risk would be to exclude all intersegmental transactions for the purposes of Amount A. However, in some instances this would result in the misallocation of profits between segments – e.g. where one segment incurs substantial costs in developing an intangible that is then profitably exploited in another segment. To address the challenges associated with intersegmental transactions, consideration is being given to requiring a group to combine relevant segments where intersegmental transactions exceed a given percentage of the revenue attributable to a segment.

Step 3(c): Computing Amount A based on alternative segments

468. The few groups that are not able to compute the Amount A tax base on a group basis or based on their disclosed segments could be required to perform that computation on the basis of alternative segments. This alternative approach would be determined based on the definition of a segment for the purposes of Amount A, as outlined above. It would be expected that this alternative approach would in most instances merely require a group to further break down the profit or loss account of an existing segment or segments and that the group may have an existing internal reporting framework on which to base this alternative segmentation.

469. A taxpayer could determine (or tax administrations, through the tax certainty process could require) that Amount A should be applied on the basis of an alternative segmentation. Hence, this option should deter taxpayers that may otherwise seek to use their approach to segmentation as a tool for tax planning.

5.3.5. Next steps

470. As a next step, further work will be undertaken to finalise the following specific areas of the segmentation framework:

- The exemption from segmentation (step two), especially:
    - The appropriateness of the level of the global revenue thresholds, including the threshold that would apply for the transitional period, informed by the data and analysis of the impact of the different global revenue thresholds on the number of groups required to segment their tax base (see Table 2.1).
    - The regime of this exception, and whether it should be mandatory (exemption) or optional (a safe harbour).
    - Possible additional exceptions or safeguards to override the exemption in some circumstances (e.g. in the case where a group that has out-of-scope revenue in excess of [x%] of total revenue and a group profit margin below the agreed profitability threshold or a group below the threshold has two disclosed operating segments, one that falls within scope of Amount A and one that falls out-of-scope).
- The definition of a segment based on the hallmarks (step three), especially:

  - Whether to include a third-party revenue requirement to prevent groups from using segments that consist primarily of revenue and costs generated by inter-group transactions.
  - Whether to include a materiality threshold to ensure that the definition does not lead to a proliferation of small, low-value segments (as this substantially increases the compliance costs and administrative burden associated with applying Amount A). For example, this materiality threshold could require a group to aggregate identified segments that generate less than an agreed percentage of the group's consolidated revenue and/or an absolute amount of revenue.
- The computation of the PBT measure on a segmented basis (step three), especially the treatment of regional segments disclosed in financial accounts, the use of a revenue-based allocation keys for indirect costs, and the treatment of intersegment transactions.

471. In this work, important considerations will include simplicity of administration (and compliance costs) and ensuring a level playing field between taxpayers.

5.4. Loss carry-forward rules

472. To account for losses, the Amount A tax base rules will apply consistently at the level of the group or segment (where relevant) irrespective of whether the outcome is a profit or loss. Any losses arising from a taxable period will be preserved and carried forward to subsequent years through an "earn-out" mechanism. This means that Amount A losses will be reported and administered through a single account for the relevant group or segment, and kept separate from any existing domestic loss carry-forward regime.

5.4.1. Objectives

473. Consistent with the legislation of many Inclusive Framework member jurisdictions, the loss carry-forward regime will seek to ensure that Amount A is based on an appropriate measure of net profit.[23] It is necessary to offset tax losses of earlier years against current year taxable profits to enable all businesses to recoup losses reflecting costs of their investment, and place businesses with volatile profit in the same position as those with more stable profit. This is consistent with the objective of taxing only economic profit (or ability to pay principle),[24] and improves the neutrality of Amount A by ensuring a proper matching of revenues and expenses for all types of business activities.[25]

474. Loss carry-forward is also a way to preserve the taxing rights of residence jurisdictions, for example because they have already accepted (and will continue to accept) the deduction of losses generated by a business under the existing ALP-based system. Accounting for losses ensures that the residence jurisdiction of a business bearing the initial downside of a business activity (e.g. at a start-up level) will be able to recover these losses before a portion of the profit generated by the same activity is allocated to another jurisdiction under Amount A.

5.4.2. Calculation of losses

475. The Amount A tax base will be computed consistently whether a business earns profits or incurs losses (symmetry). This means that the calculation of "in-regime" losses (losses incurred after the introduction of Amount A) will be derived from the consolidated financial accounts after making the relevant book-to-tax adjustments (see section 5.2.2). This may apply to the level of the adjusted group PBT as a whole or, where the segmentation framework applies and Amount A will be measured at the level of the segment, to each segment (see section 5.3).

476. Where there is no segmentation[26], all profits and losses linked to different business activities (including potentially out-of-scope activities) within the group will be mixed within the same tax base for Amount A purposes.[27] In contrast, where the Amount A tax base is segmented, the segmentation approach

will require that losses and profits incurred by different segments within the group are computed separately, and that losses incurred by a segment are generally not available to reduce the profit of another segment (i.e. there will be no cross-segment blending of profits and losses). Additional work will be required to finalise specific aspects of these computation rules, such as identifying exceptions for business reorganisations (see section 5.4.4), specific requirements to address the effects of inter-segment transactions (typically, to prevent abusive shifting of profits and losses, see section 454), and other implications of symmetry in the application of the Amount A tax base rules.

477. Consistent with the Outline and guiding principles established by the Inclusive Framework (see above section 1.1), a transitional regime is being considered which would allow certain net pre-regime losses (losses incurred before the introduction of Amount A that exceed profits earned during that pre-regime period) to be preserved and deducted against Amount A in-regime profits up to a certain time limit. To avoid complexity, no distinction would be made between pre-regime losses and in-regime losses under the carry-forward regime, i.e. the features of the carry-forward regime (including potential restrictions) would apply similarly to pre-regime and in-regime losses. This transitional regime would seek to allow groups to recover the costs of investment undertaken before the introduction of Amount A (i.e. distortions arising from the timing of introduction of the new taxing right), and prevent a reallocation of profit under Amount A where there is no economic profit. But it is recognised that this approach would also treat pre-regime losses and pre-regime profits differently, creating an asymmetry in the calculation of losses which would reduce the Amount A profit potentially reallocated to market jurisdictions. Some members of the Inclusive Framework consider that profit and losses should apply symmetrically and therefore, in principle are opposed to accommodating any pre-regime losses. They argue that in case pre-regime losses are considered, pre-regime profits of the relevant period must also be brought forward for distribution. In addition, retroactive identification and calculation of Amount A losses based on past financial accounts could present practical challenges. To address these challenges and to reduce compliance and administrative costs, a time limit beyond which pre-regime losses would no longer be considered could be introduced. Along with other considerations regarding this approach, further work and discussion will be required to determine this duration.[28]

478. Depending on the length of this period for pre-regime losses, and the availability of historical data, some simplifications to the Amount A tax base rules (e.g. book-to-tax adjustments, segmentation rules), or to the rules developed for business reorganisations, may also need to be considered to facilitate administration. For example, if a lengthy period of pre-regime losses is accepted then it will be necessary to devise rules which deal with the impact of changing approaches to segmentation throughout such a period to ensure that an appropriate measure of pre-regime losses is available for offset against in-scope profits (e.g. using an allocation key based on revenue).

5.4.3. Carry-forward regime

479. Unlike profits, losses generated over a given period will not be allocated to market jurisdictions through a formula. Allocating these losses to market jurisdictions would be complex and burdensome to administer,[29] and could produce outcomes that are difficult to rationalise. For example, Amount A could be allocated to new markets that a group has recently entered in profitable years, even if in previous years the losses incurred (e.g. in developing a digital platform) were allocated to other markets in which the group has been operating for a longer period. Similarly, losses might be allocated to a market jurisdiction that cannot be offset later against any future profits of the group due to changes in the activity of the group in that market jurisdiction (e.g. lower sales activity in that jurisdiction, termination of the activity in that jurisdiction).

480. To avoid such difficulties and with a view to simplifying the process of dealing with losses, Amount A losses will be preserved and pooled in a single account at the level of the group (or segment where relevant) and carried forward to subsequent years through an "earn-out" mechanism.[30] This means that a

positive tax base for Amount A (in excess of the profitability threshold determined under the formula) would arise only after all historic losses accumulated in the loss account of the group (or segment where relevant)[31] have been absorbed through an earn-out mechanism.

5.4.4. Potential restrictions

481. Although loss carry-forward rules are an essential feature to tax net profits and avoid distortions, many Inclusive Framework jurisdictions restrict the deduction of some carry-forward losses for a number of reasons such as addressing tax planning strategies or ease of administration of the system. For Amount A, further work is required to assess the possibility of including time restrictions, and to develop specific rules for business reorganisations. In this work, relevant considerations will include the impact of these rules on complexity and administration, as well as on the allocation of taxing rights.

Time limitations

482. In the legislation of many Inclusive Framework members, the period over which carry-forward losses can be used is limited; after a certain period, the taxpayer's right to offset losses against profits may lapse, wholly or in part. Beyond revenue concerns, time limitations are imposed for practical and administrative reasons, such as the difficulty of retaining information over a long period and to simplify tax administration arrangements.

483. For Amount A losses, a trade-off exists between the practical and administrative constraints that may justify the introduction of a time limitation, and the adverse impact that any limitation may have on appropriately measuring net profit (e.g. costs of investments made before the time limitation), delivering neutrality (e.g. business models with volatile profit) or on the allocation of taxing rights (e.g. residence jurisdictions that have accepted the deduction of unrelieved losses under the existing ALP-based system at an entity level). Further work is therefore required to assess the best approach to deal with this trade-off, interactions with provisions on statute of limitations (and tax audit), and determine whether unlimited carry-forward could be retained without creating excessive administrative challenges.[32]

Business reorganisations

484. In legislation across the membership of the Inclusive Framework, loss carry-forward regimes include specific rules for business reorganisations within an MNE group or between different groups.[33] These rules generally seek to prevent avoidance opportunities by ensuring that the business claiming the loss deduction is not economically different from the business that sustained the loss. Some of these restrictions are focused on changes of ownership, for example by providing that the right of a company to carry forward losses is forfeited in the event of a change in identity of its controlling shareholder (e.g. share transactions leading to a transfer of control). Other restrictions are focused on changes in business activity, and impose what is essentially a "continuity of business enterprise" test by denying loss relief when the profit against which the deduction is claimed is not produced by substantially the same business activity that incurred the loss. Finally, some legislation includes a combination of both approaches. In all cases, these rules are complex and burdensome for taxpayers and tax administrations alike, with substantial variations in scope and impact (e.g. the definition of what constitutes a "change of ownership" or "change of business activity"). Such rules create a rich source of disputes and uncertainty.

485. For Amount A, specific rules will be developed to deal with the treatment of unrelieved losses in the context of business reorganisations (e.g. creation of a new business, modification of an existing business, sale (or purchase) of whole or part of a business to a third party). These rules would seek to ensure that unrelieved losses are transferred to (and carried forward in) the relevant group (or segment where relevant) where the relevant business activity is continued. They would also seek to prevent the trading of losses and related tax avoidance arrangements. Important considerations in the development of

these rules will include: complexity (and administration) issues; definitional issues; interactions with segmentation rules (including changes over time of the segmentation basis) and the need to guard against tax avoidance arrangements; and possible impact on the allocation of taxing rights. Accordingly, a number of simplifications will be considered to deliver these results, including, for example, the use of allocation keys to allocate unrelieved losses.

5.4.5. Interactions with domestic carry-forward regimes

486. Consistent with the features described above, and the fact that Amount A has its own tax base, the Amount A carry-forward regime will be kept separate from any existing domestic loss carry-forward regime. This means that losses generated at entity level under the ALP-based profit allocation system ("entity-level losses") would not alter the Amount A tax base, nor would Amount A unrelieved losses affect the separate tax base of an MNE group entity determined in accordance with the ALP. In practice, this means that:

- A group entity liable to pay Amount A (or part of it) would not be able to reduce or eliminate that liability with entity-level losses;
- Amount A losses of a group (or segment where relevant) would not be offset against the profit of an entity determined under the ALP-based profit allocation system; and
- Entity-level losses under the ALP-based profit allocation system would generally not be affected by Amount A profit (or tax).[34]

487. There is a separate question whether entity-level losses, if not considered for computing the Amount A tax base, could be taken into account for determining the identity of the entity or entities in the group (or segment) that would bear the Amount A tax liability (for the purpose of eliminating double taxation). The mechanism to eliminate double taxation arising from Amount A is based on different steps (e.g. activity test, profitability test), and including in one of these steps the consideration of entity level losses is under consideration as part of the work on elimination of double taxation (see section 7.2.6.).

5.4.6. Profit shortfalls

488. Some Inclusive Framework members proposed that the Amount A carry-forward regime should accommodate, in addition to economic losses, "profit shortfalls". They consider that where the Amount A profit of a group (or segment) in a given period falls below the agreed profitability threshold of the Amount A formula, the Amount A carry-forward regime should treat the difference between this profit and the level of the profitability threshold (i.e. profit shortfalls) as a "loss" that can be carried forward to the next taxable periods. Profit shortfalls would thus be preserved and potentially give rise to a tax relief in subsequent profitable years for Amount A purposes (see illustration in Annex C, Box C.1.).

489. For the proponents of this approach, a carry-forward regime that includes profit shortfalls would improve neutrality by ensuring that Amount A does not apply differently to taxpayers with volatile profits from one period to the next (see Group X and Y in the example in Annex C, Box C.1.).[35] They note that in conventional tax systems which tax the first unit of profit above zero, zero profitability (where losses begin) is the "pivot point" for carryovers. They suggest that in a system like Amount A that only reallocates residual profits above a fixed positive profit threshold, neutrality requires that the pivot point for carryovers be the residual profit threshold. In addition, this approach would also allow Amount A to better adapt to unpredictable economic situation. Some of these members note that transfer pricing methods, such as the TNMM, rely on average financial data over a number of years; and that a carry-forward rule for profit shortfalls is consistent with this approach, but without the administrative difficulties of an averaging method. In addition, they consider that this approach would improve the accuracy of the measure of residual profit subject to the Amount A formula, by ensuring that only profit in excess of the profitability threshold calculated over a longer period (and business cycle) is reallocated to market jurisdictions. It would thus

contribute to preserving the taxing rights of residence jurisdictions over Amount A profits not only by recovering previously deducted losses, but also by improving the measure of the profit that remains subject to the existing ALP-based allocation system (so-called "deemed" routine profit of the business, see section 6.2.1). The residence jurisdiction where the business is bearing costs and taking risks would benefit for longer from its taxing right under existing rules on the approximation of routine profit. These members also generally consider that the same rules should apply to losses and profit shortfalls – a single carry-forward system (including for potential time restrictions) – and that this approach would not add any complexity and be easy to administer.

490. In contrast, for another group of members, accounting for profit shortfalls would not be justified in principle, and would also introduce a source of complexity and increase compliance and administrative burdens. From a policy standpoint, these members note that most existing income tax rules do not average profits over multiple years (including where there is a progressive tax rate), and also suggest that loss carry-forward regimes are designed only to enable taxpayers to recoup losses reflecting costs of their earlier investments. Because profit shortfalls are not a cost that impairs the ability of a group to recoup its past investments, they see them as fundamentally different from losses, and take the view that there is no justification for allowing their carry-forward. These members also take the view that disregarding profit shortfalls has no or a limited impact on the tax burden of the taxpayer (depending on income tax rate differentials), and hence on neutrality, as it only changes the allocation of profit (and the jurisdiction where the taxpayer needs to pay its income tax). In addition, they consider this proposal inconsistent with the rationale of the Amount A profitability threshold, which is a simplified convention introduced to limit interactions between Amount A and existing profit allocation rules, and simplify the calculation of Amount A profit. In their view, this threshold does not seek to replicate the concept of residual profit used in transfer pricing rules, is not intended to apply to the profit of an MNE group (or segment where relevant) over multiple years, and involves an accepted degree of approximation. Finally, these members are concerned that this proposal would present practical difficulties. In their view, the different policy objective of "income averaging" would require a separate treatment of losses and profit shortfalls, and create the complexity of dealing with two distinct carry-forward regimes. Specifically, they consider that stricter time limits would need to apply to profit shortfalls compared with losses, on the basis that accounting for profit shortfalls over an excessively long period would lead to inappropriate results. For example, a business with a low profit margin could accumulate unrelieved profit shortfalls over 10 or 15 years which would not be justified from a policy standpoint, and would create opportunities for tax planning. These members also note that profit shortfalls would increase the amount of losses administered by the Amount A carry-forward system, and hence the need for strict and complex anti-avoidance rules to prevent the trading of these losses (including in case of business reorganisations).

491. A decision will be necessary to determine whether the Amount A carry-forward should be extended to profit shortfalls. To facilitate this decision, further work will be conducted to estimate the impact of accounting for profit shortfalls on the amount of losses administered by the Amount A carry-forward regime (and on the Amount A profit of in-scope MNE groups), and in turn on reducing the quantum of Amount A. Relevant considerations will include possible implications and spill-overs of this proposal on other features of this carry-forward regime or of Amount A, such as time limitations for the use of losses (see section 5.4.4), or the level of the profitability threshold in the Amount A formula (see section 6.2.1).

5.4.7. Administration

492. The approach under consideration requires potentially all MNE groups in scope of Amount A to compute their Amount A tax base to identify and preserve losses incurred over a given period, including in periods where MNE groups may not foresee profit in the near or medium term that would be relevant for Amount A purposes (in excess of the profitability threshold).[36] To manage the loss account(s), these groups will also be subject to specific filing and documentation requirements, such as keeping records at group level (or segment where relevant) of carried-forward losses (including pre-regime losses) for each period

from the introduction of the new taxing right. This compliance burden could, however, be substantially mitigated by the development of a simplified and centralised compliance framework for Amount A (including standardised filing requirements), where one entity in the group would be responsible for administration and compliance with Amount A (see section 10.2.1). Further, other procedures developed to facilitate the administration of Amount A are likely to be relevant for the proposed loss carry-forward regime, such as the opportunity to obtain early certainty (e.g. calculation and allocation of pre-regime losses, impact on unrelieved losses of a business reorganisation).

5.4.8. Next steps

493. As a next step, further work will be undertaken on the specific aspects of the loss carry-forward regime that need to be finalised, including:

- The issue of pre-regime losses, and what specific time limit, if any, would be needed to limit administration and compliance costs.
- The impact of business reorganisations (including changes over time of the segmentation basis), and the specific rules that need to be developed to prevent the trading of losses and related tax avoidance arrangements.
- The question of time limitations, and the implications of adopting unlimited carry-forward.

494. In this discussion, important considerations will include simplicity of administration (and compliance costs), ensuring net-basis taxation, neutrality and the possible impact on the allocation of taxing rights.

495. Separately, as part of the discussion on the quantum of Amount A (see section 6.5), a decision will be necessary to determine whether this regime should apply exclusively to economic losses or be extended to cover profit shortfalls.

Notes

[1] These include, in addition to IFRS, the generally accepted accounting principles of Australia, Canada, Hong Kong (China), Japan, New Zealand, the People's Republic of China, the Republic of India, the Republic of Korea, Singapore and the United States.

[2] The quantum of Amount A profits allocable to an eligible market jurisdiction will result from applying the Amount A formula (including the allocation key based on in-scope revenue) to the consolidated tax base. This would mean that even though the calculation of the Amount A tax base would not distinguish between in and out-of-scope activities, market jurisdictions would still not be allocated Amount A profits for out-of-scope activities. In effect, the group or segment profit margin would be used as a proxy for the profit margin of in-scope activities.

[3] This safe harbour approach could, however, substantially increase the number of MNE groups that would elect to compute the Amount A tax base on a segmented basis, with ensuing administrative burdens for tax administrations. The safe harbour approach would be to the benefit of taxpayers, as it would allow a group with a high profitability out-of-scope business and a low profitability in-scope business to elect to calculate its Amount A tax base on a segmented basis, thereby reducing its potential Amount A tax liability.

[4] Where an MNE group is within the segmentation exemption but has one disclosed segment in scope of Amount A and one segment out of scope, it may be preferable to exclude the MNE group from the exemption. Further work will be undertaken on this issue.

[5] Not all transactions between associated enterprises as defined in Article 9 of the OECD Model Tax Convention (MTC) will necessarily be eliminated through the process of consolidation. The reason for that is that the definition of "control" for accounting purposes is typically narrower than the definition of associated enterprises under Article 9 of the OECD MTC.

[6] Even where MNE groups are not required to prepare audited consolidated financial accounts, there are also a number of constraints associated with the financial reporting process (e.g. incentives, checks and balances) that contribute to the reliability of the information provided by the financial accounts.

[7] IFRS is a set of accounting standards issued by the IFRS Foundation and the IASB. It is the most commonly used and accepted financial accounting standard worldwide (see https://www.ifrs.org/use-around-the-world/use-of-ifrs-standards-by-jurisdiction/). This widespread use across the world makes it a useful and pragmatic reference point for assessing differences between local GAAP when computing the Amount A tax base.

[8] See chapter 4 (section 4-7) of GloBE rules.

[9] Furthermore, many of the potential differences between GAAP are of a qualitative nature, which would impede the quantification and the adjustment of such divergences in a reliable manner to compute Amount A tax base.

[10] The statement of "profit or loss" is one of the five inter-related statements that comprise an MNE group's consolidated financial accounts. It contains at the bottom a total for "profit or loss" that includes, in principle, all income and expenses of an MNE group for a given period. The only exception being income and expenses presented in the "other comprehensive income" statement.

[11] For instance, an unrealised accrued gain may be relevant for a group's shareholders, but would typically not give rise to an income tax charge until it is realised and, accordingly, would not be included in the Amount A tax base. Most unrealised accrued gains are accounted for in the "other comprehensive income" statement and, therefore, not reflected into the "profit or loss" statement until the realisation of the gain. Therefore, MNE groups recognising unrealised accrued gains in the "other comprehensive income" statement would not need to make adjustments to compute the Amount A tax base, which would make the approach relatively simple to apply.

[12] IFRS defines "income taxes" for these purposes as including "*all domestic and foreign taxes which are based on taxable profits. Income taxes also include taxes, such as withholding taxes, which are payable by a subsidiary, associate or joint arrangement on distributions to the reporting entity.*" For instance, in the specific case of partnerships that are not subject to CIT, the tax expense would merely account for the withholding tax levied upon distribution of the profits to the partners.

[13] This includes income taxes on excluded income for the purposes of computing the Amount A tax base.

[14] See chapter 4 (section 4-7) of GloBE rules.

[15] See chapter 4 (section 4-7) of GloBE rules.

[16] For more details on the equity method of accounting, see chapter 4 (section 4-7) of GloBE rules.

[17] Under IFRS and a number of GAAP, income and expenses are classified and included either in the statement of "profit or loss" or in the "other comprehensive income" statement. As a general rule, non-realised income or expenses are recognised in the "other comprehensive income" statement in the period

where they are accrued. These items are subsequently reclassified ("recycled") from the "other comprehensive income" statement into the statement of "profit or loss" in a future period, usually when they are realised.

18 To calculate the PBT attributable to standardised and bespoke cloud computing services would require a group to apportion substantial shared costs between these activities using allocation keys (likely including revenue). The reliance on allocation keys to apportion a potentially broad range of different costs brings into question whether the PBT that would be determined for each of these separate activities would accurately reflect the underlying economic reality of each business. It would also be challenging to verify such allocations.

19 This will include consideration of whether it may be appropriate to only require a taxpayer to segment its tax base between in and out-of-scope activities, in line with the scope of Amount A.

20 An operating segment is defined under IFRS 8 as the "*component of an entity a) that engages in business activities from which it may earn revenues and incur expenses (including revenues and expenses relating to transactions with other components of the same entity), b) whose operating results are regularly reviewed by the entity's chief operating decision maker to make decisions about resources to be allocated to the segment and assess its performance, and for which discrete financial information is available*." International Accounting Standards Board, *International Financial Reporting Standard 8: Operating Segments*, paragraph 5.

21 International Accounting Standards Board, *International Account Standard 14: Segment Reporting*, paragraph 9.

22 *International Account Standard 14: Segment Reporting*, paragraph 9 includes a definition of a "geographical segment" which may be relevant in developing this aspect of the "segmentation hallmarks".

23 Although some jurisdictions' CIT legislation includes loss carry-back rules, whereby losses can be transferred to reduce or eliminate the CIT paid in a prior tax year, such rules are not considered in the context of Amount A because of their complexity and uncertainty. Loss carry-back regimes have proven difficult to administer as they require reopening a taxpayer's assessment for prior tax periods. They also make it difficult for jurisdictions to forecast tax revenue as they require the refunding (possibly in years of economic decline) of taxes paid in previous years.

24 In this Report, ability to pay refers to the ability of a taxpayer to pay its income tax without impairing its original investment.

25 For example, this is relevant for high-risk business activities requiring heavy investments in innovation and technology, where the risk of making losses is greater than for other (low-risk) business activities. Many highly digitalised businesses start their business cycle with a "scale up" period during which they undertake substantial investment to develop their business model and launch their international growth to capture new markets. During this period, they can experience large losses even if in the long term they become efficient and highly profitable. Loss carry-forward is necessary to ensure that those risk-taking businesses with high fluctuations in profit can recoup the costs associated with their initial investments, and hence not be subject to a relatively higher income tax burden than other business activities with a faster route to profit.

26 As a result of the different exemptions available to determine whether segmentation is required, it is expected that only a limited number of MNEs in scope of Amount A would be required to segment their consolidated accounts for the purpose of computing the Amount A tax base (see section 5.3.3).

[27] This means that if a profit margin-based approach is adopted (see section 6.2.4), the MNE group will calculate the quantum of losses for Amount A purposes by multiplying its consolidated negative profit margin by its total in-scope revenue.

[28] This time limit on the calculation and reporting of losses incurred before the introduction of Amount A would not necessarily apply to the carry-forward of these pre-regime losses to subsequent years (see section 5.4.4).

[29] An approach allocating losses to market jurisdictions would require the development in each market jurisdiction of loss carry-forward rules for Amount A purposes, presumably in accordance with some harmonised standards to ensure that market jurisdictions are not able to render the loss allocation ineffective (e.g. through prohibitive time limits on relief). Taxpayers would need to administer the allocated losses in each market jurisdiction separately, and submit in each market jurisdiction a claim for tax relief once profit is allocated to that same jurisdiction under Amount A in subsequent years.

[30] Comparable mechanisms are used in the legislation of different Inclusive Framework jurisdictions, such as for the treatment of certain investment vehicles (typically, to offset profit and losses generated by a portfolio of assets over multiple years before redistributing profit to the investors).

[31] If the Amount A carry-forward regime is extended to certain pre-regime losses, the loss account would also include those pre-regime losses.

[32] Some members of the Inclusive Framework consider the taxation of Amount A profit net of any losses as the priority, and support unlimited carry-forward (typically, jurisdictions with no time limitations in their domestic carry-forward regimes). Other members are concerned about the administrative challenges created by unlimited carry forward, including the opportunities for manipulation and abuse. They therefore favour a time limit. These members also generally consider that the need for time limitations is proportionate to the amount of losses at stake, and hence that the possible inclusion of profit shortfalls should be considered in deciding this issue.

[33] A business reorganisation here means any situation where one or more members of the MNE group, or one or more business asset or branch within the group, are transferred and become part of another group, or another business or branch within the same group. This includes therefore changes to the organisation of a business that leads to changes to the segmentation basis (see section 5.3).

[34] Members of the Inclusive Framework will remain free as a matter of domestic tax policy to reduce an Amount A allocation to their jurisdiction by entity-level losses that the same MNE has incurred through an entity in that jurisdiction.

[35] Volatility of profits may be the result of different factors in the context of Amount A, including timing differences in the treatment of revenue and expenses between different accounting standards (see section 5.2.1).

[36] The treatment of losses incurred by MNE groups that are not in scope of Amount A because they fall below one of the two revenue thresholds (see section 2.3) will also need to be considered. For example, the transitional regime developed to accommodate pre-regime losses (see section 5.4.2) could be extended and apply similarly to losses incurred during periods where the MNE falls below the scope revenue thresholds.

6 Profit allocation

6.1. Overview

6.1.1. The formula to determine the quantum of Amount A

496. The calculation and allocation of Amount A will be delivered through a formula that is not based on the ALP. This formula will apply to the tax base of a group (or segment where relevant), and will involve three distinct components represented in the steps below:

- **Step 1:** A profitability threshold to isolate the residual profit potentially subject to reallocation, and limit any interactions between Amount A and the remuneration of routine activities under conventional transfer pricing rules. To avoid complexity, this threshold would be based on a simplifying convention, which will be a PBT to revenue ratio.
- **Step 2:** A reallocation percentage to identify an appropriate share of residual profit that can be allocated to market jurisdictions under Amount A (hereafter, the "allocable tax base"). This will ensure that other factors such as trade intangibles, capital and risk, continue to be remunerated and allocated residual profit. To avoid complexity, this allocable tax base will be determined through a simplifying convention, which will be a fixed percentage.
- **Step 3:** An allocation key to distribute the allocable tax base amongst the eligible market jurisdictions (i.e. where nexus is established for Amount A). It will be based on locally sourced in-scope revenue determined by applying the rules on scope, nexus and revenue sourcing (see Chapter 4).

497. This three-step formula to determining the Amount A quantum could be delivered through two approaches: a profit-based approach or a profit margin-based approach. A profit-based approach would start the calculation with the Amount A tax base determined as a profit amount (e.g. an absolute profit of EUR 10 million), whereas a profit-margin approach would start the calculation with the Amount A tax base determined as a profit margin (e.g. a PBT to revenue of 15%). Both approaches would apply the three-steps of the allocation formula similarly, and hence would deliver the same quantum of Amount A taxable in each market jurisdiction. The administration of each approach may, however, present some variations (e.g. foreign currency exchanges), and these practical differences will inform the choice of the most appropriate approach to calculate and allocate Amount A. These two approaches are explored in more detail in Annex B.

Potential differentiation mechanisms

498. As part of the comprehensive agreement still needed, it will be necessary to determine whether the formula should incorporate any "differentiation" mechanism. That is, whether the different components of this formula should apply similarly in all circumstances, or whether some variations (for example the profitability threshold under step 1 and/or the reallocation percentage under step 2) should sometimes be applied to increase (or decrease) the quantum of profit reallocated to market jurisdictions for certain business activities. No agreement has yet been reached on either the policy merits of these variations or

their feasibility from a technical design perspective. There will also be some remaining issues around questions of regional and jurisdictional segmentation.

The issue of double counting

499. The Outline highlighted an important question as to whether the interactions between Amount A and existing taxing rights of market jurisdictions could, in some circumstances, result in a market jurisdiction being able to tax twice the residual profit of an MNE group: once under its existing taxing rights, and again through Amount A (the issue of "double counting"). The issue of double counting is expected to be addressed, at least partially, through the mechanism to eliminate double taxation (see Chapter 7). This is because where an entity is allocated significant residual profit in a market jurisdiction under existing profit allocation rules, this entity may be identified as a "paying entity" within the group for the purpose of eliminating double taxation which would bear a portion of the Amount A tax liability (resulting in a "netting-off" effect). However, some members of the Inclusive Framework suggest that, on its own:

- This may not fit with the overall rationale for Pillar One (and Amount A specifically) which has always been to adapt the income tax system where businesses have an active and sustained engagement in a market jurisdiction, but the existing profit allocation rules do not give that jurisdiction taxing rights over residual profits generated in that market. So, if Amount A did apply to businesses that already realise residual profits in the market, the problem Pillar One is trying to solve may not seem to be present.
- Applying the mechanism to eliminate double taxation to decentralised businesses that realise residual profits in a large number of entities and jurisdiction will be complex. Specifically, it may be difficult to calibrate this system to ensure that a full-risk distributor entitled to residual profit is identified as the paying entity for the Amount A allocated to the jurisdiction in which it is resident. For this reason, it may be preferable to develop a method that would reduce pressure on the elimination system, allowing this system to focus on more centralised businesses where it will be comparably easy to identify the paying entities.

500. The marketing and distribution profits safe harbour described below is an approach that seeks to address these issues related to double counting, as well as a number of other issues expressed by Inclusive Framework members and stakeholders. It would be an additional step in the Amount A formula to adjust the quantum of Amount A allocated to eligible market jurisdictions in specific circumstances. Consideration is also being given to other approaches to deal (or alleviate) double counting beyond the mechanism to eliminate double taxation, such as a domestic business exemption.

Marketing and distribution profits safe harbour

501. The premise of the "marketing and distribution profits safe harbour" is that Amount A should be allocated to a market jurisdiction that is not allocated residual profits under the existing profit allocation rules but should not be allocated to a market jurisdiction where (for its in-scope activities) an MNE group already leaves sufficient residual profit in the market. It would not be a traditional safe harbour, but would instead "cap" the allocation of Amount A to market jurisdictions that already have taxing rights over a group's profits under existing tax rules. Conceptually, it would consider the income taxes payable in the market jurisdiction under existing taxing rights and Amount A together, and adjust the quantum of Amount A taxable in a market jurisdiction, on the basis of limiting it where the residual profit of the MNE group is already taxed in that jurisdiction as a result of the application of the existing profit allocation rules. Where an MNE qualifies under the safe harbour in the market jurisdictions where it operates, it would need to calculate Amount A, but would otherwise remain subject to the existing rules including on transfer pricing and the elimination of double taxation.

502. Under the safe harbour, where an MNE group has a taxable presence in a market jurisdiction conducting marketing and distribution activities connected to locally sourced in-scope revenue (either a

resident entity or a permanent establishment), the group would determine the profits allocated to the market jurisdiction under existing profit allocation rules for the performance of these marketing and distribution activities (the "existing marketing and distribution profit").[1] The MNE group would then compare this with the "safe harbour return", which would be the sum of two components:

- Amount A, as computed under the Amount A formula; and
- A fixed return for in-country routine marketing and distribution activities, which could include a regional, and industry uplift.

503. The safe harbour return represents the cap, by reference to which the quantum of Amount A allocated to a market jurisdiction would be adjusted. It would be applied by an MNE group separately to each market jurisdiction in which they operate and would give rise to three possible outcomes:

- Where the existing marketing and distribution profit is lower than the fixed return, the MNE group will not be eligible for the safe harbour;
- Where the existing marketing and distribution profits exceeds the fixed return, but falls below the safe harbour return, the quantum of Amount A allocated to that jurisdiction would be reduced to the difference between the safe harbour return and the profit already allocated to the local presence; and
- Where existing marketing and distribution profit exceeds the safe harbour return, no Amount A would be allocated to that jurisdiction.

504. In-scope MNE groups that for commercial reasons (given their particular business models) operate without an existing taxable presence in a market jurisdiction or only allocate a relatively limited return (e.g. on a cost-plus basis) to local marketing and distribution activities would not come under the safe harbour rule and thus would pay Amount A in the majority of market jurisdictions in which they operate. In contrast, more traditional CFB businesses, particularly those with decentralised business models and full-risk distributors, may already allocate profits to market jurisdictions that exceed the safe harbour return. Hence, though these businesses would need to calculate Amount A (to determine that they have met the safe harbour), they would in many instances ultimately not need to pay Amount A or apply the mechanism to eliminate double taxation.

A domestic business exemption.

505. This mechanism would exclude from the scope of Amount A profits derived by an ADS or CFB business in a market jurisdiction which can be seen as autonomous from the rest of the group, i.e. sale of goods or services that are developed, manufactured and sold in a single jurisdiction. As in this scenario residual profit is typically already allocated to the market, this exemption would prevent the risk of double counting in those circumstances.

506. Further work will be required to assess the effectiveness, the efficiency and the feasibility of the different options to deal with double counting, in close coordination with the work on the mechanism to eliminate double taxation and in light of the policy objective of Amount A (see Chapter 7). This will also include consideration of the interactions between Amount A and certain withholding taxes collected by market jurisdictions.

6.2. The formula to determine the quantum of Amount A

6.2.1. Step 1 – The profitability threshold

507. Amount A represents a simplified proxy of the portion of the residual profit of a business that can reasonably be associated with the sustained and significant participation of that business in the economy

of a market jurisdiction. To isolate the residual profit of a business (group or segment where relevant) potentially subject to reallocation under Amount A, the formula includes a profitability threshold. This threshold is based on a simplified convention (i.e. a fixed percentage), and will apply to the Amount A tax base after the deduction of any available losses carried forward (see section 5.4).

508. One reason for introducing and using a fixed threshold, rather than a variable percentage based on facts and circumstances or related transfer pricing analysis, is to reduce complexity. The profitability threshold will materially reduce the scale of interactions of Amount A with conventional transfer pricing rules (e.g. remuneration of routine activities), and hence the complexity that these interactions create to eliminate double taxation (and double counting, see below Section 6.4). This threshold will not alter the allocation of profit derived from routine activities under the current transfer pricing rules (given that Amount A operates as an overlay to the existing profit allocation rules), but will simplify the identification and calculation of the residual profit subject to the new taxing right.

509. To achieve these results, the profitability threshold will be based on a simplifying convention (i.e. proxy). Consistent with the logic adopted for tax base determinations, and to facilitate both administration and compliance, the profitability of an MNE group (or segment) would be assessed through an Amount A PBT to revenue ratio (i.e. a percentage).[2] The determination of this figure will not rest on any MNE-specific economic assessment nor necessarily correspond with underlying transfer pricing arrangements. The impact of different profitability thresholds is shown in the Table 6.1 below.

Table 6.1. Estimated Impact of Different Profitability Thresholds

Number and share of MNE groups above the residual profit threshold.

Profitability Threshold	Estimated number of MNE groups in scope	Estimated Global residual profit (USD trillion)
8%	~990	0.60
10%	~780	0.49
15%	~430	0.29
20%	~240	0.17
25%	~150	0.10

Note: Data are for 2016. MNEs with consolidated revenue below €750 million are excluded from this estimate. Only MNEs with a primary activity in ADS and CFB sectors are included. The classification across sectors is based on the primary activity of each group. This estimate does not account for the scope threshold based on foreign source in-scope revenue, the fact that groups may have different business lines or units operating in different sectors (i.e. impact of segmentation), and the possible impact of accounting for profit shortfalls in the calculation of Amount A profit (see section 5.4.6). This suggests that the total amount of global profit designated as residual profit in this table could be lower in practice. It does not take into account that groups may have different business lines or units operating in different sectors.
Source: Secretariat calculations. Further details are provided in CTPA/CFA/WP2/NOE2(2020)65 and CTPA/CFA/WP2/NOE2(2020)6.

510. More data and analysis is available in the economic impact assessment.[3] With these estimates, Inclusive Framework members will be able to take an informed decision when setting the threshold. The decision on the level of the profitability threshold will seek to combine different objectives, such as ensuring the amount of profit to be reallocated is modest but meaningful, proportionate to compliance costs and administrative burden, and that the number of groups impacted is kept at an administrable level. For the purpose of illustration, it is noted that based on a 10% threshold of PBT to revenue, the above estimates in Table 2.1 suggest that about 780 MNE groups potentially in scope of Amount A would have residual profits. This would represent about 35% of MNE groups subject to CbCR with a primary activity in ADS and CFB sectors. Further, the combined residual profit of these MNE groups would be USD 0.51 trillion.

6.2.2. Step 2 – The reallocation percentage

511. Under Pillar One, only a portion of the residual profit of a group (or segment where relevant) is attributable to Amount A. This is because MNE groups perform a variety of activities unrelated to Amount A that generate residual profit, and hence a substantial portion of the group's residual profit should continue to be allocated under existing rules to factors such as trade intangibles, capital and risk, etc.

512. The formulaic calculation of Amount A thus requires an additional step: the reallocation percentage. For simplicity, the share of residual profit that is attributable to the market jurisdiction will be determined by a simplifying convention (i.e. proxy) not based on the particular circumstances of the MNE group or the ALP. Such a convention could be residual profit multiplied by a fixed percentage. Consistent with the estimates provided above in Table 6.1, some estimates of the impact of different reallocation percentages (in combination with different possible profitability thresholds) on the amount of global residual profit allocable to market jurisdictions are shown in the Table 6.2 below.

Table 6.2. Effect of profitability threshold and allocation percentage on residual profits

Profitability Threshold	Allocation Percentage	Estimated global residual profit allocable to market jurisdiction (USD billion)
8%	10%	60
	20%	120
	30%	180
10%	10%	49
	20%	98
	30%	147
15%	10%	29
	20%	58
	30%	87
20%	10%	17
	20%	34
	30%	51
25%	10%	10
	20%	20
	30%	30

Note: Data are for 2016 (see above Table 6.1).
Source: Secretariat calculations (see above Table 6.1).

513. More data and analysis is available in the economic impact assessment.[4] With these estimates, Inclusive Framework members will be able to take an informed decision on the reallocation percentage. This decision will seek to combine different objectives, such as ensuring that activities and factors generating residual profit unrelated to Amount A would continue to be taxed under the existing ALP-based profit allocation system. For the purpose of illustration, it is noted that based on a 10% profitability threshold and 20% reallocation percentage, the above estimates in Table 6.2 suggests that using 2016 financials USD 98 billion would be allocated to market jurisdictions. Under this approach, 80% of the residual profit of an MNE group (or segment where relevant) calculated for the purpose of Amount A would thus continue to be taxed in accordance with the existing ALP-based profit allocation system, and the other 20% would constitute the allocable tax base for Amount A purposes.

6.2.3. Step 3 – The allocation key

514. Once the calculation of the allocable tax base for Amount A is completed, that profit needs to be allocated to the various eligible market jurisdictions based on an allocation key. This allocation is based on in-scope revenue derived from each eligible market jurisdiction (for revenue sourcing rules, see Chapter 4.2).

515. The application of this allocation key will require a clear definition of revenue. Under accounting standards, revenues are typically booked on a gross basis, net of certain types of taxes (including sales, use, value added and some excise taxes). Further work will be required to determine if the existing definitions of revenue provided by accounting standards and shown in financial statements (which are relied upon for CbCR) could be used to define revenue for the purposes of applying the Amount A formula (as well as to apply the threshold tests for scope, see section 2.3).

516. The application of the revenue-based allocation key will differ depending on whether the formula is implemented through a profit-based or a profit-margin approach (see section 6.2.4). Under a profit-based approach, the allocable tax base (a profit amount, i.e. PBT) could be multiplied by the ratio of locally sourced in-scope revenue to total revenue of an MNE group (or segment where relevant) used in computing the tax base, including revenue from ineligible market jurisdictions (where no nexus would be established for Amount A purposes) and potentially out-of-scope revenue. Under a profit-margin approach, the allocable tax base (a profit ratio, i.e. PBT / revenue) could be multiplied by locally sourced in-scope revenue.

517. Both of these approaches would ensure that Amount A profits attributable to revenue sourced in ineligible market jurisdictions are not allocated to other eligible market jurisdictions, and remain instead taxed under the existing profit allocation system (a so-called "throwback" system). In practice, given the likely level of the nexus revenue thresholds, (see section 3.2.1), the Amount A profit attributable to ineligible market jurisdictions is likely to be small. Both approaches would also ensure that where the calculation of the Amount A tax base (at the level of a group or segment) includes profit from out-of-scope revenue, the portion of the Amount A tax base that relates to out-of-scope revenue will not be reallocated to market jurisdictions.[5]

518. Another possible approach would be to allocate the entire allocable tax base (as determined by steps 1 and 2) between eligible market jurisdictions, and allocate Amount A profits related to revenue sourced in ineligible market jurisdictions to eligible market jurisdictions (the "throw-in" system). This would modify the application of the revenue-based allocation key described above in paragraph 516, and require determining the source of all in-scope revenue (including revenue sourced in non-eligible market jurisdictions).[6]

6.2.4. Approaches to implement the formula

519. To summarise, a three-step process will be required to calculate the quantum of Amount A taxable in each eligible market jurisdiction. This process could be implemented by either using absolute amounts of profit (the "profit-based approach") or, alternatively, profit ratios (the "profit margin-based approach"). A profit-based approach would start the calculation from the Amount A tax base determined as a profit amount (e.g. an absolute profit of EUR 10 million), whereas a profit-margin approach would start the calculation from the Amount A tax base determined as a profit margin (e.g. a PBT to revenue of 15%). Both approaches would apply the above-described steps without changes or variations, and hence would provide the same quantum of Amount A taxable in each market jurisdiction. As a next step, the Inclusive Framework will determine which approach will be used to implement the Amount A formula. The profit-based approach and profit margin-based approach are discussed in more detail in Annex B.

6.3. Potential differentiation mechanisms

520. The technical work has considered whether the different components of the formula described above should apply similarly in all circumstances, or whether some variations are necessary to increase (or decrease) the amount of profit reallocated to market jurisdictions in some cases (the "differentiation mechanisms"). Such variations could have a significant impact to the general application of the Amount A rules.

521. Consistent with proposals formulated by some Inclusive Framework members, a differentiation mechanism could potentially be introduced to:

- Account for different degrees of digitalisation between in-scope business activities (e.g. based on the ADS definition used for scope), and increase the quantum of profit reallocated for certain types of business activities (hereafter, "digital differentiation"). This would seek to target businesses with lower marginal costs that are seen as deriving greater benefits from scale without mass.
- Account for substantial variations in profitability between different market jurisdictions, and increase the quantum of profit reallocated to market jurisdictions where the profitability is significantly higher than the average profitability of the segment (hereafter, "jurisdictional differentiation"). Such differentiation could be a simplified alternative to the jurisdictional segmentation examined in the context of tax base determination, which in many instances raises questions about feasibility and administration (see section 5.3).

522. Various mechanisms are available to provide for these types of differentiation. These include: (i) variations to the calculation of the allocable tax base, for example by increasing the reallocation percentage (step 2) in specific circumstances; (ii) variations to the allocation key used to distribute the allocable tax base between market jurisdictions (step 3), for example by weighting the amount of revenue derived from market jurisdictions; and (iii) other variations, such as adding a specific "routine return" for certain digital activities (e.g. ADS) that can be conducted without any physical presence in market jurisdictions.

523. The existing gaps between Inclusive Framework members on this policy issue will need to be resolved as part of the discussion of the quantum of Amount A.

6.3.1. Digital and other differentiation mechanisms

524. In the discussions so far, Inclusive Framework members have different views on whether some form of "digital differentiation" is necessary in the design of the Amount A formula. Accordingly, various options are under consideration, including:

- **No differentiation at all** – The Amount A formula would apply to all in-scope business activities in the same way, and in all circumstances.
- **Digital differentiation through adjustments to Amount A** – A lower profitability threshold under step 1 of the formula, or a higher reallocation percentage under step 2, would apply to MNE groups (or segments where relevant) providing primarily ADS. Though intuitively simple, any such differentiation approach would also require exploration as regards its technical and conceptual feasibility considering issues related to businesses segmentation and implications for the respective scope rules.
- **Differentiation of Amount A through a profit escalator** – A progressive reallocation percentage under step 2 of the formula would be introduced based solely on the profitability of the group (or segment where relevant). This mechanism would not seek to directly account for different degrees of digitalisation between in-scope businesses, but would be premised on the assumption that higher returns reflect at some point a greater contribution of the market to the profitability of the MNE group (e.g. monopolistic rents). The allocable tax base would thus be determined by reference to one or more bandings (e.g. X% for profit margins between a-b%,

X+Y% for profit margins between b-c%, X+Y+Z% for profit margins in excess of c%), but without any distinction based on the underlying nature of the in-scope business involved.

525. Further, some members consider that where ADS or CFB businesses make remote sales in a jurisdiction by using digital means to connect with customers, this jurisdiction should also receive an allocation of routine profits for the remote performance of marketing and distribution activities. In their view, once the new nexus threshold under Amount A is reached, it is unfair to deny market jurisdictions taxing rights over businesses that thanks to digitalisation are able to participate in the economic life of their jurisdiction remotely (i.e. making sales, marketing and distributing their products, collecting payments and addressing customer grievances). These members consider that in addition to Amount A, for businesses that operate in a market remotely certain marketing and distribution activities should be seen as taking place in the market jurisdiction and that in such circumstances profits would be allocated to the market jurisdiction. Such reallocated profits could be determined as an agreed percentage (e.g. 30%) of the deemed routine profit margin or the actual profit margin of the MNE group (or segment, where relevant), whichever is lower, subject to a minimum return (e.g. x% of sales) for the deemed routine marketing and distribution activities. Members that favor this approach recognizes that such allocation of deemed routine return for remote marketing and distribution activities needs to address the issue of double taxation. They are of the view, however, that such double taxation can be eliminated under the existing rules. Further, they believe it is important to reduce the incentives MNE groups face to conduct marketing and distribution remotely from a lower tax jurisdiction and to create neutrality between marketing and distribution conducted physically in a market jurisdiction and similar activities conducted remotely thanks to digital technologies. Other members take the view that there would be no case for reallocating both routine profit from distribution activities and residual profit.

6.3.2. Jurisdictional differentiation

526. The *Outline* identified the need to explore the rationale and technical feasibility of jurisdictional or regional segmentation as a way to account for variations in profitability across regions. For businesses that do not operate on a regional basis, regional segmentation would be technically challenging because, like segmenting between ADS, CFB and out-of-scope activities, it would require that potentially significant portions of central costs are apportioned among different regions using allocation keys. It is also recognised that regional or jurisdictional differentiation is mainly a question for CFB businesses and not for ADS businesses.[7] Whilst further technical work will be conducted on this issue, the work so far suggests that regional segmentation may not be sufficient to account for significant variations in profitability across jurisdictions (which are particularly significant in the CFB sector). Consideration has been given to whether the Amount A formula could be weighted to allocate more profits to more profitable markets. However, again the challenges of calculating the profits attributable to a market, mean it can be difficult to accurately identify more or less profitable markets.

527. Conceptually, incorporating jurisdictional differentiation within the Amount A model is particularly challenging, because it is inconsistent with the overall approach which is to calculate the profits allocable to a market jurisdiction on a group or segment basis. However, there are a number of features of Amount A that will help ensure that its introduction does not result in profits from more profitable market jurisdictions, being reallocated to less profitable market jurisdictions:

- **Mechanism to eliminate double taxation.** The mechanism to eliminate double taxation (see Chapter 7) could include an activities test and a market connection priority test. These two tests would significantly reduce the likelihood of the profits of in-market distributors being reallocated to other markets as a result of the introduction of Amount A.
- **Domestic business exemption.** As explained in more detail below, a "domestic business exemption" could be developed to exclude profits derived from the sale of goods or services that are developed, manufactured and sold in a single jurisdiction from the Amount A tax base.

However, by requiring that profits from domestic businesses are excluded from the Amount A tax base, this exemption would add significant complexity to the determination of the Amount A tax base.

6.4. The issue of double counting

528. Amount A will be allocated as an overlay to the existing income tax system. This means interactions between Amount A and the existing income tax system are inevitable.[8] The interactions between Amount A and the existing taxing rights of market jurisdictions on business profit, including withholding taxes, is conceptually challenging and an area where members have expressed different views. An important issue identified by the Outline is whether some of these interactions (i.e. between Amounts A and existing ALP-based profit allocation rules) could result in a duplicative taxation of the same profit of an MNE group in a particular market jurisdiction, which could be inconsistent with the policy intention of Pillar One (the issue of "double counting"). [9] The concern is that the market jurisdiction may get to tax the same item of residual profit twice: once through an existing taxable presence under transfer pricing rules, and again through Amount A. The issue of double counting is expected to be addressed, at least partially, through the mechanism to eliminate double taxation (see Chapter 7). This is because where an entity is allocated significant residual profit in a market jurisdiction under existing profit allocation rules, this entity may be identified as a "paying entity" within the group for the purpose of eliminating double taxation which would bear a portion of the Amount A tax liability (resulting in a "netting-off" effect). However, some members of the Inclusive Framework suggest that this approach on its own has a number of drawbacks:

- It may seem counterintuitive. As explored below, the mechanism to eliminate double taxation may address this issue through a "netting-off" effect, but fundamentally Amount A would still be allocated to a market jurisdiction that already has taxing rights over an MNE group's residual profits.
- It may be inconsistent with the overall rationale for Pillar One (and Amount A specifically) which has always been to adapt the income tax system where businesses, both ADS and CFB, have an active and sustained engagement in a market jurisdiction, but the existing profit allocation rules do not give that jurisdiction taxing rights over residual profits generated in that market. So, if Amount A did apply to businesses that already realise residual profits in the market, the problem Pillar 1 is trying to solve may not seem to be present.
- Applying the mechanism to eliminate double taxation (see Chapter 7) to decentralised businesses that realise residual profits in a large number of entities and jurisdictions will be complex. Specifically, it may be difficult to calibrate this system to ensure that a full-risk distributor (already allocated residual profit) is identified as the paying entity for the Amount A allocated to the jurisdiction in which it is resident. For this reason, it may be preferable to develop a method that would reduce pressure on the elimination system, allowing this system to focus on more centralised businesses where it will be comparably easy to identify the paying entities.

529. These challenges are variations on the same theme. Amount A can be easily rationalised when it is applied to businesses (both ADS and CFB) that realise residual profit in a handful of jurisdictions, but may be more difficult to rationalise and hence design when it is applied to businesses with less centralised business models that already leave residual profits in the market. It is also true that businesses have consistently pointed out that the ability to leverage off their existing systems that support their current in country distribution activities would seem simpler and would be very welcome. At the same time, discussions are ongoing on the issue of double counting, including on whether marketing and distribution profit allocated to a market jurisdiction under the ALP in excess of a fixed return may be seen as duplicative

with Amount A profit. This will include assessing the implications of considering the income taxes payable in the market jurisdiction under existing taxing rights and Amount A together.

530. Consequently, consideration is being given to different options to deal with issues of double counting beyond the mechanism to eliminate double taxation, such as the marketing and distribution profits safe harbour and the domestic business exemption.

6.4.1. The impact of the mechanism to eliminate double taxation

531. The elimination of double taxation process is an important element in dealing with any potential double counting in the market jurisdiction, or at least materially reduce it. This is because where an entity is allocated significant residual profit in a market jurisdiction under existing profit allocation rules, this entity may be identified as a "paying entity" within the group for the purpose of eliminating double taxation (see below Section 7.2). Identifying this entity as a "paying entity" for Amount A purposes will, in turn, result in a "netting-off" effect: the residual profit allocated under existing rules to the market jurisdiction will, in effect, be reduced by the method used to relieve double taxation from Amount A (including Amount A allocated to other market jurisdictions). There is a question however as to whether this framework can deliver such netting-off effect in all cases, and hence whether it should be the sole basis to deal with double counting issues.

532. As illustrated in Annex C (see Box C.3.), the netting-off effect can be easily identified when it is applied to an MNE group with a centralised business model (both ADS and CFB) that allocates residual profit to a limited number of jurisdictions, but is more difficult to assess when applied to a group with a decentralised business model that leaves residual profit in multiple market jurisdictions (see Annex C, Box C.4.). For example, the proposed mechanism to eliminate double taxation may not identify an in-market full-risk distributor entitled to residual profit under existing rules as a paying entity (or allocate to it the full responsibility for relieving double tax) if it does not meet the profitability test articulated in section 7.2.3, while other group entities (in different jurisdictions) would satisfy such test. Views differ as to the appropriate result in this situation. The efficiency of this approach on its own needs therefore to be further tested when applied to diverse situations, alongside with other approaches that could be developed in combination with this elimination of double taxation process to deal more effectively with double counting issues.

6.4.2. The marketing and distribution profits safe harbour

533. The "marketing and distribution profits safe harbour" would start from the premise that Amount A should be allocated to a market jurisdiction that is not allocated residual profits under existing profit allocation rules, but where a group already allocates and actually earns residual profit in the market on in-scope revenue then there should be no Amount A allocation. This would mean an MNE group would have to compute Amount A under the above rules, but would not allocate it to a market jurisdiction to the extent it already allocates and earns residual profit in that jurisdiction. The marketing and distribution profit safe harbour seeks to deliver this outcome. It would not be a traditional safe harbour, but would instead "cap" the allocation of Amount A to market jurisdictions that already have taxing rights over a group's profits under existing tax rules. Conceptually, it would consider the income taxes payable in the market jurisdiction under existing taxing rights and Amount A together, and adjust the quantum of Amount A taxable in a market jurisdiction, on the basis of limiting it where the residual profit of the MNE group is already taxed in that jurisdiction as a result of the existing profit allocation rules.

534. Under this approach, the basic mechanics of Amount A would be retained, and the formula itself would remain unchanged. A safe harbour return would be determined which would combine the residual profit that an MNE group would be expected to allocate to a market jurisdiction, with an additional fixed return to compensate the local marketing and distribution presence (more below). The safe harbour would

recognise that there are two ways that residual profits relevant to Amount A could be allocated to the market jurisdictions. All MNE groups would calculate Amount A and would then either benefit from the safe harbour or pay Amount A through the new Amount A system.

How would this safe harbour work in practice?

535. Where a group has a taxable presence in a market jurisdiction conducting marketing and distribution activities connected to locally sourced in-scope revenue (either a resident entity or a permanent establishment), the group would determine the profits allocated to the market jurisdiction under existing profit allocation rules for the performance of these marketing and distribution activities (the "existing marketing and distribution profit").[10] The MNE group would then compare the existing marketing and distribution profit with the "safe harbour return", which would be the sum of two components:

- Amount A, as computed under the Amount A formula; and
- A fixed return for in-country routine marketing and distribution activities, which could include a regional, and industry uplift.

536. The safe harbour return represents the cap, by reference to which the quantum of Amount A allocated to a market jurisdiction will potentially be adjusted. It would be applied by an MNE group on a market-by-market basis and would give rise to three possible outcomes:

- Where the existing marketing and distribution profit is lower than the fixed return, the MNE group will not be eligible for the safe harbour;
- Where the existing marketing and distribution profit exceeds the fixed return, but falls below the safe harbour return, the quantum of Amount A allocated to that jurisdiction would be reduced to the difference between the safe harbour return and the profit already allocated to the local presence; and
- Where the existing marketing and distribution profit exceeds the safe harbour return, no Amount A would be allocated to that jurisdiction.

537. In situations where an MNE group is eligible for the safe harbour in a market jurisdiction (second and third scenario above), it should be noted that it is possible that an entity resident in that jurisdiction may still be identified as a paying entity for Amount A allocated to other jurisdictions under the mechanism to eliminate double taxation if the other rules and requirements articulated in the Section 7.2, including potentially the market connection priority test, are met.

538. Further, in-scope MNE groups that, for commercial reasons (given their particular business models), operate without an existing taxable presence in a market jurisdiction or only allocate a relatively limited return (e.g. on a cost-plus basis) to local marketing and distribution activities, would not come under the safe harbour rule and thus would pay Amount A in the majority of market jurisdictions in which they operate. In contrast, more traditional CFB businesses, particularly those with decentralised business models and full-risk distributors, may already allocate profits to market jurisdictions that exceed the safe harbour return. Hence, though these businesses would need to calculate Amount A (to determine that they have met the safe harbour), they would in many instances ultimately not need to pay Amount A or apply the mechanism to eliminate double taxation. An example of its application is outlined in Annex C (see Box C.2.).

539. The safe harbour may be particularly relevant for decentralised businesses that realise residual profits in a large number of entities and jurisdictions, where it is conceptual challenging to identify the entity or entities within the group that should bear the Amount A tax liability. The adoption of the safe harbour may reduce in some cases the pressure of the mechanism to eliminate double taxation arising from Amount A and could allow the mechanism to eliminate double taxation to be developed with a focus on businesses with more centralised operating models that are less likely to be impacted by the safe harbour.

540. At the same time, the safe harbour would maintain the need to calculate Amount A, while introducing new rules to implement and administer the capping mechanism. Further, the application of the safe harbour would need to take into account any subsequent transfer pricing adjustments that changed marketing and distribution profits allocated to a market jurisdiction under the existing ALP-based profit allocation rules. For example, if a market jurisdiction made an upwards adjustment to the profits it was allocated for marketing and distribution activities, it would need to recalculate whether a MNE group would be eligible for the safe harbour, with any additional tax due under the existing profit allocation rules being offset against the tax that would no longer be due under Amount A.

Determining the fixed return for the safe harbour

541. Under the marketing and distribution profits safe harbour, the formula for calculating Amount A would remain unchanged. However, it would be necessary to determine a fixed return for in-country routine marketing and distribution activities. This will raise a number of technical and design challenges that will need to be addressed within the context of the safe harbour.

542. The fixed return would not necessarily seek to replicate an arm's length return, nor would it limit the profits allocable to marketing and distribution activities. Jurisdictions that are entitled to a higher return for the performance of marketing and distribution activities under the ALP would continue to be entitled to this return. Instead, this fixed return (which would only be relevant for large in-scope MNE groups) would act as a test to identify situations when allocating Amount A to a market jurisdiction would give rise to double counting.

543. For example, if the fixed return were set at a return on sales of 4%, it would mean that any profits allocated to a market jurisdiction in excess of this return would be deemed to duplicate the return allocated to a market jurisdiction under Amount A. So, if a market jurisdiction were allocated a 3% return under existing profit allocation rules it would receive a full allocation of Amount A, but if it were allocated a 5% return, its allocation of Amount A would be reduced by 1% (the difference between the return it receives under the existing profit allocation rules and the fixed return). If a lower fixed return were agreed, the safe harbour would apply to cap the allocation of Amount A more frequently than if a higher return were agreed.

544. The fixed return could be computed in a variety of different ways, but perhaps the simplest approach would be to agree a single fixed return on sales that would be applied to in-scope locally sourced revenue (as determined under the revenue-sourcing rules). This approach would draw on an existing component of the Amount A formula and would therefore avoid some of the challenges that would arise under a different approach, specifically in defining the base (e.g. sales or costs) to which a margin or mark-up would need to be applied.

545. Although the fixed return would not seek to be consistent with the ALP, it could be agreed that the fixed return could vary by region or industry (but probably not based on functions). For example, it may be argued that as pharmaceutical distributors are typically allocated a higher return under the ALP, the fixed return for pharmaceutical businesses could also be higher under the safe harbour. This would mean that a pharmaceutical business would need to allocate a higher return to a market jurisdiction under the existing profit allocation rules than a comparable business in another sector to benefit from the safe harbour. However, for simplicity it could also be agreed that there should be a single fixed rate applicable across all regions and industries.[11]

546. Hence, further consideration of this safe harbour will require additional work on a number of challenges, including for defining the fixed return for routine marketing and distribution activities.

6.4.3. The domestic business exemption

547. The development of a "domestic business exemption" to reduce the instances of "double counting" is also considered, together with the mechanism to eliminate double taxation and the safe harbour. There

are two potential types of domestic business exemptions. The first, and simplest, would exclude from the scope of Amount A large, domestically-focused business with a minimal level of foreign income. This would be implemented through the exemption of groups whose foreign source in-scope revenue falls below an agreed threshold from the scope of Amount A (see above section 2.3.2).

548. The second, more complex exemption, would seek to exclude from Amount A part of a group's business that is primarily or solely carried on in a single jurisdiction. This may occur for instance, where a group acquires a business operating in another jurisdiction that it does not subsequently integrate within its broader operations. In this scenario, it may be difficult to justify why Amount A should apply to this portion of a group's business, as it could result in the residual profits from this business, which are demonstrably only derived from one jurisdiction, being reallocated to other jurisdictions around the world. It could also result in residual profits generated from other parts of the business being allocated to the jurisdiction in question; despite the fact that the said jurisdiction already has taxing rights over the residual profits (to the extent they arise) associated with the relevant sales. Another possible view is that this is simply a logical consequence of the formulaic nature of Amount A applicable to the group as a whole.

549. The "domestic business exemption" would address some instances of double counting by excluding from Amount A profits derived from the sale of goods or services that are developed, manufactured and sold in a single jurisdiction.

550. There are two challenges that would need to be overcome to develop this domestic business exemption. First, it would be necessary for a taxpayer to isolate and segment out the profits of this standalone domestic business from the other activities of the group. This would require a remodelling of the segmentation framework that would increase complexity and the associated compliance costs and administrative burden. That said, on the assumption that the business is operated on a standalone basis, it may be relatively easy for the taxpayer to perform this additional segmentation.

551. Second, it is unlikely that there are many examples of MNE groups with completely standalone domestic businesses. This is because in most instances these businesses will be integrated to some extent in the broader activity of the group, whether through shared development of intellectual property (IP), intragroup financing activities, or other central services. For large CFB in particularly, royalty payments in relation to IP may be a significant expense in many market jurisdictions. Even where groups manufacture and sell goods in a single jurisdiction using local IP, these goods may include input purchased from a related party in another jurisdiction or produced using manufacturing know-how for which a licence fee is paid.

552. For this reason, if the exemption were only available for a portion of a group's business that was conducted in a single territory and had no transactions with related parties in other jurisdictions, it is unlikely that many, if any, MNE groups would be able to utilise it. Therefore, it would likely be necessary to develop a quantitative threshold to identify "domestic businesses" eligible for the exemption as those that retained over a given percentage (e.g. 90%) of the total profits derived from a market, or alternatively as those that derive only revenue sourced in their domestic market and have no or only limited transactions with related parties in other jurisdictions. This would create its own challenges. It would be difficult to reach agreement on the percentage of profits that would need to be retained in the market for the "domestic business exemption" to apply. Agreeing a single threshold would create a cliff-edge effect where a business just above the threshold would be excluded from Amount A, but a business just below the threshold would be not be excluded. If this threshold was applied on an annual basis, the domestic business could move in and out-of-scope of the exemption, creating additional complexity. Even calculating whether the threshold had been met would be difficult, as to determine the profits generated from a market, it would also be necessary to identify all the costs incurred in relation to that market, recognising that some could be incurred in other jurisdictions. This is likely to give rise to disputes over the allocation of shared costs, such as management expenses or global advertising campaigns. These issues mean that though the "domestic business exemption" is conceptually appealing, it may be very difficult to design in practice.

553. Setting aside these challenges, it is also important to emphasise that the "domestic business exemption" would only reduce the occurrence of "double counting". For example, it would not address situations where a market jurisdiction had taxing rights over the residual profits arising from the activities of a distributor not eligible for the "domestic business exemption". Therefore, the "domestic business exemption" could only be developed in combination with another mechanism to address double counting.

6.5. Next steps

554. As a first next step, drawing on the data and the analysis prepared as part of the impact assessment of different percentages for the profitability threshold (step 1) and the reallocation percentage (step 2), a decision of the Inclusive Framework members will be necessary to determine the quantum of Amount A, including whether the formula should incorporate any "differentiation mechanism". Relevant considerations in this discussion will include, for example, the amount of residual profit to be reallocated (including proportionality to compliance costs and administrative burden), the possible impact on this amount of residual profit of accounting for profit shortfalls (see section 5.4.6), and the number of MNE groups impacted. There will also be some remaining issues around questions of regional and jurisdictional segmentation.

555. In addition, further work will be required to assess the different options to deal with double counting (and their possible combinations), in close coordination with the work on the mechanism to eliminate double taxation (see Chapter 7). This will also include consideration of the interactions between Amount A and certain withholding taxes collected by market jurisdictions. For the safe harbour, issues where further work is required include:

- Assessing the implications of considering the income taxes payable in the market jurisdiction under existing taxing rights and Amount A together (e.g. whether marketing and distribution profit allocated to a market jurisdiction under the ALP in excess of a fixed return may be seen as duplicative with Amount A);;
- Defining the fixed return for routine marketing and distribution activities, including determining whether this return should vary by industry and/or region;
- Identifying and isolating the profit from marketing and distribution activities in the market jurisdiction that are covered by the safe harbour; and
- Developing a mechanism to deal with transfer pricing adjustments, lagged threshold permanent establishment claims or denial of deduction for shared costs that are made after the safe harbour has been applied in the market jurisdiction.
- Considering how common/prevalent the double counting issue is, and whether the practical and administrative challenges in designing the safe harbour are commensurate with this double counting issue; and
- Clarifying the treatment of withholding taxes collected by the market jurisdiction.

Notes

[1] Where a market jurisdiction is allocated profits for other activities, e.g. manufacturing, or marketing and distribution activities relating to out-of-scope revenue this would not be taken into account for the purposes of the safe harbour.

[2] For the purpose of calculating and applying Amount A, further work will be required to define the term "revenue" (see paragraph 515).

[3] see CTPA/CFA/WP2/NOE2(2020)10).

[4] see CTPA/CFA/WP2/NOE2(2020)10).

[5] For example, if a segment had total in-scope revenue of 80 (all of which was sourced to eligible market jurisdictions under the nexus rule) and 100 total revenue (including out of scope revenue), the allocation key would mean that only 80% of the Amount A tax base would be allocated to market jurisdictions under Amount A. The 20% would remain unallocated because it relates to revenue derived from out of scope activities.

[6] The calculation of Amount A already requires MNE groups to determine the total revenue used in computing the Amount A tax base (and where relevant attributable to each segment). Hence, only data on revenue sourced in one eligible jurisdiction would need to be verified to calculate a market specific Amount A tax liability under a throwback system. In contrast, under a throw-in system, the calculation would require verification of the revenue sourced in all market jurisdictions.

[7] Business models for MNE groups in ADS industries typically entail early and ongoing centralised development of intellectual property (IP) and the incurring of other costs aimed at developing the service offering as a whole, which then may be rolled out to new markets at limited marginal cost. Consequently, significant costs are centralised and the variation of profit between regions and jurisdictions is materially affected by the allocation of those costs to entities that operate in the various market jurisdictions and that benefit from the initial and ongoing development. This implies that regional or jurisdictional differentiation will be less relevant for ADS businesses.

[8] As noted above, the profitability threshold of the Amount A formula is designed to limit interactions between Amount A and existing taxing rights of market jurisdictions based on the ALP.

[9] It could also be argued that the interactions between Amount A and some withholding taxes could give rise to double counting, i.e. that a market jurisdiction would tax twice the same item of profit if they were allocated Amount A on top of certain existing withholding tax liabilities. For example, assume an entity in the MNE group outside the market jurisdiction is receiving a royalty payment from an entity in the market jurisdiction for the use of branding or licensing rights in respect of sales in that jurisdiction. Assume the royalty is subject to withholding tax in the market jurisdiction. If the royalty is contributing to residual profits, then the market jurisdiction can be seen as already taxing a share of this residual via the withholding tax. It is important to emphasise that members have different views on this issue, some consider that this interaction could give rise to double counting, whilst others argue that it does not.

[10] Where a market jurisdiction is allocated profits for other activities, e.g. manufacturing, or marketing and distribution activities relating to out-of-scope revenue, this would not be taken into account for the purposes of the safe harbour. Further rules may be required to determine the existing marketing and distribution profit (e.g. book-to-tax adjustments).

[11] The pharmaceutical industry typically has higher returns than most other industries and so even under a single fixed return approach, the total safe harbour return (i.e. Amount A plus the fixed return) would, when compared to other industries, still be relatively high for most pharmaceutical groups.

7 Elimination of double taxation

7.1. Overview

556. Amount A will apply as an overlay to the existing profit allocation rules. As the profit of an MNE group is already allocated under the existing profit allocation rules, a mechanism to reconcile the new taxing right (i.e. calculated at the level of a group or segment), and the existing profit allocation rules (i.e. calculated at an entity basis) is necessary to prevent double taxation.

557. This is the purpose of the mechanism to eliminate double taxation from Amount A described in this chapter. To reconcile the two profit allocation systems, it identifies which entity or entities within an MNE group bears the Amount A tax liability, which effectively determines which jurisdiction or jurisdictions need to relieve the double taxation arising from Amount A. This mechanism is based on two components: (i) the identification of the paying entity (or entities) within an MNE group (or segment, where relevant); and (ii) the methods to eliminate double taxation.[1]

Component 1: Identifying the paying entities

558. Amount A will be calculated at a group or segment-level using a simple formula, incorporating a profitability threshold and reallocation percentage. For this reason, it could be argued that a similar formulaic approach should be adopted to identify entities that will bear the Amount A tax liability (the paying entities[2]) for example, as those entities with a PBT to revenue ratio in excess of the agreed profitability threshold. The process to identify the paying entities will include a profitability test. However, there are two technical reasons why the profitability test applied at entity level cannot be the same test as that applied to the group:

- **Using the same formula to calculate residual profit at a group and entity-level could be distortive:** The most logical starting point for this profitability test would be to use the same formula used to calculate Amount A at a group or segment level (PBT / revenue, in excess of x%). However, there are two reasons why this approach is considered not appropriate. First, entity-level accounts include intragroup transactions that are eliminated on consolidation. As a result, the consolidated revenue of a group will be less (potentially substantially less) than the total (unconsolidated) revenue of entities within the group. This means that where a group has a profit margin in excess of x%, it is at least theoretically possible that there will not be any entities within that group with a profit margin in excess of x%. Second, the inclusion in entity-level accounts of intragroup transactions means that an entity's revenue and hence profit margin can be easily distorted or manipulated by the way intragroup transactions are structured.
- **Differences between local GAAPs of group entities:** At a group or segment-level, the use of consolidated accounts means that for most MNE groups the financial information necessary to compute the Amount A tax base and apply the Amount A formula will be readily available and prepared under a comparable accounting standard. In contrast, at an entity-level financial information will be less readily available, or may be prepared under local accounting standards, which means, even within the same group, the financial statements for different entities may not

be comparable. That said, as discussed below, this issue could be overcome by using the entity-level accounts used by a group to prepare its consolidated group accounts.

559. Conceptually, different approaches can be considered. For example, consistent with the formulaic nature of Amount A, one option would be to identify the paying entities using a quantitative approach similar to that used to calculate Amount A. This approach would prioritise simplicity, as it could limit the need to enter into detailed facts and circumstances functional and transactional analyses using transfer pricing concepts to identify the entities that should bear the Amount A tax liability. This would be consistent with the fact that Amount A itself is designed independently of these considerations. Another option would start from the basis that conceptually, the different features of Amount A suggest that paying entities should not only be profitable, but should be those that (individually or collectively) make material and sustained contributions to an MNE group's residual profits,[3] rather than those that perform only activities that generate routine profits. In addition, from a conceptual standpoint it could be argued that a paying entity should perform activities that relate to an MNE group's engagement in a market jurisdiction for which it bears an Amount A tax liability, as opposed to non-market related activities or activities that relate to other markets. These options could also be combined, in a variety of different ways, as outlined in the four-step process discussed below.

560. The process to identify the paying entities could have up to four steps.[4] These are to:

- **Step 1:** Identify the entities within an MNE group that perform activities that make a material and sustained contribution to the group's ability to generate residual profits.
- **Step 2:** Apply a profitability test to ensure the entities identified have the capacity to bear the Amount A tax liability.
- **Step 3:** Allocate, in order of priority, the Amount A tax liability to the entities that have a connection with the market(s) where Amount A is allocated.
- **Step 4:** Allocate, on a pro-rata basis, where no sufficiently strong connection(s) is (or are) found or where those with a market connection lack the necessary amount of profit.

Step 1: Activities test

561. An activities test would require that taxpayers undertake a qualitative assessment to identify the entities within the MNE group that make material and sustained contributions to a group's residual profits. This reflects the fact that conceptually, it is these entities within the MNE group collectively that should earn the residual profits corresponding to Amount A profit.

562. Practically, the activities test would include a general principle describing the type of relevant activities that a paying entity would be expected to perform, and this would be supplemented by a list of indicia that would support the application of this principle. These indicia would include the functions, asset and risk (FAR) profile of an entity, an entity's characterisation for transfer pricing purposes and the transfer pricing method used to determine the remuneration of an entity. Where possible, the documentation that taxpayers are already required to collect and report and that tax administrations already review will be used for this purpose.[5] These existing documents and any additional documents that may be required would be included in the single standardised documentation package that would be submitted as part of the Amount A tax certainty process. This should limit any additional compliance costs and administrative burden arising from this test.

563. As part of the activities test, where an MNE group computes the Amount A tax base on a segmented basis, it would be necessary to identify the potential paying entities that relate to each segment.

Step 2: Profitability test

564. The profitability test would ensure that the potential paying entities have the capacity to bear the Amount A tax liability. The profitability test would ensure that an entity making routine, low profits or losses is not identified as a paying entity, and is consistent with the decision of the Inclusive Framework to limit the application of Amount A to in-scope MNE groups that earn residual profits, rather than all in-scope MNE groups irrespective of their profitability. For simplicity, this profitability test could be aligned with the substance carve-out that is being developed for Pillar Two, where there will be a combined payroll and tangible assets profitability test.

565. In combination, the objective of the activities test and profitability test is to identify the entities that earn residual profits relevant to Amount A (as calculated at a group or segment level). The activities test, by incorporating concepts imported from transfer pricing, will identify entities within a group that derive residual profits from the performance of non-routine activities that relate to the engagement of the group in market jurisdictions. The profitability test, like the Amount A formula, will be applied to financial, rather than tax accounts. This will mean that the entities identified through these two steps will perform non-routine activities and report residual profits in their financial accounts.

Step 3: Market connection priority test

566. The application of the activities and profitability test (or the profitability test if applied on a standalone basis) will identify a pool of potential paying entities on an MNE group or segment basis (depending on the basis on which the Amount A tax base is calculated). However, there will be instances where these potential paying entities derive profits from only a limited number of market jurisdictions allocated taxing rights over Amount A. This is because an entity should only bear an Amount A tax liability that relates to a market jurisdiction(s) in which it is engaged. A market connection priority test could be introduced to require that, in the first instance, the Amount A tax liability for a market jurisdiction is allocated to a paying entity that is connected to a market jurisdiction through the performance of activities identified under the activities test. This test may establish a connection between a market jurisdiction and a single or multiple paying entities.

Step 4: Pro-rata allocation

567. Where the entity or (entities) identified under the market connection priority test do not have sufficient profits to bear the full Amount A tax liability for a given market jurisdiction(s), other paying entities within the group or segment will be required to bear the remaining portion of the Amount A tax liability. This portion of the Amount A tax liability would be apportioned between these entities on a formulaic pro-rata basis. This would provide a "back-stop" position where it is not possible to establish a sufficient connection between any paying entity and a market jurisdiction allocated Amount A. Consideration could also be given to alternative "back-stop" positions, as discussed in more detail below.

568. Under a two-step approach relying primarily on the profitability test, where more than one entity is found to meet the test, the Amount A tax liability would be apportioned among them on a pro-rata basis according to the amount of profits earned by each entity that exceeds the agreed profitability test.

Other issues

569. In addition, when identifying the paying entity, it may in some circumstances be necessary to take into account transfer pricing adjustments and entity-level losses as determined under domestic entity-level loss carry-forward regimes.

Component 2: Methods to eliminate double taxation

570. The second component of the mechanism to eliminate double taxation deals with the methods to eliminate double taxation. The application of these methods will ensure that a paying entity is not subject to tax twice on the same profits in different jurisdictions, once under the current CIT rules and once under the new Amount A system. Today, jurisdictions apply two main methods to eliminate international juridical double taxation, the exemption method and the credit method. Under the exemption method, a paying entity would simply exempt from taxation the portion of its profits that had been allocated to market jurisdictions under Amount A. Under the credit method, the residence jurisdiction of a paying entity would provide a credit against its own tax for the tax paid in another jurisdiction.

571. The Blueprint contemplates that tax on Amount A could be relieved by paying entities using either the exemption method or the credit method. Given the current tax rates in market jurisdictions, both methods may ultimately deliver the same outcome.

7.2. Component 1: Identifying the paying entities

572. Amount A will be calculated at a group or segment level using a simple formula, incorporating a profitability threshold and reallocation percentage. This section explains how this calculation of residual profit at a group or segment level (which is allocated to market jurisdictions under Amount A) is broken down to an entity level. This is necessary as the mechanism to relieve double taxation arising from Amount A operates at an entity rather than a group or segment level. The Blueprint uses an approach that combines tax and accounting concepts, as well as simplifying conventions, to identify the entities within the MNE group that earn the residual profit under existing tax rules corresponding to Amount A and that are therefore designated as paying entities for the purposes of Amount A.

573. It could be argued that the same or a similar formulaic approach used to determine Amount A should be adopted to identify entities that will bear the Amount A tax liability – the paying entities – for example as those entities with a PBT to revenue ratio in excess of the agreed profitability threshold.

574. The most logical starting point for this profitability test would be to use the same formula used to calculate Amount A at a group or segment level (PBT / revenue, in excess of x%). However, there are two reasons why this approach is not considered appropriate. First, entity-level accounts include intragroup transactions that are eliminated on consolidation. As a result, the consolidated revenue of a group will be less (potentially substantially less) than the total (unconsolidated) revenue of entities within the group. This means that where a group has a profit margin in excess of x%, it is at least theoretically possible that there will not be any entities within that group with a profit margin in excess of x%. Second, the inclusion in entity-level accounts of intragroup transactions means that an entity's revenue and hence profit margin can be easily distorted or manipulated by the way intragroup transactions are structured.

575. In addition, at a group or segment level, the use of consolidated accounts means that for most MNE groups the financial information necessary to compute the Amount A tax base and apply the Amount A formula will be readily available and prepared under a comparable accounting standard. In contrast, at an entity-level, financial information will be less readily available or may be prepared under local accounting standards, which means that even within the same group, the financial statements for different entities may not be comparable. That said, as discussed below, this issue could be addressed by using the entity-level accounts used by a group to prepare its consolidated group accounts. These factors mean that the test of profitability used at entity level in designating paying entities must be structured somewhat differently from that applied at group level in the determination of Amount A.

576. Conceptually, different approaches can be considered. For example, consistent with the formulaic nature of Amount A, one option would be to identify the paying entities using a quantitative approach similar to that used to calculate Amount A. This approach would prioritise simplicity, as it could limit the need to

enter into detailed facts and circumstances functional and transactional analyses using transfer pricing concepts to identify the entities that should bear the Amount A tax liability. This would be consistent with the fact that Amount A itself is designed independently of these considerations. Another option would start from the basis that conceptually, the different features of Amount A suggest that paying entities should not only be profitable, but should be those that (individually or collectively) make material and sustained contributions to an MNE group's residual profits, rather than those that perform only activities that generate routine profits. In addition, from a conceptual standpoint it could be argued that a paying entity should perform activities that relate to an MNE group's engagement in a market jurisdiction for which it bears an Amount A tax liability, as opposed to non-market related activities or activities that relate to other markets.

7.2.1. The process to identify the paying entities

577. There will be a process with potentially up to four steps to identify the paying entities. Step 1 will be an activities test that will identify entities within a group or segment that perform activities that make material and sustained contributions to an MNE group's ability to generate residual profits. Under Step 2, an MNE group will apply a profitability test to ensure the entities identified under Step 1 have the capacity to bear the Amount A tax liability. Step 3 will require that these paying entities have a connection with the market jurisdictions allocated Amount A, and that as a priority rule, the Amount A tax liability for these jurisdictions is relieved against the profits of these entities. Finally, if the entities connected to a market jurisdiction do not have sufficient profits to relieve the full Amount A tax liability, then the remainder will be apportioned on a pro-rata basis between other paying entities within the group or segment that do not have a connection to the relevant market jurisdiction. This will in effect provide a "back stop" where it is not possible to establish a "sufficient connection" between a market jurisdiction, allocated Amount A, and a paying entity with sufficient profits to bear the Amount A tax liability.

578. A two-step process could also be envisaged, whereby: a profitability test would be used to identify entities in the group that earn residual profits; and where more than one entity is found to meet the test, the Amount A liability would be apportioned among each entity on a pro-rata basis according to the amount of profits earned by each that exceeds the agreed profitability threshold.

7.2.2. Step 1: Activities test

579. An activities test would require that taxpayers undertake a qualitative assessment to identify entities within the group that make material and sustained contributions to an MNE group's ability to generate residual profits. This reflects the fact that conceptually these are the entities that should bear the Amount A tax liability It is important that the activities test is developed in a way that is clear and simple to apply in practice, and draws on the existing transfer pricing analysis and documentation prepared by MNE groups. By doing so it will limit the additional compliance costs of MNE groups. Nevertheless, any additional documents that may be required would be included in the standard Amount A documentation required for the tax certainty process. At the outset, it is important to emphasise that Amount A would only apply to large MNE groups, that meet or exceed a number of threshold tests and have in-scope revenue. This section outlines the concepts that could underpin the activities test and explains how this test could be applied in practice.

580. The transfer pricing master file and relevant local files prepared by MNE groups provide a first point of reference for the application of the activities test, taking into account that this documentation should describe an arm's length allocation of assets and risks based on the functional analysis of the MNE group. For many groups, particularly those with centralised operating models that perform the activities that make material and sustained contributions to an MNE group's ability to generate residual profits in only a handful of locations, the application of this test should be straightforward. For groups with a comparatively decentralised operating model, more entities may be identified under this test. However, where activities that make material and sustained contributions to an MNE group's ability to generate residual profits are

performed in market jurisdictions, the application of the marketing and distribution profits safe harbour may mean that these groups do not need to apply the mechanism to eliminate double taxation, or only need to do so for a limited number of jurisdictions. In any case, the application of the activities test, alongside all other parts of the mechanism to eliminate double taxation, will be covered by the Amount A tax certainty process. Within the Amount A tax certainty process, tax administrations would be able to request additional information from taxpayers and challenge their self-assessed application of the activities test. The Amount A tax certainty process will be important to ensure that any disputes arising from the application of this test are resolved in a timely manner and do not give rise to unrelieved double taxation.

Determining the activities

581. The conceptual development of the activities test requires the identification of the set of activities that are likely to make a material and sustained contribution to an MNE group's ability to generate residual profits, and potentially to specifically to identify the activities that relate to their engagement in market jurisdictions. The activities that relate to an MNE group's engagement in a market jurisdiction would extend beyond the ownership of (or entitlement to income derived from) relevant marketing intangibles and would, for example, include the ownership of (or entitlement to income derived from) product or technology intangibles that help to support sales as well as the oversight/control of economically significant risks and decisions relating to the business. As set out in more detail in section 7.2.4 the activities performed by an entity may relate to its engagement in a market jurisdiction, even where there is no direct transactional connection between a market jurisdiction and an entity.

582. The OECD Transfer Pricing Guidelines (TPG) identify a series of factors that may entitle an entity to participate in the residual profits generated by an MNE group for transfer pricing purposes that will also be relevant for identifying the paying entities. These include the following:[6]

- First, the paying entity should oversee some of the core strategic and operational activities that generate residual profits for the MNE group, and specifically exercise control and decision-making authority over key aspects of those activities. The activities identified should also relate to the MNE group's engagement with the market.
- Second, the activities of the paying entity will likely consist of the performance of some or all of the important functions related to the development, enhancement, maintenance, protection and exploitation of intangible assets of the MNE group that are specific to the MNE group's market engagement. This would include intangibles related to technology that facilitates market engagement, such as technology used in the ADS businesses to gather user data and content contributions.
- Third, a paying entity would perform the activities that would mean it should have the entitlement to some or all of the residual profits arising from valuable intangible assets that relate to the engagement of the MNE group with the market where they have been acquired and were not self-developed.[7]
- Fourth, the paying entity should both assume economically significant risks that relate to the MNE group's engagement in the market, and exercise decision-making functions and control over the assumption of those economically significant risks.[8] This would at least include (i) the capability to make decisions to take on, lay off, or decline a risk-bearing opportunity,[9] together with the actual performance of that decision-making function, and (ii) the capability to make decisions on whether and how to respond to the risks associated with the opportunity, together with the actual performance of that decision-making function. It may also include (iii) the capability to mitigate risk, meaning the capability to take measures that affect risk outcomes, together with the actual performance of such risk mitigation.

583. It may be considered that the provision of intragroup financing is not an activity that makes material and sustained contributions an ADS or CFB business' ability to generate residual profits, specifically as it

relates to their engagement in market jurisdictions. Therefore, the provision of intragroup financing alone would not be sufficient to identify an entity as a paying entity. The provision of an intercompany loan or guarantee, while representing an activity that would result in the assumption of an economically significant risk, relates solely to the assumption of financial risks and results in residual profits associated with financial risks being generated. This return is typically fixed and does not vary after the instrument/guarantee is entered into. Further, the return does not sufficiently relate to the performance of functions and the materialisation of risks related to non-routine activities in the market itself.[10] Alternatively, it could be argued that the provision of intragroup financing alone should be sufficient to identify an entity as a paying entity and that adopting this approach would require the design of the activities test to be revisited.

Practical application of the activities test

584. To facilitate ease of compliance and reduce complexity, the activities test is structured as follows. A general principle derived from the activities identified above will govern the identification of paying entities and will assist with clarifying the expected FAR profile of a paying entity. The application of this general principle, which will be based on concepts already included in the TPG, will be supported by a more specific list of indicia that will either positively identify features associated with a paying entity, or negatively identify features not associated with a paying entity. The identification itself will primarily leverage from the transfer pricing master file and local files of an in-scope MNE group.

585. The proposed general principle is to identify paying entities as "*the member or members of an MNE group (or segment) that perform functions, use or own assets and/or assume risks that are economically significant, for which they are allocated residual profits relevant to Amount A*". This principle seeks to reflect the types of activities that would be regarded as giving an entity the right to participate in a group's residual profit. As noted above, this general principle draws on a series of concepts that already form part of transfer pricing today.

586. The application of this general principle will be supported by a list of indicia that would make it easier for taxpayers and tax administrations to apply this general principle in practice. To limit compliance costs associated with applying these indicia, they will be based on information that taxpayers are already required to collect and report and that tax administrations already review. In particular, a group's master file and local file already include information on the functions performed, assets used and risk assumed by most entities in an MNE group.[11] These documents typically characterise the primary activities of an entity, information that is also collated for CbCR purposes. Finally, transfer pricing documentation identifies the transfer pricing method (or methods) that is used to establish whether the profits allocated to an entity are arm's length given its FAR profile. Hence, there are at least three indicia that could readily be used as part of the activities test. These are:

- The functions performed, the assets used and risks assumed by an entity;
- The characterisation of an entity, derived from existing transfer pricing documentation; and
- The transfer pricing method used to determine an entity's arm's length profits.

587. How would these indicia be applied in practice? An entity that is entitled to the entrepreneurial profit from exploiting key intangibles, from assuming economically significant risks; which is characterised as an entrepreneurial principal entity; and which should receive the residual profit according to the transfer pricing method (typically, but not always, in the form of a variable return), from a group's value chain would, under a positive approach, be identified as a potential paying entity. In this context, the characterisation of an entity and the transfer pricing method used to determine its arm's length profits should reflect and will be indicators of its FAR profile.

588. For example, an entity that makes unique and valuable contributions to activities that generate residual profits for the MNE group, and/or is entitled under the ALP to exploit and derive non-routine profit from intangible assets, and/or assumes or shares the assumption of economically significant risks, would

be caught under the first indicator. In the transfer pricing documentation, it would likely be characterised as an entrepreneurial principal entity, thus meeting the second indicator. The third indicator may show that the remuneration for such an entity is determined through a transactional profit split method (TPSM) or by taking residual profits after remunerating a routine-function, limited-risk entity through the TNMM or other methods. Such an entity would be identified as a potential paying entity and so would, through the positive approach, be included in the pool of potential paying entities.

589. In contrast, an entity that does not own key intangibles or manage economically significant risks; is characterised as a limited risk entity or contract service provider (such as, a sales agent); and receives a fixed, benchmarked return determined using, say, the TNMM or cost-plus method would not be identified as a potential paying entity and so would on a negative approach, be excluded from the pool of potential paying entities.

590. As part of the activities test, where an MNE group computes the Amount A tax base on a segmented basis it will be necessary to determine the segments within which a potential paying entity is part of. For example, if a pharmaceutical group applied Amount A separately for its pharmaceutical and consumer healthcare segments, then it will need to identify its paying entities on the same basis.

591. Further work will be undertaken by the Inclusive Framework to refine the activities test and, specifically, the general principle and list of indicia on which basis it would be applied. This will include determining the types of activities that a paying entity should perform or the intangibles it should own. This will include further work on specific issues, including:

- The guidance that should be included alongside the list of indicia, to facilitate the application of these indicia by taxpayers, including the interactions between the general principle and the positive and negative lists.
- The type of documentation that could be used to develop and ultimately apply the list of indicia, which will include the identification of any additional or improvements to documentation that may be requested as part of the standard Amount A documentation included within the tax certainty process and how this documentation can be shared through appropriate exchange of information (EOI) agreements.
- The feasibility and additional guidance that will be required to facilitate the segmentation on the basis of entity-level accounts, where required.
- The interactions between the application of the activities test and existing ALP-based profit allocation rules. For example, that there would be a requirement for taxpayers to take consistent positions for the purposes of the activities test and the application of ALP-based profit allocation rules, and whether tax administrations would retain the option to take inconsistent positions.

7.2.3. Step 2: Profitability test

592. The profitability test would ensure that the potential paying entities have the capacity to bear the Amount A tax liability. The profitability test would ensure that an entity making low profits (or losses) is not identified as a paying entity, and is consistent with the decision of the Inclusive Framework to limit the application of Amount A to in-scope MNE groups that earn residual profits (rather than all in-scope MNE groups).

593. In combination with the activities test, the objective of the profitability test is to identify the entities that earn residual profits relevant to Amount A (as calculated at a group or segment level). The activities test, by incorporating concepts imported from transfer pricing, will identify entities within a group that derive residual profits from the performance of non-routine activities that relate to the engagement of the group in market jurisdictions. The profitability test, like the Amount A formula, will be applied to financial, rather than tax accounts. This will mean that the entities identified through these two steps will perform non-routine activities and report residual profits in their financial accounts.

594. The Inclusive Framework is considering a profitability test aligned with the substance carve-out that is being developed for Pillar Two, which is based on expenditures for payroll and tangible assets (calculated by reference to depreciation expenses for certain assets including land).[12] In a Pillar Two context, the policy objective behind the carve-out is to exclude a fixed percentage of income from substantive activities within a jurisdiction. The use of payroll and tangible assets as indicators of substantive activities is justified because these factors are generally expected to be less mobile and less susceptible to lead to tax induced distortions. Conceptually, excluding a fixed percentage of income from substantive activities focuses Pillar Two on "excess income", such as intangible-related income, which is most susceptible to remaining BEPS risks. This objective may also be relevant when identifying the potential paying entities for Amount A, as Amount A has been designed to allow jurisdictions to retain sole taxing rights over the routine (or non-Amount A profits) of entities resident in their jurisdiction.

595. In an Amount A context, a profitability test would identify entities that earn income in excess of a fixed return for payroll and tangible assets. A combined test based on payroll and tangible assets would take into account the varying substance profiles of different types of entities, including labour-intensive and asset-intensive businesses. It would level the playing field by acknowledging the contributions of both employees and tangible assets to an entity's routine profits. Such an approach is preferable to a profitability test based on a single factor, either payroll or tangible assets, given that a single factor approach would favour entities performing one type of activities over another, though the Inclusive Framework will continue to explore other potential profitability tests.

596. There are two sources of readily available financial information that could be used to apply the profitability test outlined above, namely tax accounts and financial accounts. It would not be appropriate, however, to apply this test using tax accounts. This is because there are significant jurisdictional variations in how tax bases are determined, which means that, as an example, the design of a jurisdiction's R&D tax incentives would impact the reported profitability of an entity. Therefore, and to align with Pillar Two, the profitability test will apply based on entity-level financial accounts used by a group to prepare its consolidated accounts. These accounts will be prepared under IFRS or a comparable accounting standard used by the group to prepare its consolidated accounts. Such an approach will be more consistent than reliance on entity-level accounts prepared under domestic accounting standards (where there can be significant variation between jurisdictions).

597. Where a potential paying entity derives profits from more than one segment (as defined under the Amount A segmentation framework) it will be necessary to subdivide the entity-level accounts between these two or more segments in order to apply the profitability test. This is necessary to ensure that the different segments are not pooled together, which could result in an entity being inappropriately identified or not identified at alas a paying entity. Further, the definition of PBT developed to compute the Amount A tax base, will exclude dividend income and gains or losses from the disposal of shares, and may also exclude other types of income. To ensure symmetry between the computation of Amount A and the identification of the paying entities, the profitability test will need to be based on a comparable measure of PBT.

598. The Inclusive Framework will further review the relevance and application of the Pillar Two substance-based carve out, in the context of Pillar One, to determine whether any modifications to this test are required. It will also continue to consider other quantitative methods that could be used in combination with, or as an alternative to the profitability test outlined above. This includes a proposal to identify paying entities as those that earn in excess of an agreed percentage of an MNE group's profit, either on an individual or aggregate basis.

7.2.4. Step 3: Market connection priority test

599. The application of the activities and profitability test would identify a pool of potential paying entities on an MNE group or segment basis (depending on the basis on which the Amount A tax base is calculated).

There will be instances where these potential paying entities derive profits from only a limited number of market jurisdictions allocated taxing rights over Amount A. A simple example is a group that has two regional principals that are entitled to all the residual profits derived from their region. In this scenario, it could be argued that each regional principal should only bear the Amount A tax liability that arises in respect of the market jurisdictions from which it derives residual profits. Therefore, a market connection priority test could be introduced, whereby, in the first instance an Amount A tax liability for a given market jurisdiction would be relieved against the profits of a paying entity that performs, in relation to a given market, the activities identified as part of the activities test.

600. As Amount A will apply on a group or segment basis, without taking into account the profitability of different regions or sub-segments, this approach could result in situations arising where it is not possible to identify a paying entity that meets the profitability test. Returning to the example outlined above, there could be instances where one regional principal does not by itself earn the necessary quantum of Amount A. In this scenario, other paying entities within a group or segment will be required to bear the remaining portion of the Amount A tax liability (see Step 4: Pro-rata allocation below).

601. For each market jurisdiction allocated Amount A, a taxpayer will be required to determine which (if any) of the potential paying entities identified have a sufficient connection to be identified as a paying entity for that market jurisdiction. It will be possible to establish a direct or indirect connection between a market jurisdiction and a variety of different entities within a group. For example, an entity may sell goods or services to related or unrelated parties resident in that market; or, it may license intangible assets that are subsequently exploited in that jurisdiction. For the purpose of this test, it cannot be assumed that any connection between a paying entity and a jurisdiction will be sufficient to establish a connection for Step 3. Instead, this connection should be linked to the activities identified as part of the activities test.

602. For many groups it will be relatively straightforward to identify the paying entities connected to different markets. For example, where a single entity within the group has the global rights to exploit intangible assets and receives residual profits from every market jurisdiction, it will have a sufficient connection to every market jurisdiction. In contrast, where a group has a regionally centralised operating model, where different entities within the group have the right to exploit intangible assets and receive residual profits from the market jurisdictions within its region, then each of these entities will have a sufficient connection with the market jurisdictions in their region (but will not have a sufficient connection to market jurisdictions in other regions).

603. As a result, in many instances it should be relatively easy to establish a sufficient connection between a paying entity and a market jurisdiction. This is because most MNE groups will have legal entity structures and legal agreements that clearly document which entities in the group have the rights to exploit specific intangible assets in and receive residual profits from specific markets. For example, a legal agreement giving an entity the right to exploit an intangible in a region would provide evidence of a connection between that entity and market jurisdictions in that region. Similarly, the direct license of an intangible from an entity to a market jurisdiction would also provide evidence of a connection between a paying entity and a market. In many instances, this information will already be available to tax administrations through a group's master file or other transfer pricing documentation.

604. In the development of this priority rule it is important to highlight a number of design principles that will be relevant when defining what constitutes a "sufficient connection":

- The transactions that give rise to the connection should be linked to the activities identified under the activities test. For example, if an entity performs certain routine support services, in addition to non-routine activities that result in it being identified as a paying entity, there would not be a sufficient connection between that entity and a market jurisdiction that received only routine support services. Similarly, the provision of intra-group financing to an entity resident in a market jurisdiction would not be sufficient to establish a connection, as the performance of intra-group financing activities is not sufficient to identify an entity as a paying entity.

- A paying entity should derive profits that are ultimately connected to sales to third parties in a particular market jurisdiction. For example, if an entity receives a fee for the provision of manufacturing support services from a related party manufacturer, this would not be sufficient to establish a connection between the entity that receives the fee and the jurisdiction in which the manufacturer is resident (which may also be a market jurisdiction).
- It would not be necessary for a paying entity to have a direct transactional connection with a market jurisdiction. For example, where a royalty payment is made from a market jurisdiction to a conduit entity (that bundles together royalty payments from a variety of markets) and then pays them to an ultimate recipient, there could be a sufficient connection between the market jurisdiction and the ultimate recipient. The same would be true in the event of a chain of conduit entities.

605. The Inclusive Framework will undertake further work to develop this test and seek to analyse the types of arrangements and transactions that could be used to establish a sufficient connection between a paying entity and a market jurisdiction and the evidential basis through which these arrangements and transactions could be identified. It will also look at situations where a market jurisdiction may be sufficiently connected with multiple paying entities and explore whether there should be a hierarchy so that the Amount A tax liability would first be allocated to the paying entity with a direct or otherwise the "strongest" connection. To the extent that this paying entity did not have sufficient profits[13] to bear the full Amount A tax liability, it would then be allocated to the entity with an indirect or otherwise less "strong" connection until the tax liability had been fully allocated. Conversely, the Inclusive Framework will also consider whether in this scenario, the fairest and simplest approach would be to apportion the relevant Amount A tax liability between the paying entities with a sufficient connection to a market jurisdiction on a pro-rata basis (as explored in more detail in section 7.2.5).

606. These two approaches would deliver different outcomes. For example, assume that an MNE group has an operating model where a regional trading principal in Country A is entitled to the majority of the residual profits from a market jurisdiction and is determined to have the strongest connection to that market, but the ultimate parent entity in Country B (which performs some DEMPE functions in relation to intangibles owned and exploited by the regional trading principal) retains an entitlement to a small proportion of the residual profits from the relevant market jurisdiction. Under a hierarchical approach, the relevant Amount A tax liability would first be allocated to regional principal and would only be allocated to the parent entity where the regional principal did not have sufficient profits to bear the full Amount A tax liability. In contrast, under a pro-rata approach the relevant Amount A tax liability would simply be apportioned between the regional principal and parent entity on a formulaic basis assuming both have a sufficient connection with the relevant market jurisdiction.

607. Some Inclusive Framework members believe that there is a tension between calculating Amount A on a global basis and then requiring that profit allocated to a market jurisdiction to be paid by entities with which there is a market connection. These members support removing the market connection priority test and apportioning the Amount A liability between entities identified in Steps 1 and 2 on a pro-rata basis, as outlined under Step 4. To the extent that there are concerns about the profits of a regional principal being allocated to markets with which the regional principal has no transactional connection, these members think that these concerns should be considered as part of the debate on regional segmentation i.e. whether Amount A should operate on a geographically segmented basis in certain situations.

7.2.5. Step 4: Pro-rata allocation

608. As paying entities will only be entities that earn above a routine return, as defined under the Step 2 profitability test, it can be argued that after applying the mechanism to eliminate double taxation a residence jurisdiction should, at a minimum, retain taxing rights over this portion of routine profit. This is consistent with the rationale underpinning the inclusion of a profitability threshold in the Amount A formula. Therefore, a paying entity will be deemed to have no profits to bear a further Amount A tax liability, once

the taxing rights of the residence jurisdiction have been reduced to a routine return, as defined under the profitability test.

609. There is a risk that in some circumstances the paying entities that are sufficiently connected to a market jurisdiction (through the market connection priority test) will have insufficient profits to bear the full Amount A tax liability. This is in addition to situations (such as that outlined in the example above) where it may not be possible to identify a connection between any paying entity and a market jurisdiction. In order to ensure that the Amount A does not lead to double taxation, if the paying entities connected to a market do not have sufficient profits to bear the full Amount A tax liability, then as a "back-stop" any outstanding liability will be apportioned between all other potential paying entities within a segment.

610. This step could also be designed so that the residence jurisdiction retains taxing rights over a portion of a resident entity's residual profits. This could be delivered through this step, for example by deeming a paying entity to have no profits to bear a further Amount A tax liability after x% of their residual profits (as defined through the application of Step 2) had been allocated to market jurisdictions under Amount A.

611. Under either approach, the apportionment will be on a formulaic pro-rata basis. This formula will based on a paying entity's PBT in excess of routine profit (as defined under the profitability test) and/or the profitability of the entity (i.e. PBT / revenue). Both of these approaches would be designed so that the apportionment of the Amount A tax liability between paying entities will ensure that at a minimum the relevant residence jurisdictions retain taxing rights over the profits earned by any paying entity that are attributable to routine activities. Again, a paying entity will be deemed to have no profits to bear a further Amount A tax liability, once the taxing rights of the residence jurisdiction have been reduced to a routine return. If the market connection priority test were not adopted, due to perceived tensions with the global nature of Amount A, this pro-rata allocation could be used as the only method to apportion an Amount A tax liability between multiple paying entities.

612. This formulaic pro-rata approach (including the application of the market connection priority test) can be illustrated through two simple examples. First, assume for a given market jurisdiction two paying entities are identified under Step 3 with an equally strong connection to the relevant market and that after allocating each entity a routine return (based on the profitability test) the entities earn residual profits of 60 and 40 respectively. The first paying entity would bear 60% of the Amount A tax liability and the second paying entity would bear 40% of the Amount A tax liability for the jurisdiction in question. Second, assume that for a given market jurisdiction a single paying entity is identified under Step 3, but that after allocating this entity a routine return (based on the Step 2 profitability test) it has insufficient profits to bear the full Amount A tax liability of the market jurisdiction in question. In this scenario, the paying entity identified under Step 3 would bear the portion of Amount A tax liability that would reduce the taxing rights of the jurisdiction in which it was resident to the routine profits attributable to the entity. The remaining Amount A tax liability would then be apportioned between other paying entities within the group or segment that were not identified as having a connection to the market under Step 3 on a pro-rata basis.

613. There are other alternative or additional "back-stop" rules that could be considered and on which Inclusive Framework members have different views. One approach would be that where it is not possible to identify a paying entity connected to a market with sufficient profits to bear the full Amount A tax liability, the Amount A allocation to a market jurisdiction could be reduced or eliminated. However, others members consider that this would be conceptually inconsistent with the Amount A nexus and profit allocation rules, which would apply alongside and on an equal basis to the existing rules. Further, these members argue that this approach would place significant additional pressure on the application of Step 3 and would likely significantly increase the controversy surrounding the application of this step. An alternative could be that in this scenario the Amount A tax liability could also be relieved against the routine profits that would usually remain taxable in the residence jurisdiction, or that the Amount A tax liability would be carried forward and would only become payable in a market jurisdiction in future years when a paying entity connected to a

market had sufficient profits to bear the outstanding liability. It is acknowledged however that this would exacerbate the tensions that some members perceive to exist between the market connection test and the global basis for calculating Amount A, as referred to in 607. A further alternative would be to designate an entity (or entities) within the group as the paying entity of last resort. This could for example be the ultimate parent entity or an entity identified under the Global Anti-base Erosion Proposal (GloBE) as being subject to below an agreed minimum level of taxation. This approach could also be used to identify a paying entity in the unlikely event that no potential paying entities were identified following the application of Step 1 and Step 2 (outlined above). Alternatively, consideration could be given to the design of the steps before the pro-rata allocation which ensures that identified entities always have sufficient profits to bear the Amount A tax liability. If the development of such process is achieved, back-stop rules would not be needed.

7.2.6. Other issues

614. Discussions in the Inclusive Framework are ongoing on various other issues notably transfer pricing adjustments and entity-level losses. These discussions reflect some of the challenges that arise from integrating the new Amount A tax right into the existing tax system.

Transfer pricing adjustments

615. Tax administrations can make transfer pricing adjustments to increase the profits allocated to an entity to reflect the profits that would have been earned at arm's length. Typically, it can take tax administrations three to five years to make transfer pricing adjustments, due to the detailed audit work required to make an adjustment. When a tax administration makes a transfer pricing adjustment, a taxpayer can request, through the MAP, that a corresponding adjustment is made to reduce the taxable profits of the counterparty entity in another jurisdiction. The MAP process can again take a number of years to complete. This means there may be situations where a paying entity has its profits reduced through a corresponding adjustment. This may reduce its capacity to bear the Amount A tax liability (as determined under Step 3 or 4), or, in extreme cases, may mean it no longer satisfies the conditions required to identify it as a paying entity. [14] Transfer pricing audits may also lead to a reassessment of an entity's FAR profile, its characterisation for transfer pricing purposes and the transfer pricing method used to determine its arm's length profits, which may have an impact on whether the entity has been correctly identified (or not identified) as a paying entity.

616. In many instances, reductions to an entity's profits as a result of a corresponding adjustment will be small in relative terms, and it will not be necessary to take account of these adjustments for the purposes of Amount A. In addition, as part of the Amount A tax certainty process, the Inclusive Framework is considering how existing compliance processes could be used to reduce the likelihood of transfer pricing adjustments being made that have a significant impact on the identification of the paying entity (see Chapter 9). However, where these adjustments are "material", the mechanism to eliminate double taxation under Amount A will take this into account. It would be very challenging to make retrospective changes to the elimination of double taxation arising from Amount A, because this would require the reopening of the tax certainty process and the reassessment of the application of Amount A. However, it may be possible to make prospective adjustments, for example by adjusting the future Amount A tax liability of a paying entity based on a transfer pricing adjustment for a past period. Alternatively, in some instances it may be possible to consider whether the apportionment of the Amount A tax liability could be taken into account as part of the MAP, where for example a transfer pricing adjustment results in the transfer of profit between two paying entities. The Inclusive Framework will undertake further work to develop this mechanism, including a definition of what constitutes a "material" adjustment, (which may be framed as a relative threshold or an absolute amount – for example, a "material" adjustment may exceed x% of an entity's profits or EUR Xm). This work will also consider how transfer pricing adjustments can be taken into account where changes are made to an entity's tax accounts, but not their financial accounts.

Entity-level carried forward losses

617. The rules to compute the Amount A tax base will incorporate loss carry-forward rules that will be separate from existing domestic loss carry-forward rules. This group-level loss carry forward regime should ensure that most taxpayers continue to benefit from domestic loss carry-forward regimes at an entity-level. However, there may be situations where groups are required to allocate Amount A profits to market jurisdictions, even when some paying entities within the group have carried-forward losses under existing domestic rules. This may arise where a jurisdiction's domestic loss regime provides for the accelerated expensing of depreciation or amortisation expenses, or simply because there are some loss-making principal entities within a group that are profitable on a consolidated level.

618. To address these situations, it could be argued that domestic carry-forward losses should be accounted for when determining the paying entities for the purposes of Amount A. This would require a modification of Steps 3 and 4, to deem an entity to have insufficient profits to bear an Amount A tax liability when it has domestic carried-forward losses. This would avoid the risk that an entity bears an Amount A tax liability, even when it does not pay tax in the jurisdiction where it is resident due to domestic carry-forward losses. This outcome could be perceived as inequitable as it would, in effect, give market jurisdictions taxing rights over an entity, before a resident jurisdiction. It would also reduce the value to an MNE group of carry-forward losses, potentially discouraging investment.

619. However, developing rules to account for entity-level losses specifically would equally create fairness concerns if it resulted in a paying entity in one jurisdiction bearing the full Amount A tax liability of a group, because a paying entity in another jurisdiction has large amounts of carried forward losses, especially where the difference is simply the result of different loss carry forward rules in the two jurisdictions concerned. It could also create opportunities for manipulation. The risk of manipulation arises because there are situations where MNE groups can artificially generate carry-forward losses at an entity level. Therefore, if entity-level losses were to be taken into account in the process of identifying the paying entity, it may be necessary to develop additional protections to prevent this opportunity for manipulation, creating significant additional complexity for taxpayers and tax administrations. The Inclusive Framework is continuing to examine this issue.

7.3. Component 2: Methods to eliminate double taxation

620. The second component of the mechanism to eliminate double taxation concerns the methods to eliminate double taxation. The application of this method (or methods) will ensure that a paying entity is not subject to tax twice on the same profits in different jurisdictions, once under the existing profit allocation rules and once under Amount A. The identification of paying entities under Component 1 is structured such that the entities which earn residual profits under existing rules are designated as paying entities. The result is that the double taxation that will arise is juridical in nature (the taxation by two jurisdictions of one person on the same income). These paying entities are potentially subject to tax on the profits reflected in Amount A by both their jurisdiction of residence under existing tax rules and by the market jurisdiction which is given a new taxing right with respect to Amount A. This suggests the use of either the exemption or credit method would be appropriate. If the double taxation was economic in nature (where two persons are taxed on the same economic income), the reallocation method used under transfer pricing rules (effected by corresponding adjustments) would likely be more appropriate.

621. Today, jurisdictions apply two main methods to eliminate international juridical double taxation: (i) the exemption method (a version of which is found in Article 23 A of the OECD and UN Models); and (ii) the credit method (Article 23 B of the OECD and UN Models).

622. The exemption and credit methods are not simply different ways to deliver the same mechanical outcome. Under the credit method, the residence jurisdiction retains secondary taxing rights over the profits

of a paying entity where these profits are taxed in the market jurisdictions at a rate that is lower than the rate in the residence country. Whereas, under the exemption method, the residence jurisdiction would not retain secondary taxing rights over the profits of a paying entity because those profits are exempted or removed. However, as outlined below, the initial economic analysis of Pillar One estimates the current average rate of tax in market jurisdictions at 26% (noting, however, that rates may change over time) and, therefore, there will be meaningful secondary taxation rights only for jurisdictions with relatively high tax rates. The Blueprint contemplates that a jurisdiction will be able to opt for the exemption method or the credit method to relieve double tax arising on Amount A. Where both methods produce the same or a similar result, member jurisdictions would likely opt for the simplest method.

623. This chapter shows how either the exemption or credit methods could be used to eliminate double taxation arising from Amount A. In situations where a group has a local subsidiary in a market jurisdiction, an alternative "reallocation method" could be contemplated. Under this approach, the Amount A profit allocated to a market jurisdiction would be deemed to arise in the local subsidiary and an upward adjustment to its profits would be made for tax purposes, resulting in the local subsidiary being liable to pay Amount A. Double taxation would be relieved by providing a deduction or downward adjustment to the profits of the relieving entity. This deemed transfer of Amount A profits between these two entities would be similar to the economic double taxation relief mechanism under Article 9(2). For the relieving jurisdiction, this would deliver an equivalent outcome to the exemption method. For the local entity, however, it would be difficult to justify paying tax on the Amount A profits if the entity does not own those profits. Therefore, the MNE would likely want to make a secondary adjustment to actually transfer the Amount A profits to the local entity for legal and accounting purposes so that they align with the tax accounts. This accounting transfer, which might be characterised as a loan or a contribution of capital, and subsequent transactions to repatriate the profits may have secondary spill-over tax effects (for example, withholding tax) which would be considered undesirable. If the MNE group does not have a local subsidiary in the market jurisdiction, the relieving jurisdiction would still have to provide either a credit or exemption for Amount A tax in that jurisdiction. A reallocation method may also be difficult to adapt to (or undo many of the benefits associated with) the centralised and simplified administration system discussed in Chapter 10. For those reasons, the reallocation method does not appear to be appropriate to eliminate double taxation under the current design of Amount A and Component 1. But, as work progresses, new features may emerge which could demonstrate a benefit to using this method, and so it may be revisited in due course.

7.3.1. Exemption method

624. Under the exemption method, a paying entity would simply exempt from taxation the portion of its profits that had been allocated to market jurisdictions under Amount A.

625. This means that the exemption method would effectively eliminate double taxation arising from Amount A and would be relatively simple to apply. That is because a residence jurisdiction would not be required to determine the rate at which profits allocated under Amount A had been taxed, but simply identify the proportion of the relevant paying entity's profits that had been reallocated under Amount A.

626. While the exemption method may have the advantage of simplicity in certain cases, there will be a broader set of considerations taken into account when deciding which method to apply, including the absence of secondary taxing rights under the exemption method[15] and the possibility that taxpayers could have less tax to pay overall under the application of the Amount A system with the exemption method (considered below). Further technical work will be done to identify the advantages and disadvantages of these two methods.

7.3.2. Credit method

627. Though more complex than the exemption method, certain jurisdictions may have a preference for using the credit method to relieve double taxation of Amount A.

628. Under the credit method, tax applied to Amount A in the market jurisdictions would be available as a tax credit to the paying entity or entities. The available credit would then be capped at the lower of the tax applied in the market jurisdiction and the tax that would have been paid on the Amount A allocation in the relieving jurisdiction. Considerations for a jurisdiction that would want to opt for the credit method are described below.

Per jurisdiction or blended limit

629. The Blueprint contemplates that the credit method could potentially be applied either jurisdiction by jurisdiction, or using a blended approach. Under a jurisdiction-by-jurisdiction approach, the limit on the available credit is determined by comparing the tax that would have been paid in the relieving jurisdiction to the tax applied to Amount A in each market jurisdiction separately. If a blended approach applies, the limit on the available credit would be determined by comparing the tax that would have been paid in the relieving jurisdiction to the tax applied on the total Amount A liability allocated to each paying entity. A blended approach would permit tax applied to Amount A in low tax markets to be blended with tax paid on Amount A in high tax markets (this approach could be referred to as a "blended cap"). Jurisdictions operating a blended cap will typically provide a higher level of relief for double taxation on Amount A than those operating a per jurisdiction cap. The net effect of applying a blended cap may not be dissimilar to the effect of applying the exemption method where the tax that would have been paid in the relieving jurisdiction is lower than the weighted average tax rate applied to Amount A in the market jurisdictions.

630. It could be argued that the operation of a blended cap more closely reflects the multilateral nature of Amount A, although it is noted that the operation of the market connection priority test should facilitate the operation of a per jurisdiction cap. In order for the credit method to apply on a per jurisdiction basis, it will be necessary to first identify specific market jurisdictions where a paying entity incurs an Amount A tax liability. This will be possible where a connection is established between a specific market jurisdiction and paying entity under the market connection priority test. In this scenario it would be possible to operate the cap on a per country basis.

631. Where a market jurisdiction's Amount A tax liability is simply allocated between paying entities on a pro-rata basis, the per jurisdiction cap would be applied by reference to the amount allocated to each paying entity on a per jurisdiction basis.

Secondary taxing right

632. One of the main benefits of applying the credit method for relieving jurisdictions is that secondary taxing rights remain available to the residence state. However, as mentioned above, the value of such a right is expected to be relatively limited as it is expected that the average rate applied to Amount A would be relatively high. With a view to testing this position, some initial analysis was undertaken to compute the average CIT rate across market jurisdictions. That initial analysis indicated that for ADS, the average CIT rate in market jurisdictions based on the data would be at present 26.0%, and for CFB it would be 26.3%. Under such scenario, and noting that rates may change overtime, a jurisdiction with a CIT rate below 26% would have no additional collected under the secondary taxing right in respect of Amount A if the credit method is applied using a blended cap.[16] Where the credit method is applied using a per jurisdiction cap, some additional tax may be collected by relieving jurisdictions with lower tax rates.

Outcome for MNE

633. Another argument made in favour of the credit method over the exemption method is that the exemption method could put taxpayers in a better position than before if the profits allocated to market jurisdictions were taxed at a lower rate in the market jurisdiction. Under the exemption method, taxing rights on residual profits are moved from relieving jurisdictions to market jurisdictions. If the tax rates in relieving jurisdictions are higher than the tax rates in market jurisdictions, globally the MNE group may be paying less tax under Amount A with the exemption method than it would under existing rules. However, the initial economic analysis on average tax rates referenced above would tend to indicate that this should not be a significant risk. Further, since Amount A is intended to effect a transfer of taxing rights to market jurisdictions, and some jurisdictions do not view this transfer as conditional on the level of taxation in the market, if in a particular case it results in a reduction in tax, this is not necessarily an inappropriate result.

Differences in sourcing rules

634. Another consideration for applying the credit method is that domestic foreign tax credit regimes tend to have "sourcing" rules that can result in part of the income that was taxed in the source country being regarded as domestically sourced income in the country of residence. As a result, double taxation can arise and go unrelieved.

635. Amount A will be agreed multilaterally under a single system along with the Amount A allocations to market jurisdictions and the Amount A that should be relieved by each relieving jurisdiction. Given the multilateral nature of Amount A, there should be no opportunity for having different domestic legislation and sourcing rules that would lead to unrelieved double tax on Amount A.

Information requirements

636. Another consideration when using the credit method to relieve double taxation on Amount A is that more information is required by the jurisdiction providing the double tax relief in relation to the tax treatment of Amount A in the market jurisdiction (for example, the applicable rate in the market jurisdiction) than is required to apply the exemption method.

7.3.3. Facilitating use of both methods

637. Allowing jurisdictions to select which of the two methods they would apply to relieve double taxation would introduce some additional complexity.

638. Where jurisdictions are permitted to select the method, once the paying entities of an MNE group were identified (through the process outlined in Component 1), the method to eliminate double taxation adopted by the jurisdiction in which a paying entity was resident would apply. So if the group identifies two paying entities – the first resident in a jurisdiction that applies the exemption method and the second in a jurisdiction that applies the credit method – in the first jurisdiction, the profits of the paying entity would be exempt from tax. But the second jurisdiction would tax those profits and provide a credit against that tax for the tax paid in eligible market jurisdictions.

639. MNEs typically operate a multitude of credit and exemption methods in their tax returns and while the possibility of an MNE group having to operate two methods will involve an amount of additional complexity, it would be incremental only. No paying entity would be required to operate more than one method of relief in respect of Amount A as each jurisdiction would be required to select one method only.

640. It is noted that if an MNE considers that one method produces more favourable outcomes, there may be a risk that it could seek to manipulate the application of Component 1 so that paying entities in jurisdictions that operate that method are identified. At the same time, the operation of the rules outlined in Component 1 is not anticipated to provide scope for manipulation and will be subject to the tax certainty

process which should go some way to alleviating any such concern. However, this issue will be further explored.

7.3.4. Conclusion on the choice of a method

641. The exemption and credit methods may ultimately deliver similar outcomes. But some jurisdictions have a strong preference for one method over the other and so it is expected that both the credit and the exemption method should be available to jurisdictions to eliminate double tax on Amount A.

7.3.5. Other technical issues

642. Technical issues that require further work include:

- ***Interaction of Pillar 2 and the application of the exemption method.*** Further analysis must be undertaken on how Pillar 2 might impact an MNE group where the exemption method is used to eliminate double taxation on Amount A.
- ***Interaction of the methods with existing domestic law.*** Further consideration must be given to how the methods will interact with existing domestic rules governing relief of double tax.
- ***Interaction of the method and the centralised and simplified administration system and the tax certainty process for Amount A.*** Further work will involve the examination of the application of each of the methods in the context of other work streams such as the centralised and simplified administration system and the tax certainty process for Amount A covered in Chapters 9 and 10.
- ***Interaction between Amount A and certain withholding taxes collected by market jurisdictions.*** As noted in Chapter 6 (see section 6.4), further work will consider the interaction between Amount A and its double tax relief system and withholding taxes by which market jurisdictions may already be taxing a share of residual profits and how any double counting that might arise can be resolved.

7.4. Application of the marketing and distribution profits safe harbour

643. The application of the marketing and distribution profits safe harbour would adjust (and in some cases reduce to zero) the quantum of Amount A allocated to market jurisdictions where an MNE group has an existing marketing and distribution presence. This may give rise to the question of whether an MNE group could choose to adjust their transfer pricing in order to access the safe harbour and use their transfer pricing system as an alternative mechanism to eliminate double taxation.

644. In addressing this question, it is important to emphasise that the marketing and distribution profits safe harbour is not an alternative way to allocate Amount A to a market jurisdiction, but rather a method to determine whether allocating Amount A to a market jurisdiction would give rise to double counting. Correspondingly, where an MNE group already allocates the safe harbour return to a market jurisdiction under the existing profit allocation rules, there would be no allocation of Amount A, and hence no need to apply the mechanism to eliminate double taxation.

645. The principle-based nature of ALP-based profit allocation rules means that the safe harbour contains some limited flexibility for an MNE group to increase the profits it allocates to a market jurisdiction and correspondingly reduce (or even eliminate) a potential Amount A tax liability. However, the safe harbour would not permit a group to use transfer pricing to allocate profits to a market in excess of an arm's length amount. For market jurisdictions where the safe harbour return is not met, a taxpayer would be required to rely on the Amount A mechanism to eliminate double taxation in order to identify the paying entities and relieve double taxation. For example, where MNE groups have adopted limited risk distribution structures, it may not be feasible to increase the profits of such entities so that the quantum of Amount A

would be allocated through the transfer pricing system, as the entity characterisation and transfer pricing method would not allow for non-routine profits to be allocated to a limited risk distribution entity.

646. It should also be noted that where an MNE group meets the marketing and distribution profits safe harbour in a given market jurisdiction, this should not prevent an entity resident in that jurisdiction being identified as a paying entity for other jurisdictions. Though the non-allocation of Amount A in this scenario could be seen to disadvantage a jurisdiction, this is in fact not the case.

7.5. Next steps

647. For Component 1, the process to identify the paying entities, the Inclusive Framework will need to make a final decision on the design of the tests outlined above. This will include agreeing the elements of the tests and the ordering and design of their various components. Further work will also be undertaken on specific aspects of Component 1, including:

- the set of activities included in the positive and negative lists;
- the practical application of the profitability test;
- the practical aspects of implementing a market connection priority test; and
- Consideration of other back-stop positions for any remaining Amount A tax liability not allocated after application of the process

648. For Component 2, the method to eliminate double taxation on Amount A, further work will be required to provide guidance to jurisdictions in selecting and applying each method and, in particular to:

- analyse the interaction of the application of methods to relieve tax on Amount A and Pillar 2;
- consider the interaction between the methods to eliminate double taxation and existing domestic law;
- consider the interactions between Amount A and certain withholding taxes collected by market jurisdictions; and
- examine the application of each of the methods with other work streams including the centralised and simplified administration system and the tax certainty process.

Notes

[1] Under the marketing and distribution profits safe harbour, an MNE group would not be required to allocate Amount A to market jurisdictions, where doing so would duplicate a jurisdiction's existing taxing rights over the residual profits of the group. In this scenario, there would be no allocation of Amount A, and hence the mechanism to eliminate double taxation arising from Amount A would not apply. Instead, an MNE group that meets the safe-harbour with respect to a particular market jurisdiction remains subject to the existing profit allocation and nexus rules.

[2] The "paying entities" are the entities that will bear the Amount A tax liability and hence the jurisdictions in which they are resident will be required to relieve the double taxation arising from Amount A. These entities will not necessarily be required to physically pay the Amount A tax liability in each market jurisdiction, as the simplified administration system may allow a single entity within a group to pay the Amount A tax liability (as agent) to each market jurisdiction (see Chapter 10).

[3] At the level of a group or segment, the term "residual profit" for Amount A purposes refers to profit in excess of an agreed profitability threshold (see above Chapter 6). This differs from the transfer pricing concept of "residual profits", which are the profits (or losses) that remain after remunerating activities that

can be reliably benchmarked using comparables. Unless specifically noted, the term residual profits used in this chapter refers to profit in excess of the profitability threshold pursuant to the Amount A formula.

[4] For ease of reference, the rest of this Blueprint will refer to paying entities (in the plural), though in some instances there may be only one paying entity for a group or segment.

[5] This will include a group's master file, relevant local files, CbCR and other transfer pricing documentation that groups may already prepare. It is recognised that at present this documentation may not be available in all jurisdictions that would be impacted by Amount A, but this can be addressed within the context of the tax certainty process contemplated for Amount A (as discussed in Chapter 10).

[6] OECD (2017), *Transfer Pricing Guidelines for Multinational Enterprises and Tax Administrations*, OECD Paris, paragraphs 1.60, 1.61, 6.51 and 6.56 constitute primary sources of reference, together with further examples derived from the concepts outlined.

[7] The ownership of assets and/or provision of funding alone is not sufficient in this sense, but the entitlement to residual profits from exploiting intangible assets that have been acquired is an indicator of the performance of the value-adding activities, including the DEMPE functions.

[8] Risk is not considered in isolation, but is directly associated with decision-making authority over the potentially residual profit-generating activities of the group.

[9] Inclusive of the deployment of capital in relation to the same.

[10] The return to financing activities is affected by the performance of activities in the market if the performance of the borrower in the market is such that a default or other credit event materialises; however, the financing activity does not sufficiently relate to the actual performance of the in-market borrower. This is to be distinguished from situations where an entity provides decision-making control over commercial and operational functions and the assumption of risks that drive the performance of the in-market entity.

[11] It is recognised that not all jurisdictions require taxpayers to file this information with tax administrations contemporaneously, however, in most instances it would still be expect that they would hold much of the information required on file internally.

[12] See chapter 3 (section 3.7) of GloBE rules.

[13] It is not intended that under Amount A, taxing rights over an entity's entire profits would be allocated to a market jurisdiction. Instead, as discussed further in paragraph 608 at a minimum a resident jurisdiction should retain taxing rights over an entity's routine profits, as determined under the profitability test.

[14] While the profitability test starts with the financial accounts, corresponding (or tax) adjustments will typically be made in the tax account. Further work is therefore required to align this issue.

[15] For example, if the rate of tax in the relieving jurisdiction is 28% and the average rate of tax in market jurisdictions is 26%, an exemption from tax will, in effect, be worth 28% of the exempted income while a foreign tax credit would normally be capped at 26%.

[16] The rates used in the analysis were the statutory CIT rates, combining national and subnational rates, in 2019, based primarily on OECD Corporate Tax Statistics. The average was weighted by the estimated amount of MNE sales into each jurisdiction, so that larger markets have more influence over the average than smaller markets. This is an average computed across all MNEs, and individual MNEs could face lower or higher average rates depending on the exact location of their sales.

8 Amount B

8.1. Overview

649. Amount B aims to standardise the remuneration of related party distributors that perform "baseline marketing and distribution activities" in a manner that is aligned with the ALP. Its purpose is two-fold.

650. First, Amount B is intended to simplify the administration of transfer pricing rules for tax administrations and reduce compliance costs for taxpayers. Second, Amount B is intended to enhance tax certainty and reduce controversy between tax administrations and taxpayers. In these ways, Amount B has the potential to address certain challenges that tax administrations face in evaluating the arm's length nature of the pricing of distribution arrangements adopted by MNE groups. Distribution arrangements constitute an area of concern for tax administrations and taxpayers alike and are a frequent focus of domestic transfer pricing controversy. They are often the subject of dispute between tax authorities, and require settlement under the MAP[1] provided for in bilateral tax treaties. For these reasons, many governments and businesses view improvements in this area as a key deliverable of Pillar One, on the presumption that the design features of Amount B are such that these key benefits may be realised in practice.

651. This chapter sets forth the framework that would enable the implementation of Amount B. It starts with a discussion of the entities and transactions that are anticipated to be in scope. Next, it proceeds to outline the way in which the in-scope baseline activities would be defined.[2] It then turns to the assessment of the quantum of Amount B and finally considers the implementation of Amount B.

652. It currently assumes that distribution and marketing activities would be identified as in scope based on a narrow scope of baseline activities, set by reference to a defined 'positive list' and 'negative list' of activities that should and should not be performed to be considered as in scope. Quantitative indicators would then be applied to further support and validate the identification of in-scope distributors. Pending further technical work to be performed, it is anticipated that Amount B could be based on a return on sales, together with potentially differentiated fixed returns to account for the different geographic locations and/or industries of the in-scope distributors. Further technical work is also required to both define the precise calculation of the return on sales and the in-scope geographic locations and industries. But given the narrow scope of Amount B, there is currently no provision for Amount B to increase with the functional intensity of the activities of in-scope distributors.[3] Finally, Amount B would not supersede advanced pricing agreements (APAs) or MAP settlements agreed before the implementation of Amount B.

653. Under one proposal, the implementation of Amount B would operate under a rebuttable presumption: namely that an entity that acts as a buy/sell distributor and performs the defined baseline marketing and distribution activities qualifying for the Amount B fixed return would render it in scope – but that it will be possible to rebut the application of Amount B by providing evidence that another transfer pricing method would be the most appropriate to use under the ALP.[4] The burden of proof for this will rest with the taxpayer. For example, the presumption would be rebuttable if a sufficiently reliable CUP was available, which under specific circumstances would be the most appropriate transfer pricing method to use. As the Amount B fixed return will be set by reference to a narrow scope of baseline activities and

determined through a benchmarking analysis based on third party comparables, it is intended to approximate results determined under the ALP [5] and hence with existing domestic and treaty law.[6]

654. While a group of Inclusive Framework members prefer a narrow approach, which is discussed in detail in this chapter, another group of Inclusive Framework members wish to have a broader scope – e.g. one that provides for standardised remuneration also for commissionaires or sales agents, or for distribution entities whose profile differs from the baseline marketing and distribution activities just mentioned. Such a broader scope would also raise issues that would require further work, including how to reconcile the fixed return profile for these activities with the ALP.

655. Further, some Inclusive Framework members have expressed an interest to see Amount B first delivered in a pilot programme, which would have the objective of evaluating whether Amount B can meet its aims of simplification and reduced disputes, would allow for monitoring of behavioural change of MNE groups in response to the implementation of Amount B, would allow for phased introduction in Inclusive Framework member jurisdictions and would entail an assessment of the ease of implementation on a phased basis. The means of implementation of Amount B and the potential implementation of a pilot programme is subject to further technical work and discussion between the members of the Inclusive Framework.

656. As a next step, the members of the Inclusive Framework will need to decide how to proceed with Amount B, in particular regards the question of using a narrow or a broader scope. In addition, further technical work will need to be undertaken to set the fixed return profiles for the defined baseline activities, including establishing the benchmark for the to-be-defined profit level indicator, and accounting for the agreed-upon regions and industries in scope. In this task, it will be possible to draw on the wider work currently undertaken by the Forum for Tax Administration (FTA) MAP Forum and the FTA.

8.2. Key design features of Amount B

657. The key design features of Amount B cover: (i) scope, (ii) quantum and (iii) implementation. This section provides an update on the progress made for each of these features.

8.2.1. Scope

658. As Amount B would apply to the enterprises of MNE groups that perform the defined baseline marketing and distribution activities in a market under an accurately delineated transaction[7], it is not subject to the scope limitations of Amount A. The accurately delineated transaction should consider the five comparability factors outlined in Chapter I of the OECD Transfer Pricing Guidelines. In particular, the functions performed, assets owned and risks assumed in the accurately delineated controlled transaction should be similar to those identified as being within the baseline marketing and distribution activities. Accordingly, it is necessary to define what controlled transactions and baseline marketing and distribution activities would qualify for the fixed return which is Amount B. In particular, defining the baseline marketing and distribution activities will be achieved by reference to a positive and a negative list of qualitative factors that closely relate to the performance of marketing and distribution activities, with further reference to a set of quantitative indicators that relate closely to the performance of these activities.

Definition of entities and transactions covered by Amount B

659. Amount B is the remuneration of group enterprises resident in (or in the case of a permanent establishment[8] located in) a market jurisdiction (either a subsidiary or a permanent establishments of a foreign party) that perform baseline marketing and distribution activities for the distribution of products for the MNE group (hereinafter, "distribution entity").[9]

660. The controlled transactions in scope could consist of:

- The purchase of products from a foreign associated enterprise for resale to unrelated customers predominantly[10] in its country of residence, and the associated performance of defined baseline distribution activities; and
- The performance of the defined baseline marketing and distribution activities by the distribution entity in its state of residence, transacting or dealing with a foreign associated enterprise.[11]

661. An accurate delineation of the controlled transaction, taking into account all of the relevant comparability factors inclusive of the functional analysis on which the defined in-scope activities are based, will determine whether a distribution entity is engaged in a transaction in scope of Amount B. Accordingly, the guidance in Chapter I of the OECD TPG will be relevant for purposes of identifying entities in an MNE group that are within scope of Amount B. No assumption is made about the functional profile of a distribution entity based on how it is labelled or characterised by the MNE of which it is a member.

662. Amount B would apply to a distribution entity that, according to the accurate delineation of the transaction, performs functions, owns assets and assumes risks that would characterise it as a routine distributor at arm's length.[12]

Definition of baseline activities and negative indicators

663. For simplicity of administration and to limit the potential for disputes over what is in the scope of Amount B, the in-scope baseline marketing and distribution activities are first defined by reference to a list of typical functions performed, assets owned and risks assumed at arm's length by routine distributors.[13] This 'positive list' is based on a narrow scoping definition that aims to qualitatively measure the profile of typical routine distributors. Second, a 'negative list' of typical functions that should not be performed, assets not owned and risks not assumed at arm's length by routine distributors are included to qualitatively measure the additional factors that would cause a distributor to be outside the scope of Amount B. Taken together, the positive and negative lists demonstrate the qualitative indicia of the baseline activities and risk assumption expected of a distribution entity within the scope of Amount B.

664. Certain quantitative indicators would also be used to further support the identification of in-scope activities, and are described in the next section. The qualitative factors and quantitative indicators are used together to test if a distribution entity is in scope.

665. If the accurately delineated transaction results in a characterisation of the in-market enterprise as a routine marketing or sales support service provider[14] (i.e. performing fewer functions and assuming less risk than is defined under the baseline marketing and distribution activities) then it would not fall within the scope of Amount B and the return should be measured by the ALP as it applies today.[15] In the same way, if the accurately delineated transaction results in a characterisation of the in-market enterprise as performing more than routine functions and assuming more than routine risks than are defined under the baseline marketing and distribution activities, the remuneration commensurate with such activities and risks will also be outside the scope of Amount B.

666. Typically, an in-scope distribution entity would perform at least sufficient activities for it to be characterised as a routine distributor for which the return on sales profit level indicator would be appropriate at arm's length. For this purpose, the guidance on the functional analysis in Section D.1.2 of Chapter I of the TPG will be relevant. It should be noted that the required sufficiency of functions performed, assets used and risks assumed in performing the baseline marketing and distribution to be considered as in scope is subject to refinement through further technical work, as is the definition of functions, assets and risks themselves as well as the meaning of terms such as "limited" or "routine" when referring to them.

Functions

667. The baseline marketing and distribution functions typical of the performance of distribution activities by distribution entities in scope of Amount B may include:

1. Importation of products for resale within the market[16] and customs clearance, including charge of freight, insurance and customs costs;
2. Purchase of goods for resale within the market; Development and execution of sales budgets and plans within the market, within the MNE group's guidelines and under its oversight and/or subject to the MNE group's approval;
3. Development and maintenance of local customer relationships within the market;
4. Determination or negotiation of pricing and other contract terms with third party customers, within the MNE group's pricing guidelines or price lists and under its oversight or approval where necessary (e.g. to adapt based on market demand, competition and currency, or to allow certain discounts);
5. Processing of orders and contracts with customers; Inventory: monitoring and routine management of inventory (e.g. on the books or by means of joint systems or by receiving regular updates from an entity providing storage and logistics services);
6. Management of logistics, warehousing and transportation of products to customers (which includes situations when these are outsourced to another entity);
7. General administration functions, e.g. sales invoicing, process and collection of payments, accounts, and financial and tax reporting obligations;
8. Routine input into demand planning activities undertaken by the MNE group; and
9. Marketing activities:
    a. Pre-sale services: provision of product information to prospective customers (e.g. product demonstrations);
    b. Execution of global marketing plans in local jurisdictions with no further material adaptation (advertising campaign, trade shows);
    c. Translation of marketing and advertising material and business website to local language;
    d. Market research for planning and marketing purposes, e.g. provision of input to foreign related party on trends, customers, consumers, demands, local input; and
    e. Routine after-sales services: including processing complaints, and providing non-technical support.

668. Conversely, Amount B is not intended to cover distribution entities that perform any of the following activities:

1. The performance of activities related to the development, enhancement, maintenance or protection of marketing intangibles (other than local customer lists/customer relationships). For instance, this may be exhibited by:
    a. The lack of centralised structure and control of the group's intangibles;
    b. Decision-making by the distribution entity about investments and associated investment and development costs; or
    c. Developing and taking primary responsibility for maintaining, improving the technology supporting on-line sales and interaction with customers.
2. The performance of strategic sales and marketing functions in the local market, such as:
    a. Development of strategic marketing policies;
    b. Development of pricing and negotiation of pricing outside of parameters set by the MNE group;

c. Product development functions; or

d. Any marketing and advertising functions that are non-routine or where expenditures are made without an arrangement with the legal owner of the intangibles for reimbursement.

3. Activities related to the assumption of entrepreneurial risks and responsibilities in the controlled transaction.

4. Activities related to the resale of products mainly to government entities or government contractors, as companies performing such activities may face different contractual terms and competition compared with companies distributing to private companies; however, some Inclusive Framework members do not consider that this should be in the negative list and consequently be out-of-scope. Further technical work will be performed to evaluate this concern.

Assets

669. The assets used by the distribution entity in the performance of baseline activities in scope of Amount B may include:

- Ownership/lease of offices, product display premises;
- Ownership/lease of warehousing facilities;
- Limited ownership of inventory;[17]
- Customer list/customer relationships for their own local customer relationships;
- The right to sell in a market and use product name and brands;[18] and
- Local registrations or licences for products.

670. The distribution entity should not have the ownership of valuable marketing intangibles, such as local trademarks, brands, trade names, whether or not these are included as an asset in the distribution entity's balance sheet.

Risks

671. The risks assumed by the distribution entity in the performance of baseline activities in scope of Amount B may include:

- Limited market risks, for example on the basis that other entities within the MNE group assume material market risks, by developing strategic marketing plans, define pricing and undertake brand development activities, but where a local distributor may assume some risk of variable sales volumes in its specific market through reduced revenues;
- Between no to limited credit risks, for example where the routine distribution entity makes sales within its market and where it develops and maintains the customer relationship;
- Between no to limited inventory risk, to the extent that the routine distribution entity holds inventory; and
- Between no to limited foreign exchange risk, where the routine distribution entity purchases products or services for resale and either resells them in a different currency or bears operating costs in a different currency.

672. Typically, these entities would not be expected to assume risks that were economically significant for the MNE group as a whole. Determining whether a risk is economically significant is part of the functional analysis and the broader delineation of the related party transaction.

Quantitative indicators that may be used as proxies to identify entities and transactions out-of-scope of Amount B

673. In conjunction with considering the qualitative factors highlighted above, quantitative indicators could be used to identify in-scope distribution entities.

674. These aim to provide means of ascertaining whether the distribution entity does in fact perform baseline marketing and distribution activities and has the profile of a routine distributor, or whether it performs additional activities and assumes additional risks that may render it out-of-scope. They therefore take the form of quantitative thresholds that are closely linked to typical marketing and distribution activities. Consequently, if the thresholds are exceeded, it may indicate that the distribution entity performs more than the baseline marketing and distribution activities, inclusive of owning assets and assuming risks commensurate with the profile of a routine distributor, and therefore its activities may fall within the negative list described in the section above.

675. The quantitative indicators may also help analyse the consistency between the qualitative description of the functions performed, assets owned and risks assumed and how that is represented in the financial and operating structure of the business.

676. Technical work has so far focused on identifying appropriate quantitative indicators that are associated with activities in excess of the baseline. The following indicators may constitute appropriate quantitative proxies to support the determination of what may be an in- or out-of-scope distribution entity and transaction:[19]

- For the performance of activities related to the development, enhancement, maintenance or protection of marketing intangibles (other than local customer lists/customer relationships), and for the performance of strategic sales and marketing functions in the local market:
    a. Marketing and advertising expenses exceeding a fixed proportion of the total costs of the distribution business and for the account of the business incurring the expense; and
    b. R&D costs (on the basis that such costs relate to the generation of potentially valuable marketing intangibles for the MNE group within its industry) exceeding a fixed proportion of the total costs of the distribution business (again for its own account).
- For the ownership of potentially valuable marketing intangibles: The above indicators, plus the presence of amortisation costs in excess of the total costs of the distribution business.
- For the performance of activities related to the assumption of entrepreneurial risks and responsibilities in the controlled transaction:
    a. Finished product inventory of the distribution entity is greater than a fixed proportion of the annual net sales of the distribution entity, calculated on the basis of the average inventory held on the last day of each of the four quarterly periods during the relevant taxable year of the distribution enterprise;
    b. Inventory write-downs are greater than a certain fixed proportion of total inventory; and
    c. Accounts receivable are greater than a fixed proportion of total finished product inventory.

677. Further work is required on these proxies[20], with a view to clarifying the precise quantitative indicator to be used and the basis on which each one will be applied. For example, this may set ratios or absolute levels, depending on the required measurement, and subsequently benchmarking will be undertaken to fix the level of the relevant proxies. The basis on which the indicators will apply, together with the qualitative tests, will also be further evaluated. In addition, some Inclusive Framework members have the view that the quantitative indicators should also attempt to evaluate circumstances where the required threshold of activities to be considered as being in scope has not been met. Further technical work will be performed in this regard.

678. The application of Amount B would be prospective, i.e. Amount B would not supersede MAP settlements or APAs (unilateral, bilateral or multilateral) entered into before the implementation of Amount B.

Amount B and multifunctional entities

679. A distribution entity performing a controlled transaction in scope of Amount B may also perform other activities, such as R&D, manufacturing or back-office services. In those cases, it will be necessary to determine whether Amount B can still be applied to the controlled activities in scope.

680. In principle, the ALP should be applied on a case-by-case basis, and thus the application of Amount B to entities with controlled transactions in scope should be possible, even when those entities are engaged in other activities.[21] In practice, however, this determination will depend on the facts and circumstances of each case. For instance, when the additional activities do not relate to the products being distributed, the distribution entity may be able to apply Amount B, and separately determine the remuneration for the additional activities under a full transfer pricing analysis.

681. The determination may be different where a distribution entity performs other activities which relate to other aspects of the value chain of the product being distributed. In some situations, the accurate delineation of the transactions may indicate that the Amount B activities and the additional transactions are so closely linked or continuous that they may need to be considered in the aggregate.[22] In these cases, it would be likely that such transactions would be outside of the scope of Amount B, although further technical work will need to be performed to establish this.

682. The availability of reliable segmented financial information for the different activities will also play a key role in deciding whether to price each type of activity separately or to adopt a holistic approach and consider the overall functionality of the entity.[23]

683. Further, some Inclusive Framework members have expressed the view that consideration be given to situations where related manufacturing and distribution activities are performed domestically but are fragmented, opining that such entities should be considered to be in scope. Additional technical work will continue to assess this concern.

Commissionaires and sales agents

684. On the assumption of a narrow scope, commissionaires, sales agents and other businesses that perform non-baseline marketing and distribution activities[24] would not be within the scope of Amount B.[25] This is principally due to the increased breadth of the work needed if they were to be included as in scope, the additional technical complexity and specificity that their inclusion would require, and the issue that the inclusion of both of these models would render it more difficult to reach consensus. Subject to the overall direction of the work on amount B, further work would then need to be undertaken to assess the feasibility of including commissionaires, sales agents and other businesses that perform non-baseline marketing and distribution activities in scope of Amount B. If they are included in scope, it will be appropriate to determine commensurate remuneration under Amount B that is consistent with the ALP. Some members of the Inclusive Framework favour a broader scope inclusive of commissionaires and sales agents, whereas others prefer the current narrow scoping criteria. For example, some members want commissionaires and sales agents to be included within the scope of Amount B because they think that there is only a thin line that separates commissionaires and sales agents from entities that perform routine marketing and distribution activities. Further technical work will be carried out to evaluate this issue.

8.2.2. Quantum

Structure

685. The fixed return provided to remunerate baseline marketing and distribution activities under Amount B is intended to deliver a result that approximates results determined in accordance with the ALP. The TNMM is set forth in this Blueprint as the most appropriate transfer pricing method associated with the adequate remuneration for the baseline marketing and distribution activities performed by distribution entities in scope of Amount B. For example, net profit indicators are less affected by transactional differences and more tolerant to some functional differences between the transactions being compared).[26]

686. For the appropriate profit level indicator, a return on sales could be used[27] as a fixed return for the transactions in scope and with the numerator to be defined based on further technical work (e.g. EBIT or EBT). Further work would also consider what is included in the denominators of the various profit indicators that are specified under this approach (e.g. whether revenue should include product returns and refunds and foreign currency gains and losses).

687. Under one proposal, Amount B would operate on the basis of a rebuttable presumption, namely that a distribution entity that acts as a buy/sell distributor and performs the defined baseline marketing and distribution activities qualifying for the Amount B fixed return would be in scope. But it would be possible to rebut the application of Amount B by providing evidence that another transfer pricing method would be the most appropriate to use under the ALP.[28] For example, the presumption would be rebuttable if a sufficiently reliable CUP[29] was available and under the specific facts and circumstances the CUP is the most appropriate transfer pricing method to use. As the Amount B fixed return will be determined through a benchmarking analysis based on third party comparables, it is intended to approximate results determined under the ALP[30] and hence existing domestic and treaty law.

Differentiated returns by region

688. The TPG explains that arm's length prices may vary across different markets even for the distribution of the same or similar products. This can be due to a number of factors, such as (i) geographic location; (ii) the size of the markets; (iii) the extent of competition in the markets and the relative competitive positions of the buyers and sellers; (iv) the nature and extent of government regulation of the market; (v) transport costs; and (vi) the level of the market (e.g. retail or wholesale).[31] There may therefore be differentiated returns by region, with further technical work being required to establish the specific regions and to understand the variance in arm's length returns by region. .

689. Accordingly, as a next step, the work may develop differentiated returns for certain defined geographic regions. Ways of measuring the appropriate return will be explored, including the use of standard reference benchmarking sets and quantitative approaches. As reference benchmarks that rely on comparables will be considered, further technical work is needed to consider how to overcome any lack of publicly available information in certain regions for purposes of identifying comparables and evaluating their financial data (see further comment in the section "Process for determining the quantum of fixed returns").

Differentiated returns by industry

690. The fixed return could need to vary by industry. This responds to the view that two distributors operating in different industries (for instance, the pharmaceutical industry and motor vehicle industry) may experience divergences in their remuneration for a number of reasons (e.g. the type of products sold (high value products v. commoditized products) or the intensity and effort required to perform the marketing and distribution function).

691. Accordingly, further technical work is necessary to develop potentially different industry-based returns. These are likely to include: pharmaceutical, consumer products, automotive, and information and

communication technology (ICT), but this list may be refined and others may be included on the basis of further technical work. These industries are likely to be the most relevant for the largest number of jurisdictions.

Differentiation by functional intensity

692. Under the ALP, greater functionality should generally be accompanied by a higher profit potential (or loss potential). Conversely, lower functionality should generally be accompanied by a lower but less variable profit potential. On the assumption that the narrow scope of Amount B set out here is the one used, no attempt is made to account for functional intensity, as broadening the scope of baseline activities may increase complexity and increase the areas for dispute. However, functional intensity adjustments may be required if commissionaires and sales agents are included in the scope of Amount B, as these types of entities may receive lower returns than buy/sell distributors.[32]

Process for determining the quantum of fixed returns

693. Establishing the specific fixed return for the baseline marketing and distribution activities will require the preparation of reference benchmarking sets for each of the regions to which differentiated returns should apply. To finalise each reference set will also require a consistent definition to be developed for each of the industries for which a reference benchmarking set will be prepared. The development of the reference sets will proceed by locating potentially comparable independent companies within each industry and region for which a benchmarked return on sales will be calculated. This will in turn require the development of a specific search strategy to find such comparable companies, including a fixed definition of independence, the specific use of industry classification codes and other qualitative and quantitative criteria by which potentially comparable companies may be reviewed to ascertain whether or not they should be included in the reference set. Finally, the profit level indicator will be calculated (with the potential to make certain comparability adjustments which are to be defined) to establish the range of potentially appropriate fixed returns.

694. Consistency with the ALP requires that the determination of the quantum of fixed returns for Amount B be informed by benchmarking studies based on publicly available information (noting the comments above). To this end, consideration will be given to issues such as:

- Whether to use data for a single year or a weighted average of multiple years to determine the fixed return;
- The selection of the database(s) to be used for the benchmarking exercise, as there are several databases with diverse coverage and level of detail in terms of regions, financial and non-financial information;
- The selection of the search strategy, which includes the search parameters and screening criteria. For instance, identification of the relevant industry classification codes to capture the scope of Amount B; identification of the filters to be applied in the screening procedure (number of years of available financial data, independency criteria, consolidation, etc.); and
- The evaluation of necessary adjustments to enhance comparability.

695. Further work will also need to be undertaken regarding analysing how often the benchmarking will need to be updated and how often the underlying search process to develop the reference sets will need to be reviewed. The specific benchmarking with regional and industry variation will be developed alongside the current FTA MAP forum benchmarking exercise.

8.2.3. Implementation

696. Implementing Amount B in a coordinated and uniform fashion will reduce the risk of double taxation and double non-taxation.

697. A narrow scope of Amount B may facilitate reaching a consensus by a large number of Inclusive Framework members as it would be easier to agree on the appropriate set of baseline marketing and distribution activities, including the qualitative and quantitative indicators according to which distribution entities may be out-of-scope, and the appropriate means to be applied to set the fixed returns. It would also provide flexibility to assess out-of-scope distribution returns according to the existing operation of the ALP. A narrow scope for Amount B could also be developed more efficiently, as it would negate the possible need to differentiate the returns based on the differing functional intensity of a broader spectrum of marketing and distribution entities.

698. On the presumption that Amount B will be implemented at the same time as Amount A, and to ensure that it can be applied in a coherent manner by all jurisdictions, it would need to be implemented in three main ways. First, implementation of Amount B may need to be effectuated under domestic law or regulation. As noted above, the narrow approach articulated in this Blueprint carries the additional benefit that, as a simplified means of establishing the arm's length remuneration to narrow baseline activities, it would more likely be consistent with existing domestic law and treaties. Second, although two jurisdictions with an existing tax treaty can resolve disputes over Amount B through that treaty, where there is no treaty in place, a new treaty based dispute resolution relationship may be required (see Chapter 9). Third, guidance to accompany domestic legislation and treaty provisions may be required, although the narrower approach to scope may again limit this requirement.

699. There is interest by some Inclusive Framework members in exploring the feasibility of broadening the scope of Amount B, e.g. through an evaluation of how the remuneration may be standardised for commissionaires and sales agents, or distribution entities that have a profile wider than the narrow scope marketing and distribution activities set out in this Blueprint. This raises issues that will need to be further explored, to ensure that the fixed return profile for such activities is set in a manner that approximates results determined under the ALP.

700. In particular, should a broader scope to Amount B be implemented, in addition to the above considerations (and depending on the extent of scoping additions) this may also require further amendment to Article 9 of the OECD Model Tax Treaty and for this to be implemented in bilateral tax treaties, which would further complicate the implementation of Amount B. Finally, as there is some interest to explore the feasibility of implementing Amount B through a pilot programme, further discussions will occur to evaluate this.

8.3. Next steps

701. The next step will require a decision by the members of the Inclusive Framework on what scope and within which context the work on Amount B should be advanced and implemented.

702. In addition, further technical work will need to be undertaken and will include:

- Finalising the determination of the profit level indicator to be applied, including what should be incorporated into in the numerator and denominator for the calculation of the return on sales;
- Identifying what baseline marketing and distribution activities should be in the positive list, what activities, functions and risks should be in the negative list, and the quantitative indicators and specific thresholds that may indicate activities below or in excess of the baseline;

- If sales agents and commissionaires are to be in scope, the definition of equivalent baseline marketing and distribution activities, an appropriate negative list, quantitative indicators and profit level indicators to use to set the fixed returns;
- Determining the regions and industries to which differentiated returns should apply;
- Considering the risk of double non-taxation as a result of divergence between the fixed Amount B and a lower amount taken into account in the jurisdiction(s) of the other party(ies) to the transaction;
- Conducting the benchmarking to set the required returns using the agreed basis;
- Establishing and articulating the process to implement Amount B, including developing the implementation requirements through a multilateral instrument and a specific Amount B guidance document, including processes to resolve disputes and the process by which the benchmarks will be completed and periodically updated;
- Considering the impact of other intercompany transactions for an entity that may be in the scope of Amount B, inclusive of the treatment of multifunctional entities and how to address the effects of potential transfer pricing adjustments for out-of-scope transactions, where the entity in scope for Amount B is the recipient entity, for example services; and
- Considering the merits and objectives of a potential pilot programme.

Notes

[1] In the past, these concerns led to the work on business restructurings, which provides tax administrations and MNE groups with a framework to analyse and price arrangements resulting from the restructuring of an MNE group's operations. OECD (2017), *OECD Transfer Pricing Guidelines for Multinational Enterprises and Tax Administrations 2017,* Chapter IX "Transfer Pricing Aspects of Business Restructurings"

[2] A 'narrow scope' would standardise the return for a more limited and narrower range of baseline marketing and distribution activities and would not seek to address the standardisation of the remuneration for distributors performing other activities, whether performing more value-add activities, assuming greater risks or (in particular) undertaking less than sufficient baseline activities. Several Inclusive Framework members favour a broader scope, including a broader range of marketing and distribution activities. Further technical work will be performed to address this concern.

[3] In this regard, it should be noted that some Inclusive Framework members are of the view that even narrowly defined routine distributors may have differing levels of functional intensity and that may require differential levels of return. Some Inclusive Framework members have suggested that analysis be performed to measure this.

[4] Some Inclusive Framework members do not support the use of a rebuttable presumption, as they believe it to undermine the simplification benefits of Amount B. Because this is a relatively recent proposal, other Inclusive Framework members have requested additional explanation of how the rebuttable presumption would work (including whether the taxpayer and the tax administration would have the ability to rebut) where they assess that another transfer pricing method would be the most appropriate method under the arm's length principle. Further discussion will occur on this matter.

[5] Meaning that the TNMM and the return on sales should represent the most appropriate transfer pricing method and profit level indicator respectively, and be consistent with the operation of the ALP under the existing transfer pricing guidelines.

[6] This approach is consistent with the approach in the OECD Transfer Pricing Guidelines. That is, the Amount B fixed return could be applied as the most appropriate method, but potentially rebutted where a CUP may be applied as the most appropriate method.

[7] A comparison of all the economically relevant characteristics of the transaction is relevant to establish comparability of the controlled transaction with the relevant uncontrolled transactions used to fix the return for Amount B purposes, to retain its consistency with the arm's length principle. This determination is subject to further technical work.

[8] Several members of the Inclusive Framework have highlighted that including in-scope permanent establishments located in jurisdictions where the Authorised OECD Approach in the 2010 report on the "Attribution of Profits to Permanent Establishments" is not followed may entail inconsistencies in the application of Amount B and create implementation challenges. Further technical work will be required to address this concern, including the determination of whether PE's would be in scope. Further, some Inclusive Framework members have highlighted the need to consider situations where both an in-scope PE and distribution entity is within a market jurisdiction. Further technical work will be required to address whether returns in such situations are aggregated or measured separately.

[9] The same rules will apply to a local permanent establishment of a foreign enterprise. It is not a resident, but for simplicity the analysis in this chapter refers only to local resident entities.

[10] The term "predominantly" would require that at least [50%] of the products be sold in the state of residence of the distribution entity.

[11] There may be situations where the first test is met, but the distribution entity does not perform a sufficient level and/or breadth of marketing and distribution activities to warrant it being in the scope of Amount B. In such circumstances remuneration based on the existing ALP will be appropriate.

[12] As noted, this may have different functional intensity and the appropriate fixed remuneration under Amount B in such circumstances is being considered in further technical work. In particular, some Inclusive Framework Members consider that routine distributors have sufficiently variant functional profiles such that different return levels may be warranted. The ongoing technical work will further consider this concern.

[13] For definitional purposes, this may refer to distribution entities performing routine functions that use routine assets in the course of their distribution operations, and assume routine risks. Further work needs to be undertaken to clearly define these terms, to clarify the in-scope activities and to clarify the meaning of a routine distributor or limited risk distributor, noting the views of some Inclusive Framework members that these are not considered to be the same in character and return profile.

[14] Or, potentially, a distribution entity that would perform functions more akin to logistics services to which a return based on the return on sales profit level indicator may not be appropriate.

[15] As Amount B is currently intended to operate on the basis of a narrow scope, applying the positive and negative lists outlined in this chapter, certain types of entities may not typically be included in scope. One example would be commodity marketing hubs, depending on the nature of the activities performed by the hub.

[16] Noting that Amount B will apply for entities where up to [50%] of the products distributed may be to customers outside the market where the distribution entity is resident (or where the PE is situated).

[17] Including on a flash title basis for Routine Distributors that may be classified as Limited Risk Distributors, but not limited to this – entities that assume routine inventory risks and own routine levels of inventory may also fall within scope.

[18] Under an accurately delineated distribution arrangement.

[19] Further technical work is required to establish and benchmark these proxies.

[20] One Inclusive Framework member suggests a proxy as follows: entities that in the 3 years prior to the adoption of Amount B have reported a profit level for in-scope activities that is above the highest fixed return determined under Amount B (considering the relevant region, industry and functionality level). This and other proxies will be subject to further discussion and evaluation.

[21] See para. 3.9 TPG.

[22] See para. 3.9 TPG.

[23] See para. 2.74 and 3.37 TPG.

[24] Other marketing and distribution activities might include other service providers that do not take title to the goods or businesses that do take title but perform marketing and distribution functions different than the baseline.

[25] This may also be relevant for other entities that perform a more limited set of marketing and distribution activities that collectively fall below the required set of baseline marketing and distribution activities to be considered in scope.

[26] See para. 2.68 and 2.69 TPG.

[27] See para. 2.96 TPG.

[28] There are divergent views between some Inclusive Framework members on the scope and operation of the rebuttable presumption – including whether it should be included in any form – which will be subject to further discussion.

[29] This approach is consistent with the approach in the OECD TPG. That is, the Amount B fixed return could be applied as the most appropriate method, but potentially rebutted where a taxpayer seeks to apply a CUP as the most appropriate method.

[30] Meaning that the TNMM and the return on sales set at the EBIT level should represent the most appropriate method and PLI respectively, and be consistent with the operation of the ALP under the existing transfer pricing guidelines.

[31] See paragraph 1.110 TPG.

[32] It may also be required in other circumstances where an accurately delineated transaction may be a distribution relationship and where Amount B may apply on the basis that the deemed distribution entity performs the baseline marketing and distribution activities. The correct profit level indicator in areas where functional intensity differs will also be considered in further technical work.

9 Tax Certainty

9.1. Overview

703. Securing tax certainty is an essential element of Pillar One. Providing and enhancing tax certainty across all possible areas of dispute brings benefits for taxpayers and tax administrations alike and is key in promoting investment, jobs and growth, and G20 Finance Ministers have recognised the importance of international cooperation to ensure tax certainty as an integral part of arriving at a consensus-based solution to the tax challenges of the digitalisation of the economy.[1]

704. The Blueprint breaks down the tax certainty dimension of Pillar One into two segments: dispute prevention and resolution for Amount A; and dispute prevention and resolution beyond Amount A.

705. With respect to Amount A, the Inclusive Framework recognises that it would be impractical, if not impossible, to allow all affected tax administrations to assess and audit an MNE's calculation and allocation of Amount A and to address potential disputes through existing bilateral dispute resolution mechanisms. That is why this Blueprint contains a clear and administrable mandatory binding dispute prevention process that would provide early certainty, before tax adjustments are made, to prevent disputes related to all aspects of Amount A. Such disputes could concern, for example, the correct delineation of business lines, allocation of central costs and tax losses to business lines, the existence of a nexus in a particular jurisdiction, or the identification of the relieving jurisdictions for purposes of eliminating double taxation. The process described in this Blueprint remains under discussion and may be revised as work continues.

706. The process is based on a representative panel mechanism that would carry on a review function and involve both a review panel and, where necessary, a determination panel to ensure that early certainty is achieved. Where an MNE accepts the outcomes of the tax certainty process, these outcomes would be binding on the MNE and tax administrations in all jurisdictions affected by the calculation and allocation of Amount A, including jurisdictions that did not participate directly on the relevant panel. Where it does not accept the outcomes of this process, an MNE group may rely on domestic measures. Where an MNE does not elect into the early tax certainty process, and disputes arise, the new approach also provides enhanced dispute resolution features. However, given the benefits of the early certainty process, the expectation is that most in-scope MNEs would make use of it.

707. Importantly, rules for dispute prevention and resolution would be embedded in the same instrument that introduces the rules for the taxation of Amount A, ensuring that the new taxing right would be linked to the availability of the new tax certainty approach.

708. To provide tax certainty beyond Amount A, the Blueprint takes an approach based on a number of main steps – from dispute prevention (Step 1) and the existing MAP (Step 2) to a new and innovative mandatory binding dispute resolution mechanism (Step 3). While ongoing work to improve and enhance the dispute prevention and resolution tools and the MAP has already been important separate from work on the tax challenges of the digitalisation of the economy, that ongoing work has gained further momentum in light of the fundamental importance of tax certainty as an element of Pillar One.

709. Inclusive Framework members continue to have different views on the scope of application of a new mandatory and binding dispute resolution mechanism beyond Amount A. Some strongly support a

mandatory binding dispute resolution mechanism with broad application, while others consider that disputes unrelated to Amount A should be resolved through the existing MAP framework and non-binding administrative tools. To bridge these different views, the Blueprint explores the following approach based around four elements:

- **In-scope taxpayers**. For MNE groups with global revenue and foreign in-scope revenue above the relevant Amount A thresholds, the approach contemplates a new mandatory and binding resolution process for all disputes related to transfer pricing and permanent establishment adjustments to any of their constituent entities. This is designed as a last resort and would follow the exhaustion of all other dispute prevention and resolution tools, which would be expanded and improved, including as part of the 2020 review of BEPS Action 14. The process would cover adjustments related to in-scope activities, but also extend to other (out-of-scope) activities of MNEs that are subject to the new taxing right, possibly subject to a materiality condition. The new process would not apply where disputes are already covered by existing mandatory and binding dispute resolution mechanisms, which would continue to apply.
- **Other taxpayers**. All other taxpayers would benefit from improvements to the MAP and other existing dispute prevention and resolution tools. For these taxpayers, the Inclusive Framework will also examine new and innovative dispute resolution mechanisms for material transfer pricing and permanent establishment-related disputes that competent authorities are unable to resolve in a timely manner through the MAP. In this regard, the next steps of this work will explore the benefits of two approaches: a mandatory binding dispute resolution process and a mandatory but non-binding dispute resolution process coupled with aspects of peer review and statistical reporting.
- **Amount B**. A key purpose of Amount B is to prevent transfer pricing disputes regarding baseline marketing and distribution activities through the use of agreed standardised returns to objectively defined activities, supported by quantitative indicators. Any disputes related to the application of Amount B (for example, whether a taxpayer falls within the definition of "baseline marketing and distribution activities"), which create risks of double taxation, would also be subject to mandatory binding dispute resolution, as a last resort and following the exhaustion of all other dispute prevention and resolution tools.
- **Developing economies with no or low levels of MAP disputes**. Where developing economies have no or almost no MAP cases in inventory and therefore limited or no experience with the MAP, it would seem disproportionate to require them to commit to and implement a potentially complex mandatory binding dispute resolution process to address a situation that in their current circumstances may not present a material risk to taxpayers or other tax administrations. Instead, for issues not related to Amount A, these jurisdictions would commit to an elective binding dispute resolution mechanism that would be triggered where both competent authorities agree that the mechanism should be used to resolve unresolved MAP issues. In determining appropriate levels of MAP inventory to be included in this category of jurisdictions, reference would be made to the principles of the Action 14 peer review process (in particular the criteria for deferral of a jurisdiction's peer review), which considers the number of MAP cases in inventory as well as access limitations that may have prevented cases from entering the MAP process and appearing in inventory.
- The mechanisms described above could be coupled with a peer review and reporting framework to monitor the effectiveness of all elements of the new dispute prevention and resolution mechanisms.

710. Further work will be undertaken to finalise the different technical features of the tax certainty process for Amount A, including ways to minimise the resource burden and administrative costs of the process and how these costs should be borne. However, it is noted that, while there will be a cost implication of a new process, in aggregate and over time this should be significantly lower than the cost to both tax administrations and MNE groups from an un-coordinated application of Amount A by tax administrations in all jurisdictions where an MNE group has a constituent entity or a market. This work will

also consider any other issues where further practical guidance on the Amount A tax certainty process is needed for its implementation.

711. A decision on the scope of application of a new mandatory and binding dispute resolution mechanism beyond Amount A will be necessary to progress technical work on that mechanism and its implementation. Such technical work will include exploring how the implementation of Amount A could include extending the application of that new dispute resolution mechanism to circumstances in which there is not currently a bilateral tax treaty that includes a MAP article between the relevant jurisdictions (and thus no existing obligation or common legal standard that could form the substance of a dispute).

9.2. A new framework for dispute prevention and resolution for Amount A

712. This section contains a detailed draft outline of the approach to provide early tax certainty with respect to Amount A for MNE groups that are within scope.

713. The process comprises a number of elements and stages[2], which are discussed further below.

- Development of a standardised Amount A self-assessment return / documentation package and centralised filing, validation and exchange of this information.
- Request for tax certainty by an MNE group.
- An optional initial review by the lead tax administration and determination if a panel review is needed.
- Constitution of the review panel, the review panel process and approval by affected tax administrations.
- Constitution of the determination panel and the determination panel process.
- Cases where an MNE group does not accept a panel conclusion.
- Other opportunities to provide greater certainty concerning Amount A.
- Transfer pricing adjustments and other adjustments in subsequent years.

9.2.1. Development of a standardised Amount A self-assessment return / documentation package and centralised filing, validation and exchange of this information

Standardised Amount A self-assessment return and documentation package

714. As described in Chapter 10, to facilitate a consistent implementation of Amount A by MNE groups and tax administrations, a standardised Amount A self-assessment return and documentation package will be developed, for use in all jurisdictions. These will be used by MNE groups irrespective of whether a particular MNE group makes a request for early tax certainty.

- The self-assessment return will set out each stage of the MNE group's determination and allocation of Amount A between jurisdictions, including identification of relieving entities. An XML schema could be developed for use by MNE groups, which should facilitate electronic filing and exchange of returns. Where an MNE group applies Amount A separately to a number of lines of business, separate self-assessment returns should be prepared and submitted together as a package in order to ensure common elements (e.g. business line segmentation and allocation of central costs) are consistent.
- The standard documentation package will be designed to contain sufficient background information and evidence to assess the MNE group's self-assessment of Amount A based on the information provided, while further information may be requested by tax administrations if needed. This will include a detailed description of the methodology and controls applied by the

MNE group to ensure the integrity of its data and processes for applying Amount A, as well as a list of jurisdictions where the MNE group has a constituent entity or revenues that meet the applicable market jurisdiction threshold in the relevant fiscal year or the prior fiscal year. Further work will consider ways to ensure that all market jurisdictions are identified.

715. The format and content of these items will be developed at a later stage, but the use of a standardised self-assessment return and documentation package should have a number of benefits for MNE groups and tax administrations, including the following.

- It would reduce the burden on MNE groups, which would be able to provide the same documentation in each jurisdiction where they have activity.
- Consistency in the application of Amount A by MNE groups would be improved, as the return would require the same specific information to be provided and calculations to be performed by each MNE group.
- It would aid tax administrations in reviewing an MNE group's determination and allocation of Amount A, as they would gain experience in working with standardised templates, which may also make it easier to identify comparable MNE groups that are taking different approaches.
- It would facilitate exchange of information and multilateral approaches by tax administrations, because competent authorities would be working with exactly the same information.
- Guidance could be developed to support MNE groups and tax administrations in completing and using standardised templates.

Filing of the self-assessment return and documentation package by the Amount A co-ordinating entity with its lead tax administration

716. To minimise the burden on MNE groups and ensure the same information is available to all relevant tax administrations, an Amount A co-ordinating entity within an MNE group will file a single self-assessment return and documentation package on behalf of the entire MNE group, with its lead tax administration, by an agreed filing deadline. In setting this deadline, different options will be explored but an approach could be such that jurisdictions are free to set the filing deadline up to 12 months after the end of the relevant fiscal year. This allows jurisdictions to align the filing date with their normal tax return filing deadline if they wish to do so.

717. In the majority of cases, the lead tax administration will be in the jurisdiction where the UPE of an MNE group is resident. However, there may be cases where the tax administration in that jurisdiction may be unable to act (e.g. because it is in a jurisdiction that is not a member of the Inclusive Framework or has not implemented Amount A) or where another tax administration may be more suitable (e.g. because the MNE group only has nominal activity in that jurisdiction or if the tax administration does not have the resources to act).

718. To deal with these cases, an approach will be developed to identify a "surrogate lead tax administration" for the MNE group. One option could be for tax administrations that in principle are prepared to act as lead tax administrations for these MNE groups would identify themselves and be included on a list of "surrogate lead tax administrations" that is made publicly available. Where the tax administration in the jurisdiction of an MNE group's UPE is unable to act as lead tax administration, or agrees that other tax administrations may be more suitable, the UPE may contact one of the tax administrations on this list (directly or via their UPE tax administration) to request that they act as lead tax administration. In the first instance, no tax administration would be required to agree to be lead tax administration for a particular MNE group (e.g. a tax administration may wish to decline if the MNE group has no or little activity in its jurisdiction or if its capacity is filled). However, if no tax administration agrees to act as lead tax administration for a particular MNE group, a process will be identified to ensure that every MNE group within the scope of Amount A has access to a lead tax administration. Another option would be for clear

objective criteria to be agreed (e.g. based on revenues or the location of key functions), to determine which tax administration that should act as surrogate tax administration.

719. A surrogate lead tax administration should only be used if the UPE jurisdiction is not a member of the Inclusive Framework, if the jurisdiction has not yet implemented rules for Amount A, or if the UPE tax administration agrees to the MNE group using a surrogate lead tax administration. In cases where the UPE tax administration is in an Inclusive Framework member jurisdiction that has implemented Amount A, and is able and willing to act as lead tax administration, it should do so.

720. The co-ordinating entity should also provide to its lead tax administration an agreement signed by all entities in the MNE group undertaking residual profit activities (i.e. those which could be paying entities for the purposes of Amount A), confirming their agreement to be bound by the self-assessment return, as well as any amendments to this return agreed by the co-ordinating entity, including as part of any early certainty process. Depending upon the final design of Amount A, this agreement may also need to be signed by other constituent entities in the MNE group. Where legal or practical issues mean it is not possible for a constituent entity to agree in advance to be bound by decisions of the co-ordinating entity, the process described in this Blueprint will be amended to reflect this and further work will consider how this can be done (e.g. by requiring these constituent entities to confirm their agreement before outcomes become binding). Further work will be undertaken to understand the extent to which these legal or practical issues may arise in practice and how these can be avoided. It is expected that in the significant majority of cases all constituent entities will accept the position agreed by the co-ordinating entity, which applies Amount A across the MNE group and avoids double taxation. In exceptional cases, if a constituent entity takes a position with respect to its Amount A assessment which differs from that filed by the co-ordinating entity, this is likely to have an impact on the assessment of Amount A for other entities in the group.

Validation of the self-assessment return by the lead tax administration

721. Following filing of the MNE group's self-assessment return and documentation package, the lead tax administration would be expected to conduct a validation of these items for completeness and consistency, which should be completed before the deadline for exchanging this information described below. Guidance would support lead tax administrations in performing a validation and other tax administrations in understanding the extent of the validation expected. In conducting a validation, the lead tax administration is not expected to independently confirm the accuracy of information provided by the MNE group or the application of rules for determining and allocating Amount A, but should request clarification or additional information from the co-ordinating entity where any element appears incomplete or if there is inconsistency within the information and documentation provided. In other words, this process is intended to identify obvious errors before information is exchanged with other tax administrations, but is not intended to involve any substantive review of the MNE group's self-assessment.

722. In some cases, an MNE group may be required to submit a corrected self-assessment return and/or documentation package addressing these points. In most cases, the corrected self-assessment return and/or documentation package should be provided by the co-ordinating entity in the MNE group within [one month] of receiving instruction from the lead tax administration.

Exchange of the self-assessment return and documentation package

723. The self-assessment return and documentation package will be exchanged by the lead tax administration with tax administrations in other jurisdictions where the MNE group has a constituent entity and those where it has a market that meets the applicable threshold, or did so in the previous fiscal year (jointly referred to as "affected tax administrations"). These jurisdictions will be identified by the lead tax administration using information provided by the MNE group. Jurisdictions where an MNE group had a constituent entity or a market in the previous fiscal year are included to ensure that, where the MNE group reports that it no longer has a constituent entity or a market in such a jurisdiction, these tax administrations

have the opportunity to review this and object if necessary. Later in this section a possible accelerated early certainty process is described for cases where a tax administration believes that its jurisdiction should be included on an MNE group's list of market jurisdictions, but it has not been included on the list by the MNE group.

724. The usual deadline for the exchange of CbCRs under BEPS Action 13 is 15 months after the end of the relevant fiscal year and a similar approach could be applied to Amount A information. Where the lead tax administration is awaiting a corrected self-assessment return from the MNE group, it should inform affected tax administrations and then exchange the revised self-assessment return and documentation package within [one month] of receiving it from the co-ordinating entity. Provisions may be needed within the planned multilateral instrument and/or domestic law to allow what would in effect be part of a domestic tax return to be received under exchange of information rather than directly from the relevant taxpayer and most likely at a point which is later than the deadline for filing a domestic tax return.

725. To ensure information is available to all affected tax administrations, it will be necessary for a comprehensive network for the exchange of information to be put in place (possibly under the envisaged multilateral instrument or the existing Multilateral Convention on Mutual Administrative Assistance in Tax Matters), together with up-front consent as appropriate for the on-sharing of this information to ensure tax administrations are able to discuss it with each other.[3] Currently, bilateral double tax conventions and tax information exchange agreements alone may not provide a sufficiently complete network for the necessary exchange and on-sharing of information. This exchange framework could be supplemented by a secondary mechanism for local filing of the self-assessment return and documentation package where exchange of information cannot or does not take place. This secondary mechanism would in principle be similar to local filing of an MNE group's CbCR, but would not be subject to some of the limits on local filing imposed under BEPS Action 13. Further work will be required to ensure that jurisdictions which have to rely on local filing are able to engage in the early certainty process, given exchange of information is a vital element.

726. These exchanges (and local filing where needed) will take place irrespective as to whether an MNE group makes a request for tax certainty (i.e. this process would be followed to ensure that consistent information is available to all relevant tax administrations in cases where an MNE group plans to rely on domestic remedies to resolve areas of disagreement). The exchange of information could potentially be simplified by the development of a central administrative platform to hold information on Amount A provided by MNE groups.

9.2.2. Request for tax certainty by an MNE group

A voluntary mechanism for MNE groups

727. The approach to achieve early certainty for Amount A will be voluntary on the part of an MNE group, and triggered by a request from an MNE group's co-ordinating entity to its lead tax administration. In this context, references to "early certainty" refer to certainty before tax administrations have made any adjustments to the tax position filed by an MNE group (i.e. during the dispute prevention stage, compared with dispute resolution which is needed once a tax administration requires a tax adjustment to be made which results in double taxation). Later in this section there is a discussion on circumstances where a modified certainty process may be initiated following the request of a tax administration.

728. There are two levels with respect to which tax certainty may be requested by an MNE group:

- Whether an MNE group is within the scope of Amount A. It is likely that this certainty would only need to be provided once, or only periodically.
- Whether an MNE group's determination and allocation of Amount A is agreed, including the identification of paying entities and the relief from double taxation that should be provided by relieving jurisdictions. This certainty may be requested annually, though for some MNE groups

only a high-level review may be required. As mentioned below, after the first year(s) tax administrations may feel comfortable to provide early certainty for some MNE groups without any review by a panel, if they are confident the MNE group's processes for applying Amount A are robust and nothing material has changed since the previous review was undertaken.

Submission of a request to the lead tax administration

729. A request for early certainty will be submitted by the MNE group's co-ordinating entity to its lead tax administration, which in most cases should be in the MNE group's UPE jurisdiction. This request should be submitted by an agreed deadline, say within [six months] of the end of the relevant fiscal year end. Within [1 month] of receiving the request, the lead tax administration should send a notification to competent authorities in all jurisdictions where the MNE group has a constituent entity or a market, based on information provided by the MNE group.

730. As mentioned above, the MNE group should have provided an agreement signed by all constituent entities undertaking residual profits activities confirming that they agree to be bound by any changes to the MNE group's Amount A self-assessment return agreed by the co-ordinating entity. Depending upon the final design of Amount A, this agreement may also need to be signed by other constituent entities in the MNE group. In addition, the request for tax certainty should include confirmation from these constituent entities that:

- they agree to the suspension of time limits on domestic compliance activity for the period of the review, to the extent this is possible under each jurisdiction's law. This is to ensure that, in the event an MNE group does not accept the outcomes of a review and chooses to rely on domestic remedies, tax administrations are still able to conduct their own enquiries, and
- they understand that any binding tax certainty provided as a result of this process may fall away if
  - any member of the MNE group later pursues domestic remedies with respect to Amount A for the relevant fiscal year or
  - it is later discovered that information provided by the MNE group to tax administrations for the purposes of its review is inaccurate, incomplete or misleading.

731. If these elements are provided, the lead tax administration will inform the co-ordinating entity as soon as possible or within [one month] that its request for Amount A tax certainty is accepted. Incomplete requests will not be accepted and the lead tax administration will advise the co-ordinating entity as to any outstanding items that should be provided. In exceptional cases, where the lead tax administration is aware or is made aware (e.g. by the MNE group or an affected tax administration) that an MNE group's financial statements or other information relied on in calculating Amount A are likely to change or be re-stated and this will have an impact on Amount A, the lead tax administration may decline the MNE's request for certainty, but may agree that a request can be submitted once the final position is known. There is no other opportunity for a complete request for tax certainty from an MNE group to be declined.

732. With respect to domestic compliance processes (e.g. tax audit), affected tax administrations should not commence any compliance activity or issue assessments with respect to topics specific to Amount A for the relevant tax year pending the outcomes of the review. This does not extend to any other compliance activity or assessments (i.e. with respect to other aspects of the MNE group's taxation, including transfer pricing issues beyond Amount A, compliance activity may continue) and does not suspend the collection of Amount A tax due in accordance with the MNE group's self-assessment. Specifically, affected tax administrations are not restricted from conducting audits or other compliance activity concerning issues that may impact the level of residual profits in a jurisdiction, even though these may have a consequential effect on the identification of relieving jurisdictions and the amount of double tax relief they should provide. The interaction of these issues with an early certainty process for Amount A

is considered later in this section. Further work will be undertaken to explore how to deal with cases where a jurisdiction's law does not permit the suspension of time limits on domestic compliance activity.

9.2.3. An optional initial review by the lead tax administration and determining if a panel review is needed

733. This part and the following parts of this section focus on cases where an MNE group has made a request for certainty concerning its determination and allocation of Amount A, including the identification of relieving entities. A discussion later in this section considers other occasions where the architecture described may be used to provide wider tax certainty for Amount A.

Optional initial review by lead tax administration

734. In addition to and simultaneous with the validation described above, where an MNE group has made a request for early certainty, the lead tax administration may also conduct an initial review of the MNE group's self-assessment return in order to filter out lower-risk groups, based on agreed criteria, where tax administrations may be willing to provide certainty without a review by panel. This could be a useful mechanism to reduce the overall tax administration resources needed in the first year of operating Amount A and even more so in subsequent years.

735. The extent of this review may vary depending upon, among other factors, the robustness of the MNE group's processes and controls over its application of Amount A, whether it has previously been reviewed by a panel and, if it has, the outcomes of those reviews. In conducting an initial review, the lead tax administration may request some clarification or additional information from the MNE group, but a need for significant extra information may suggest that a panel review is needed. As a result of its initial review, the lead tax administration may propose changes to an MNE group's self-assessment return which, if accepted by the MNE group, could be reflected in a revised return provided to the lead tax administration, typically within [one month]. Guidance will clarify the level of comfort that a lead tax administration should seek to achieve in conducting an initial review, and how the outcomes of that review should be presented.

736. Leaving flexibility around whether an initial review is conducted is intended to allow lead tax administrations to identify lower risk MNE groups that may be provided with certainty quickly, without the need for a panel review, reducing the resources required from all tax administrations. However, an initial review does not need to be undertaken, for example where a lead administration does not have the resources or capacity to conduct an initial review, or it feels that in any case a review by panel is needed (e.g. because it is the MNE group's first year of applying Amount A and the lead tax administration believes a review conducted by a panel of tax administrations would be beneficial).

737. As the initial review is intended to be high-level and only filter out relatively low-risk MNE groups rather than deal with more complex cases, it is anticipated that in most cases a review should be completed by the time the self-assessment return and documentation package are exchanged with other tax administrations. As described above, this could be 15 months after the end of the MNE group's fiscal year. If this approach is adopted, this would mean three months for an initial review if the filing deadline in the lead tax administration's jurisdiction was 12 months after the end of the fiscal year, but the time available for the review would be longer if the filing deadline in that jurisdiction was earlier (e.g. if the lead tax administration required filing nine months after the fiscal year end, this would leave six months for the initial review).

738. Where an initial review is still underway at the point of the deadline for exchange, the MNE group's self-assessment return and documentation package will be exchanged with affected tax administrations as normal. If any revisions are subsequently required as a result of the initial review, an amended self-assessment return and documentation package will be exchanged when available. In the event that the initial review is still incomplete at the end of [three months] following the deadline for exchange (or shortly

thereafter), the initial review will end without reaching a conclusion. Work undertaken to date by the lead tax administration will contribute to any subsequent review by panel.

739. When the lead tax administration exchanges the MNE group's self-assessment return and documentation package with affected tax administrations, this will be accompanied with one of the following.

- A statement that the lead tax administration has not conducted an initial review of the MNE group's Amount A self-assessment (or an initial review was conducted which ended without reaching a conclusion) and so a review by panel is required.
- A statement that the lead tax administration has conducted an initial review and concluded that a review by panel is required. This may be accompanied by a summary of the review undertaken by the lead tax administration and particular issues it considers should be discussed by the review panel.
- A statement that the lead tax administration has conducted an initial review and, based on the outcomes of this review, a recommendation that a review by panel is not required. This must be accompanied by a summary of the review undertaken by the lead tax administration and the basis for its conclusion that each element of the MNE group's application of Amount A poses a low risk to the jurisdictions of affected tax administrations (including both market jurisdictions and relieving jurisdictions).
- A statement that the lead tax administration is in the process of conducting an initial review that is not yet complete (in which case the conclusions of this initial review, if any, should be exchanged with other tax administrations as soon as they are available).

Decision as to whether a review panel is required

740. Where the lead tax administration has conducted an initial review and recommended that a review by panel is not needed, other affected tax administrations have [three months] to consider this and submit comments, which may fall into one or more of four categories:

- A proposal to establish a panel based on concerns that could impact the MNE group's Amount A tax liability in that tax administration's jurisdiction (e.g. that there may be errors in the determination and allocation of Amount A or the identification of relieving entities that affect the jurisdiction in question). This should be accompanied by a description of the specific concerns the affected tax administration has (e.g. that aspects of the MNE group's self-assessment do not reflect published guidance or are inconsistent with the approach applied by comparable MNE groups) and, if possible, the tax impact in its and other jurisdiction(s).
- A preference that a panel be formed that is not linked to specific concerns.
- Observations that the affected tax administration would like to raise but that do not result in a proposal to form a panel. This could include technical issues with an MNE group's self-assessment that the tax administration does not consider material for the relevant fiscal year but would like to have recorded in case the issues become material in the future.
- An expression of interest to participate in any review panel that is established. In the event that a panel review is undertaken, the review panel will be drawn first from a list of tax administrations that indicated an interest in participating.

741. The issues underpinning proposals to establish a panel and observations by affected tax administrations will be discussed by the lead tax administration with the co-ordinating entity of the MNE group. If the co-ordinating entity is able to address the concerns underlying a proposal to the satisfaction of the affected tax administration, without impacting the position in any other jurisdiction, the affected tax administration should withdraw its proposal to establish a panel, and may replace this with a general preference that a panel be formed. Observations do not require any specific action on the part of an MNE

group, but it should consider taking them into account in applying Amount A in future fiscal years, if relevant.

742. A panel of tax administrations (the review panel) could be established in all cases where an MNE group has requested certainty and either:

- the lead tax administration has not conducted an initial review or did not reach a conclusion as a result of such a review;
- the lead tax administration has conducted an initial review and concluded a panel review is needed;
- any affected tax administration has submitted a proposal that a panel review be conducted together with an explanation of its specific concerns and this proposal has not been subsequently withdrawn; or
- [three or more] affected tax administrations have indicated a preference that a panel be formed (this number may be reduced where an MNE group has constituent entities in a very small number of jurisdictions). Alternatively, rather than an absolute number, this option could be based upon a minimum percentage of affected tax administrations, which may be subject to a *de minimis* number (e.g. at least five per cent of affected tax administrations subject to a minimum of three).

743. Further work will consider whether a panel should be formed in each of the above scenarios, or if modifications to these scenarios should be made. Where none of these conditions are met and a review panel is not to be established, the lead tax administration will inform the MNE group that the position set out in its self-assessment (reflecting any agreed changes) is accepted. This position is then binding on the MNE group's constituent entities and on tax administrations in all Inclusive Framework member jurisdictions. Tax administrations should undertake any steps needed in their jurisdiction to implement this assessment. Further discussions will consider issues that tax administrations may encounter in implementing the outcomes of a mandatory binding process, with domestic law issues dealt with by each jurisdiction as necessary, to ensure implementation of these outcomes. These discussions will also consider how the outcomes of the Amount A certainty process will interact with domestic court decisions or other "binding" rulings in a jurisdiction (e.g. in cases where these conflict).

744. In the event that any constituent entity in an MNE group subsequently seeks to reduce its liability to Amount A tax via domestic remedies, the tax administration in the relevant jurisdiction will inform the lead tax administration and other affected tax administrations that the MNE group is not complying with its commitments under the tax certainty process. This will be raised with the MNE group's co-ordinating entity by the lead tax administration and, if this situation is not addressed, affected tax administrations will be informed by the lead tax administration that the binding tax certainty provided to the MNE group no longer applies with respect to the relevant fiscal year.

745. It is anticipated that a significant majority of MNE groups within the scope of Amount A will submit a request for tax certainty for the first year(s) following the introduction of the rules. The approach set out in this section could include elements to limit the resources required to undertake panel reviews during this initial period. However, there is a risk that tax administrations will indicate a preference for a panel to be established in all or almost all cases, which could exceed the capacity of tax administrations to undertake these reviews. This may be a particular concern for tax administrations that are commonly lead tax administrations, given the likely concentration of the UPEs of in-scope MNE groups in a reasonably small number of jurisdictions and the need for a lead tax administration to co-ordinate the panel review. However, this situation should not limit the ability of MNE groups to obtain certainty following the introduction of new taxing rights. In light of this challenge, it may also be possible to reduce the burden on tax administrations and MNE groups by phasing in rules for Amount A, beginning with the largest MNE groups and/or initially excluding some elements of the rules such as business line segmentation.

9.2.4. Constitution of the review panel, the review panel process and approval by affected tax administrations

Constitution of the review panel

746. If a review panel is established, tax administrations participating on the panel will be drawn from the list of affected tax administrations that indicated an interest in taking part, based on criteria to be agreed.

747. The criteria for determining the constitution of a review panel could include the following elements, which may be revised as experience is gained:

- Panels should ideally comprise 6-8 tax administrations. The number of tax administrations on a particular panel may depend on the geographic spread of an MNE group (e.g. MNE groups with a very wide geographic spread may justify a larger panel than an MNE group with a narrower, localised footprint). This location of the UPE of the MNE group will not be taken into account in considering the geographic spread of an MNE. This is to ensure that market jurisdictions and relieving jurisdictions that are geographically close to the UPE jurisdiction have the opportunity to be represented on a panel.
- The profile of tax administrations participating on a panel could reflect an agreed categorisation of all jurisdictions' economies as large or small and as developed or developing, such that a panel includes broadly the following mix of tax administrations (assuming sufficient affected tax administrations from each category express an interest in participating):
    - the lead tax administration;
    - 2-3 tax administrations from other jurisdictions that provide relief for Amount A (the lead tax administration will typically also be from a relieving jurisdiction, increasing this number to 3-4); or
    - 3-4 tax administrations from jurisdictions that receive an allocation of Amount A, ensuring that at least one small economy and one developing economy are included (unless no such jurisdictions are recipients of Amount A for the particular MNE group).
- Tax administrations on the panel should broadly reflect the geographic spread of the MNE group.
- It is necessary to ensure that all tax administrations have the opportunity to participate in the panel process (though not necessarily on all panels), taking into account their interest and capacity. With respect to capacity constraints, this may be a reason for a tax administration choosing to limit the number of panels in which it participates. However, capacity building will be undertaken to ensure tax administrations from developing economies are able to participate in panels if they wish to do so.
- Where an MNE group has several business lines within the scope of Amount A, the panel should ideally include tax administrations from jurisdictions involved in each allocation, though there may be cases where this will not be possible.
- The reasons given by a tax administration for wishing to participate in a particular panel (e.g. the value of potential tax revenue at stake) and any general considerations provided, such as an overall limit on the number of panels a tax administration has the capacity to participate in, albeit that tax administration may express interest in joining a greater number of panels (anticipating that there may be cases where a panel is not formed or it is not invited to participate).

748. The agreed criteria could be applied and a review panel identified by the lead tax administration, ensuring a streamlined process in which the lead tax administration is fully involved. Alternatively, if a

secretariat is to be established, application of agreed rules and procedures by the secretariat could be viewed as more objective.[4] This may also better ensure that all jurisdictions have balanced representation across different panels (as the secretariat would have information on the constitution of all review panels whereas a lead tax administration may only be aware of the constitution of review panels on which it participates). Other than providing the list of constituent entity and market jurisdictions and other information required to apply the agreed criteria (e.g. sales by jurisdiction), the MNE group would not participate in identifying the review panel or agreeing its membership.

749. In the event that a panel is to be established but an insufficient number of affected tax administrations expressed an interest in participating, the lead tax administration or secretariat will inform all affected tax administrations that this is the case. Affected tax administrations will then have a further opportunity to express interest in participating. A review panel will be formed from affected tax administrations that expressed interest, reflecting to the extent possible the criteria described above (e.g. if no affected tax administrations expressed an interest in joining the panel, this category of jurisdictions cannot be reflected).

750. As mentioned above, it is critical that all Inclusive Framework members are able to participate fully throughout this tax certainty process, and in particular in the panel reviews at the heart of the process. As such, the development and deployment of tools for capacity building will be important to support developing economies. These could include, among others, the preparation of guidance and manuals, online and face-to-face training, and direct support via the OECD Tax Inspectors Without Borders (TIWB) programme.

The review panel process

751. To ensure a streamlined process, all engagements with an MNE group with respect to the early certainty review will be conducted via the lead tax administration. Following the establishment of the review panel, the lead tax administration will contact the co-ordinating entity of the MNE group and agree a start date for the review. In most cases this should be as soon as possible, but a short delay may be appropriate (e.g. if key staff at the MNE group are engaged in transactions, or if the lead tax administration is leading a large number of reviews and these need to be co-ordinated). The start date will also be agreed with other affected tax administrations on the review panel and, given their expression of interest in joining the panel, panel members should be as flexible as possible in agreeing to this.

752. The review panel will conduct a review of an MNE group's self-assessment, including each element of the determination and allocation of Amount A, including the identification of relieving entities. The review may also include testing factual information provided by the MNE group, to ensure the accuracy of information. This process should include a number of conference calls and email exchanges which may be co-ordinated by the lead tax administration or secretariat and chaired by the lead tax administration. Where an affected tax administration not on the panel identifies a possible concern with an MNE group's self-assessment of Amount A, it should raise this with the lead tax administration at the earliest possible opportunity. This issue will then be addressed directly by the lead tax administration or included as a specific consideration in the panel review of the MNE group's self-assessment return. This will reduce the risk of delays later in the tax certainty process where an affected tax administration raises an objection that could have been dealt with during the panel review.

753. In some cases it may be necessary for additional information or clarification to be requested via the lead tax administration, or for the MNE group to join a conference call with members of the review panel to present on specific issues (e.g. business line segmentation) and respond to questions. In a small number of cases a face-to-face meeting with an MNE group may be needed, but it is anticipated that this will not usually be the case. Any approach to achieve early tax certainty relies upon active and transparent participation by an MNE group. Wherever additional input is requested, it is critical that an MNE group endeavours to provide the information or clarification as quickly as possible, reflecting timeframes agreed with the panel (taking into account the volume and availability of the information requested). This additional

information may be provided on request to affected tax administrations not participating in the review panel, or may be made directly available to these tax administrations. Wherever possible, the panel review should be completed within [three months] from the start date.

754. If, in the view of review panel members, an MNE group is persistently late in providing information to the review panel without explanation, is acting in an un-cooperative or non-transparent manner, including by providing inaccurate or incomplete information, or where information provided proves to be unreliable or changes (or is expected to change), this issue will be raised with the co-ordinating entity by the lead tax administration. Where this issue is not resolved and where objective criteria to be developed are met, the co-ordinating entity may be informed that the review panel is not able complete the review as requested. These are the only circumstances in which an MNE group may not be provided with certainty after having submitted a request, and it should instead rely on domestic remedies. In cases where a review cannot be completed because information provided by the MNE group has changed or is expected to change, but the MNE group has acted in goodwill and informed the lead tax administration of any uncertainty it is aware of, it may be agreed that a review of the MNE group's application of Amount A may re-start once it is confident that relevant information is no longer subject to change.

755. It may be possible for information to be made available to tax administrations via a secure virtual data room maintained by the MNE group. Affected tax administrations may then download the information they require. This is based on an approach adopted in the pilots for the FTA ICAP for a co-ordinated risk assessment of large MNE groups, ensuring access to information while reducing the burden on the lead tax administration. However, it does require a tax administration to access each virtual data room to obtain information, which could be problematic if there are technical issues in accessing the data. It would also require MNE groups to establish virtual data rooms, which adds to their burden.

756. In the event that any member of the review panel is not able to reach a conclusion within [three months], the lead tax administration should inform the co-ordinating entity that more time is needed to complete the panel review, which may involve further requests for information. The overall length of time needed for a panel review will vary, but it is anticipated that in the majority of cases these will be completed within [nine months] from the start date. In particular, it is envisaged that, after the first year, in many cases an MNE group's review may be completed more quickly, as it may not be necessary to review all elements of the MNE group's determination and allocation of Amount A or such review may not need to be so detailed (e.g. a review of an MNE group's delineation of business lines and the identification of residual profit activities entities may not be needed after the first year if there have been no significant changes).

757. If at any point it becomes clear to the lead tax administration that the review panel is unable to reach agreement and this is unlikely to be resolved within the panel, it should consider ending the panel review with a conclusion that no agreement was reached. It is expected that any panel review that extends to [12 months] from the start date should be brought to an end with no agreement reached. This should provide an incentive for the review panel to reach agreement if possible and, where this is not possible, it allows the process to move on to the determination panel stage, ensuring certainty for the MNE group within a reasonable timeframe.

758. Following the panel review process, review panels may make recommendations to the MNE group for improvements to its processes and controls for applying Amount A, that may or may not be agreed by the MNE group. Where an MNE group's processes and controls appear weak, and in particular if a review panel has previously recommended changes but these were not implemented, this may mean that a more detailed review of the MNE group's determination and allocation of Amount A is needed.

759. While tax administrations on a review panel will work closely together, each may have its own view as to whether an MNE group's self-assessment is in accordance with globally agreed rules on the operation of Amount A or whether any adjustments are needed. Where these views differ, panellists should seek to understand the reason for these differences and agree a common position if possible. For example, if there are a number of possible acceptable approaches under Amount A (e.g. as a basis for the allocation of

central costs) and the majority of panellists agree as to which is most suitable, other panellists should consider if they can accept this approach even if it is not their preferred outcome. However, while tax administrations on a review panel should endeavour to reach agreement, they are not committed or required to do so.

760. At the end of the panel review, the MNE group is informed as to the result. Where the review panel has reached agreement that changes are required to the MNE group's assessment of Amount A, the MNE group will be asked to agree that these changes be made. There are therefore three broad possible outcomes from this process:

- The review panel agrees with an MNE group's assessment of Amount A, which either corresponds with the self-assessment submitted by the MNE group or the MNE group agrees to revise its self-assessment to reflect changes required by the panel (which will now be submitted to other affected tax administrations for approval).
- The review panel reaches agreement, which does not correspond with the self-assessment submitted by the MNE group, and the MNE group does not agree to revise its self-assessment.
- The review panel fails to reach agreement.

Submission of assessments agreed by the review panel for approval

761. If the review panel reaches agreement with the MNE group's self-assessment (either as filed or reflecting adjustments to the self-assessment agreed by the MNE group), this self-assessment and a panel recommendation that the self-assessment be accepted is sent by the lead tax administration to all affected tax administrations not on the panel. This is accompanied by a summary of the review undertaken by the panel and the basis for its conclusion that each element of the MNE group's application of Amount A should be agreed by affected tax administrations. The summary would be prepared by the lead tax administration, supported by the secretariat, and agreed with panel members. Affected tax administrations will also have access to any other information provided the MNE group in the course of the panel review. Depending upon the volume of such information, it may be exchanged by the lead tax administration at the same time as the panel recommendation, or a list of the information may be exchanged with the indication that the information itself is available on request.

762. In most cases the summary of the work undertaken by the review panel and the information it used as a basis for its decision should be sufficient for affected tax administrations to form a view as to whether or not they agree to the review panel's recommendation but, if needed, a tax administration may request additional information. This will be provided by the lead tax administration if it concerns information that was already supplied by the MNE group, or else may be requested by the lead tax administration from the MNE group.

763. If no affected tax administration objects to the review panel's recommendations within [three months], their acceptance is assumed and the MNE group is informed by the lead tax administration. The assessment of Amount A agreed by the review panel and approved by affected tax administrations is binding on the MNE group's constituent entities and on tax administrations in all Inclusive Framework member jurisdictions.

764. If any affected tax administration objects to the review panel's recommendation, all affected tax administrations will be informed and invited to provide any comments on these objections within [two weeks]. The review panel will have up to [two months] to consider whether an adjustment is needed to the MNE group's assessment of Amount A and discuss this with the MNE group, though this process should be completed more quickly if possible.

765. If the review panel and MNE group agree that adjustment is needed (or accepted), the lead tax administration will re-circulate a revised assessment of Amount A and recommendation reflecting this to affected tax administrations for any further objections. At this point objections should be raised within a

period of [one month] and should only concern or be consequential to elements that have changed since the previous version was circulated. This process continues, with [one month] for additional objections concerning new elements, until no objections are received. At this point, the lead tax administration informs the MNE group that the assessment has been accepted. The amended assessment of Amount A agreed by the review panel and approved by affected tax administrations is binding on the MNE group's constituent entities and on tax administrations in all Inclusive Framework member jurisdictions.

766. If the review panel is unable to accommodate objections raised by an affected tax administration, the lead tax administration will explain the reasons for this to the affected tax administration and invite the affected tax administration to withdraw its objection. If the affected tax administration accepts this explanation and withdraws its objection, assuming no other objections remain, the assessment of Amount A becomes binding on the MNE group's constituent entities and on tax administrations in all Inclusive Framework member jurisdictions as if no objection was made. If the affected tax administration does not withdraw its objection, the lead tax administration will inform the MNE group and all affected tax administrations that relevant questions will be referred to a determination panel for a conclusive outcome. The process for approving review panel recommendations will be reviewed as tax administrations gain experience.

767. In the event that the review panel reaches agreement, which does not correspond with the self-assessment submitted by the MNE group, and the MNE group does not agree to revise its self-assessment, the MNE group is treated as not accepting panel conclusions (see below).

Submission of assessments not agreed by the review panel for comments

768. If the review panel fails to reach agreement on an MNE group's self-assessment, the MNE group and all affected tax administrations will be informed by the lead tax administration that relevant questions will be referred to a determination panel for a conclusive outcome. A summary of the review undertaken by the panel identifying the elements where the panel was able to agree and those where agreement was not possible is sent by the lead tax administration to all affected tax administrations. This will be prepared by the lead tax administration, with support from the secretariat as appropriate taking into account the need for strict taxpayer confidentiality, and agreed with other panel members. As before, additional information obtained from the MNE group in the course of the review is also available to all affected tax administrations.

769. Affected tax administrations have [three months] to raise objections to the points that the review panel could agree and make comments on the points where it did not agree. This process ensures that, whether or not the review panel reaches agreement, all affected tax administrations have the opportunity to provide input before the determination panel process commences.

9.2.5. Constitution of the determination panel and the determination panel process

770. If the review panel is unable to reach agreement, or if it is unable to accommodate objections by other tax administrations, relevant questions would be submitted to a second panel (the determination panel), which is obligated to reach a decision. This ensures that certainty is offered to MNE groups in all cases where it is requested and the MNE group co-operates in the process. These questions would be accompanied by relevant comments from affected tax administrations, including those that participated in the review panel and those that did not. In light of the amount of time and resource required to undertake a tax certainty process involving two panels, a possible option which will be considered in further work could be for a condition to be imposed that questions will only be put to a determination panel for a conclusive outcome if an MNE group agrees to be bound by the determination panel's decision.

Constitution of the determination panel

771. Disputes concerning Amount A are likely to impact a significant number of jurisdictions, including those that may not have been involved in detailed discussions concerning the dispute in question (i.e. jurisdictions that were not on the review panel and that have not raised any objection to the review panel's recommendation). In light of this impact, clear, objective rules will be developed to identify members of the determination panel where it is to consider questions concerning Amount A.

772. With respect to a determination panel to consider disputes concerning Amount A only, work on the appropriate constitution of a panel focuses on a number of fundamental issues. The Inclusive Framework will address a number of issues on which members hold different views, including by considering how panels are currently constituted in other contexts. These issues include:

- Whether panellists should be serving tax officials, retired (or non-serving) tax officials or independent experts, or a combination of these groups.
- Whether panellists should be drawn from a pool with rotating membership of individuals. For example, individuals could initially be appointed to the pool for a period of either two or four years, and then for a period of four years, so that half of all pool members would be replaced every two years. This would ensure that, after an initial period, panels include members with experience in resolving Amount A disputes. If this approach is adopted, members of the pool that are serving tax officials would be appointed by members of the Inclusive Framework. A process for appointing other members of the pool will be explored.
- Whether a pool member from the lead tax administration and/or other tax administrations participating on the review panel may participate on the determination panel.
- Whether determination panellists that are tax officials should be from affected tax administrations, from non-affected tax administrations or a combination of affected and non-affected tax administrations (or, in light of the possible difficulty in adopting one approach that applies to all in-scope MNE groups, whether they should be appointed with no reference to this criterion).
- Whether small economies and developing economies should always be represented on a determination panel, to the extent these jurisdictions appoint pool-members.
- Whether a determination panel should have a Chair who is responsible for co-ordinating discussions and would have an additional vote in the event of no overall majority, to decide between two or more outcomes which otherwise have equal support. The Chair could be a named individual appointed by the Inclusive Framework (e.g. a suitable senior serving or retired tax official) or drawn from a small pool of such individuals (given that there may be a number of panels required in the first year(s) of applying Amount A).
- Whether a Chair who is a tax official should be from a tax administration that is not an affected tax administration (or, in the case of a retired or non-serving tax official, one that did not previously work for an affected tax administration).
- Whether a determination panel should include an odd number of panellists (including the Chair), which would facilitate a decision being reached by simple majority, where consensus proves impossible.

Determination panel process

773. The review panel will develop specific questions for consideration by the determination panel, together with written analyses of the different positions held by members of the review panel, by affected tax administrations that raised objections to the review panel's recommendation and by other affected tax administrations (i.e. the determination panel will use a "last best offer" approach to decision-making, choosing from among these alternative responses and will not re-open elements that were already settled

by the review panel and agreed by all affected tax administrations). All affected tax administrations will have the opportunity to view and comment on the questions to be submitted. The format of these questions, and whether they deal with each objection in turn or whether they deal with a number of objections that are linked, will be determined by the review panel on a case-by-case basis. To the extent possible, interactions between questions will be identified and explained by the review panel, as will any consequences of the determination panel's choice of response to one question for other questions put to it. Further work will consider if, where possible, the review panel could also include an indication as to the level of support each objection has, but this should not by itself determine the outcome of a question. As time goes on and experience is gained in framing questions possibly involving a number of different objections and interactions, this process may be revised.

774. Where possible, the determination panel should endeavour to reach agreement on each question by consensus, taking into account the views of all panel members. Where this is not possible, a decision by simple majority on each question may be accepted. Where even simple majority does not provide a clear outcome (e.g. where there are numerous possible answers to a particular question and there is no majority view on the determination panel), the Chair of the determination panel would have an additional vote, to decide between two or more answers which otherwise have equal support. To the extent possible, the determination panel should seek to reach a decision within [six months] following referral from the review panel. The Chair of the determination panel should then prepare a short summary of its conclusions, setting out the key reasons for its decisions, which is made available to affected tax administrations by the lead tax administration.

775. In the event the determination panel confirms an approach that has already been agreed by the MNE group (i.e. the position as filed in its self-assessment return or reflecting changes agreed by the MNE group), this assessment of Amount A is binding on the MNE group's constituent entities and on tax administrations in all Inclusive Framework member jurisdictions. If the determination panel reaches any other conclusion, the lead tax administration will invite the co-ordinating entity of the MNE group to accept the outcomes of this process. If it does, the outcome becomes similarly binding. If, as a result of further work to be conducted, it is agreed that a case will only progress to a determination panel stage if the MNE group commits to being bound by the panel's decision, then the determination panel's conclusions will be binding in all cases.

776. Work will be undertaken to develop a control framework for the determination panel, setting out specific rules for the determination of the Chair and panel members, and procedures for undertaking a review and reaching decisions. This may also include the development of guidance as needed, supported by the secretariat, to promote consistency in the decisions of later determination panels considering similar issues. This guidance may also be made available to tax administrations for use in conducting panel reviews and, where appropriate, to MNE groups for use in preparing an Amount A self-assessment return. This should facilitate reviews being completed more quickly and reduce the need for questions to be referred to a determination panel which concern issues that have been dealt with previously.

9.2.6. Cases where an MNE group does not accept a panel conclusion

777. If an MNE group does not agree with the recommendations of the review panel (including any adjustments agreed by the panel based on objections raised by other tax administrations) or the conclusions of the determination panel, as appropriate, it may withdraw its request for early certainty (unless the MNE agrees in advance to being bound by the determination panel's decision). The MNE group may then rely on domestic procedures in each jurisdiction.

778. The lead tax administration will inform affected tax administrations not on the panel that the MNE group has withdrawn its request for early certainty. It will also provide these tax administrations with a copy of the review panel's recommendation (if the MNE group did not agree with the review panel's conclusions)

or with a copy of the determination panel's conclusions (if the MNE group did not agree with these conclusions).

779. With respect to cases where an MNE group withdraws its request for tax certainty after a review panel recommendation has been agreed by all affected tax administrations or after a determination panel has completed its review, further discussions will be conducted to consider whether tax administrations should still be bound by panel conclusions. As the MNE group has withdrawn its request for early certainty, it may be appropriate that tax administrations are also not bound by these conclusions. However, given they reflect an approach that has already been reviewed and that would determine and allocate Amount A between jurisdictions consistently while eliminating double tax, there may be a benefit in tax administrations still being bound by panel conclusions, unless a constituent entity in a tax administration's jurisdiction appeals the assessment to a domestic court or a tax administration is required to comply with a court decision that is different. In particular, the consistent implementation of panel outcomes by all affected tax administrations could remove the risk of double taxation and prevent disputes arising at a later point. Where an MNE group withdraws its request for tax certainty at any other point (e.g. before a review panel's recommendation is agreed by affected tax administrations or before questions are submitted to a determination panel), tax administrations are not bound and may conduct their own enquiries. However, even if tax administrations are not bound by panel conclusions, they may take work conducted by the review panel and determination panel (if relevant) into account in conducting these enquiries.

780. It is expected that in the significant majority of cases all constituent entities will accept the position agreed by the co-ordinating entity, which applies Amount A across the MNE group and avoids double taxation. If, in exceptional cases, legal or practical issues mean it was not possible for a particular entity within an MNE group to agree in advance to be bound by decisions of the co-ordinating entity, and the entity does not accept a panel conclusion, the tax certainty provided to other entities in the MNE group may also fall away, even though they have accepted panel outcomes. This will depend upon the circumstances of each case (e.g. if the entity that does not accept the panel conclusion is an Amount A paying entity vs an entity in a market jurisdiction). Further work will be undertaken to understand the extent to which these legal or practical issues may arise in practice and how these can be avoided.

9.2.7. Other opportunities to provide greater certainty concerning aspects of Amount A

Whether an MNE group is within the scope of Amount A

781. Depending upon the final scope of Amount A agreed by the Inclusive Framework, a number of MNE groups may also seek certainty from tax administrations as to whether they are within or outside of this scope. However, unlike the process described in the rest of this chapter (which could be an annual process for some MNE groups), it is likely that an MNE group would only require certainty that it is within the scope of Amount A once, or periodically following any change to its business, structure, revenues or profitability. A possible approach to provide MNE groups with certainty as to whether they are within the scope of Amount A is described below.

- A specific self-assessment return and documentation package to determine whether an MNE group is within the scope of Amount A could be developed. This would focus on each element of the definition of scope.
- MNE groups that require certainty as to whether they are within scope should make a request early. Ideally this should be before the end of the first fiscal year when the MNE group could be within scope (recognising that any outcome would be dependent on information on revenue and profit levels for that fiscal year, which would not be available until after the year-end), but in all cases an MNE group should seek to make a request for certainty at least six months before the relevant filing deadline for the MNE group's Amount A self-assessment return.

- Where the UPE of the MNE group is resident in a jurisdiction that has introduced Amount A, this request should be submitted to the tax administration in this jurisdiction. Where the UPE jurisdiction has not introduced Amount A, the request may be submitted to any tax administration on a list of potential surrogate lead tax administrations.
- The UPE tax administration should conduct an initial review of the MNE group's self-assessment and the application of each element of the definition of an in-scope MNE group.
- Where the UPE tax administration does not agree with the MNE group's assessment as to whether it is in scope, this should be discussed with the MNE group to understand the different perspectives and see if agreement can be reached. The MNE group may modify its position as a result of this discussion.
- Where the UPE tax administration agrees with the MNE group's assessment as to whether it is within scope (as filed or following discussion with the MNE), the MNE group's self-assessment return as to scope and the associated documentation package should be exchanged with tax administrations in all Inclusive Framework member jurisdictions that have implemented Amount A, together with a recommendation that the MNE group's position be accepted. These items are sent to all member jurisdictions that have implemented Amount A as there is the potential for any jurisdiction to become a relieving jurisdiction or market jurisdiction in the future and the decision as to whether a particular MNE group is in scope should not change as a result of this. In other words, all member jurisdictions with Amount A rules have a potential interest in whether any given MNE group is within scope of Amount A and should be given the opportunity to comment.
- If the MNE group and UPE tax administration continue to disagree as to whether the MNE group is within scope, the MNE group's self-assessment return and documentation package is exchanged with tax administrations in all Inclusive Framework member jurisdictions that have implemented Amount A, together with an explanation as to why the UPE tax administration disagrees with this assessment and a recommendation that the UPE tax administration's position be supported.
- Tax administrations are given [12 weeks] to provide comments or objections to the UPE tax administration's recommendation. Objections should be accompanied by a clear explanation of the specific elements where there is disagreement. It is anticipated that in the significant majority of cases, if rules for the scope of Amount A are clearly articulated, tax administrations should agree with this recommendation. If no objections are received, the UPE tax administration's recommendation is approved and communicated to the MNE group.
- If one or more tax administrations object to the UPE tax administration's recommendation, the UPE jurisdiction should discuss these with the relevant tax administrations and consider whether its recommendation should be changed or if the tax administrations will withdraw their objections. In the event this does not happen, the question as to whether the MNE group is within scope should be referred to a determination panel for a conclusion.
- An MNE group is given certainty subject to a commitment that they will inform their UPE tax administration (or lead tax administration for MNE groups within scope) of any change that impacts this decision. Until such a change occurs, the certainty provided is binding on all Inclusive Framework member tax administrations. This means that:
    - MNE groups that have been given certainty they are in scope should not be denied relief from double taxation in accordance with rules for Amount A; and
    - MNE groups that have been given certainty they are out-of-scope should not be subject to penalties or compliance action as a result of not filing an Amount A self-assessment return.

- Measures will be considered to ensure that an MNE group informs its UPE tax administration (or lead tax administration, as appropriate) in a timely manner. This could include, for example, an annual reporting requirement to confirm whether any changes have occurred, a periodic review by tax administrations, or penalties for late or incomplete notification of changes. Following a change that impacts a decision as to whether an MNE group is within scope, an MNE group may request a new review, which will benefit from work undertaken in the earlier process.

Whether a jurisdiction is a market jurisdiction of an MNE group

782. As mentioned above, an MNE group will be required to provide to its lead tax administration a list of all Inclusive Framework member jurisdictions that are market jurisdictions. For these purposes, a market jurisdiction is defined as a jurisdiction in which the MNE group:

- had pro-rata in-scope revenue equal to the threshold for an allocation of Amount A in the most recently ended fiscal year or in any fiscal period ending in the prior 12 months (i.e. in most cases this will mean the most recent fiscal year and the one before that); and
- any "plus factor" described in chapter 3, as appropriate.

783. This approach should ensure that Inclusive Framework member jurisdictions where an MNE group is likely to have in-scope revenue close to the threshold for an allocation of Amount A receive a copy of the MNE group's Amount A self-assessment return and documentation package. The tax administrations in these jurisdictions can then review these to determine whether the in-scope revenue is above the applicable threshold.

784. An issue remains however, where an MNE group does not include a particular jurisdiction on its list of market jurisdictions in circumstances where the tax administration in that jurisdiction takes the view that it should be a market jurisdiction. A possible approach to address this concern is summarised below.

- An MNE group will be required to provide to its lead tax administration a list of its market jurisdictions, which will be made available to tax administrations in all Inclusive Framework member tax administrations. Therefore, tax administrations that believe they are in a market jurisdiction can review this list and confirm if their jurisdiction is included.
- Where a tax administration sees that its jurisdiction is not included on the list, it may contact the lead tax administration with any evidence it has to support its position that the MNE group has in-scope revenues (and, if applicable, a relevant constituent entity) in its jurisdiction such that it should be included in the list, and request that it be added to the list. The deadline for this request should be no later than [9 months] after the end of the relevant fiscal year, in order that this process may be completed prior to the exchange of the MNE group's self-assessment return and documentation package with affected tax administrations.
- The lead tax administration will share this information with the co-ordinating entity of the MNE group and invite the co-ordinating entity to update its list of market jurisdictions, or to provide a response to the other tax administration's comments.
- If the MNE group is willing to include the jurisdiction on its list of market jurisdictions (noting that the jurisdiction will only receive an allocation of Amount A if it has in-scope revenues above the applicable threshold and not simply by reason of being included on the list), this will address the tax administration's concerns.
- If the MNE group is not willing to include the jurisdiction on its list of market jurisdictions it should provide an explanation as to why this is the case (e.g. provide information on the level of in-scope revenues in that jurisdiction to illustrate they are lower than 75% of the threshold and, if applicable, the nature and activities of constituent entities in the jurisdiction). If the tax administration accepts this explanation it should withdraw its request.

- If the MNE group and the tax administration continue to disagree on this issue, a determination panel may be formed including the tax administration, the lead tax administration and the Chair of the determination panel (or a Chair where there is more than one). This panel will consider information provided by the tax administration and the MNE group and reach a conclusion as to whether the tax administration's jurisdiction should be considered a market jurisdiction. This decision will be reached by majority, so if either the lead tax administration or the Chair supports the tax administration's position, its jurisdiction will be considered a market jurisdiction. It is suggested that the Chair of the determination panel should be included in these discussions even if it is already clear that the lead tax administration supports the tax administration position.
- If the panel supports the tax administration position, the MNE group is informed and the tax administration will be included as an affected tax administration for the purposes of exchanging the MNE group's Amount A self-assessment return and documentation package, as well as for any Amount A early certainty process for the relevant tax year. If the panel supports the MNE group's position, the tax administration will not be included as an affected tax administration for the relevant fiscal year.

Whether an MNE group's self-assessment of Amount A is correct in the absence of a request for tax certainty

785. This chapter describes a process to provide early certainty over the operation of Amount A to MNE groups on request. There are also advantages in a process for tax administrations to jointly consider the application of Amount A to a particular MNE group, even if the group has not requested certainty and the outcomes of this review are not binding on it.

- Even where an MNE group does not make a request for early certainty, its Amount A self-assessment return and documentation package will still be filed with its lead tax administration and exchanged with other affected tax administrations.
- The lead tax administration and affected tax administrations could be given the opportunity to propose that a panel review of an MNE group's application of Amount A be undertaken. Affected tax administrations may also express an interest in participating on such a panel.
- Whether or not the lead tax administration proposes the panel, it may agree to co-ordinate a multilateral review of the application of Amount A by any MNE group. Where the lead tax administration is not willing to co-ordinate the panel review, or does not have the resources to do so (e.g. taking into account its commitment to co-ordinate panel reviews where an MNE group has made a request for certainty), another affected tax administration may offer to co-ordinate the review. The lead tax administration may join the panel even if it does not co-ordinate the review, and it is noted that the participation of the lead tax administration (which will often be in the MNE group's UPE jurisdiction) will typically benefit the review process for all tax administrations.
- An MNE group could be informed that the review panel will be constituted and given the opportunity to submit a late request for tax certainty. This would benefit tax administrations as the MNE group would then be engaged in the process, which should aid the review. It would also benefit the MNE group, as it would obtain tax certainty as a result.
- The review panel would be conducted largely consistent with the process described in this chapter. An MNE group should provide information requested for use by a panel even if it does not choose to make a request for early certainty.
- At the end of the panel review, the panel's recommendation that the MNE group's self-assessment (or elements of its self-assessment) are acceptable, and any changes that it

proposes, are shared with affected tax administrations for their comments and agreement. Any comments from affected tax administrations may be taken into account by the panel.

- Where tax administrations are unable to reach agreement, the review panel could in principle refer questions to a determination panel for a conclusive answer. As this could prove useful in specific situations it is suggested that this possibility is left open, but it is expected that, unless an MNE group has agreed to submit a late request for tax certainty, affected tax administrations will typically not wish to take this step if, in any case, the end result is not binding.
- Where an MNE group agrees to submit a late request for tax certainty, the potential outcomes are as described earlier in this chapter. Where an MNE group does not submit such a request, there are a number of potential outcomes from this process:
    - Where tax administrations agree that all or parts of an MNE group's self-assessment are acceptable, may not be binding on them, but could be agreed and implemented by each tax administration within their domestic framework without undertaking significant further work, minimising duplication of work across affected tax administrations. Alternatively, it could be agreed that, if tax administrations agree that an MNE's self-assessment of Amount A is acceptable, this should be binding on tax administrations even where an MNE has not requested certainty, unless a constituent entity in a tax administration's jurisdiction appeals the assessment to a domestic court or a tax administration is required to comply with a court decision that is different.
    - Where tax administrations agree that changes should be made to an MNE group's self-assessment, these could be proposed to the MNE group. The MNE group may be willing to accept these changes to avoid double taxation that could arise if changes were proposed unilaterally by tax administrations in some jurisdictions.
    - Where tax administrations do not reach agreement or wish to undertake their own review they are free to do so, but their future enquiries may benefit from work undertaken by the panel.

Whether an MNE group can seek dispute resolution in cases where it did not submit a request for early certainty

786. Connected with the previous issue, there may be cases where an MNE group does not make a request for tax certainty and subsequently is subject to tax adjustments with respect to its self-assessment of Amount A in one or more jurisdictions. In these cases, an MNE group may seek to address this through domestic processes, or may seek to rely on MAP if available. However, given the likely complexity of a MAP involving potentially all jurisdictions where an MNE group has constituent entities or a market, it may be preferable from a tax administration perspective to rely on a panel process.

787. To recognise the resource commitment of tax administrations to the panel process and encourage MNE groups to seek early certainty, later requests for tax certainty could be subject to the agreement of affected tax administrations. In other words, complete requests for early certainty should always be accepted, whereas there may be cases where a late request for certainty is not accepted, and an MNE group that did not request early certainty is required to rely on domestic remedies to deal with any disputes that arise. However, it is anticipated that, in the majority of cases, a request would be accepted and further work will be undertaken to explore how MNE groups can be encouraged to seek early certainty. For these cases, work will be undertaken to consider how the experience and positions of tax administrations that have already undertaken enquiries domestically may be taken into account (e.g. by participation on a review panel, or by providing the results of their enquiries to the review panel).

9.2.8. Transfer pricing and other adjustments in subsequent years

788. The process for providing early tax certainty described in this section includes identification of an MNE group's relieving jurisdictions (i.e. those where double tax relief will be provided to compensate for Amount A allocated to market jurisdictions). The process to determine these jurisdictions under Pillar One will be based wholly or in part on the level of profit attributed to each jurisdiction under the ALP.

789. As mentioned above, a request for certainty with respect to Amount A does not prevent tax administrations from commencing compliance activity with respect to an MNE group's other tax matters, including transfer pricing issues. There is therefore a risk that any material transfer pricing adjustments made after an MNE group has been provided with early certainty with respect to Amount A could require the identification of relieving jurisdictions, and the amount of relief they should give, to be re-considered.

790. Until the design of Amount A is agreed, it is not possible to fully finalise an approach to address this issue. One option to reduce (though not remove) this risk could be if an MNE group is able to request a co-ordinated risk assessment of its transfer pricing and permanent establishments in key jurisdictions under the ICAP. This would allow an MNE group to help identify the jurisdictions where it is most likely to be subject to a transfer pricing adjustment, taking into account the nature of its activities and previous experience. Work will progress on other solutions to address this issue, which will also link to tax certainty beyond Amount A.

9.3. Dispute prevention and resolution beyond Amount A

791. As noted above, Inclusive Framework members continue to have different views on the scope and nature of new approaches to provide greater certainty beyond Amount A, and in particular the application of a new mandatory and binding dispute resolution mechanism to these issues. To help bridge those differences this Blueprint uses an approach that is built around four elements, which are described in more detail below. Discussions of the scope of mandatory and binding dispute resolution beyond Amount A will continue in the Inclusive Framework, with a view to achieving a balance that provides greater certainty to MNE groups where it is needed most while recognising the concerns, challenges and constraints of a number of members.

792. Work on tax certainty beyond Amount A has not, however, focused solely on mandatory and binding dispute resolution. The approach to tax certainty beyond Amount A comprises a number of main steps – from dispute prevention (Step 1) and the existing MAP (Step 2) to mandatory binding dispute resolution (Step 3). While ongoing work to improve and enhance dispute prevention tools and the MAP has already been important separate from work on the tax challenges of the digitalisation of the economy, that ongoing work has gained further momentum in light of the fundamental importance of tax certainty as an element of Pillar One. This part of the chapter describes these four steps and how a novel dispute resolution mechanism would apply to different categories of disputes and jurisdictions.

9.3.1. Step 1: Improvements to dispute prevention processes

793. The most effective approach to dealing with tax disputes is to prevent them from arising in the first place. This section considers a number of enhancements and improvements to existing dispute prevention tools, including existing projects undertaken as part of the FTA tax certainty agenda. These would sit alongside and complement new dispute resolution mechanisms.

- ***ICAP.*** The ICAP is a voluntary programme for a co-ordinated risk assessment of potentially all of an MNE group's transfer pricing and permanent establishment risk by tax administrations in a number of jurisdictions where the MNE group has activity, including its headquarter jurisdiction. ICAP does not provide an MNE with legal certainty as may be achieved, for example, through an advance pricing arrangement (APA), but does give comfort and assurance where tax administrations participating in an MNE's risk assessment consider a covered risk to be low. Where an area is identified as needing further attention, this may be addressed through a defined "issue resolution" process within the programme or, if needed, work conducted in ICAP can improve the efficiency of actions taken outside the programme. First launched in 2018, ICAP is currently in a second pilot including tax administrations from 19 jurisdictions. Following the conclusion of this pilot, the programme could be widened to include more tax administrations and MNEs. This could be particularly beneficial to MNE groups within the scope of Amount A, given the possible interactions between an MNE group's transfer pricing and permanent establishment issues and Amount A (see below). A multilateral ICAP-like mechanism could also be used to facilitate greater certainty and a more consistent outcome as to whether an MNE group's activities in a number of jurisdictions represent baseline marketing and distribution functions (and so are within the scope of Amount B) or go beyond this.

- ***Joint audits.*** Early co-ordinated intervention in the form of a joint audit may be more effective than having several tax administrations each perform their own transfer pricing audits of an MNE group, with the resulting potential for inconsistent positions and disagreements between tax administrations. Work is currently being done within the FTA to support greater use of joint audits and this could be a useful addition to support tax certainty for MNE groups within the scope of Amount A, again given the possible interactions between transfer pricing disputes and Amount A.
- ***Improved processes for bilateral and multilateral APAs.*** Multilaterally co-ordinated risk assessment and assurance (through ICAP) could be coupled with enhanced bilateral and multilateral APAs to provide advance certainty and avoid potential transfer pricing disputes. Work on bilateral and multilateral APA processes is currently being undertaken by the two FTA Focus Groups (on Improving the APA Process and on Multilateral MAP and APAs).[5]
- ***Use of standardised benchmarks in common transfer pricing situations.*** The use of standardised benchmarks in common transfer pricing situations between jurisdictions has the potential to improve tax certainty for MNE groups in a number of ways, either for dispute prevention (where benchmarks used at the risk assessment or audit stages allow MNE groups to be de-selected from further enquiries) or for dispute resolution (to resolve MAP cases more quickly). The FTA is currently undertaking work to explore how this work can be supported in key areas that give rise to the greatest tax uncertainty and MAP.
- ***Time limits to make transfer pricing and permanent establishment adjustments.*** The January 2020 *Outline* provided that Inclusive Framework members could explore limiting the time during which any adjustments with respect to transfer pricing issues could be made. The Inclusive Framework is currently exploring such limits and their scope, as well as the conditions under which they could apply.
- ***Suspension of tax collection.*** The *Outline* also provided that jurisdictions could explore the limitation or suspension of tax collection for the duration of any disputes. Further work would be required to define and agree the conditions under which such a suspension would be available. As recognised in the Report on Action 14, the requirement to pay tax for MAP access may create significant financial difficulties for taxpayers. Such a requirement may also make it more difficult for a competent authority to enter into good faith MAP discussions in circumstances where that competent authority could likely have to refund taxes already collected as a result of any compromise reached through the MAP. The proposals to strengthen the Action 14 minimum standard being considered in the context of the 2020 review of the standard include a proposal under which it would be explored whether it could be possible to suspend tax collection for the duration of the MAP process under the same

conditions as are applicable under domestic rules. Work on suspension of collection on this basis will thus be continued as part of the 2020 review.

9.3.2. Step 2: Improvements to the MAP

794. Although enhancements and improvements to the existing dispute prevention framework should reduce the number of disputes, bilateral and multilateral MAPs will continue to be necessary to resolve the disputes that do arise. The ongoing implementation and peer review of the Action 14 minimum standard will contribute to the continual strengthening of existing MAP infrastructure and processes.

795. The 2020 review of Action 14 will also provide a vehicle to advance the broader tax certainty agenda through the consideration of additional options to enhance the robustness and effectiveness of the MAP. In particular, in the context of the 2020 review, the FTA MAP Forum and Working Party 1 are exploring the addition of a number of proposed elements to the Action 14 minimum standard, including the following:

- Introduce the obligation to establish a bilateral APA programme for jurisdictions with more than 10 transfer pricing MAP cases per annum over the past three years.
- Introduce the obligation to roll-out the Global Awareness Training Module or a similar training programme.
- Provide criteria for determining whether access to MAP should be given as well as to define what information taxpayers (as a minimum) should include in their MAP requests. Jurisdictions should reflect both items in their MAP guidance.
- Introduce the obligation that tax collection is suspended during the period a MAP case is pending, under the same conditions as are available to taxpayers under domestic rules.
- Jurisdictions should ensure that penalties/interest charges are aligned in proportion to the outcomes of the MAP process.
- Jurisdictions should ensure that all MAP agreements can be implemented notwithstanding the expiration of domestic time limits.
- Jurisdictions should implement appropriate procedures to permit, in certain cases and after an initial tax assessment, requests made by taxpayers which are within the time period provided for in the tax treaty for the multiyear resolution through the MAP of recurring issues with respect to filed tax years, where the relevant facts and circumstances are the same and subject to the verification of such facts and circumstances on audit.

796. The implementation of a mandatory and binding dispute resolution mechanism beyond Amount A should itself contribute to more effective MAP processes. While the effects of mandatory and binding dispute resolution mechanisms such as MAP arbitration may be difficult to separate from the effects of other initiatives to improve competent authority operations, experience has generally shown that the adoption of mandatory and binding dispute resolution mechanisms has contributed to more constructive competent authority collaboration, with the result that competent authorities are generally able to reach agreement within a timeframe that avoids triggering those mechanisms. A mandatory and binding dispute resolution mechanism beyond Amount A should reasonably be expected to produce a similar effect – that is, the broader dispute resolution mechanism should be expected to provide competent authorities with strong incentives to bridge their differences to reach agreement and should accordingly be triggered only exceptionally.

797. The options explored will include broader support for low-capacity jurisdictions' MAP programmes through the ongoing work of the FTA MAP Forum. Such support could include an adapted form of the Tax Inspectors Without Borders (TIWB) programme to provide technical assistance to these jurisdictions'

competent authorities as well as training and other capacity building activities delivered through the Inclusive Framework and other international organisations such as the United Nations.

798. Work to improve the MAP as it relates to issues beyond Amount A will be carried out within the overall framework of the continuing relevant work streams of the FTA MAP Forum, given that body's broad mandate to work collectively to improve the effectiveness of the MAP to meet the needs of both governments and taxpayers in the global tax environment.

9.3.3. Step 3: A binding dispute resolution mechanism beyond Amount A

The scope of dispute prevention and resolution beyond Amount A

799. As already noted, there remain differences in the views of Inclusive Framework members as to the extent to which Pillar One should incorporate new tax certainty approaches beyond Amount A. Some strongly support a mandatory binding dispute resolution mechanism with broad application, while others consider that disputes unrelated to Amount A should be resolved through the existing MAP framework and non-binding administrative tools.

800. To bridge these different views on the scope of dispute prevention and resolution beyond Amount A, the Blueprint explores the following approach based around four elements:

- **In-scope taxpayers.** For MNE groups with global revenue and foreign in-scope revenue above the relevant Amount A thresholds, the approach contemplates a new and innovative mandatory and binding resolution process for all disputes related to transfer pricing and permanent establishment adjustments to any of their constituent entities. This is designed as a last resort and would follow the exhaustion of all other dispute prevention and resolution tools, which would be expanded and improved including as part of the 2020 review of BEPS Action 14. The process would cover adjustments related to in-scope activities, but also extend to other (out-of-scope) activities of MNEs that are subject to the new taxing right, possibly subject to a materiality condition. The new process would not apply where disputes are already covered by existing mandatory and binding dispute resolution mechanisms, which would continue to apply.
    - This approach to in-scope taxpayers is motivated principally by the potential impacts of transfer pricing and permanent establishment disputes on Amount A. Although Amount A's approach to allocating part of an MNE group's residual profits to market jurisdictions does not use traditional transfer pricing techniques, disputed transfer pricing adjustments may have effects on the application of Amount A, in particular when identifying paying entities and determining the amount of double tax relief available in relieving jurisdictions. In addition, depending upon the final design of the rules, questions as to whether or not there is a permanent establishment in a jurisdiction may be relevant in determining if there is nexus in that jurisdiction. As such, while the approach described earlier in this chapter will provide MNE groups with certainty regarding their assessment of Amount A, this certainty could be undermined if a subsequent transfer pricing or permanent establishment dispute means that the underlying assumptions upon which Amount A is based for a particular fiscal year are changed.
    - This approach to in-scope MNE groups also recognises that they will be required to implement new processes and controls to comply with innovative new rules, and to engage with new approaches to demonstrate their compliance. This implies a burden for in-scope MNE groups that is on top of any additional tax paid to market jurisdictions that cannot be relieved against existing taxes (e.g. because of differences in tax rates between market jurisdictions and relieving jurisdictions). Broader certainty beyond Amount A could be viewed as a possible *quid pro quo* for these MNE groups. If rules for Amount A are to be phased in, this could also imply a phased approach to the introduction of new tax certainty rules in step with the rules for

Amount A, giving jurisdictions time to gain experience before potentially applying them more widely in the future.

- **Other taxpayers**. All other taxpayers would benefit from improvements to the MAP and other existing dispute prevention and resolution tools. For these taxpayers, the Inclusive Framework will also examine new and innovative dispute resolution mechanisms for material transfer pricing and permanent establishment-related disputes that competent authorities are unable to resolve in a timely manner through the MAP. In this regard, the next steps of this work will explore the benefits of two approaches: a mandatory and binding dispute resolution process; and a mandatory but non-binding (advisory) dispute resolution process coupled with aspects of peer review and statistical reporting. A mandatory and non-binding mechanism could increase some jurisdictions' familiarity and comfort with the processes involved and, together with a complementary review and reporting framework, would monitor progress in resolving both the disputes that are submitted to the mandatory non-binding process and those that are not.
- **Amount B**. A key purpose of Amount B is to prevent transfer pricing disputes regarding baseline marketing and distribution activities through the use of agreed standardised returns to objectively defined activities, supported by quantitative indicators. Any disputes related to the application of Amount B (for example, whether a taxpayer falls within the definition of "baseline marketing and distribution activities"), which create risks of double taxation, would also be subject to mandatory binding dispute resolution, as a last resort and following the exhaustion of all other dispute prevention and resolution tools. Mandatory binding dispute resolution is needed to protect the benefits of Amount B, which will be undermined if certainty is limited to the remuneration of baseline activities and there are unresolved disputes as to whether or not particular arrangements or structures are within the scope of Amount B.
- **Developing economies with no or low levels of MAP disputes**. In the course of the Action 14 peer preview, more than 50 developing economies were identified that had no or only a very small number of MAP cases in inventory. Given these jurisdictions' lack of MAP experience, the limited capacity of their competent authorities and the circumstance that other jurisdictions did not identify areas of these jurisdictions' MAP regimes that required improvements, the peer review of these jurisdictions was deferred. For these developing economies, their small or non-existent MAP inventories would not justify the creation of the infrastructure for mandatory binding dispute resolution for issues not related to Amount A. Requiring these jurisdictions to commit to and implement a potentially complex dispute resolution process to address a situation that currently does not appear to present a material risk could be considered disproportionate:
    - These jurisdictions would, however, commit to an elective binding dispute resolution mechanism that would be triggered when their competent authorities were unable to resolve a MAP case within an agreed defined period. The mechanism would reflect the features of the mandatory binding mechanism developed for disputes beyond Amount A but would be triggered only where both competent authorities agreed that the mechanism should be used to resolve unresolved issues in a specific case. The mechanism would increase these jurisdictions' familiarity and comfort with the processes involved.
    - In determining appropriate levels of MAP inventory to be included in this category of jurisdictions, reference would be made to the principles of the Action 14 peer review process (in particular the criteria for deferral of a jurisdiction's peer review), which considers the number of MAP cases in inventory as well as access limitations that may have prevented cases from entering the MAP process and appearing in inventory.
- The mechanisms described above could be coupled with a peer review and reporting framework to monitor the effectiveness of all elements of the new dispute prevention and resolution mechanisms.

The mandatory and binding dispute resolution mechanism for disputes beyond Amount A

801. The new and innovative dispute resolution mechanism would apply for those MAP cases that remain unresolved after an agreed period and within the context developed above. It is recognised that the exploration of a mandatory binding dispute resolution mechanism represents a significant step for a number of Inclusive Framework jurisdictions that have historically opposed their use to resolve tax matters. Some Inclusive Framework jurisdictions take the view that the new and innovative dispute resolution mechanism should be separate and distinct from the mechanism and framework to provide tax certainty with respect to Amount A and, in particular, reflect the primarily bilateral nature of most MAP cases.

802. The mechanism for disputes beyond Amount A itself would operate in a broadly similar manner regardless of whether it was mandatory and binding, mandatory and non-binding, or elective and binding.[6] The mechanism would become part of the existing MAP infrastructure and, in general terms, would have the following features:

- As now, taxpayers would set in motion the MAP with respect to transfer pricing and profit allocation disputes through a request for competent authority assistance within the deadline established by the MAP article of the applicable tax treaty. The ongoing peer review of the Action 14 Minimum Standard will ensure that taxpayers have access to MAP in all appropriate cases.
- The dispute resolution mechanism would then be triggered if the competent authorities were unable to reach an agreement to resolve a MAP case after a defined period. The Inclusive Framework would agree on the defined period after which the dispute resolution mechanism would be triggered. In such cases, only the issue or issues that competent authorities were unable to resolve by mutual agreement would be submitted to a panel of experts (a determination panel) who would reach a decision.
- There is agreement that existing mandatory binding dispute resolution mechanisms (such as MAP arbitration provisions in bilateral treaties or the EU tax dispute resolution directive) should apply by default and that a new dispute resolution mechanism should only apply in the absence of an existing mandatory binding dispute resolution mechanism, or where treaty partners expressly agreed that the new mechanism should take priority over an existing mechanism. Ongoing technical work is addressing the relationship between the determination panel and existing mandatory binding dispute resolution mechanisms, including related implementation issues (which may be different depending on whether the relevant mechanism is provided for by a tax treaty or some other legal instrument such as EU law).
- Discussions are ongoing regarding the constitution of the determination panel. Different considerations will apply in the selection of members of a panel that resolves primarily bilateral transfer pricing disputes, as compared with the determination panel described above that would resolve disputes related to Amount A with potential effects in dozens of market and/or relieving jurisdictions. Parties to a bilateral dispute (or a multilateral dispute involving a small number of jurisdictions) will generally not accept a process in which they are not permitted to name at least one member of the determination panel. The development and design of the determination panel is thus exploring how the jurisdictions involved in a MAP case should be represented on a determination panel. Work to design a framework for the constitution of the determination panel is addressing issues that include:
    - Whether some or all members of the determination panel should be serving tax officials, recognising the importance of impartiality and independence to robust decision-making by the panel.
    - Whether members of the determination panel could be chosen from a sitting pool of potential members agreed by the jurisdictions involved in the MAP case, as well as how the determination panel could be selected from such a pool (for example, at

random, based on objective criteria or based on nominations by the jurisdictions involved).

- The number of members on a determination panel, which should reflect the decision-making process used by the panel (for example, a determination panel that made decision by majority should have an odd number of members). The size of a determination panel should also seek an appropriate balance between representation, effectiveness and resource and administrative burdens associated with the panel.
- Clear agreed deadlines for competent authority designation of determination panel members, including robust default rules to ensure that members of a determination panel are designated in the absence of competent authority action within the agreed deadline.

- The determination panel would resolve the specific issue or issues that prevented a competent authority agreement to resolve the MAP case. Two main issues are being addressed in the ongoing technical work regarding the decision-making process used by the determination panel:
  - First, how the panel would make its decisions. While most Inclusive Framework members prefer decision-making by majority, the work is exploring other possible decision-making models (such as consensus or consensus-minus-one decision-making). This work will develop agreed default rules to deliver an outcome in circumstances in which the determination panel would be deadlocked or otherwise unable to decide. The work will also explore models that, where necessary, would be suited for multi-jurisdiction disputes with multiple possible outcomes (such as a transfer pricing dispute involving an integrated series of transactions between associated enterprises in three jurisdictions); such models could include a voting system in which determination panel members ranked possible outcomes.
  - Second, the authority of the determination panel to decide. A majority of Inclusive Framework members favour a last-best offer approach in which the determination panel chooses between alternative outcomes submitted by the jurisdictions involved in the MAP case as the default rule, unless the competent authorities agree that a different approach should be used. Work is exploring a number of subsidiary issues, which include how to accommodate some jurisdictions' preference for independent opinion decision-making and whether the determination panel should provide a rationale for its decisions.
- Work on the determination panel process will also establish clear agreed deadlines for the determination panel to deliver its decision, including robust default rules to deliver an outcome in circumstances in which the determination panel fails to reach a decision within the agreed deadline.
- The decision of the panel would generally be binding on the competent authorities (including in circumstances where the proposed elective dispute resolution mechanism applicable to developing economies has been triggered). Where the panel process was binding, its outcomes would be implemented through a competent authority mutual agreement in the same way as any other resolution through the MAP. As noted above, the work is also exploring the benefits of a mandatory non-binding (advisory) dispute resolution mechanism for taxpayers outside the scope of Amount A.
- A mandatory non-binding dispute resolution mechanism would be coupled with statistical reporting on the results of this process to provide information on whether the panel opinion was followed and/or whether double taxation was otherwise addressed. The effectiveness of this mechanism could then also be subject to peer review.

- It is contemplated that the determination panel process would interact with domestic remedies under the same general principles that apply in any other MAP case resolved by competent authorities through a mutual agreement, according to which:
  - In many jurisdictions, a taxpayer cannot pursue simultaneously the MAP and domestic legal remedies. Where domestic legal remedies are still available, competent authorities in these jurisdictions will generally either require that the taxpayer agree to suspend these other remedies or, if the taxpayer does not agree, will delay the MAP until these remedies are exhausted. For jurisdictions that have adopted MAP arbitration, however, that form of mandatory binding dispute resolution is not available if a decision on the relevant issues has been rendered by a court or administrative tribunal of either jurisdiction.
  - Where the MAP is first pursued and a competent authority agreement has been reached, the taxpayer and other persons directly affected by the case are offered the possibility to reject the agreement and pursue any domestic remedies that had been suspended. Conversely, if these persons prefer to have the agreement apply, they will have to renounce the exercise of domestic legal remedies as regards the issues covered by the competent authority agreement.
  - Where the domestic legal remedies are first pursued and are exhausted in a jurisdiction, a number of Inclusive Framework members will only allow a taxpayer to pursue the MAP to obtain relief of double taxation in the other jurisdiction. Once a legal decision has been rendered in a particular case, most members would not override that decision through the MAP and would therefore restrict the subsequent application of the MAP to trying to obtain relief in the other jurisdiction. Mandatory binding dispute resolution would thus not be available as part of the MAP process in these circumstances.
- Ongoing work is exploring how a binding outcome can be achieved, with some Inclusive Framework members favouring the creation of a legal obligation on competent authorities to implement the determination through a mutual agreement (in the international law instrument used to adopt the new dispute resolution mechanism).

9.4. Next steps

803. As a next step, further work will be undertaken to finalise the different technical features of the tax certainty process for Amount A, including how to implement a binding outcome in jurisdictions, as well as to consider any other issues where further practical guidance on the Amount A tax certainty process is needed for implementation.

804. A decision on the scope of application of a new mandatory and binding dispute resolution mechanism beyond Amount A will be necessary to progress technical work on that mechanism and its implementation.

Notes

[1] See the Final Communiqué of the G20 Finance Ministers & Central Bank Governors Meeting, 22-23 February 2020, Riyadh, Saudi Arabia (available at: https://g20.org/en/g20/Documents/Communique%CC%81%20Final%2022-23%20February%202020.pdf).

[2] Throughout this chapter, draft timeframes have been included as estimates of how long each stage of the process is likely to take. However, these are currently included in square brackets and will be revised as work progresses. In any case, any process is likely to take longer in the first years of operation until experience is gained and efficiencies are identified. However, it is useful to have some measure of how long the process is expected to take and to retain reasonably challenging target timeframes where appropriate, recognising that in some cases more time will be needed. Based on the approach in this Blueprint, a simple case where no panel review is needed could be completed in as little as [6-9 months] following the filing of an MNE group's Amount A self-assessment return, whereas a complex case could take [two years] from the establishment of a review panel to a final decision by a determination panel. It is likely that that complex cases with longer timeframes should reduce over time as processes become more efficient and both MNE groups and tax administrations gain experience in applying rules consistently year on year.

[3] Inclusive Framework members will consider whether these information exchange mechanisms will need to take into account the information needs of sub-national jurisdictions that levy taxes on corporate income.

[4] In all cases, work undertaken by a secretariat in supporting a tax certainty process for Amount A will only be where appropriate and will respect strict tax confidentiality.

[5] This work includes the exploration of a possible APA-equivalent for non-transfer pricing issues.

[6] See paragraph 801 for a description of how the mechanism would apply to different categories of disputes and jurisdictions.

10 Implementation and administration

10.1. Overview

805. The development of the implementation framework for Pillar One is at an earlier stage than other work streams. This is because the Inclusive Framework focus has been on the design and development of the key operational components of Pillar One, including: scope, revenue sourcing, nexus, tax base, elimination of double taxation and tax certainty. Implementation design is dependent on decision points in these areas and with the progress now made in these work streams, a focus of the coming months of the project is to ensure that Pillar One can be implemented swiftly, effectively, consistently and in a coordinated manner.

806. The implementation of Pillar One will require action across three different dimensions: (i) domestic law; (ii) public international law; and (iii) guidance to supplement (i) or (ii) or both.

807. It is expected that any consensus-based agreement under Pillar One must include a commitment by members of the Inclusive Framework to implement this agreement and at the same time to remove relevant unilateral actions.

808. The implementation of Amount B is covered in Chapter 8

10.2. Implementation

10.2.1. Domestic law implementation

809. The operative sections of Pillar One will need to be translated into domestic law. Although the particular form of domestic law implementation required will depend on the legal framework and the particular circumstances of each jurisdiction, domestic legislation would need to achieve the following four outcomes:

- Create a domestic taxing right consistent with the design of Amount A. This would require rules that implement the following essential elements of a taxing right: the identification of the taxpayer, object of taxation, the tax base, the tax period, and the tax rates (see (i) below);
- Provide for the relief of double taxation where a resident entity is identified as a taxpayer under the preceding section. This would authorise the elimination of double taxation and specify the method to be used (see (ii) below);
- Incorporate procedures for administering the new taxing right as well as relief from double taxation for those resident entities identified as taxpayers under the new taxing right, including measures facilitating the centralised and simplified administration system and the tax certainty process in respect of Amount A (see(iii) below); and

- Include processes to improve tax certainty beyond Amount A, notably by providing for effective dispute prevention and resolution mechanisms (see (iv) below).

(i) Determination of the essential elements of a new Amount A tax

810. A jurisdiction will first need to transpose into its domestic law the rules agreed by the Inclusive Framework that are to be applied to determine when an MNE group is subject to tax in that jurisdiction on the basis of Amount A. Without the creation of a domestic taxing right for Amount A, the jurisdiction would have no authority to impose tax on Amount A.

811. The essential elements of a new taxing right are:

- *The identification of the taxpayer and the object of taxation:* the new taxing right will be imposed on "paying entities" that are a member of an MNE group that exceeds the threshold limitations, has domestic source in-scope revenue and meets the nexus requirements (see Chapter 2 Chapter 3 Chapter 4. For the identification of the paying entity see section 7.2).
- *The tax base, the tax period, and the tax rates.* A jurisdiction will also need to incorporate into its domestic law the rules governing the calculation and allocation of Amount A (see Chapter 5 on tax base determination, and Chapter 6 on profit allocation). Determinations on the tax period and the tax rate would follow applicable domestic rules.

(ii) Elimination of double taxation

812. Jurisdictions will also need to include in their domestic law the agreed rules on the elimination of double taxation. This is to ensure that the entities that are subject to the new taxing right can benefit from the Amount A mechanisms to eliminate double taxation.

813. This will require the implementation of the rules or principles on approaches to identifying the group entities that will pay tax on Amount A (the paying entities), and the method(s) that will be applied to eliminate double taxation arising from the payment of Amount A for those entities (see Chapter 7).

(iii) Procedure, administration and Amount A related tax-certainty processes

Procedure and administration:

814. It is also essential to implement procedures to administer, levy and collect the new Amount A tax in domestic law administrative rules.

815. The simplified administration process that is currently being developed could be based on, and be explored in parallel to, the centralised and simplified tax certainty process that is discussed in Chapter 9. It would be designed to centralise the computation of Amount A and related compliance activities in a single entity, possibly the UPE as required for CbCR under BEPS Action 13. Centralising the process of applying Amount A through a single entity should generate a material reduction in compliance costs. It could also reduce the burden this process would create for tax administrations, which would be provided with a single coherent Amount A tax return, a standardised documentation package and possibly a single Amount A payment from each MNE group. Provisions may be needed within the planned multilateral instrument and/or domestic law to allow this more centralised process (e.g. to allow a domestic tax liability to be satisfied by a single tax payment made by a non-resident entity in another jurisdiction).

816. There are a variety of different elements that could be considered as part of a simplified administration process. These include allowing a single entity to:

- Compute Amount A on behalf of the group and file tax returns on behalf of the paying entities (including the reporting of losses);

- Manage the Amount A tax certainty process on behalf of the group, including by accepting any adjustments proposed;
- Pay the Amount A tax liability in the market jurisdictions on behalf of the paying entities (acting as an agent); and
- Assume primary liability for compliance with all aspects of Amount A in the market jurisdictions, including being the primary entity against which these jurisdictions could seek legal redress.

Amount A tax certainty process:

817. On dispute prevention and resolution for Amount A, the administrable and binding dispute prevention process will provide early certainty, before tax adjustments are made, to prevent disputes related to all aspects of Amount A. Chapter 9 provides further information on related tax certainty process.

818. Although the innovative approach is developed within a multilateral framework, jurisdictions will need to incorporate into their domestic law all necessary references to the new tax certainty process for Amount A, including the implementation of the panel decision and other procedural aspects.

(iv) Other tax-certainty processes beyond Amount A

819. The approach to tax certainty beyond Amount A spans a range of steps from dispute prevention and the existing MAP to a mandatory binding dispute resolution mechanism.

820. To benefit from the enhancements and improvements to existing dispute prevention tools, which include projects undertaken as part of the Forum on Tax Administration tax certainty agenda, jurisdictions will need to ensure that their domestic law allows for their use.

821. Similarly, features of the MAP and the new dispute resolution mechanism may need to be reflected in domestic law. As for the new dispute resolution mechanism, the domestic law would need to provide for the possibility of submitting cases to a panel of experts that would reach decisions that could be binding.

10.2.2. Public international law implementation

822. Existing tax treaties contain provisions that would generally prevent the application of Amount A, even after it has been implemented in domestic legislation. Furthermore they are unlikely to contain rules on relief of double taxation that would work for Amount A. Nor do they include rules governing the administration of Amount A, including the new rules on dispute prevention and resolution.

823. The best way to remove treaty obstacles to the implementation of Pillar One and to do so in a way that ensures consistency and certainty in the application and operation of Amount A is to develop a new multilateral convention. The multilateral convention would remove existing barriers in tax treaties to the application of Amount A and would also contain the four elements discussed in the previous section.

A. The removal of treaty barriers for the determination of a new Amount A tax

824. Even if a jurisdiction transposes into its domestic law the rules that will govern Amount A – e.g. the rule that gives a market jurisdiction the right to tax a portion of an MNE's profits in the absence of traditional physical presence – existing bilateral treaties are likely to prevent the application of those rules. That is because, for example, most existing treaties permit a market jurisdiction to tax the profits of a non-resident entity only if it has a permanent establishment in that jurisdiction. Changes to bilateral treaties are therefore necessary to allow the Amount A rules to operate as intended.

825. The implementation of rules for the determination of Amount A in an international public law instrument on tax would only strictly be necessary for those jurisdictions that have these restrictive bilateral tax treaties in force; where there is no treaty, the rules could, at least in theory, be implemented purely

under domestic legislation. However, in order to ensure consistent coherent implementation of Amount A among jurisdictions, it is recommended to include in the multilateral convention implementation rules for the determination of all aspects of Amount A for all jurisdictions irrespective of tax treaties. In other words, the multilateral convention should apply to limit the right to tax to the agreed parameters on scope, nexus, thresholds, etc., including the rules on dispute prevention and resolution for Amount A, and represent a commitment to provide double tax relief in accordance with the agreed framework.

826. However, the section of the multilateral convention that will include the rules on the determination of Amount A tax would still be relevant for those jurisdictions because it would serve as a reference for the application of the section of the convention on dispute prevention and resolution for Amount A.

827. It will therefore be necessary to implement through the multilateral convention all the essential elements of a new taxing right (the rules on the identification of the taxpayer and the object of taxation and those on the tax base, the tax period, the tax rates, etc.) consistent with the design of Amount A and domestic legislation.

828. As bilateral tax treaties would remain in force and continue to govern cross-border taxation outside Amount A, the new multilateral convention would coexist with the existing tax treaty network. But its provisions would generally supersede provisions in existing bilateral tax treaties where there was a conflict.

829. Unlike the MLI, the multilateral convention would not seek to modify the wording of existing treaty provisions (e.g. the new nexus rule would not change the existing permanent establishment definition in a particular tax treaty). Instead, new standalone treaty provisions would be developed to govern the new taxing rights and those would prevail for the taxation of in-scope MNEs.

B. Elimination of double taxation

830. Changes to the present rules on the elimination of double taxation that will operate for Amount A will be necessary. These rules will provide for the relief of double taxation where a resident entity is identified as the paying entity for the purposes of Amount A. The rules could also specify the method to be used – e.g. exemption or credit.

831. In contrast to the rules on the determination of Amount A itself, however, implementing rules on the elimination of double taxation in an international public law instrument may not be necessary as most jurisdictions could, in principle rely on their domestic legislation (amended as necessary) to eliminate double taxation[1]. However, domestic foreign tax credit regimes tend to have limitations that can sometimes result in unrelieved double taxation (for example, if the income taxed in the market jurisdiction is regarded as domestically sourced income in the relieving jurisdiction). There should not be different domestic sourcing rules that would lead to unrelieved double tax on Amount A. Therefore, it would be preferable to include in the multilateral convention those rules which would be relevant for all jurisdictions, regardless of the existence of bilateral tax treaties. This would ensure that relief from double taxation is effective and coordinated among jurisdictions. Including such a section would also ensure the effective operation of the dispute prevention and resolution processes for Amount A.

C. Procedure, administration and Amount A related tax-certainty processes

832. It will be essential to implement the new simplified administration process and the processes for dispute prevention and resolution for Amount A in the multilateral convention to ensure consistency and certainty on Amount A.

833. Unlike the sections of the multilateral convention on the determination of Amount A and the elimination of double taxation, the section on procedure, administration and the tax certainty processes would be relevant for all parties to the convention, whether or not they have an existing treaty between them. Existing bilateral tax treaties would not prevent the application of these procedures, administrative and tax certainty provisions and so the multilateral convention would not need to supersede them. For

provisions relating to the new dispute resolution mechanism beyond Amount A, it is envisaged that they would apply only in the absence of an existing mandatory binding dispute resolution mechanism, or where treaty partners had expressly agreed that the new mechanism should take priority over an existing mechanism.

D. Other tax-certainty processes beyond Amount A

834. Implementing new rules on tax certainty beyond Amount A through the multilateral convention may help ensure that the processes introduced are consistent with those that apply for Amount A. A dedicated part of the convention could likely be used, governing the different steps of the tax certainty processes beyond Amount A, including dispute prevention, MAP processes and the mandatory binding dispute resolution mechanism.

835. Further consideration needs to be given to the question how this part of the convention should apply among jurisdictions depending on whether they have an existing bilateral treaty, or if no bilateral tax treaty applies.

E. The development of a new multilateral convention

836. To remove treaty obstacles and implement the four elements discussed in the previous section, the method used must ensure coordination, consistency and certainty, and operate in a speedy manner. The best way to do this would be through a new multilateral convention.

837. The Inclusive Framework initially considered using the *Multilateral Convention to Implement Tax Treaty Related Measures to Prevent Base Erosion and Profit Shifting* (MLI)[2] (or creating another instrument that works in the same way to modify existing tax treaties) to implement Pillar One, but ultimately agreed that it would not be a suitable instrument: implementing measures that need to be part of a multilateral framework would not always be feasible (e.g. multilateral dispute resolution mechanisms) nor would implementing changes and measures between jurisdictions that do not have a bilateral tax treaty be possible (e.g. the dispute prevention and resolution processes for Amount A).

838. As bilateral tax treaties would remain in force and continue to govern cross-border taxation outside Amount A, a new multilateral convention would need to coexist with the existing tax treaty network and, for its parts on the determination of Amount A tax and elimination of double taxation, supersede and prevail over existing bilateral tax treaties for the taxation of in-scope MNEs. Further work will also be required on the relationship of the multilateral convention with bilateral tax treaties concluded after its entry into force (see paragraph 851).

839. The new multilateral convention would thus operate differently than the MLI, which was used to directly modify existing provisions in tax treaties. The new multilateral convention would provide a multilateral framework to facilitate the coordinated and effective implementation that is necessary between multiple jurisdictions and would, for its parts on the determination of Amount A tax and elimination of double taxation, supersede all bilateral tax treaties in force.

840. As noted above, there would not be treaty barriers that would need to be removed between jurisdictions that currently do not have a treaty with respect to those parts and those jurisdictions could rely on their domestic legislation to apply and administer Amount A. The part of the multilateral convention that would implement the features of the new simplified administration process and the tax certainty-related processes would apply to all parties and would also close the gaps in treaty coverage. That part would also make the appropriate linkages for all signatories to the rules that govern the application and operation of Amount A.

841. If developing a multilateral convention is the ideal way to ensure a legal obligation to apply and administer Amount A in the same way, and better coordination and speedier international public law implementation. However, some jurisdictions may need to explore whether they could exceptionally make

all necessary treaty changes by amendments to their existing bilateral treaties and domestic law within a reasonable timeframe. Under such an approach, a jurisdiction may be able to agree with its treaty partners to bilaterally amend its existing treaties to remove obstacles for the determination of Amount A tax and elimination of double taxation and then rely on its domestic legislation to apply and administer Amount A. Allowing a jurisdiction to require a bilateral approach would, however, place an additional burden on partner jurisdictions who would be required to implement on both a bilateral and a multilateral basis. Also, it is not clear that the multilateral dispute prevention process for Amount A could be implemented other than by a multilateral convention given the need to coordinate results among multiple jurisdictions.

842. As part of this work on possible bilateral amendments to treaties, further thoughts could be given on the development of a separate instrument that would deal with the features of the new simplified administration process and the tax certainty-related processes.

10.2.3. Guidance and accompanying instruments

843. Guidance will also need to be developed for many aspects of Pillar One to support and supplement domestic legislation and provisions in public international law instruments (for example, multilateral competent authority agreements, commentary on the multilateral convention, guidelines for the determination and application of Amount A, etc.).

844. The guidance, which would serve tax administrations and taxpayers alike, will, for instance, contain detailed guidelines for the tax base determinations for Amount A, financial accounting, segmentation, and the treatment of losses.

845. The guidance could be revised or updated periodically. Some revisions or updates could be implemented without changing domestic legislation or treaties while others may require such changes. The revisions would be based upon input received and experience in the practical implementation of Amount A.

846. Further work will be required to determine which aspects can be included in guidelines as opposed to the multilateral convention or domestic law.

10.3. Removal of unilateral measures

847. As stated in the Outline, it is expected that any consensus-based agreement must include a commitment by members of the Inclusive Framework to implement this agreement and at the same time to withdraw relevant unilateral actions, and not adopt such unilateral actions in the future.[3]

10.4. Next steps

848. The next steps on implementation will require further work on the multilateral convention. This will include work on the architecture of the convention and its legal functioning. It will also include work to determine the core elements of the rules on the determination of Amount A and elimination of double taxation that will need to be implemented in the multilateral convention to ensure all treaty barriers are removed.

849. Once the core elements of the rules will have been identified, the Inclusive Framework will start to work on the design of the treaty provisions that will be inserted in the multilateral convention.

850. More work will also be required on different challenges that could arise in developing the multilateral convention. Those will include work on the design of the provisions on entry into force and effect to ensure that parallel and conflicting rules for the taxation of in-scope MNE groups do not arise and that the multilateral convention starts to take effect only once a critical mass of jurisdictions have fully

implemented it. This will include establishing a timeline for implementation, and clarifying the meaning of a "critical mass" of jurisdictions.

851. In order to ensure consistency with the legal framework established by a multilateral convention and to ensure that bilateral tax treaties concluded after its entry into force do not create new barriers to the exercise of the new taxing right, further work will also be required on the relationship of the multilateral convention with these later tax treaties, taking into account legal frameworks that may not permit clauses that bind future Parliaments.

852. The next steps on the "removal" of unilateral measures will require work on what constitutes a "relevant" unilateral measure that would need to be removed, and any transitional framework to do so. As noted above, members of the Inclusive Framework agree that one element of an agreement on Pillar One should be a commitment to withdraw relevant unilateral measures that would undermine the stability of the agreed framework and to refrain from introducing new ones.

853. Lastly, the implementation of Pillar One on a safe harbour basis requires continued consideration and development by the Inclusive Framework.

Notes

[1] Treaty provisions on elimination of double taxation impose an obligation on the state of residence to relieve foreign tax. They would not typically prevent a jurisdiction from taking on additional obligations to relieve double taxation – such as would be required for Amount A.

[2] To use the MLI, the instrument would need to be amended (pursuant to its Article 33) or supplemented by a protocol (pursuant to its Article 38). A Party to the MLI would not automatically be bound by an amendment or protocol implementing the changes in their tax treaties unless it ratified the amendment or protocol. Implementing Pillar One through the MLI would require a jurisdiction that is not currently a Signatory or Party to the MLI to join it. The MLI, which currently only covers agreements that have been specifically notified (the Covered Tax Agreements) by its Parties, may also involve requiring Parties to expand their list of covered agreements. Amendment to the MLI or the development of a protocol would establish another layer of complexity requiring matching as the changes to bilateral tax treaties would only have effect where the jurisdictions were parties to both the MLI and the amendment or protocol.

[3] See paragraphs 9 and 89 of the Outline. Also, as stated in paragraph 90 of the Outline, considerations will be given to the implications of the safe harbour proposal for unilateral measures.

Annex A. Detailed Process Map of Amount A

Application of Amount A

Steps 1-2: Scope tests (revenue and *de minimis*)

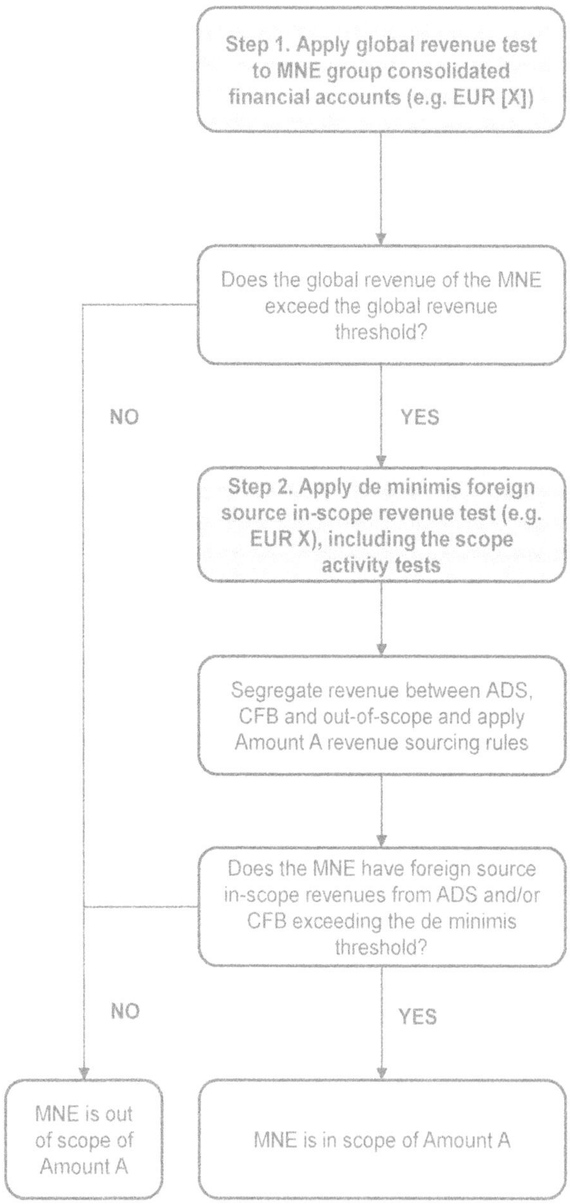

Step 1. Global revenue test

- Global revenue test applied to total MNE group revenue.
- *Potential Phased Approach*: Threshold could be set at [EUR X] in the first year and drop to [EUR X] over a number of years or be applied for a longer period and then start the reductions after a post-implementation review has been undertaken.
- The revenue figure for determining whether the threshold is met will be drawn from the MNE group's consolidated financial statements.

Step 2. Apply de minimis foreign source in-scope revenue test

- The de minimis test would be applied to all foreign in-scope revenue, with MNE groups falling below this threshold excluded.
- *Potential Phased Approach*: Threshold could be set at [EUR X] in the first year and drop to [EUR X] over a number of years or be applied for a longer period and then start the reductions after a post-implementation review has been undertaken.
- Amount A revenue sourcing rules would be applied to determine source of in-scope revenue. See Step 6(a).
- This simplifies the application of Amount A, where the majority of profits will be allocated to/from the same jurisdiction, and also excludes MNE groups with de minimis foreign in-scope revenue.

Application of Amount A

Step 3: Make required adjustments to consolidated financial accounts

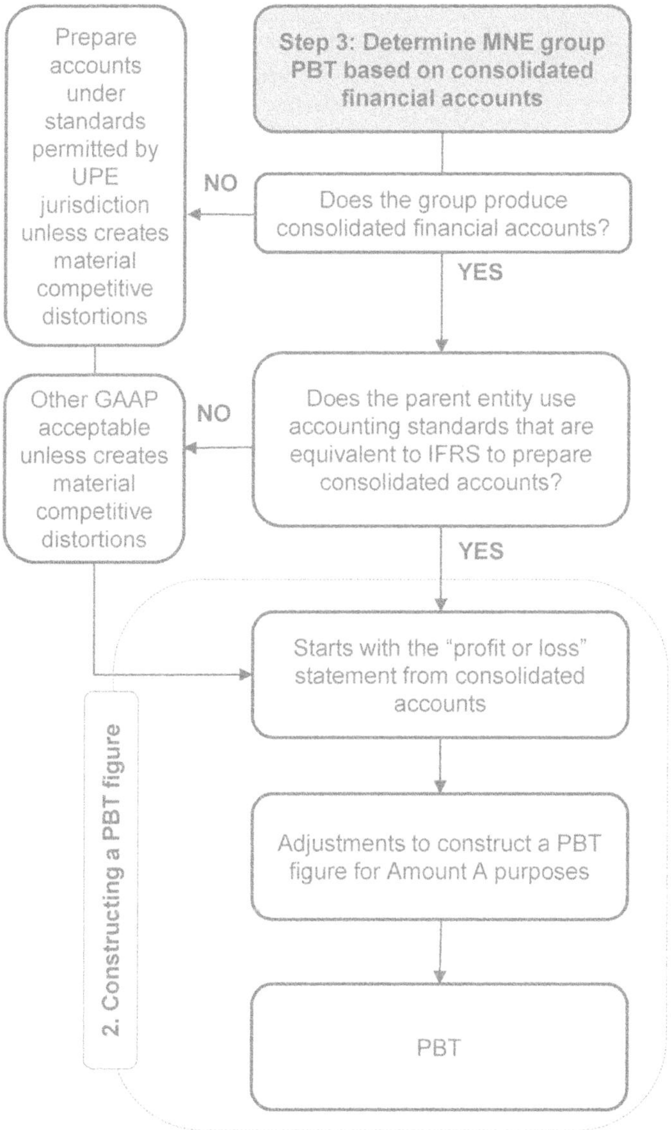

Step 3: Determine MNE group PBT

1. Identify and test consolidated financial accounts

- MNE groups that prepare consolidated financial accounts that produce equivalent or comparable outcomes to consolidated financial accounts prepared under IFRS – including GAAP of Australia, Canada, Hong Kong (China), Japan, New Zealand, the People's Republic of China, the Republic of India, the Republic of Korea, Singapore, and the United States – would use these as the starting point. Other MNE groups are estimated to be less than 10% of groups in scope.
- Privately held MNE groups that do not produce consolidated accounts would be required to prepare consolidated accounts under standards permitted by their UPE jurisdiction, provided that those standards qualify as eligible or, otherwise, do not result in material competitive distortions.
- MNE groups that use GAAP not equivalent to IFRS will be permitted to compute Amount A under that GAAP unless it creates material competitive distortions.

2. Constructing a PBT figure

- Potential book-to-tax adjustments include: (1) income tax expense; (2) dividend income and gains or losses arising in connection with shares; and (3) expenses that are typically not deductible or limited for public policy reasons (e.g. fines).

Application of Amount A

Step 4-5: Segmentation and losses

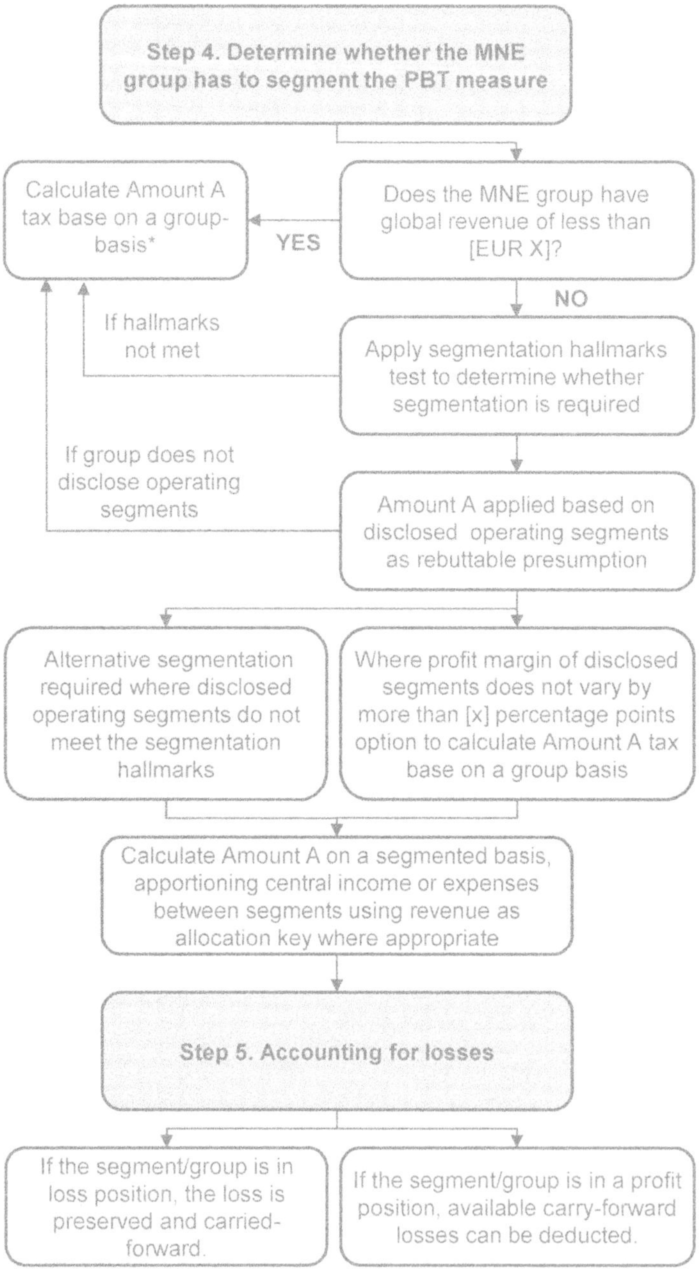

Step 4: Scope of segmentation

- Simplified rules to limit the number of MNE groups that compute Amount A tax base on a segmented basis. This approach is expected to limit the compliance burden created by Amount A and to make the tax certainty process manageable.
- Apply exemption or safe harbour* from segmentation based on global revenue: MNE groups with global revenue of less than [EUR X] would apply Amount A on a group basis. This threshold would be increased to [EUR X] for a five-year transition period.
- MNE groups not eligible for the exemption/ safe harbour will apply the segmentation hallmark tests to determine whether they are required to segment their Amount A tax base and on what basis.
- As a rebuttable presumption, MNE groups would be required to apply Amount A on the basis of their disclosed operating segments, except:
  - MNE groups that do not disclose operating segments should apply Amount A on a group basis, and
  - MNE groups can apply Amount A on a group basis where the profit margin of their disclosed segments do not vary by more than [x] percentage points.
- Where Amount A is computed on a segmented basis, an MNE group would be required to apportion central or unallocated costs, using revenue as an allocation key where appropriate.

Step 5. Accounting for losses

- If in the current period, the segment/group has a loss, this is calculated and carried-forward to offset against future profits.
- If in the current period, the segment/group has a profit, available carry-forward losses are automatically offset against these profits for the purposes of determining Amount A.
- Loss carry-forward rules could be extended to certain pre-regime losses (i.e. losses incurred by group/segment before the introduction of the new taxing right).

Application of Amount A
Step 6: Nexus and Revenue Sourcing

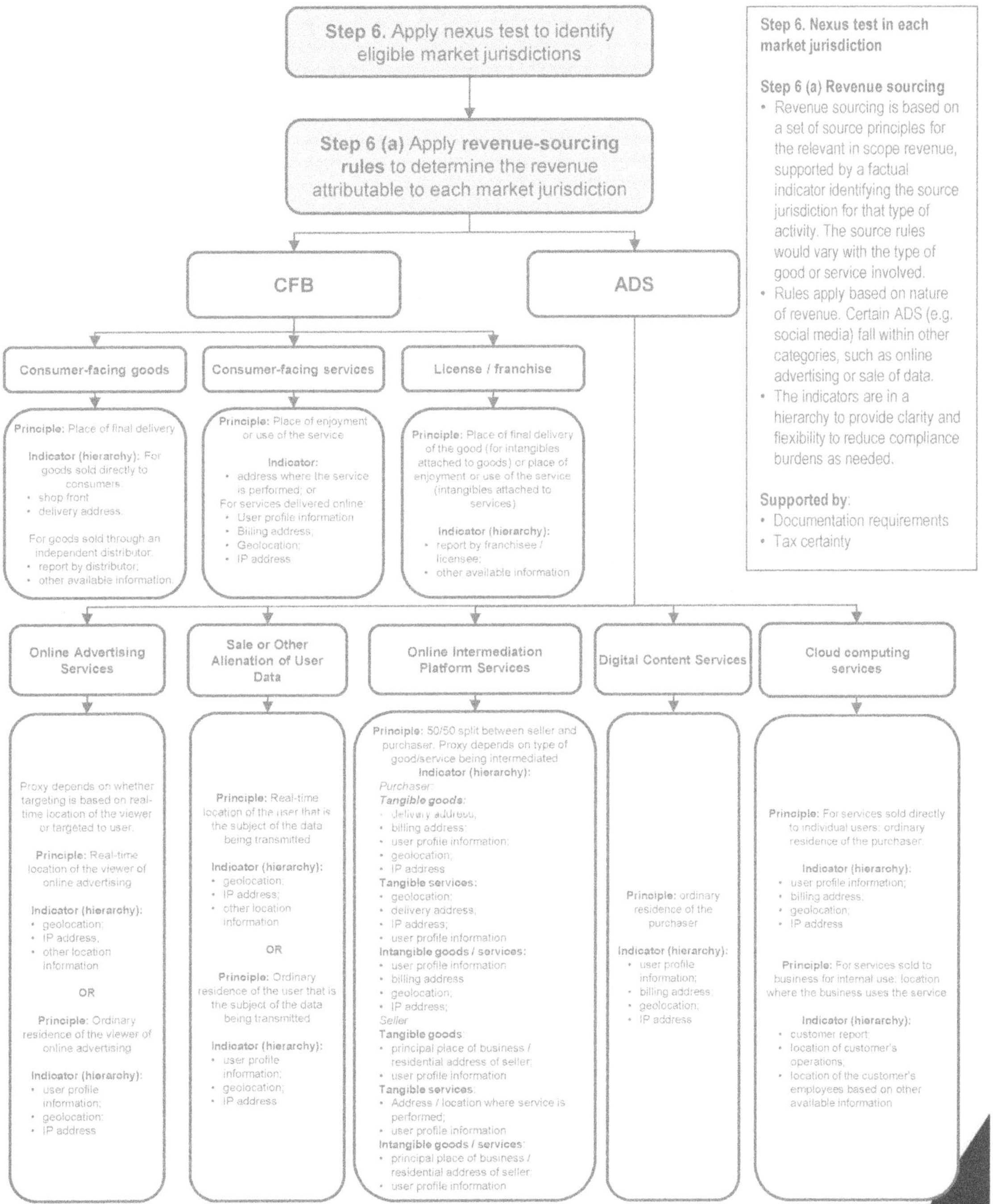

Application of Amount A

Step 6: Nexus and Revenue Sourcing (continued)

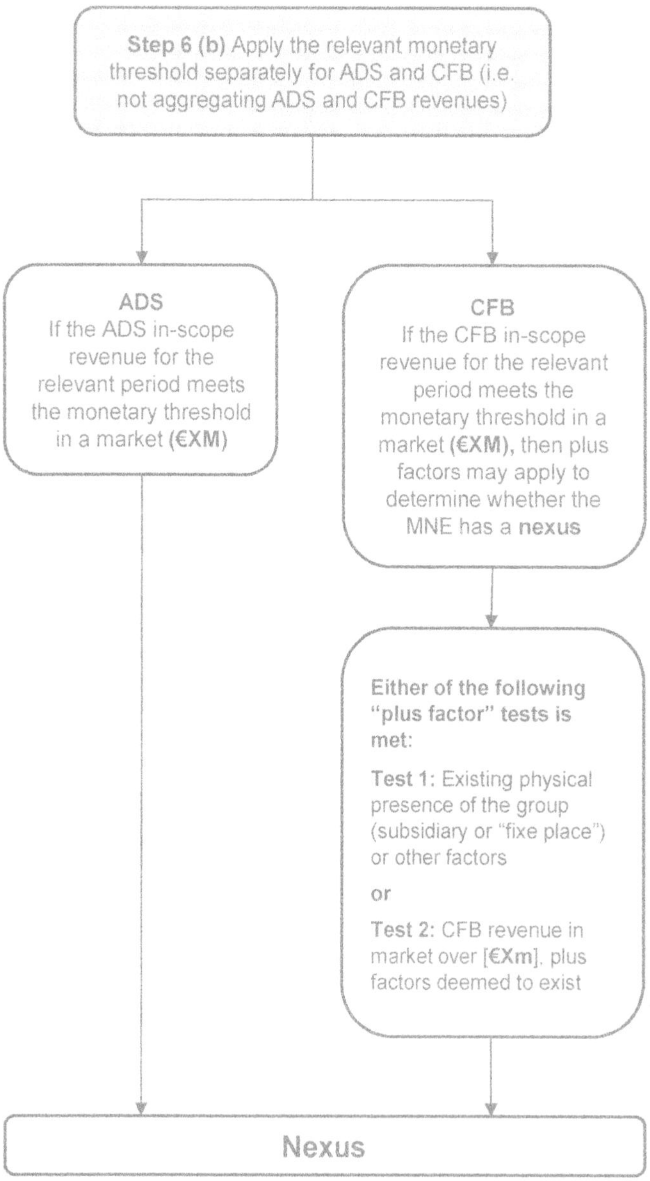

Step 6 (b) Apply the relevant monetary threshold

- The nexus rules will establish whether the MNE group has a significant/active and sustained engagement in a particular market jurisdiction. The primary nexus test (and the only one for automated digital services) will be a revenue threshold.
- If there is a **segmentation**, the nexus rule is likely to follow the segmentation approach.
- Using a temporal requirement spanning only one year would avoid the complexities of a multiyear testing period.
- **For CFB,** the "sales" may not a sufficient factor to establish nexus in a market jurisdiction, and hence that the country-specific revenue thresholds is to be **complemented by "plus factors"** which could be:
  - Physical presence of the MNE group in the form of a subsidiary or a fixed place of business; or
  - Other form of presence of the MNE group in the market jurisdiction.
  - Simplification: a possible way to simplify the administration of the "plus factors" would be to deem these factors to exist once the sales of the MNE group exceed a certain amount in the market jurisdiction.

Application of Amount A

Step 7-8: Calculation and Allocation of Amount A

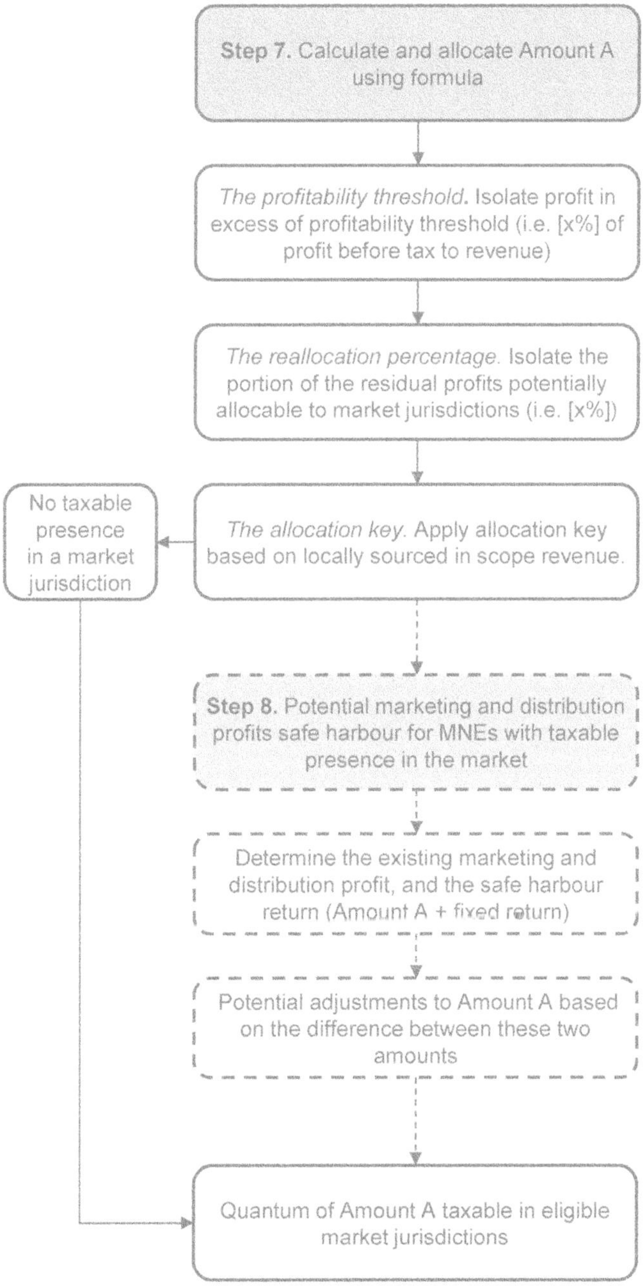

Step 7. Formulaic allocation of Amount A

- The quantum of Amount A will be calculated through a formula that will apply to the tax base of a group (or segment where relevant), with three steps:
- *A profitability threshold* to isolate the residual profit potentially subject to reallocation. As a simplifying convention, this will be a profit before tax to revenue ratio.
- *A reallocation percentage* to identify the appropriate share of residual profit to be allocated to market jurisdictions under Amount A. This will be a fixed percentage.
- *An allocation key* to distribute the allocable tax base amongst the eligible market jurisdictions (i.e. where nexus is established for Amount A). It will be based on locally sourced in scope revenue.
- The quantum of Amount A could be weighted (through variations to the formula) to account for different degrees of digitalisation between in-scope business activities (so called "digital differentiation"), or to account for variations in profitability between different market jurisdictions (so-called "jurisdictional segmentation").

Step 8: Potential marketing and distribution profits safe harbour

- An option under consideration is to provide a safe harbour where an MNE has a taxable presence in a market jurisdiction to deal with some potential double counting issues
- Determine the existing marketing and distribution profits, and determine the safe harbour return, the sum of: (i) Amount A; and (ii) a fixed return for in-country routine marketing and distribution activities.
- Compare the safe harbour return with the existing marketing and distribution profits, to determine a potential cap to the Amount A allocation and hence the quantum of Amount A taxable in eligible market jurisdictions.
- Where the existing marketing and distribution profit exceeds the safe harbour return, there will be no allocation of Amount A to that market jurisdiction.
- NB: Other options are being considered to deal with potential double counting issues.

Application of Amount A

Step 9: Elimination of double taxation

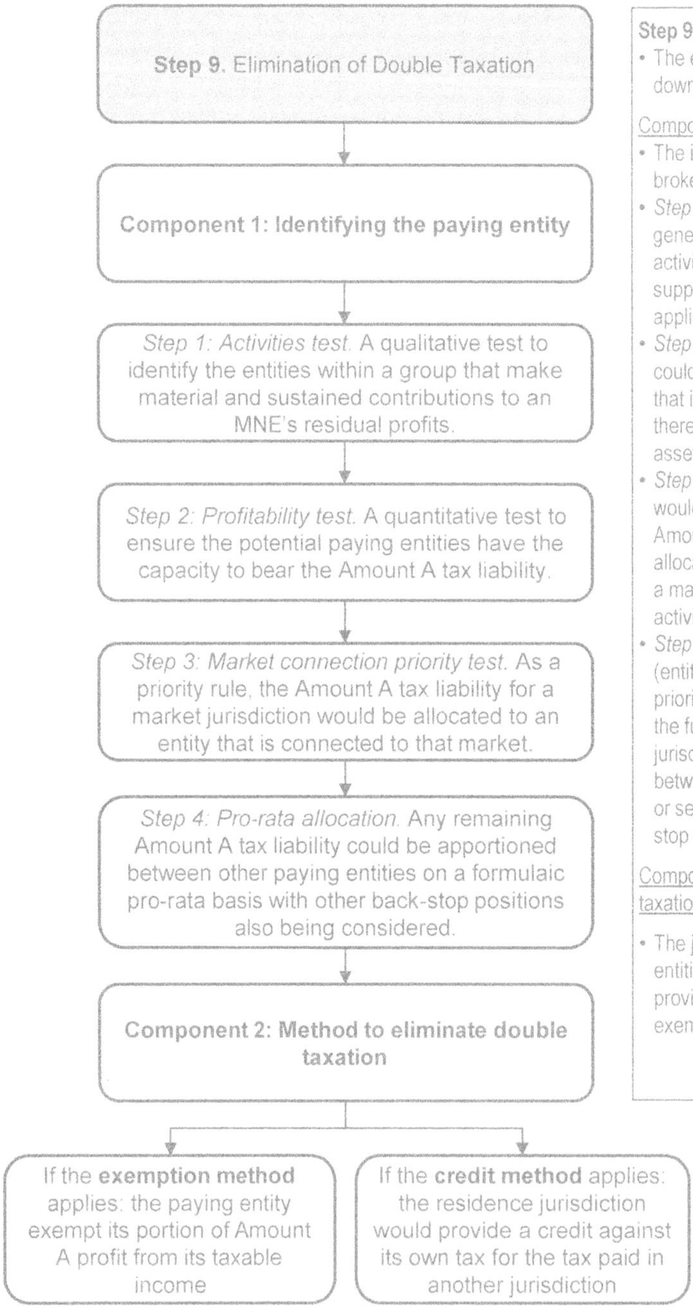

Step 9: Elimination of Double Taxation

- The elimination of double taxation is broken down into two components

Component 1: Identifying the paying entities

- The identification of the paying entities will be broken down into up to four steps:
- *Step 1: Activities test.* This test will include a general principle describing the types of activities a paying entity will perform and supplemented by a list of indicia to support its application.
- *Step 2: Profitability test.* For simplicity, this test could be aligned with the substance carve-out that is being developed for Pillar Two, where there will be a combined payroll and tangible assets profitability test.
- *Step 3: Market connection priority test.* This test would require that, in the first instance, the Amount A tax liability for a market jurisdiction is allocated to a paying entity, that is connected to a market jurisdiction through the performance of activities identified under the activities test.
- *Step 4: Pro-rata allocation.* Where the entity or (entities) identified under the market connection priority test do not have sufficient profits to bear the full Amount A tax liability for a given market jurisdiction that liability ~~will~~ could be apportioned between other paying entities within the group or segment on a pro-rata basis with other back-stop positions also being considered.

Component 2: Methods to eliminate double taxation

- The jurisdiction(s) in which the paying entity (or entities) are resident will then be provide to provide relief for double taxation using the exemption or credit method.

Application of Amount A

Step 9: Elimination of double taxation (continued)

Step 9 (ctd): Paying Amount A to the market jurisdiction

↓

The MNE group nominates a **co-ordinating entity** who computes the Amount A profits and tax liability and apportions the profit and tax liability to the paying entities in proportion determined under Component 1

↓

This computation gets approved by all of the jurisdictions involved under the tax certainty process
(see Step 10)

↓

The paying entities pay their share of Amount A tax due by the **co-ordinating entity**

↓

The **co-ordinating entity** pays Amount A tax to market jurisdictions (or pays the local entity who will then pay the market jurisdiction)

<u>Step 9 (ctd): Paying Amount A to the market jurisdiction</u>

- The MNE group nominates a single entity to bear all of the administrative responsibility and legal liability for the payment of any and all tax due under Amount A by the MNE.
- Jurisdictions would apply either the exemption method or the credit method to ensure that double taxation under Amount A is fully relieved.
- The payment and liability for Amount A tax could be at the level of the nominated co-ordinating entity, or, if the MNE prefers leveraging its **local subsidiary** in the market jurisdiction, at the level of that local entity.

Application of Amount A

Step 10: Submission of self-assessment through common platform and early certainty process

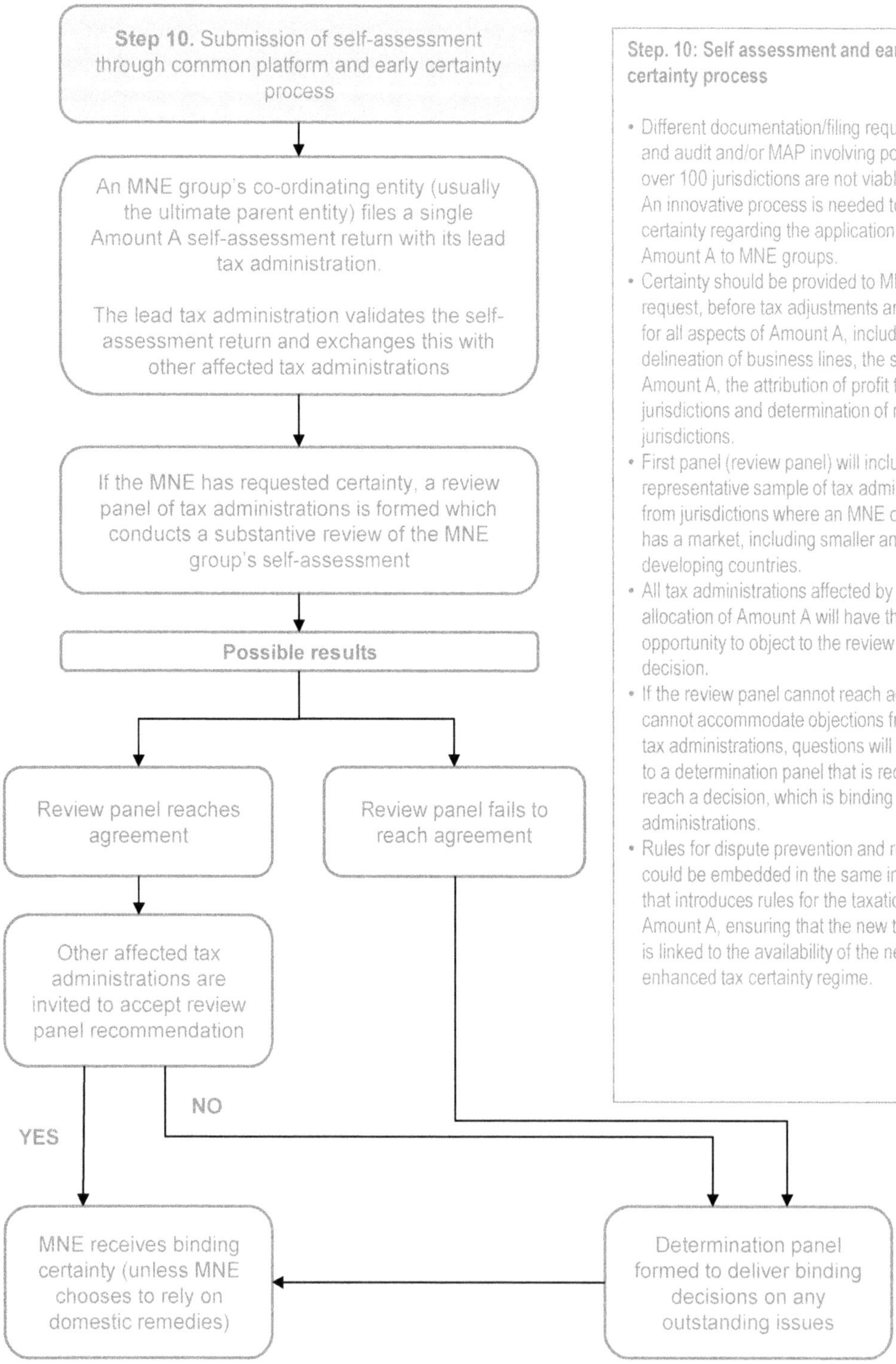

Step. 10: Self assessment and early certainty process

- Different documentation/filing requirements and audit and/or MAP involving potentially over 100 jurisdictions are not viable options. An innovative process is needed to provide certainty regarding the application of Amount A to MNE groups.
- Certainty should be provided to MNEs upon request, before tax adjustments are proposed, for all aspects of Amount A, including the delineation of business lines, the size of Amount A, the attribution of profit to market jurisdictions and determination of relieving jurisdictions.
- First panel (review panel) will include a representative sample of tax administrations from jurisdictions where an MNE operates or has a market, including smaller and developing countries.
- All tax administrations affected by an allocation of Amount A will have the opportunity to object to the review panel's decision.
- If the review panel cannot reach agreement or cannot accommodate objections from other tax administrations, questions will be referred to a determination panel that is required to reach a decision, which is binding on all tax administrations.
- Rules for dispute prevention and resolution could be embedded in the same instrument that introduces rules for the taxation of Amount A, ensuring that the new taxing right is linked to the availability of the new and enhanced tax certainty regime.

Annex B. Approaches to implementing the Amount A formula

855. A three-step process will be required to calculate the quantum of Amount A taxable in each eligible market jurisdiction. This process could be implemented by either using absolute amounts of profit (the "profit-based approach") or, alternatively, profit ratios (the "profit margin-based approach"). Both approaches would apply the above-described steps without changes or variations, and hence would provide the same quantum of Amount A taxable in each market jurisdiction. This identical outcome is illustrated below in algebraic form, as well as through examples in Box B.1. and B.2. But the administration of each approach may present some variations, and these differences would inform the choice of the most appropriate approach to calculate and allocate Amount A.[1]

Profit-based approach

856. Consistent with the three steps described above, the profit-based approach can be described in algebraic form as follows.[2]

- **Step 1:** Isolate the residual profit (if any) by excluding the profit of the group or, where relevant, the segment that does not exceed an agreed level of profitability, e.g. a percentage of PBT to revenue ("z"). Assuming that the Amount A tax base for the relevant group or segment is "P", revenues of the group or segment are "R", and the profit margin of the group or segment is "P/R", this means that Amount A applies only if "P/R" is greater than z%, and that a positive residual profit "W" can be calculated as:[3]

$$W = P - (R \times z)$$

- **Step 2:** Separate "W" between the portion of residual profits attributable to Amount A (the allocable tax base, "A") and other factors ("X"). Where W = A + X. If the agreed portion of residual profit attributable to Amount A is, for example, a percentage ("y"), then "A" can be calculated as:

$$A = y \times W$$

- **Step 3**: Distribute the allocable tax base "A" among the market jurisdictions that meet the new nexus threshold. This would be done through an allocation key based on revenue (i.e. ratio of local revenue to total revenue). Assuming that in a particular market jurisdiction the group or, where relevant, the segment local revenue is "S", then the allocation key is "S/R". Therefore, the quantum of Amount A profit allocated to that particular market, expressed as "M", can be calculated as:

$$M = \frac{S}{R} \times A$$

857. After bringing the three components together, the Amount A formula under a profit-based approach becomes:

$$M = S/R \times y \times [P - (R \times z)]$$

Box B.1. Example – profit-margin based approach

For the purpose of this example, it is assumed that the Amount A formula includes a 10% profitability threshold (step 1) and 20% reallocation percentage (step 2).

Facts

Group A is a large MNE group providing exclusively in-scope ADS via an online platform. It is assumed that Group A is treated as one segment for Amount A purposes and that it has the following simplified income statement:

	in million EUR
Revenue (**R**)	25,000
Profit before tax (**P**)	6,500
PBT margin (**P/R**)	26%

It is assumed further that the revenues are sourced exclusively from three market jurisdictions.

in million EUR	Local revenue (**S**)	
Market 1	2,000	local subsidiary
Market 2	18,000	remote activity
Market 3	5,000	remote activity
Total	**25,000**	

Due to the strategic location and attractiveness of Market 1, Group A established a local subsidiary in that jurisdiction performing baseline marketing and distribution activities for the whole world. In contrast, Group A has no taxable/physical presence in Market 2 and Market 3, where services are supplied remotely by the subsidiary located in Market 1. For Amount A purposes, however, it is assumed that a new nexus will be created in Markets 2 and 3 (i.e. nexus revenue threshold exceeded).

Applying Amount A formula

<u>Step 1: Profitability Threshold</u>

Determine Group A's residual profit (W) by subtracting 10% from the PBT margin (P/R).

W = P – (R*10%)

W = 6,500 – (25,000 * 10%)

W = 4,000

<u>Step 2: Reallocation percentage</u>

Determine Group A's allocable tax base (A) by multiplying residual profit (W) by 20%.

A = 20% * W

A = 20% * 4,000

A = 800

<u>Step 3: Allocation key</u>

Allocation key based on the ratio of locally sourced revenue (S) to total revenue (R). This last step provides for the quantum of Amount A taxable in each eligible market jurisdiction (M), as described in the below table.

in million EUR	Local revenue (S)	Allocation key (S/R)	Amount A (M)
Market 1	2,000	8%	A * S/R = **64**
Market 2	18,000	72%	A * S/R = **576**
Market 3	5,000	20%	A * S/R = **160**
Total	**25,000**	**100%**	**800**

Profit-margin approach

858. Consistent with the three-steps described above, the profit-margin approach can be described in algebraic form as follows.[4]

- **Step 1:** Isolate the residual profit margin (if any) of the group or, where relevant, the segment by deducting the deemed routine profit margin – e.g. a percentage of PBT to revenue ("z") – from the total profit margin. Assuming that the Amount A tax base for the relevant group or segment is "P", revenues of the group or segment are "R", and the profit margin of the group or segment is "P/R", this means that Amount A applies only if "P/R" is greater than z, and that a positive residual profit margin "w" can be calculated as:

$$w = P/R - z$$

- **Step 2:** Separate "w" between the portion of residual profitability attributable to Amount A (the allocable tax base, "a") and other factors, such as trade intangibles, capital and risk ("X"). If the agreed portion of residual profitability attributable to Amount A is, for example, a percentage ("y"), then "a" can be calculated as:

$$a = y \times w$$

- **Step 3**: Allocate the relevant portion of residual profitability attributable to Amount A to the market jurisdictions that meet the new nexus threshold. This would be done through an allocation key based on local revenue. Assuming that in a particular market jurisdiction the group or, where relevant, the segment local revenue is "S", then the quantum of Amount A profit allocated to that particular market, expressed as "M", can be calculated as:

$$M = S \times a$$

859. After bringing the three components together, the Amount A formula under a profit-margin approach becomes:

$$M = S \times [y \times (P/R - z)]$$

Box B.2. Example – profit-margin based approach

For the purpose of this example, it is assumed that the Amount A formula includes a 10% profitability threshold (step 1) and 20% reallocation percentage (step 2).

Facts

The same as in the other example (see Box 6.4).

Applying Amount A formula

Step 1: Profitability Threshold

Determine Group A's residual profit margin (w) by deducting 10% from the total PBT margin (P/R).

w = P/R – 10%

w = 26% – 10%

w = 16%

Step 2: Reallocation percentage

Determine Group A's portion of residual profitability attributable to Amount A by multiplying the residual profit margin (W) by 20%.

a = 20% * W

a = 20% * 16%

a = 3,2%

Step 3: Allocation key

Allocation key based on locally sourced revenue (S). This last step provides for the quantum of Amount A taxable in each eligible market jurisdiction (M), as described in the below table.

in million EUR	Local revenue **(S)**	Residual profit margin attributable to Amount A **(a)**	Amount A **(M)**
Market 1	2,000	3,2%	S x a = **64**
Market 2	18,000	3,2%	S x a = **576**
Market 3	5,000	3,2%	S x a = **160**
Total	**25,000**	**n.a.**	**800**

Annex C. Examples

Box C.1. Extending the carry-forward regime to profit shortfalls

Group X is an MNE group that provides streaming services with a business model producing regular profit. It has no other business lines. In Years 1, 2 and 3, pursuant to Amount A computation rules, the group (no segmentation required) generated the following results.

In EUR million	Total Revenue	PBT	Profitability	Profit shortfalls
Year 1	100	10	10%	0
Year 2	100	10	10%	0
Year 3	100	10	10%	0
Total	300	30	10%	0

Assuming the Amount A profitability threshold is established at a 10% return on revenue, Group X has no profit in excess of that threshold in any of the three years under review, and none of the profit for Amount A purposes generated during those years would be reallocated to market jurisdictions.

Consider now a competitor, Group Y, providing similar services but with a business model producing irregular profit. In Years 1, 2 and 3, pursuant to Amount A computation rules, the group (treated as a segment) generated the following results.

In EUR million	Total Revenue	PBT	Profitability	Profit shortfalls
Year 1	100	5	5%	5
Year 2	100	5	5%	5
Year 3	100	20	20%	0
Total	300	30	10%	10

Notwithstanding the fact that this competitor has generated the same level of profit over the three-year period under review, without a carry-forward regime accommodating profit shortfalls, Group Y would have a share of its profits for Amount A purposes in excess of the profitability threshold in Year 3 reallocated to market jurisdictions, i.e. EUR 10 million.

In contrast, with a carry-forward regime accommodating profit shortfalls, the profit shortfalls generated in Year 1 (i.e. EUR 5 million) and Year 2 (i.e. EUR 5 million) would be preserved and offset against the profit in excess of the profitability threshold in Year 3 (i.e. EUR 10 million). Group Y would thus not have a share of its profit for Amount A purposes reallocated to market jurisdictions in Year 3.

Box C.2. The marketing and distribution profits safe harbour for a decentralised business model

Group X is an MNE group in scope of Amount A. Under the marketing and distribution profits safe harbour proposal, the assumption is that the Amount A profit allocated to market jurisdictions where the group does not have a physical presence is a return on sales of 1.5% (Amount A only) and the Amount A profit allocated to market jurisdictions where the group has a physical presence is a return on sales of 3.5% (Amount A plus a 2% fixed return for routine marketing and distribution activities).

IP Owner (Jurisdiction 1)

Group X has a decentralised operating model, in which an IP Owner (resident in Jurisdiction 1) develops and owns the group's trade intangibles and licenses these intangibles to full-risk distributors in market jurisdictions in exchange for a benchmarked royalty.

Full-risk distributors (Jurisdictions 2, 3, 4 and 5)

The full-risk distributors (resident in Jurisdictions 2, 3, 4 and 5 respectively) combine these licensed intangibles with their own marketing and other intangibles, in products that are then sold to third parties. The full-risk distributors realise the residual profits (or losses) from their respective markets. The group and entity-level financials for Group X are summarised below.

in EUR million	IP Owner	Distributor 2	Distributor 3	Distributor 4	Distributor 5	Total
	Jurisdiction 1	Jurisdiction 2	Jurisdiction 3	Jurisdiction 4	Jurisdiction 5	Consolidated
Revenue	1,500	1,000	800	1,200	4,000	7,000
Third party revenue	0	1,000	800	1,200	4,000	
Intragroup revenue	1,500	0	0	0	0	
Profit before tax (PBT)	450	46	256	-12	712	1,222
Profit margin (%)	30.0%	4.6%	3.2%	-1.0%	17.8%	17.5%

Application of the safe harbour

Group X would determine the safe harbour return due to each of these market jurisdictions under Amount A and the profits allocated to market jurisdictions under the existing profit allocation rules (shown in the table above). As Group X has a physical presence in each of the market jurisdictions it operates in the safe harbour return would be 3.5%.

Finally, Group X would then determine in which markets it is eligible for the safe harbour and in which market it would be required to allocate Amount A:

- In Jurisdictions 2 and 5, Group X already allocates a return in excess of 3.5%. Therefore, it would be eligible for the safe harbour and hence would not pay Amount A in these jurisdictions.
- In Jurisdiction 4, Group X incurs a loss. Therefore, it would not meet the fixed return of the safe harbour and would, therefore, be ineligible for the safe harbour.
- In Jurisdiction 3, Group X would meet the fixed return of the safe harbour but not the cap. Therefore, it would only need to allocate profit equal to an additional return of 0.3% (being the difference between the profits already allocated to Jurisdiction 3 under the existing profit allocation rules and the cap of the safe harbour return) to Jurisdiction 3 under Amount A.

Under the proposed mechanism to eliminate double taxation, the IP Owner is likely to be identified as the paying entity and hence Jurisdiction 1 would be required to provide double tax relief (through the exemption or credit method) for the Amount A profit allocated to Jurisdiction 4 and 3.

Box C.3. The netting-off effect for a centralised business model

Group A is an MNE group in scope of Amount A. The group generates EUR 20,750 million in third party revenue and earned PBT of EUR 5,323m, resulting in a profit margin of 26%. The group and entity-level financials are summarised in the table below.

Principal (Jurisdiction 1)

Group A has a centralised operating model, in which a Principal (resident in Jurisdiction 1) owns the group's trade and marketing intangibles and realises the entire residual profit of the group. Jurisdiction 1 is a large market for Group A, generating EUR 10,000 million in third party revenues that are booked by the Principal.

Other market jurisdictions (Jurisdiction 2, 3, 4 and 5)

The other entities in the group (resident in Jurisdictions 2, 3, 4 and 5 respectively) perform baseline marketing and distribution functions. Under the ALP-based profit allocation rules, these distributors are remunerated with a 3% return on sales.

in EUR million	Principal	Distributor 2	Distributor 3	Distributor 4	Distributor 5	Total
	Jurisdiction 1	Jurisdiction 2	Jurisdiction 3	Jurisdiction 4	Jurisdiction 5	Consolidated
Revenue	15,000	2,000	4,000	3,500	1,250	20,750
Third party revenue	10,000	2,000	4,000	3,500	1,250	
Intragroup revenue	5,000	0	0	0	0	
Profit before tax (PBT)	5,000	60	120	105	38	5,323
Profit margin (%)	33%	3%	3%	3%	3%	26%

Under the Pillar One solution, Jurisdictions 1, 2, 3, 4 and 5 would all (as eligible market jurisdictions where nexus is established) be allocated Amount A. Jurisdictions 2, 3, 4 and 5 would also continue to be allocated profit under the existing ALP-based profit allocation rules The results of these allocations are shown in the table below.

Prior to the elimination of double taxation, the full Amount A profit allocated to Jurisdiction 1 could be said to give rise to double counting because this market jurisdiction already exercised taxing rights over material residual profit under existing ALP-based profit allocation rules, i.e. profit amounting to EUR 5,000 million, that is, a profit margin on total sales of 33% exceeding the average return on sales of the MNE group (26%).

in EUR million	Jurisdiction 1	Jurisdiction 2	Jurisdiction 3	Jurisdiction 4	Jurisdiction 5	Total
Amount A	313	63	125	110	39	650
ALP-based allocation	5,000	60	120	105	38	5,323
Total taxable profit *	5,313	123	245	215	77	5,972
Potential double counting	313	0	0	0	0	313

* The total taxable profits exceed the taxable profits of Group A, as the double taxation arising from Amount A has not yet been eliminated.

Under the proposed mechanism to eliminate double taxation, the Principal would be identified as the paying entity[5] and hence Jurisdiction 1 would be required to provide double tax relief (through the exemption or credit method) for the EUR 650 million in profits reallocated under Amount A.

In this example, the mechanism to eliminate double taxation will entirely net-off the potential for double counting in Jurisdiction 1 (i.e. EUR 313 million), by effectively reducing the profit for which income tax will be paid in Jurisdiction 1.

in EUR million	Jurisdiction 1	Jurisdiction 2	Jurisdiction 3	Jurisdiction 4	Jurisdiction 5
Amount A	313	63	125	110	39
ALP-based allocation	5,000	60	120	105	38
Total taxable profit*	5,313	123	245	215	77
Potential double counting	313	0	0	0	0
Netting-off of profits under the mechanism to eliminate double taxation	(650)	0	0	0	0
Total taxable profits (after the elimination of double taxation)	4,664	123	245	215	77

* The total taxable profits exceed the taxable profits of Group A, as the double taxation arising from Amount A has not yet been eliminated

Box C.4. The netting-off effect for a decentralised business model

Group B is an MNE group in scope of Amount A. The group generates EUR 12,000 million in third party revenue and earned PBT of EUR 2,450 million, resulting in a profit margin of 20%. The group and entity-level financials are summarised in the table below.

IP Owner (Jurisdiction 1)

Group B has a decentralised operating model, in which an IP Owner (resident in Jurisdiction 1) owns a significant part of the group's intangibles. Under the group's transfer pricing policy, the IP Owner receives a revenue-based royalty from the distribution entities for the right to use its intangibles. Group B's products are not sold in Jurisdiction 1.

Distributors (Jurisdictions 2, 3, 4 and 5)

Each distribution entity (resident in Jurisdictions 2, 3, 4 and 5) owns the marketing intangibles relevant to their jurisdiction. Under the group's transfer pricing policy, these distribution entities realise the residual profit or loss from their activities after paying IP Owner a royalty for the right to use its intangibles.

In the year under analysis, a recession in Jurisdiction 2 means Distributor 2 only earns PBT of EUR 200 million, a profit margin of 5%. Distributors 3, 4 and 5 earn higher profits and higher profit margins, as shown in the table below. The profit margins earned by Distributor 3 exceeds those earned by Distributor 4 and 5. This could be for a number of reasons, such as the effectiveness of their local operations or the underlying economic conditions in the different markets.

	IP Owner	Distributor 2	Distributor 3	Distributor 4	Distributor 5	Total
	Jurisdiction 1	Jurisdiction 2	Jurisdiction 3	Jurisdiction 4	Jurisdiction 5	Consolidated
Revenue	2,000	4,000	2,000	3,000	3,000	12,000
Third party revenue	0	4,000	2,000	3,000	3,000	
Intragroup revenue	2,000	0	0	0	0	
Profit before tax (PBT)	750	200	650	400	450	2,450
Profit margin (%)	38%	5%	33%	13%	15%	20%

Under the new taxing right of Pillar One, Jurisdictions 2, 3, 4 and 5 would all (as eligible market jurisdiction where nexus is established) be allocated Amount A, in addition to the profit allocated under existing ALP-based profit allocation rules due to the performance of marketing and distribution activities. Jurisdiction 1 would be allocated profit under existing rules for the activities performed by the IP Owner. The results of these allocations are shown in the table below.

Prior to the elimination of double taxation, the Amount A profit allocated to Jurisdiction 3 could be said to give rise to double counting. It is more difficult to assess whether and how much of the allocation of Amount A to Jurisdictions 2, 4 or 5 constitutes double counting. These jurisdictions may have taxing rights over some residual profit derived from Group B's marketing intangibles under the existing profit allocation rules, but measuring any related double counting is more complicated due to the lower profitability of the entities in those jurisdictions.

in EUR million	Jurisdiction 1	Jurisdiction 2	Jurisdiction 3	Jurisdiction 4	Jurisdiction 5	Total
Amount A	0	83	42	63	63	250
ALP-based allocations	750	200	650	400	450	2,450
Total taxable profit *	750	283	692	463	513	2,700
Potential double counting	0	?	42	?	?	n.a.

* The total taxable profits exceed the taxable profits of Group B, as the double taxation arising from Amount A has not yet been eliminated.

Assume that under the current mechanism to eliminate double taxation, only IP Owner and Distributor 3 would be identified as potential paying entities under the activity test (step 1) and profitability test (step 2).[6] Further, assume that as a result of the market connection priority test (step 3) the IP Owner is identified as the paying entity for Jurisdiction 2, 4 and 5 and Distributor 3 is identified as the primary paying entity for Jurisdiction 3, on the basis that it has the strongest connection to this market.

In this example, the mechanism to eliminate double taxation would not entirely net-off the potential for double counting in the different jurisdictions where Group B has a distribution entity. This is because the mechanism to eliminate double taxation would not require Jurisdictions 2, 4 and 5 to provide relief for whole or part of the profits reallocated under Amount A. However, the additional profits allocated to Jurisdiction 3 under Amount A (which could give rise to double counting) would be entirely eliminated as a result of Distributor 3 being identified as the primary paying entity for this jurisdiction. It should be noted this outcome would only arise if the market connection priority test (step 3) resulted in Distributor 3 bearing Jurisdiction 3's full Amount A tax liability.

in EUR million	Jurisdiction 1	Jurisdiction 2	Jurisdiction 3	Jurisdiction 4	Jurisdiction 5
Amount A	0	83	42	63	63
ALP-based allocations	750	200	650	400	450
Total taxable profit	750	283	692	463	513
Potential double counting	0	?	42	?	?
Netting-off of profits under the mechanism to eliminate double taxation	(209)	n.a.	(42)	n.a.	n.a.
Total taxable profits (after the elimination of double taxation)	541	283	650	463	513

Notes

[1] In practice, some variances may arise for the implementation and administration of each approach. For example, using profit margins instead of profit amounts may limit the scope and relevance of some currency exchange issues (i.e. timing and determination of the appropriate conversion rate), to the extent that the locally sourced revenue is booked in the currency of the market jurisdiction (e.g. multiplying local revenue by a profit margin would not involve any currency exchange). These practical differences will be considered as part of the work on implementation and administration of Amount A, especially when designing a simplified administration system to centralise the computation and compliance of Amount A (see below Chapter 10).

[2] To facilitate the illustration, the calculation assumes that all the revenue of the MNE group (or segment where relevant) falls in the scope of Amount A (see section 2.2).

[3] As there can be no negative residual profit (W), this calculation could also be expressed as W = Max(P-R*z, 0).

[4] To facilitate the illustration, the calculation assumes that all the revenue of the MNE group (or segment where relevant) falls in the scope of Amount A (see section 2.2).

[5] In practice, the identification of the paying entity (or entities) should follow the rules articulated in the Section 7.2.

[6] The identification of the paying entity (or entities) would follow the rules articulated Section 7.2.

www.ingramcontent.com/pod-product-compliance
Ingram Content Group UK Ltd.
Pitfield, Milton Keynes, MK11 3LW, UK
UKHW051500290926
15471UKWH00008B/1325